Organizations and Society

Organizations and Society

Joseph H. Spear
James Madison University

Los Angeles | London | New Delhi
Singapore | Washington DC | Melbourne

FOR INFORMATION:

SAGE Publications, Inc.
2455 Teller Road
Thousand Oaks, California 91320
E-mail: order@sagepub.com

SAGE Publications Ltd.
1 Oliver's Yard
55 City Road
London, EC1Y 1SP
United Kingdom

SAGE Publications India Pvt. Ltd.
B 1/I 1 Mohan Cooperative Industrial Area
Mathura Road, New Delhi 110 044
India

SAGE Publications Asia-Pacific Pte. Ltd.
18 Cross Street #10-10/11/12
China Square Central
Singapore 048423

Printed in the United States of America

ISBN 978-1-0718-0220-5

This book is printed on acid-free paper.

Acquisitions Editor: Jeff Lasser
Product Associate: Tiara Beatty
Production Editor: Vijayakumar
Copy Editor: Christobel Colleen Hopman
Typesetter: TNQ Technologies
Proofreader: Benny Willy Stephen
Indexer: TNQ Technologies
Cover Designer: Candice Harman
Marketing Manager: Jennifer Haldeman

22 23 24 25 26 10 9 8 7 6 5 4 3 2 1

For my parents, Joe and Kathy Spear
If I'm able to maintain any sense of stability and sanity, it's because of a
lifetime of firm foundations provided by them.

And in memory of my mother-in-law, Barbara J. Solomon
I could write another chapter on the ways that her support has been
invaluable over the years, and she is sorely missed.

Brief Contents

Detailed Contents

PART II: FORGING THE SOCIETY OF ORGANIZATIONS 79

4 The Rise of Bureaucracy and the Question of Efficiency 81

5 The Rise of Bureaucracy and the Question of Power 101

6 The Fall of Big Business? 131

PART III: ANALYZING ORGANIZATIONS 159

7 The Machine Organization 162

8 The Human Organization 192

9 The Open Organization: Organizations and Their Environments 225

10 The Prospects for Rationality 254

11 Rationality as Constant and Variable 284

12 Final Reflections: Living With Organizations 308

Preface

This book has two main purposes. The primary purpose is to provide a reasonably short and simple introduction to the Sociology of Organizations for a general audience. It assumes no knowledge of sociology or of the study of formal organizations, and is meant to be completely readable by anyone with about a high school level of reading comprehension. It presents the field in a way that makes it relevant to general citizens rather than to the technical interests of research, management, administrative, or other professionals. It is largely meant for Sociology majors and other liberal arts students whose primary need is to be able to make sense out of themselves and the world they find themselves in—to grasp the intersections between history and biography, as C. Wright Mills so eloquently expressed it.[1] Yet anyone struggling to make sense out of our world today should find it valuable—including even research, management, administrative, or other professionals.

The secondary purpose resides in the book's basic narrative which speaks just as much to the world of professionals in Organizational Studies and Management. While much of the text is meant to provide very simple and down-to-earth overviews of standard topics of research and theory in the Sociology of Organizations, it takes on some semblance of a critical essay. The guiding concern is much more in tune with Sociology's attempt to make sense out of ourselves than it is with trying to design more effective tools for the control of social action. It is largely critical of our 150-year cultural love affair with rationalized control, and of the general fields of organizational and management studies for their participation in it. At least as far as Sociology is concerned, we are better served as citizens and as social scientists by keeping Max Weber's pessimism and warnings at the forefront of our inquiries and actions.

The book, its organization, style, and narrative are largely born of my own early-career frustrations in trying to find a model to use while introducing undergraduate students to formal organizations. I started out like a classic academic, thinking that I was supposed to bring my students some manner of contemporary literature review on the state of the art in the field—as if I was priming up classrooms full of sociologists or organizational scholars. But that doesn't work on several levels. One is that this is a very broad, complex, highly technical, and fully interdisciplinary field. It's like trying to do an entire major in a single semester in the space of what needs to be a basic introductory course. The average undergraduate student doesn't even come in knowing what an "externality" is, and still thinks that you can understand the economy by imagining neighborhood kids trying to sell lemonade on a street corner. There is a lot of "square one" work to be done before even trying to talk to people about professional research on formal organizations.

A fully related issue is that for some reason it did take me a while to realize that virtually none of my students would ever become scholars in

[1]C. Wright Mills. [1959] 2000. *The Sociological Imagination*. New York: Oxford University Press.

organizational studies, or scholars in anything else for that matter. They simply aren't there because they need to prepare for their PhD comprehensive exams. But perhaps most important of all, it took me a while to shift to the logic that, regardless of all else, they *would all* become *citizens* who did really need to grasp the intersections between biography and history. There is a "story of us" embedded (though scattered) in the history and the present of organizational studies and most people don't know much, if anything, of it. And I'm not sure how anyone can make sense out of the "blooming, buzzing confusion" around us without knowing something of the story—something of how much formal rationalization changed the world around the turn of the twentieth century, setting the stage for the middle of the twentieth, and then for the ongoing roller coaster of the late twentieth into the twenty-first century. And even as we have hit a period where we might find sentiments that formal organizations are no longer the key to understanding society, it is still impossible to fulfill the promise of the sociological imagination without understanding the "story" of formal organizations.

When I initially cast about for teaching models by looking at existing introductory materials, I never did find anything trying to tell a story about it. I did find excellent, high-quality materials. But they tended to be pitched above a basic introductory level, and built largely toward concerns internal to the field as a professional area of research. They were not created to take what the field has to offer and bring it into touch with the frameworks of mind or concerns of the average person who needs to make sense out of themselves and our social world. I myself wasn't sure what to do about it and, after a few faltering attempts at organizing an effective Sociology of Organizations course, I stopped teaching it for a few years. I then had occasion to provide a chapter for an edited volume reflecting on Amitai Etzioni's book *The Active Society*.[2] The purpose of that book was to use social science knowledge to imagine how we might build the "good society"—one that was more democratically responsive, less alienating, and more effective at meeting its goals. Much of what Etzioni did was shaped by his own involvement in organizational sociology so I evaluated it in that light. What this meant was turning the tools of organizational theory and research outward toward our larger questions of the intersections between history and biography. The result was new ideas about how a course might be pitched.

So I went back to the course with fresh ideas in mind, and I have been piecing a story together largely using primary source reading materials over which I lay a narrative through course lectures. But it has always been rough—both on me and on my students. What I really wanted was just a simple, easy-to-read, and basic text that could get the students up to speed, and leave them able to deal with primary materials in a much more productive way. Never having found anything to meet my purposes, I set out to try to do it myself.

Thus, the goal here is to write a simple, easy-to-read overview of formal organizations and their importance to modern and now postmodern societies. It contains a lot of "square one" narrative that at times may even seem ponderous. But it's just been my experience that some degree of hand-holding

---

[2]Etzioni, Amatai. 1968. *The Active Society: A Theory of Societal and Political Processes*. New York, NY: Free Press. The chapter: Spear, Joseph H. 2006. "The Actively Drifting Society." Chapter 6 in *The Active Society* Revisited. Edited by Wilson Carey McWilliams. New York, NY: Rowman & Littlefield Publishers, Inc.

is often needed for laying down foundations. The book is meant as a stepping stone rather than a full immersion. It will also favor integrative narrative over technical depth and detail. In addition to being reasonably easy to read, I tried to keep it fairly short. The goal is to do a lot of basic introductory work, but leave plenty of room for individual customization based on contingencies of contemporary events, developments in organizational studies, and/or instructor and student interests. I even want this room for myself.

What the Book Is Not

Given the above, the book is not intended to be a contemporary literature review of organizational studies, nor should it look like one or read like one. I have taken the unconventional step of trying to lay things out in such a way that constant in-text citation is not necessary. It contains the occasional footnote for various purposes such as direct quotations or highly specific references, but I tried to keep it largely note and citation free. The ideas presented are largely of the landmark type and, variations among us all notwithstanding, should be well known. In lieu of constant citations in academic form, each chapter has an annotated list of sources and further reading.

Save for the last chapter providing my final reflections, the book is also not intended to be a commentary on the current times. For example, I was trying to compose and finish a good deal of it right through the heart of the global coronavirus pandemic, but references to that are mostly confined to one small section of Chapter 11. As much as major historical events such as these seem massive while we're in the midst, their shelf life also tends to be short as compared to the timeline of getting a book to press. (One case in point is that as I am reviewing page proofs, attention to the pandemic has been eclipsed by the Russian invasion of the Ukraine). If I wanted to write a book about current events, then that is what I would be writing. My own strategy for putting the subject matter in touch with the times is simply to use supplementary readings selected according to the times. Just to take a few examples, in the Fall of 2020, I assigned a Hamilton Project paper on the effects of COVID-19 on labor market outcomes (with Chapter 3 material),[3] an article from *The Atlantic* on police culture and its potential role in discriminatory policing (with Chapter 8 material),[4] and a piece from the American Sociological Association *Footnotes* newsletter discussing COVID-19 in light of the logic of Normal Accidents theory (with Chapter 10 material).[5] The reading list for my courses can change quite rapidly, unlike the contents of the course text.

---

[3]Betsey Stevenson. 2020. "The Initial Impact of COVID-19 on Labor Market Outcomes Across Groups and the Potential for Permanent Scarring." Essay 2020–16, The Hamilton Project, Brookings Institution, Washington, DC. Retrieved 09/10/2020 (from https://www.brookings.edu/research/the-initial-impact-of-covid-19-on-labor-market-outcomes-across-groups-and-the-potential-for-permanent-scarring/).

[4]David Brooks. 2020. "The Culture of Policing is Broken." *The Atlantic*. Retrieved 08/23/2020 (https://www.theatlantic.com/ideas/archive/2020/06/how-police-brutality-gets-made/613030/)

[5]Donald Tomaskovic-Devey. 2020. "The COVID-19 Pandemic: Normal Accidents and Cascading Systems Failures." *ASA Footnotes*. 48(3): 25-26.

Basic Organization of the Text

The book is organized into three main parts:

Part I: Our Society of Organizations

Part I establishes the basic subject matter and its importance, providing an initial conceptualization of formal organization and its place in the contemporary social order largely in social power terms. It is meant to be "the hook." My experience has been that students enter the course without having any idea why they should care about understanding or studying "organizations," and need an antidote to overly individualistic visions of things like choices, achievement, and power. In the largest sense, Part I should clarify how all aspects of our lives—past, present, and future—are dependent on them, but that this wasn't always the case. The turn of the twentieth century saw an "organizational revolution," which is still under-appreciated in the public mind.

- *Chapter 1: Introduction: A Society of Formal Organizations* provides preliminary grounding for discussing the concept of formal organization and the general Weberian rationalization thesis. It leans heavily on Weber's classic ideal type of *bureaucracy*, provides students with a definition of formal organization, and situates it within the "long view" of human existence as a recently emergent mode of social organization. As a matter of course it outlines the basic rationalization thesis, including its more recent reincarnation as Ritzer's *McDonaldization* thesis.[6] The reader emerges with a clear picture of what formal rationality entails, is introduced to some of the general consequences that follow from it, and is asked to consider a view of the world as an *iron cage of rationality*. While there are alternative conceptions of organizations, such as those of Chester Barnard, those emerge at other points in the book, often as parts of qualifications to the Weberian *ideal type*.

- *Chapter 2: The Subject Is Organizations. The Issue Is Power* makes the argument that the most important aspect of formal organizations is that they represent social power instruments of the first order. (In Weber's terms "the concentration of the means of administration.") It frames the question with a basic overview of the social-scientific concept of social power, both *collective* and *distributive*, and establishes the role of organizations in that regard. It visits Robert Michels' analysis of oligarchy and the extension of that to *power elite/power structures* theories of society. It then contrasts that with alternative images of social power, such as *pluralist* conceptions. It concludes by explaining that, regardless of one's understanding of power in today's society, organizations remain the key instruments of

---

[6]For example, George Ritzer. 2019. *The McDonaldization of Society: Into the Digital Age*, 9th Ed., Los Angeles, CA: Sage Publications. While Weber's full rationalization thesis is much broader than simply the growth and spread of formal organization, it certainly does lie close to its heart. The broader notion of rationalization will not be lost.

social power, whether collective or distributive. The degree of power concentration is a crucial variable, so the emphasis becomes the question of the *conditions under which* power elite or pluralist theories of power are more or less applicable.

- *Chapter 3: Organizations and Inequality* moves the question of power down to the *life chances* of individuals. This entails sustained focus on organizations as crucial to *social stratification*. The main line of the story involves laying out major changes in organizational forms that have created and shaped labor market structures, and thus *class* structures. That is then carried over and extended to the highly variable experiences people have in labor markets based on *race/ethnicity* and *gender*. The chapter drives home the point that rationalization creates durable inequality structures, regardless of the variable activities and achievements of persons (*human capital*). Persons seeking to accomplish things and achieve a place in the social order must navigate existing organizational structures—or build new ones.

Part II: Forging the Society of Organizations

Part II provides and overview of the rise—and potential fall—of the "society of organizations" by asking what brought it about and whether or not it still makes sense to think of it in those terms. The focus is largely on business organizations as arguably lying at the center of the *organizational revolution*, and follows the basic story regarding the move from *markets to hierarchies* to...what? This is complex, and there is no way to produce a full account within the confines of a few chapters of an introductory book. None-theless, one can outline basic arguments regarding the genesis of the rise and spread of the bureaucratic form, along with those who declare its post-1970s' demise.

- *Chapter 4: The Rise of Bureaucracy and the Question of Efficiency.* The vestiges of bureaucratic organization can be found in many times and places in human history, including outside of Western societies, and its roots in the West can be traced in various ways back through the Middle Ages. Yet the central period for the organizational revolution and growth of the *iron cage* as we came to know it largely lies in the transformation of business organizations around the turn of the twentieth century. Thus Chapter 4 introduces the *managerial revolution* and *efficiency arguments*, largely from Alfred Chandler, which are generally taken to explain it.

- *Chapter 5: The Rise of Bureaucracy and the Question of Power* provides a critical consideration of Chandler's arguments, introduces alternative arguments, and provides a revised narrative for understanding how the growth of the large bureaucratic form came about. With regards to the managerial revolution, there is ample evidence to suggest that the organizational revolution was economically driven by the use of concentrated capital to pursue economic market control rather than technology and efficiency. The growth of organizations in other institutional areas of society, including even government, followed from this. While this chapter is not merely a simple distillation of Charles Perrow's *Organizing America*,[7] it is heavily inspired by it.

- *Chapter 6: The Fall of Big Business?* takes a step back for a critical assessment of concern with the growth of large formal organizations. Since at least the 1980s, it has become common to see the large bureaucratic form of organization as in decline, or even disappearing, with the rise of new networked forms of action (among other things). Organizations in some form are still important, but in this view they are becoming smaller and less bureaucratic. Similar to Chandler's arguments, the shift is often linked to technological change and the quest for economic efficiency. If the organizational base is shifting, this would mark yet another significant shift in the basic social order, and there are many arguments to that effect, including that we are no longer a *society of organizations*. However, not everyone is convinced of this. So this chapter serves to introduce what we can summarize as the *markets, hierarchies, or networks* question, including consideration of whether we are moving away from a *society of organizations*.

Part III: Analyzing Organizations

The segue here is that if organizations are the actors in society, then we had better understand them. This part often represents the main focus for entire courses, and certainly for courses in *Organizational Theory*. It provides a basic "tour" through major perspectives in organizational theory and research. Its logic will borrow much from accounts in existing texts, such as W. Richard Scott's and Gerald Davis' (though originally only Scott's) rational, natural, and open systems (RNO) or Gareth Morgan's "images,"[8] but rather than just laying differing images next to each other, eventually integrates around the central theme of rationality. Whatever else they may be, formal organizations are *intendedly rational* means for accomplishing various kinds of ends, and this is arguably the most significant key to understanding them.

- *Chapter 7: The Machine Organization* explains the basic picture of formal organizations as rational systems or machine-like structures. The reader is reminded of the Weberian ideal type as the foundation, but the key imageries here are drawn from Frederick Taylor's scientific management and the rise of Fordism. We revisit the *second industrial revolution* at the turn of the twentieth century, the heart of which was the marriage of technical and human organization into the

---

[7]Charles Perrow. 2002. *Organizing America: Wealth, Power, and the Origins of Corporate Capitalism*. Princeton, NJ: Princeton University Press.
[8]Scott, W. Richard and Gerald F. Davis. 2007. *Organizations and Organizing: Rational, Natural, and Open Systems Perspectives*. Upper Saddle River, NJ: Pearson Education, Inc.; Morgan, Gareth. 2006. *Images of Organizations*. Sage: Thousand Oaks, CA.

large industrial Fordist models of production. It is here that the managerial impulse, so widely taken for granted as "normal" by current organizational professionals, was established as dominant. This is all linked back to the lessons of Part II and to Weber's inspiration for the rationalization thesis itself. The content here corresponds to seeing organizations as *Rational Systems*.

- *Chapter 8: The Human Organization* considers the "discovery" within management sciences that human persons are rather difficult to incorporate as pieces of organizational machinery. The humans, it would seem, have always been a wrench in the works for rational systems builders. Growing initially from the famous Hawthorne Experiments, and later from the birth of new psychologically informed types of organizational consulting, the reader learns of people as complex creatures who are members of informal social groups and cultures rather than as "rabble." We see how the *Human Relations* and *Humanistic Management* movements dealt with the humans, and then learn of later sociological research on the *informal organizations* and *organizational cultures* that often lurk behind outwardly bureaucratic structures. This corresponds to seeing organizations as *Natural* and/or *Human Systems*.

- *Chapter 9: The Open Organization: Organizations and Their Environments* moves on to the issue of organizational environments as yet another thing that places limits on the ability of organizations to rationalize. The key is that formal organizations cannot simply be seen as Tayloristic machines because their primary line tasks are only one thing to be managed. An organization also must manage its environment. An overview of standard theoretical perspectives is given including *transaction cost economics, resource dependence, ecological,* and *institutional/neoinstitutional* theories. At various moments, the material links back to Chapter 8 in that the human elements inside of the organization are part of the environment that organizations need to accommodate, attempt to control, and/or incorporate. This Chapter's content corresponds to seeing organizations as *Open Systems*.

- *Chapter 10: The Prospects for Rationality* digs directly into the limits of rationality with what is sometimes called a *Neo-Weberian* view of organizations. It begins with Herbert Simon's work on *bounded rationality* and its expansion to a form of organizational theory by Simon and colleagues. It carries through on the implications to the conceptualization of *adhocracies, garbage can models,* and then *normal accidents. Normal accidents* often appear in other accounts under the rubric of *organizational dysfunctions* or *deviance.* However, they belong firmly with things such as *garbage cans* in that they share the basis of growing from systems that outstrip our ability for rational control.

- *Chapter 11: Rationality as Constant and Variable* takes in all of the foregoing from Part III and ties it together under a generalized conception of *contingency theory*. It introduces the classical contingency tradition of organizational research from the late 1950s through the 1970s, and then generalizes it to encompass and incorporate the entirety of the issues raised through Part III. The overriding emphasis is on learning to see organizations (and persons) as *intendedly rational* actors that are only capable of *varying* degrees of rationality. Sometimes Weberian bureaucracy can be closely approximated along with its control characteristics of precision, predictability, and efficiency. Sometimes it cannot be, and it is possible to produce organizational systems that we cannot fully predict or control. It is also possible to get anything in between. The original contingency theory research tradition remains largely intact as a foundation—all of the tools for understanding rationality as a variable were developed there.

  ○ Note: To the extent that the book offers something to those interested in practical and technical matters of *organizational design*, this chapter offers the best guidance. It cautions against following any of the particular fads that run through the world of organizational or management consulting because they often produce one-size-fits-all kinds of ideas.

- *Chapter 12: Final Reflections: Living With Organizations* will reflect upon the lessons of the entire book including how it all informs our current times, full as they are of various forms of widespread public frustration and disillusionment. Our culture is firmly entrenched in Enlightenment assumptions regarding the ability of human beings to make use of reason to control our own destiny. Yet, we all must confront the question of whether or not the constant march of *formal rationality* has taken us farther away from the goal of a world guided by human reason (with its much greater similarity to *substantive rationality*). Indeed, we must ask whether or not our last century of rationalizing has, ironically, made these Enlightenment dreams impossible.

Acknowledgments

I begin with thanks to my reviewers (some anonymous) who gave things their careful attention and provided many useful and insightful suggestions and observations. This work was significantly enhanced by their attention to it. In the end, I was not able to accommodate all of the concerns, and errors, omissions, and other deficits are mine alone. On that note, to the extent that this work is found useful in any respect, I am happy to hear from anyone with regards to how it could have been more useful.

In addition, my many students over the years, too numerous to mention by name, have provided an invaluable source of constant conversation and feedback regarding their experiences with formal organizations and the materials of organizational studies.

The editorial staff at Sage has been great, especially my editor Jeff Lasser. Much of the work that went into this book was underway as the world hit the COVID-19 pandemic, and the sudden need to reinvent everything with regards to my teaching responsibilities (and other aspects of life) on the fly created some significant kinks for me. Not much of anything was ever made of it, but whatever backstage acrobatics were required to provide support and make things come to fruition were handled with expert attention, patience, speed, and grace.

At various stages of conceptualization and execution, this work was supported by the James Madison University Program of Grants for Faculty Assistance. This included some summer grant assistance that was initially put in jeopardy at the onset of the COVID-19 pandemic, but was eventually worked out. So there were some other backstage acrobatics in my Dean's office in this regard, and I thank all of those whose work went to continuing what support can be offered.

And many thanks to Nina, my wife of almost 30 years, and our two now adult "children" Sam and Becky. Living with a sociologist is often no picnic, but I'm blessed that they put up with me, and even continue to be my biggest fans and to encourage me. To the extent that I care about anything at all, it's because of them.

Reviewer Acknowledgments

James I. Bowie, Northern Arizona University
Nicholas Membrez-Weiler, North Carolina State University
Junmin Wang, University of Memphis

Our Society of Organizations

Introduction
A SOCIETY OF FORMAL ORGANIZATIONS

In teaching people about culture, many like to use an old quote from anthropologist Ralph Linton who wrote that the last thing a fish would notice would be the water. For a fish, water is ever-present. It is constant. It is so ever-present and so constant that it is just taken-for-granted, and thus not notable to the fish. Large formal organizations, such as governmental agencies, business corporations, universities, churches, and the like may be like that for people today. We are educated by them. We work in them. We worship in them. We shop in them. The things that we buy when shopping are supplied by them. We pay with money that is withdrawn or borrowed from them. They are where you get your electricity, phone, cable, and internet service. They provide you with news, such that it is. They often provide how and where you go on vacation. When you need medical care, you are treated by them, and the organizations that provide medical treatment are overseen by and often paid by yet other large formal organizations. And so on. It was like this when you were born. Barring massive apocalyptic events, it will be like this when you die and your cause of death is verified and recorded in the official records of various government agencies. And you probably haven't noticed it or thought much about it.

We think that societies are made of people. But these days, it might make more sense to think of society as being made of organizations. Think of it like this: People also generally think that forests are made of trees. But why not think of forests as being made of plant cells? Trees, after all, are just made of cells. Perhaps thinking of societies as being made of people is like thinking about forests as being made of cells rather than of trees. There is a way in which it makes sense, and things can be learned with that view of forests in mind. But much is also missed. This book will be about what too often gets missed in the forest of society. We will be thinking about ourselves not as living in *societies of people*, but rather, as living in *societies of organizations*, as organizational sociologist Charles Perrow has put it.

The Idea of Organization

Human beings are social creatures and we always have been. That doesn't just mean that we like to hang around with other people. It means that we do things cooperatively in groups—we always have. We are primates. Primates are social creatures.

Depending on your cultural background, that might run contrary to some common sense notions. You might have the idea that, fundamentally speaking, society is just what all of the individuals within it choose to do on any given day or at any given time. You may have heard of some Enlightenment philosophy that takes living together in social groups to be a rational decision among individuals—the famed *social contract*. You may have the idea that this is a dog-eat-dog world where it is "every man for himself"—that all of us, as individuals, are turned loose to fight and claw and compete against one another. But all of that is just part of Western cultural myth—at least if it these kinds of things are taken to be fundamental statements about how societies are built and how people behave. Humans do not and have never lived as isolated individuals. We are social creatures—it is actually in our DNA. Human infants cannot physically survive without other, more mature humans, to take care of them. Human beings do not develop normally—biologically, psychologically, or socially—if they do not live in regular interaction with other human beings. In a general physiological sense, we are programmed for very little by our instincts and are fairly puny and weak specimens not particularly well-fit to deal with the challenges of our environments on our own. Our success as a species comes from the fact that we live in socially organized groups.

Since humans live in groups, then that means living with some form of *organization*. There are distinctive, regular, and identifiable patterns of thought, action, and relationships among people that come with rights, duties, obligations, and expectations. Individuals live out these patterns, and they do change over time, but individuals do not produce them. They are born into them. The famous, classical sociologist Emile Durkheim called them *social facts*, in contrast to *biological* or *psychological facts*. Rooted in the regular relationships between people is a way of dividing up all of the things that need to be done for a given course of action. Tasks are broken up among different actors, and all of those activities are coordinated to add up to more than just the sum of the parts. A great deal of variation notwithstanding, societies also have various kinds of authority relationships, even if it is just that elders often have more authority in a group than others. All of these things are, further-more, shaped and knitted together by cultural rules that go by different kinds of names—*norms, mores, taboos, laws*, and so on.

In the grand scheme of things, human beings have been on the planet in current biological form for about 200,000 years. For almost all of that time, and in most places, social activity has been organized according to *tradition*. In traditional modes of organizing, people organize themselves and what they do according to what is passed down to them over generations, and the primary social relations that people have with each other are often organized along the lines of extended kinship networks.

But, very, very recently—within the last 150 years (that's about 0.075% of human history)—things changed rather radically. Most of our activities now take place through, within, and around what are called *formal organizations*, and that is what this book about. The most common word that you have probably heard for *formal organization* is *bureaucracy*. Although many people would say that the bureaucratic form is only one kind of formal orga-nization we are going to start there and consider the variations later. These days bureaucracy carries a lot of connotations, most of which are negative. A lot of people, for instance, think that it is a reference to governmental agencies and the people that are in them. This is then often equated with incompetence, inefficiency, and needless complexity, or the infamous *red tape*. But virtually all of the organizations that you know of are bureaucracies. Governments are certainly networks of various bureaucracies. But business corporations are also bureaucracies, as are schools and churches, civic organizations, nonprofit organizations and universities. And that's the thing. Everywhere you look in society today, this is what you see—*formal organizations*. But it wasn't always this way. The dominance of the bureaucratic organizational form throughout all areas of society is a relatively recent and underappreciated turning point in human history.

Somewhere in your educational travels you have probably heard of dramatic turning points in human history such as the *Agrarian Revolution*, the *Industrial Revolution*, or the *Information Revolution*. This particular line of revolutions centers on economic production technologies, but they are called revolutions because they are seen to have radically changed the entire social world in terms of how people live in it. In other words, the changes are not thought to be limited to technologies or economies—the production and distribution of goods and services. They are completely transformative of society—changing politics, economics, culture, and social structure. Yet this kind of story for understanding our human past is one born of our own culture's technologically determinist assumptions. *Technological determinism*, to put it simply, is the idea that technologies, especially economic production technologies, are the single greatest force in shaping a society. But there is something very important that gets overshadowed by our romance with technological change. The something is the *Organizational Revolution*, and it is about people rather than technologies. It certainly involves technologies. But technology by itself can't do anything. People have to create it and put it into motion. The organizational revolution is arguably a revolution that is just as, if not even more, profound than any of these others because it represents a fundamental change in the very logic by which we humans organize all of our social relations and activities. It is a change that hides underneath of everything else something like the way that DNA lies behind the myriad of physical surface variation among humans. The fact that it is a little-recognized or discussed revolution (outside of those who study organizations, anyway) is real problem, because we have no hope of understanding what is going on in the world today without recognizing and understanding it and what it means. Trying to understand today's world without an understanding of organizations is like trying to understand biological organisms without knowing anything about DNA.

The Idea of Formal Organization (a.k.a. Bureaucracy)

In order to get started on the idea of formal organization, you can think very simply. Many people share a living space with other people—houses, apartments, dorm rooms. In those living spaces there are all sorts of things that need to get done. Kitchens and bathrooms need to get cleaned. The garbage needs to get taken out. The electric bill needs to be paid. There are floors to be swept, vacuumed, and mopped. Perhaps this also means that the couch needs to get moved. (I'm not saying these things *do* get done! But they probably do *need* to get done!) If you need to move a couch you'll often have help from someone else. It might be impossible to do it by yourself. It might just be easier to have some help. (This is the nature of the advantage of collective action among humans.) But if it's going to work you have to *coordinate* (organize). Each of you will need to take an end, lift at the same time, move together in the same direction, put it back down together at a specified point, and so on. If one of you tries to do her end of the couch on Tuesday and the other on Wednesday, or if one decides to go left while the other goes right, it all just doesn't work. Social life works this way—by having people fit their actions together with one another. This is true even when you're not specifically thinking about it that way. If it wasn't, then you wouldn't be able to navigate an intersection or check a book out of the library.

A lot of everyday stuff like moving couches or getting an apartment cleaned up is done by *ad hoc organization*. We just coordinate ourselves on the fly and the "organization" lasts for as long as the task. It is *informal* organization and is rooted in the decision-making of the actors at the time of the activity. Perhaps in your own living space, all of these things are just left to ride until it becomes obvious that something needs to be done (maybe because someone important is coming to visit). At that point, some kind of plan might get drawn up for covering all of the relevant tasks. This often works fairly well for very small groups of people and relatively simple and *ad hoc* tasks. But many of our activities are much more regular and routine and take place very predictably over time with large numbers of people—like the kind of organization that gets everyone showing up for work and class at regular times and places. These days things like this are a matter of *formal organization*.

In fact, some people who do share a living space will produce *formal organization* for taking care of all of the tasks. This occurs if you make a specific schedule of things to be done, when they are to be done, and by whom. We might write such a thing down and hang it on the refrigerator to keep everyone clear and on board with the program. In addition to keeping everyone clear, it also provides the basis for easy *accountability*. If something isn't done, then you know who failed to do her job. At this point, *informal organization* becomes *formal organization*, albeit on a scale which is very small and simple. In the end, this is the heart of living by formal organization—it is living by the written rule—by preset standards, schedules, routines, and procedures. These standardized procedures are either written down, or actually materially built into the world.

The latter—having rules built into our material surroundings—may sound a little bit odd, but it becomes easier with just a little bit of thought and perhaps a simple example. I work on a University campus and like many campuses we often have too much traffic, both automotive and pedestrian. There is one spot where a very busy main street cuts between two areas of the campus, and right next to this busy main street is a fairly large auditorium that is often used as a classroom. The problem is that when class lets out a lot of people have to get from one side of the main street to another. Just down the street from the auditorium in one direction is a traffic light with a crosswalk. We all know "the rules" for pedestrians. You are supposed to use the crosswalk and obey the traffic light. But we are talking about college students here. College students stubbornly walk in straight lines, and they are often in a hurry. So the deviation down the street to wait at the crosswalk was apparently too much to ask of too many. At the end of every class session in the auditorium there was fairly widespread traffic disruption as a mass of college student pedestrians flowed out of the building and into main street traffic. Since the mere written rules were apparently not effective enough, a rather intimidating-looking fence has since been built down the center of the street and along the sidewalk. It is the rule built into the world in material form. Keep this in mind as we move along through the book and as you go along through life. The world is full of rules even when they don't look like rules.

And this filling of the world with formalized rules that set down prescribed actions for us to follow is a main story line of this book. In a historically unprecedented way, for the last 150 years (or so), more and more of our lives and activities have come to be defined in terms of written rules. The rules are not merely prohibitive (specifying what you are not supposed to do) but are heavily prescriptive (specifying what you are to do). In a global and cross-cultural sense, the degree to which this applies to people is still variable. However, the march of the formal rule has been consistent and relentless, and over time fewer and fewer people on the globe and fewer and fewer aspects of our lives escape the systems of rules. A famous hero of classical sociological theory, Max Weber, has referred to it as *the iron cage of rationality.*

Max Weber's Bureaucratic "Ideal Type"

Max Weber is one of the foremost heroes of classical sociology theory. He lived and wrote during the turn of the twentieth century and was among the first people to draw attention to the *organizational revolution.* We find this in several different aspects of Weber's work, but the most central one has to do with his *ideal-type*[1] definition of *bureaucracy* and by extension his more general *rationalization thesis* from which we will get the *iron cage* imagery. In defining the bureaucracy, Weber was calling attention to a new form of organizing human activities and predicting that this form would only grow and spread to encompass more and more aspects of life. Anyone who thinks that sociologists haven't ever used their analyses to make good predictions about social change has apparently overlooked Weber because he pretty much nailed it.

The ideal-typical definition of bureaucracy, in particular, has always been a central point of reference for the study of formal organizations. To think about and keep track of the elements of the definition it is probably easiest to picture a typical organizational chart. Almost all formal organizations have them, and they generally look something like Figure 1.1. In his classic description Weber provides six primary characteristics of bureaucracy. For simplicity's sake, I will summarize all of them in terms of the first three (see Figure 1.2 for a summary).

Division of Labor/Task Specialization: Think of any organization as having a primary general goal such as administering drivers' licenses, granting Bachelor's degrees, or making toothpicks. Accomplishing those goals requires a lot of different tasks (the labor). If your organization makes toothpicks you

---

[1]This will be defined shortly. For now, note that an *ideal-type* is just a pure conceptual definition of some kind of thing that leaves aside messy details and contingencies. Its purpose is to capture the essential features of a thing so that we can do systematic comparison and contrast. An ideal-type definition will rarely, if ever, correspond exactly to any specific instance of a thing.

FIGURE 1.1   An Ideal-Typical Organizational Chart

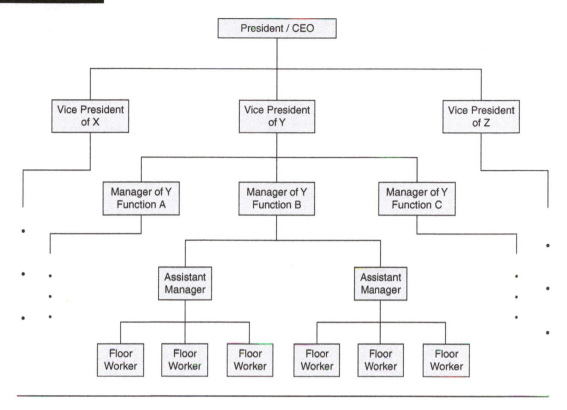

FIGURE 1.2   Summary Table of Weber's Ideal-Type Description of Bureaucracy

Division of Labor / Task Specialization
- Everyone has clearly defined roles
- Tasks are assigned according to technical competence
- Performance of task is to be the office holder's primary occupation
- All positions carry at least some authority
- Rights / duties / obligations go with the offices not the persons

Hierarchy of Authority
- Authority flows downward
- Accountability / responsibility flow upward
- Authority lies with positions, not with persons

Formalization
- Tasks and authority are specified by rules, standards, and procedures
- Authority lies in the rules themselves rather than the persons
- Written records are kept of official organizational activities

need to acquire raw materials, transport them, run machinery, maintain and repair machinery, do accounting, hire and fire employees, administer benefits, clean the bathroom, and so on. In a bureaucracy, all of these tasks are very specifically broken down and assigned to particular *offices*. The word *bureau* means office, or administrative division. The suffix *-cracy* is always about rule or authority, so the term bureaucracy just means *rule by office*. The boxes on an organizational chart represent all of those specialized tasks, or offices. Each box comes with a written job description that specifies the regular duties that are required of the person who occupies that office.

All of this carries several very important things with it. First, when people are assigned to specific positions, the only relevant question is supposed to be that of their *technical competence* for handling the role. The office holder must be qualified to perform the duties of the office above all else. In a construction company, you don't want the welders trying to do accounting or the accountants trying to do the welding. Ideally the office holder is not merely competent, but also *the most competent* person available to accomplish the tasks.

Second, the duties of a person's office become their *primary occupation*. That is, all of a person's work time and attention are to be devoted to doing the job as defined by the organization. This one obviously does vary a lot, but if you are offered a full-time job someplace, the organization expects your full working time and capacity. If you decide to moonlight on a second job, you might even be required to tell your employer about it and seek approval. (This would be written down in a contract and/or job description.)

Third, the office carries with it whatever *authority* over organizational property or other office holders is necessary for the person to carry out the duties. Perhaps most crucially, *the person and the office are strictly separate* from one another. Mixing one's official life with one's private life is not permitted. This includes your time while at work and whatever authority over people or things is carried by your office. You cannot do your personal income taxes on company time. And when you are not on company time, you don't hold any authority over the people below you in the organization, or any authority over any of the organization's resources. If you happen to leave the position, the position remains as it was, someone else occupies it and she takes on those rights, duties, and obligations. You no longer have any of them.

Hierarchy of Authority: In a typical organizational chart you also see that the boxes are arranged in what looks something like a pyramid with lines connecting higher boxes to lower boxes. You can trace chains of boxes all the way from the top to the bottom. Those lines represent lines of authority. Formal organizations are full of order-givers and order-takers where higher level offices give orders to and supervise lower level offices. Thus authority flows downward through the hierarchy. But accountability and responsibility for overseeing that things are done according to plan flows upward. As noted, the authority only goes with the office. When you are at work your boss is allowed to tell you what to do. But if you happen to run into your boss at the grocery store on the weekend, that authority does not carry over. (Remember—this is an *ideal-typical* description!) As noted above, all of the rights and duties that come with an office are strictly limited to life inside of the organization. None of it carries over into private life that is not associated with the official functioning of the organization. In fact, the authority itself, whether one has it or is subject to it, is only with the office and never with the person. Persons do not have power in organizations. Only the offices that they occupy do.

Formalization: Formalization refers to the fact that everything is written down. If you had to choose a single thing to put at the heart of bureaucracy, this is it. Weber went so far as to say that an organization really is its filing cabinet. A bureaucracy is basically a set of written rules and procedures that define what an organization is, what it does, and how it does it. Everything about the *division of labor* and *hierarchy of authority* are written down as sets of standardized rules and procedures. It is the rules themselves that carry the actual authority in an organization. Persons, as persons, don't have any authority, and no one is outside of control by the rules. Even those at the very top of an organization are under the authority of the rules and have their powers limited by them. Think about the situation where you may have created a chore chart for managing the tasks in the apartment. Once the chart is created, it is the chart that rules.

In addition to defining the organization and its activities, all official activities of the organization are written down and filed. When a meeting is held, minutes are kept. When rules and policies are changed and instituted, this is done according to the rules and recorded in the files. Office holders and agencies regularly prepare reports on their activities to be filed. These are often reviewed by other offices and reports are filed on those reports. People often refer to all of this formalization as the famed bureaucratic *red tape*. There is always a lot of paperwork. Yet, as we will come to see, this aspect of organization is crucial to the functioning of the social world as we know it (in ways that people might see as both good and bad). It is also important to keep in mind that the principles apply to all formal organizations (to varying degrees). It is not merely governmental agencies that are awash in their own paperwork and formal rules.

On the Ideal-Typical Nature of Weber's Description

It is important to recognize that Weber's description of bureaucracy, as with most of Weber's concepts, is called an *ideal (or "pure") type*. An ideal type is basically a conceptually pure way of thinking about something. In its pure form, it exists only in our heads and is rarely, if ever, found to be exactly represented in actual reality. The basic purpose of the ideal type is to allow you to make sense out of the world while also allowing for a lot of variation. Ideal types can be seen as akin to everyday concepts that you already know about. If I was to ask you to describe what a chair is, you wouldn't have to know which chair I was talking about. You could come up with a generalized description of a chair that would include the essential elements that are normally found in chairs. This might include a seat mounted on four legs with a back support. I'm sitting in a room with two chairs that fit that ideal-type description well. In the next room there are six chairs that also fit the ideal type but are of a very different appearance and design. But there are also two chairs in there that do not fit the description perfectly because neither rests on four legs. Yet they are still identified as chairs. Every actual instance of a chair represents a specific variation on a general theme. The ideal-type is the general theme. We are quite accustomed to working with ideas that have to be applied flexibly in specific instances. Weberian ideal-types are no different. We know that the world contains a great deal of variation, yet we do manage to order it with general concepts.

It is the same with organizations as it is with chairs, and this will be very important to keep in mind. Just as the specific form of chairs in the world varies a lot with each real chair only approximating the *ideal type*, so it is with formal organizations. For now just think of the Weberian ideal type as providing a baseline description for what a formal organization is and assume that any real organization approximates it only to a varying degree. Some organizations look an awful lot like the ideal type. Others look much less like it, but all carry the characteristics to a varying degree. As we will see in Part III, explaining this variation in organizational form and operation has been a central part of the field of organizational studies.

Formal Organization and the Rationalization of the World

In defining bureaucracy, Weber was actually working on something much bigger about how society was changing. It was the turn of the twentieth century, and he was witnessing the *organization revolution* as it occurred. And once it had started, he didn't think it would stop. He noted that bureaucratic forms of organization, once created, are very difficult to change or destroy and that they have a tendency to both grow and spread. As such, he saw the bureaucratic form and the logic that it carries as well on its way to becoming the most fundamental aspect of society and the basis for more and more of our activities over time. Ultimately he argued that society was in the process of becoming encased in what he called the *iron cage of rationality*.

The Tendency to Grow and Spread

By laying out day-to-day activities in terms of specific rules and duties assigned to specific offices with replaceable office holders' whose primary concerns in life are the accomplishment of those duties, bureaucracies come to take on machine-like characteristics. They operate from moment to moment, day to day, year to year in way that is much more reliable and predictable than other ways of organizing activities. Thus for most any kind of activity bureaucracies would be *technically superior* to other modes of organizing and would basically outcompete other, less formal ways of organizing. This would cause them to spread.

For Weber, this aspect of the bureaucracy is especially important when viewed next to the rise and growth of capitalist market economies. Bureaucracy was growing simultaneously in all sectors of society. The increasing formal organization of governments provided for the management of such things as banking and monetary supplies, economic infrastructure for reliable transportation and communication, and a basic legal structure for the definition and enforcement of property rights and contracts. These things stabilize the entire social environment and make things more *predictable*. This encourages and facilitates the growth of business enterprises because people can be more certain about access to things like suppliers, customers, and financial capital. Furthermore, from the point of view of business, the machine-like operations of the formal organization present the potential for *predictability* and *efficiency* both inside one's own organization and in supplier and customer organizations. This provides distinctive competitive advantages for businesses who adopt the bureaucratic form and through some combination of purposeful design and *survival of the fittest* in market econo-mies, formal organization rapidly becomes the standard form for business operations. Hence, the overall tendency of bureaucracy is to spread, but with the rise of capitalist economic systems the technical superiority of bureaucratic forms of organization takes on addition importance and hastens the process.

Difficulty of Change

Not only will bureaucratic forms spread, but once in place they are only likely to remain. They are very difficult to change and destroy for many complex reasons. To think about it simply for now, one reason is that people become encased in the organizational structure. If one thinks of the organi-zation as a large machine, the offices are cogs inside of that machinery and none of them stand outside of it. The people who occupy the offices are expected to perform their duties to the best of their ability in the interests of the organization itself. The alternative is to get fired. So, in other words, everyone who works inside of the machine is in one way or another compelled to do his part in keeping the machinery operating to the best of his ability. It is also the case that this goal of acting in the best interests of the organization according to the duties as described by the organization is the source of each person's well-being. Note that this applies especially to organizational leaders who would be those most in position to produce changes. In normal everyday terms we're talking about job performance and career advancement. If you do your job well you will continue to hold it and get paid, and perhaps get pro-motions and raises. In the simplest terms possible, the well-being of persons comes to depend on maintaining organizations.

It is not only the case that individual persons within organizations are dependent upon those organizations, but that everyone becomes dependent on their functioning. As more and more goods and services come to be supplied by formal organizations (whether public or private), people depend on them more and more for access to those good and services. Your elec-tricity service, for example, depends on the continued, routine and predict-able functioning of a very large organization which is likely a business corporation. But the functioning of something like your electric company is also interdependent with the regular and continued functioning of other large organizations such as supplier organizations, various subcontractors, banks, and regulatory agencies. So everything gets to be connected to everything else. Some of my readers might be old enough to recall US government activities to save and maintain very large corporations such as insurance companies, banks, and automobile companies during the 2008 financial crisis and its aftermath. Many of these organizations were dubbed *too big to fail* because they exist in a networked system of other organizations. On this logic, the failure of some would bring down the entire system like a string of dominoes, or perhaps like matter being sucked into a black hole.

This dependence and interdependence is not only there in instances where large-scale disruptions might take place. It is there in the minutiae of our everyday lives. The fact that bread constantly appears on grocery store shelves, gasoline at gas stations, textbooks to the college book store, that your money is good for purchasing those things, and so on owes the networks of organizations that are involved in producing, distributing, regulating, and selling these things. Once these things are built, basic dependency is the result. Any dramatic forms of change result in disruption to daily life and even to survival.

Changing Organizations Usually Means More Organizations

Note that the Weberian claim is only that change is difficult. It is not that it is impossible. It is not the case that organizations never fail or change or are destroyed. (Heck, I still miss *Circuit City* and *Radio Shack*.) Nor is it wise to reduce the humans to mere automatons. Change happens all of the time; interconnections and dependencies are variable, as is the place and importance of persons. The issues are complicated, and we will revisit them later. But for present purposes, note that even when organizations are changed or destroyed, it is most often in the face of actions by other organizations, or by turbulence in networks of organizations. If you begin to pay attention to the world as one populated by organizations rather than people, then you will begin to see that society is full of organizations acting on other organizations. Politics, for example, is about control of the state. The state itself is a large network of organizations. The main route for trying to control state organizations is through yet other organizations. Political parties are the most prominent, but the bulk of lobbying and campaign funding is also done by organizations on behalf of organizations.

With regards to the business world, business people, economists, and other commenters like to give the impression that business success is all about the customer—in the sense of individual consumers. This is certainly relevant. But first note that many customers are not individual consumers, but are other organizations. In many businesses, such as those that deal in raw materials, there might not even be any customers who are actual persons. Furthermore, in the world of business, often your most important interactions aren't with customers at all. Other relevant organizations include suppliers, distributors, regulating agencies, competitors, formally organized consumer interest groups, and the like. In fact, competition from other organizations is one of the primary drivers of attempts to change business organizations.

If you go on to study attempts to produce general social change on issues such as human rights, equal rights, environmental concerns, and so on, then you will quickly find organizations as well. In the study of social movements in sociology, for instance, the importance of the *social movement organization* (SMO) is well known. SMOs are the vehicles by which people recognize shared grievances, frame those grievances in terms of meanings, cause and remedy, and engage in collective action to seek redress. Without the organization, grievances tend to just remain *personal troubles*, in the words of C. Wright Mills. C. Wright Mills was a prominent sociologist, even if a bit of a renegade, during the middle of the twentieth century. He wrote a famous book for introducing sociology called *The Sociological Imagination* where he draws a distinction between *personal troubles* and *social issues*. Personal troubles are things about your own personal life, like being unemployed. But sometimes your own personal troubles are related to much larger *social issues*, such as the onset of a large recession or widespread decline of the industry in which you have been working. Individuals have troubles. But SMOs can turn the *troubles* of many into things recognized as social *issues*.

Thus, the observation that organizations do, in fact, change doesn't modify Weber's observation regarding the growth of the iron cage. Individual organizations certainly do change and do even disappear. But that doesn't change the picture of the world as one increasingly populated with formal organizations. Any serious attention to the question actually just serves to highlight the spread of formal organizations to an even greater extent. These are complicated issues to be sure and we will return to them.

The Iron Cage of Rationality

Once we have the basic picture of what a bureaucracy is, and we know about the tendency of this mode of organizing to spread we have the nuts and bolts of a central thread of Weber's famous *rationalization thesis*.[2] As the bureaucratic form grows and spreads it comes to encompass virtually everything in society. People now spend their lives, both over the long haul and on a day-to-day basis just moving from one rationalized structure to the next. You are born in an organizational nexus of hospital, insurance company, professional medical associations, and state regulations. You are quickly moved on into an education in other formal organizations (schools), so that you can later go work in one or more of them (businesses, government agencies, nonprofit organizations, and so on). Along the way you will get your goods and services—from gallons of milk to life insurance policies to brain surgery—through formal organizations which you will pay for in a form set up by other formal organizations such as banks that are themselves overseen by government agencies. When you die you will be ushered out of this world by formal organizations. Some will record your death and its causes. (I understand that you want to be a person, but you are *also* a number... perpetually.) Other organizations will see to it that your body is dealt with in culturally and perhaps religiously appropriate ways. There are virtually no aspects of social life that go untouched or unregulated by formal organizations.

When all of the pieces come together to the full picture you arrive at the basic, core meaning of the rationalization thesis. *Rational* activity is means-ends activity. Social actors have ends or goals—things that they need or want to do. For any given end or goal, there may be various means that will accomplish the goal. To be rational is to select the least cost means to a given end. This is a hallmark of modern social life. We don't live by old-fashioned adherence to tradition or superstition or the like. We deal in calculated reality. Our world is one that according to Weber is *disenchanted*.

Formal organizations are an expression of this rational approach to life. Organizations all have ends—to produce shoe laces, administer driver's licenses, sell insurance, promote interest in numismatics, or whatever else. The organization itself is designed as a set of means. It is the plan for how it is that the ends will be accomplished. Because the bureaucratic form is set up with full planning of tasks that are assigned to specific office holders with regular duties and all of this is designed to meet the ends of the organization, these are referred to as *rationalized structures*. More precisely for bureaucracies, they are *formally rationalized* because everything about the means is set out in writing or otherwise built into various material items such as production machinery or, more recently, computer algorithms.

---

[2]The full rationalization thesis in Weber's work is built on a lot more than his observations about bureaucracy, but that is beyond the scope of what we need to carry on here.

Formal rationalization brings a great deal of stability to social life. As summarized by George Ritzer, who has tried to rename this process the *McDonaldization of Society*, the formally rationalized world is marked by *efficiency, predictability,* and *calculability.* Ritzer basically agrees with Weber in pointing out that formal rationality has continued to spread throughout society on the basis of the same logic by which fast food is produced. The emphasis is on full standardization of all processes, activities, and products. These are designed to be the least cost means to produce and serve food. They also produce remarkable stability across time and place such that the operations and products from fast food restaurants are the same time after time and from location to location. All of that stability and efficiency also produces an emphasis on and ease of calculation. There is not only an ability to calculate but also an emphasis on things that can be quantified and calculated. What Ritzer was pointing out is that you can see the same principles in operation everywhere you look. School curricula become standardized in the form of textbooks, standardized worksheets, and standardized tests. Organizations like KinderCare have moved this packaged version of education to the preschool level. Vacations can be chosen off of a menu of services from various kinds of agencies. A great deal of uncertainty can be removed from camping by camp ground chains such as KOA. News outlets such as *USA Today* provide very short, simply packaged and "digestible" news. As Ritzer shows, the list goes on. The more you look, the more you see a world of pre-planned, pre-packaged goods and services provided by fairly large, bureaucratic organizations.

For many people, these things represent the benefits of formal rationality as they underlie the relatively smooth functioning of everyday life in industrialized areas of the globe. In a certain respect it is what Western culture celebrates about itself—we are "civilized" in that we have rationalized our social world. It is orderly and predictable. Weber himself seemed rather optimistic at times about some aspects of formal rationalization.

But there is a much darker side. Most people are familiar with the fact that standardized procedures can actually make things more cumbersome, for example. Faced with such situations, this is when people tend to complain about *bureaucratic red tape*. Such moments, if taken to characterize all of formal organization, do so only through selective observation because the clumsiness that can come from standardized routines does not cancel out many efficiencies that may go unnoticed. But nonetheless, as Ritzer also notes, while formal rationality can produce efficiency, predictability, and calculability, it can produce the opposite. Formal rationalization can have irrational consequences which go by the ironic phrase the *irrationality of rationality*. We will have more to say about that below and throughout the book. But regardless of whether one is thinking about what organizational sociologist Diane Vaughan has called the *bright side* or *the dark side* of formal organization, the process of formal rationalization does continue to grow and spread as Weber predicted.

Main Consequences of Rationalization

The rise of formally rationalized organizations has had profound effects on society as a whole, from the most general aspects of social structures all the way down to the level individual. There is no way to develop a comprehensive and all-inclusive list of such effects and we will deal with many aspects as we go through the book. For now, I will focus on some of the main elements that Weber emphasized as the most important effects.

Impersonality and Credentialing

Bureaucratic rationalization fundamentally changes what people are in their social contexts. The organizational focus on technical efficiency and qualifications makes what people are qualified to do a central aspect of their social statuses and identities. This produces a dominant concern with the question of credentials with regards to work education and experience. What people become is what they are worth to an organization in terms of the technical needs of organizations. This contributes to the persistent growth of formal schooling and constant pressures toward what has been called *credential inflation*. Most college students these days are in college for exactly this reason, and both they and their parents are prone to ask one related set of questions about education: What kind of job might I like to have and what credentials do I need to get there? Or, in other terms, what kind of cog do I want to be in what kind of organizational machinery, and how can I get the credentials that allow me to be there? In the minds of many, education is about technical qualifications, and its main purpose is to provide what is called *human capital* for people. Our primary identities, both what we are to ourselves and what we are to other people, become less and less tied to personal and meaningful things about ourselves and our significant others, and more and more tied to impersonal criteria as defined by the technical needs of formal organizations.

Value on Obedience to Authority

Not only do organizations turn you into a resume, but they also demand duty and loyalty from people. In fact, following organizational rules becomes a major component of socializing people in an organizational society. It begins very early in formal schooling where there are really several different curricula. On the surface education contains the credentialing aspects of "skilling" people. Students learn the famous "three r's": reading, 'riting, and 'rithmatic. But there are other *hidden curricula* in formal schooling, a major one being to learn the values associated with following along with organizational programs. In order to be successful with the content of schooling—the three r's—students must first learn to present themselves at preset times and places, occupy their assigned stations, punch the clock (so to speak), and follow orders. In many respects, the obedience to authority curriculum is taken even more seriously than the skill-building curriculum. Students who appropriately obey organizational routines but do not perform adequately on skill development might actually be set aside for special assistance and treatment. But those that break the organizational routines will be subject to more intensive forms of social control, including even involvement and enforcement of those rules by agents of government.

This sounds cold and creepy, and that is because it should. But in everyday understandings the authoritarian nature of formal organizations is accepted and justified for many reasons. One is that the organizational systems themselves are purported to be designed and run according to technical expertise. The "authority" is seen as being rooted in what is correct and best. Another is that each individual's well-being becomes tied to her abilities to perform the duties. Performance of duty comes with rewards, and in a sense everyone involved is given the incentive to remain dutiful and loyal to the organizational routines. The obedience is translated into basic respect for rules and for others, and, not surprisingly, many find that their own experiences in following the routines of authority have paid off.

The Dynamics of "Life's Chances"

These consequences at the individual level are part of a much larger shift in how social stratification operates. In common terms, social stratification is about issues of *social class* along with cross-cutting dimensions of *race/ethnicity* and *gender*. It refers to how people in society are unequal in terms of what resources they have, especially as those resources relate to power. We will have a lot more to say about power in the next two chapters and elsewhere, but for now note that most social power resources come under control of various formal organizations. Large business organizations, for example, possess large amounts of control over economic resources. Large political party organizations exist to attempt to control the organizations that make up the state which monopolizes political power. Media corporations, universities, and churches wield large measures of cultural power. As such, social stratification structures come to be thoroughly entangled with the structure of organizations and their offices.

For individuals this does mean that your own sources of social power are tied to your organizational position. For most people this becomes a primary life's concern. As Weber once noted, people come to see themselves as cogs in large machines and all they tend to ask about themselves is how to become a somewhat bigger cog. In common terms we call this a career ladder. But at the much larger level it means that much of a society's structure of opportunities is mapped to the structure of its organizations. If you are an ambitious person who seeks some high level of political power or wealth, you will find that the route will involve either navigating existing organizations or building a new one of your own.

Centralization of Social Power

This becomes even more important when one recognizes that the rise of formal organizations comes with what Weber referred to as the *concentration of the means of administration*. In more common language, social power becomes more and more centralized. One of the main administrative advantages of bureaucratic organizational principles is that it allows the coordination of many different actors and their activities. It provides the basis, in other words, for organizations to get really big. But recall that organizations are hierarchically organized, so vast amounts of social activity can come under the control of a relatively small number of offices in an organization.

Authority in organizations is tricky though. Paradoxically, formal organizations simultaneously centralize and decentralize power. They centralize because they do put the activities of many into the same administrative hierarchy of authority demanding obedience. Yet, by the same respect power is vested *in the rules*, not the people, and it is *distributed* throughout the hierarchy. No *one* is actually in control of a formal organization.[3] The ability to actually control an organization gets even trickier once you notice that organizations don't exist all by themselves, but in a social environment full of other

---

[3]This is still ideal-typical and we have much yet to learn about (a) why this is so and (b) how it is so in varying degrees.

organizations. In the end, formal organizations can become very large and very powerful but remain very difficult to control. They are very clumsy power tools. We will return to questions about power throughout the book.

The Irrationality of Rationality

Difficulties with organizational control are among the things that contribute to what can be called the *irrationality of rationality*. While George Ritzer is generally credited with the specific phrase, the concerns are apparent in Weber's writings on the issue. The irrationality of rationality refers to the fact that one can set up forms of organizing activity that are very much rationally planned and administered, yet the actual results of all of that activity can still turn out to be irrational. Since this sounds rather odd at first glance, we can get started by reference to a simple example from Ritzer's discussion of the issue. McDonald's obviously serves food, and food is important to humans for its nutritional value. That is, the *goal* of consuming food is related to human survival and health. There is little question that McDonald's accomplishes efficiency, predictability, and calculability in terms of providing food. Its operations are highly rationalized in the sense that all of the aspects of the business are calculated to be as efficient as possible. As far as the *means* are concerned, a McDonald's is a well-oiled machine. But what of the actual outcomes if one thinks carefully about it in terms of the *goal* of nutrition? Evaluations certainly vary, but fast food has been under a great deal of question for its nutritional value, including plenty of evidence indicating negative impacts on health. Thus rational means can produce irrational outcomes.

In order to understand the larger issue, it helps to understand that the kind of rationality that is in place in formal organizations—*formal rationality*—is only one type of rationally calculated social action. For Weber, there are three other types called *practical, theoretical,* and *substantive rationality* (see Figure 1.3 for a summary). *Practical rationality* is basically like every day decision-making in terms of very direct and pragmatic interests. If you are driving down the highway and get hungry, then you might start scanning for places to buy food. If the next highway exit has a McDonald's then you might

FIGURE 1.3   **Summary Table—Four Types of Rationality**

Practical Rationality: • Everyday, practical decision-making
Theoretical Rationality: • Decision-making informed by specialized expertise
Substantive Rationality: • Value oriented decision-making regarding the cultural/moral/ethical appropriateness of means and ends
Formal Rationality: • Decisions have already been made and are embedded in written rules or technological forms • The heart of the bureaucratic form, now dominating human action

choose to eat at it because it is a quick and easy way to satisfy your hunger. *Theoretical rationality* occurs where people attempt to develop highly holistic and systematic conceptual understandings of particular areas of activity in order to optimize on means and ends. It is often the province of various kinds of professionals whose knowledge in particular areas surpasses that of the day-to-day pragmatic social actor. If you happen to be a nutritionist who is driving down the highway hungry, then you might be ignoring places like McDonald's in the same way that you are ignoring hotels. Neither is thought to be relevant to your problem of needing some nutritious sustenance. You might instead be looking for a local farm stand or a health food store.

Substantive rationality is most heavily governed by concerns about social and cultural values. Like the nutritionist driving down the road hungry, you don't notice the McDonald's. But this is not out of any deep, theoretical and holistic knowledge regarding nutrition. Rather, you might be a union organizer driving through a right-to-work state, and you know that the McDonald's will be full of low-paid, nonunionized employees. You might instead be in search of a locally owned restaurant that is run by its proprietors, even if the decision to find one will take you more time and cost you more money. To provide your money to a nonunionized, corporate entity would counter your entire system of values.

The *formal rationality* that lies at the heart of the bureaucratic form of organization works by appealing to universally established routines and procedures. Here, people don't actually use their own rational principles to make decisions, whether practical, theoretical, or substantive. The decisions are all made beforehand and embedded in a system of rules. All the people do is follow the rules. And herein lies a central problem in Weber's darker vision of society. With the rise of formal rationality, the means become the ends. That is, in an organizational society our goals come to be the following of predefined routines and procedures that themselves are really just part of rationally planned means. As such, formal rationality eclipses other forms of rationality, most importantly substantive rationality. That is, people begin to be concerned mostly with acting upon means without similar attention to the evaluation of those means or the actual outcomes in terms of human values. As more and more human action gets bound by written rules, and our duties come to be defined according to following those rules, rule following itself becomes the highest value. Everyone contributes as directed toward keeping organizational machinery running with a relative lack of attention to what it is that the machinery actually turns out. An apt analogy can be found in the story of *The Sorcerer's Apprentice* (the old one originated by Goethe and popularized in the Disney version starring Mickey Mouse). The brooms were commanded to carry water. And carry water they did, regardless of the question of whether or not the original tasks were accomplished or whether the outcomes made sense.

But surely, one must think, humans are smart creatures who make decisions informed by their values and even common sense. We *should* know when our means are ethical and sane, and we *should* know when the outcomes are undesirable in some way, and any failure to act in these circumstances just indicates weakness or stupidity or worse. "I was just following orders" is not a culturally acceptable defense. In other words, good humans would know when to stop carrying the water and would, in fact, stop. There are no acceptable explanations for why human reason and substantive rationality would not always remain in control.

Certainly this is sometimes the case. People regularly set up organizational processes and procedures that do not have desired outcomes and irrational or undesirable things are stopped or changed. But it would be easy to overestimate the extent to which this characterizes today's world. To deepen the *Sorcerer's Apprentice* analogy, the brooms are formal organizations not people. The actual persons are to be found in the little bits and pieces of the broom—more like the cells in the wood and straw and bits of string, wire, and glue that hold the broom together. And the principles of formal rationality have all of those bits only tied to performing their own duties. Organizational leadership is not an exception to this. As noted, everyone is under the written rules of the formal organization, and organizational leadership may be under more pressures to make sure that the organizational machinery continues to operate. When it does not, organizational leaders tend to get the blame. Falling profits fall into the lap of the corporate CEO. Dropping enrollments fall in the lap of the college president. Budget deficits fall in the lap of the nation's president or equivalent. People are, after all, evaluated according to how well their actions are tied to the health of the organization for which they work.

Furthermore, organizations all construct stories about themselves that explain the values inherent in their inner workings. The people who operate in organizational positions are not only socialized into this vision of organizational life but also have their experiences shaped in such a way as to reinforce that very socialization. When organizations operate in ways that end up being branded as bad or irrational, it is often not because people inside of them understood their own actions as deviant. In fact, it is often the case that people all do exactly what they are supposed to do, and socially unacceptable events can occur regardless.

The uncomfortable message is that formal organization carries with it the tendency to actually escape human control. In a very real sense it is built into the operating logic or formal organizations. Humans are not in control of the organization. The organization is in control of the humans. To believe otherwise is to believe that you will be able to write your own job description and do just as you please whenever you get hired to do a job. To believe otherwise is to believe that the newly appointed CEO of a corporation is free to send her company into debt and monetary losses for the next several fiscal quarters if she realizes that many of the company's practices are harmful to the environment and public health. To believe otherwise is to think that organizational processes and procedures and the authority to change them at the stroke of a pen are under the control of specific individuals. Such is rarely the case. Thinking that organizations control people rather than *vice versa* is going to cut against a lot of things that people take for granted. But by the time we are through this book, the thought will be much harder to dismiss. (Of course, it will also be clear why much of this discussion is still ideal typical. There is always a lot of variation.)

The issues get even stickier when you ask about very general kinds of goals and take into account that the world is full of formal organizations, but that there is no rationalization of the totality of human activity itself. Most of the United States, for instance, is built around transportation by cars. There are extensive road networks, including an interstate highway system, large automobile companies, a vast auto parts industry, tires, fossil fuels, and so on. The current state of things was not a plan. There was no moment in history when someone or even one organization decided that the automotive world as we know it would be what it is. It continues to be the case that no one is actually in charge of it. It is what it is by virtue of the non-formally rationalized activities of the multitudes. (Many economists would say it was all the result of unplanned market activities, but all at the behest of consumer demands. In that respect, there is some "We" who actually "chose" it all.) At every point in the entire nexus, you will find people operating within rationalized structures doing perfectly rational things and for perfectly rational reasons. It all makes sense—in the bits and pieces. Yet the overall picture is questionable in terms of it meeting human goals or even being goal-directed. One set of outcomes—the effects of it all on the natural environment—can certainly be seen as irrational. One might argue that certain organizations, such as governments, are supposed to exercise some form of substantive control and do so through various regulatory agencies and laws. However, the complexity of everything involved is so intense that rational control is unlikely even if one had the authority to exercise it. Furthermore, those regulatory bodies and set of rules are yet other formally rationalized systems with similar kinds of issues, and their operations are not independent of the rest of the system or the politics of it all.

In many respects the irrationality of rationality belongs to a family of issues that have to do with things called *unintended consequences*. In economics, these kinds of things are referred to as *externalities*. The term is a little odd, but economists think of action as rational decision-making. In making rational decisions, calculations are made. All of the factors that are taken into account including the intended consequences of a decision are factors that are "internal" to the decision-making process. But one can never take all things into account or foresee all possible consequences. So many things remain outside of—or external to—the decision-making process. Thus, the term *externalities*.

Any course of human action has multiple effects in the world. You cross the room to pour a cup of coffee and as you do that you stir up a breeze, displace dust, and put more wear on your flooring. A company moves to factory farming of pork, and the increase in waste produced by the livestock ends up downstream of the farm polluting waterways. An anti-drug program administered in schools ends up piquing the curiosity of many students and actually increases drug use. Unintended consequences are part and parcel of all activity. They can't be avoided. However, within the iron cage they take on a special significance. Individuals and small, less formalized organized all produce externalities. But the larger the organizations become, and the more activities become linked together into interconnected systems, the size and practical consequences of those externalities grow in kind. Furthermore, with the frequent loss of attention to questions of substantive rationality, unintended consequences and externalities are more difficult to recognize as such. The Enlightenment promised us an intelligent world guided by the use of human reason. To many, rationality itself is the core of human reason. However, it is possible that the growth of *formal rationality* represents the defeat of human reason. Stay tuned.

Conclusion

Nothing here is meant to be stated as an absolute. Formal organizations certainly come into being and operate via the intentioned activities of people. This just does not mean that people are actually in control of things in any simple way nor does it mean that everything that happens in the world was due to reasoned decisions and choices of persons. And formal organization certainly represents rational activity in some form with rational and intended consequences, though we will eventually refer only to *intended rationality*. Yet it is just as apparent that all of this formally rationalized activity will actually spawn irrationality in many respects, and it is crucial to recognize that the irrationalities will frequently not be simply rooted in the decisions or actions of persons. What I will eventually draw out in Part III of this book is a means of understanding rationality as a variable. Things, whether people or actions or organizations or outcomes, are neither rational nor irrational all by themselves. For one thing, calling something rational requires a value judgment because it includes an assessment of the ends. But even given the ends, there are conditions under which things will be more or less rational and understanding that should really be one of the central foci of the social sciences. This question of rationality and irrationality will occupy us for most of the last third of the book.

But regardless of that question, we can be sure of one thing. Over the last 150 years or so, formally rationalized organizations have continued to spread as the dominant mode of guiding human social action. It did not happen all at once, though we will see that there was a crucial two decade period of change at the turn of the twentieth century that constitutes the core of the *organizational revolution*. Later we will come across various things that might lead to tempering this picture of the world, but for now we are still firmly in the grasp of *the iron cage of rationality*.

SOURCES AND FURTHER READING

Charles Perrow's statements regarding the **society of organizations** are frequent, but see especially:

- Perrow, Charles. 1991. "A Society of Organizations." *Theory and Society* 20: 725–62.

- ———. 2002. *Organizing America: Wealth, Power, and the Origins of Corporate Capitalism*. Princeton, NJ: Princeton University Press.

Emile Durkheim's discussion of **social facts** is found in Chapter 1 of:

- Durkheim, Emile. [1895] 1982. *The Rules of the Sociological Method: And Selected Texts on Sociology and Its Method*. Edited with and introduction by Steven Lukes. Translated by W. D. Halls. New York, NY: The Free Press.

The core of **Max Weber**'s writings most directly relevant to defining bureaucracy, the iron cage, and the consequences:

- 2013. *Economy and Society: An Outline of Interpretive Sociology*. Edited by Guenther Roth and Claus Wittich. Berkeley, CA: University of California Press.

  o See especially, Chapter III: "The Types of Legitimate Domination" and Chapter XI: "Bureaucracy."

The literature on **Social Movements and Social Movements Organizations** is voluminous. For reasonably recent basic overview of SMOs see:

- Walker, Edward T., and Andrew W. Martin. 2019. "Social Movement Organizations."In *The Wiley-Blackwell Companion to Social Movements*. 2nd ed., edited by David A. Snow, Sarah A. Soule, Hanspeter Kriesi, and Holly J. McCammon, 167–84. Hoboken, NJ: John Wiley & Sons, Inc.

- For a classic application of social movements theory to struggles for organizational control (though not mentioned in this chapter) see: Davis, Gerald F., and Tracy A. Thompson. 1994. "A Social Movement Perspective on Corporate Control." *Administrative Science Quarterly* 39: 141–73.

C. Wright Mills' discussion of **troubles and issues** is found in:

- Mills, C. Wright. [1959] 2000. *The Sociological Imagination*. New York, NY: Oxford University Press.

George Ritzer's McDonaldization thesis can be found:

- In book-length version: Ritzer, George. 2019. *The McDonaldization of Society: Into the Digital Age*. 9th ed. Thousand Oaks, CA: Sage Publications. (The original/first Edition was published in 1993).

- Or in an abridged paper-length version: Ritzer, George. 2008. "The Weberian Theory of Rationalization and the McDonaldization of Contemporary Society." In *Illuminating Social Life*.

4th ed., edited by Peter Kivisto, 41–59. Los Angeles, CA: Pine Forge Press/Sage.

A classic review of **the bright and dark sides of organizations** is in:

- Vaughan, Diane. 1999. "The Dark Side of Organizations: Mistake, Misconduct, and Disaster." *Annual Review of Sociology* 25: 271–305.

Among the earliest to raise the issue of **"credential inflation"** can be found in:

- Collins, Randall. [1979] 2019. *The Credential Society: An Historical Sociology of Education and Stratification*, Legacy Edition. New York, NY: Columbia University Press.

- *Note that, while Collins' is very much a Weberian sociologist, the account given is directly at odds with the notion that credentials are about technical competence.*

For the distillation of Weber's work that teases out the **four types of rationality**:

- Kahlberg, Stephen. 1980. "Max Weber's Types of Rationality: Cornerstones for the Analysis of Rationalization Processes in History." *The American Journal of Sociology* 85: 1145–79.

  - This is also used in Ritzer (2019, 2008), cited above.

For the sociological classic on **unintended consequences**, see:

- Merton, Robert K. 1936. "The Unanticipated Consequences of Purposive Social Action." *American Sociological Review* 1: 894–904.

The Subject Is Organizations.
The Issue Is Power

Many aspects of Weber's description of the bureaucracy are deserving of a chapter of their own. But it is possible that none is more important than the issue of social power summarized in Weber's observation that bureaucracy *centralizes the means of administration*. The rise and spread of formal organizations has shaped social power in ways that remain under appreciated. We live in a culture shaped by assumptions born of the Enlightenment. The core principle of the Enlightenment is that human action, and thus social life, is a matter of reasoned persons making informed decisions. In simplistic form, the Enlightenment overthrew old traditional, aristocratic social hierarchies of power and provided "power to the people." This was (and still is) expressed institutionally in our emphasis on market economies and participatory forms of government where we can all be our own decision-makers. While there is no manner of absolute equality envisioned, all people are, in principle, on a level playing field, able to act according to their own will, and have full participation in the conditions under which they live their own lives. Setting aside, just for the moment, that Enlightenment ideas were initially formulated with a narrow definition of people as white males, this Enlightenment vision of the world was arguably not inappropriate through the eighteenth and much of the nineteenth centuries. Significant aspects of the political and economic conditions of life were still heavily shaped "close to home," so to speak, in local communities. But as of the organizational revolution, this conception of persons and society very well may cease to apply, despite the fact that it is still widely assumed. Social power is in organizations, and to the extent that persons have any, it is either by virtue of their organizational positions or strongly conditioned by an organizational environment.

The attentive reader will be thinking that such absolute statements must be oversimplified, and indeed they are. But this is not hard to do because issues of power "in and around organizations" (as Management scientist Henry Mintzberg once put it in a famous book title) are nothing if not highly complex. This chapter will not attempt to deal with the issue in its entirety. It is unlikely that any chapter can. For now, still at the introductory beginnings of our journey, I will outline a general picture of a society in which the *means of administration* have been heavily concentrated. Our initial focus will not be typical for treatments of power found in other general overviews of organizational studies. Those are overwhelmingly concerned with how power operates on the inside of organizations or between them. This kind of focus matters greatly here too, but our foremost questions have more to do with what the rise of large formal organizations means for the general conditions of power throughout society. At other points in the book we will return to questions of power again and again, including those more often found in other treatments of organizational power.

With our attention largely on the question of organizations, the picture of power that emerges from this chapter will be most compatible with those that are called *power structures* or *power elite* orientations to understanding social power. These are generally contrasted to *pluralist* orientations. In the power literature, these orientations are taken to be opposed and in many respects they are. This goal here, however, is not to take a side or settle any questions. (This has already taken up entire books.) Although a focus on organizations as the locus of social power will inevitably lean harder in the direction of power structures orientations, my goal will be to leave us beyond polarized types of arguments and leave the attention on being sensitive to variation. But regardless of how the picture gets painted or how it leans, we arrive at the same destination. Over the last century and a half, social power has become significantly a matter of the dynamics of formal organizations, and thus has become more concentrated rather than distributed throughout the population as would be required for living up to Enlightenment ideals.

While the study of social power has always been a central point of attention for social scientists, most people probably have very fuzzy ideas regarding the subject if it has been given any thought at all. So we'll begin with a very basic overview of the general concept of social power. What I will provide isn't the only way to conceptualize power, though it is the most common one and will serve our purposes as well as any other.

What Is Social Power?

In its simplest sense, power is often defined as the ability of an actor to realize its will. In other words, if you want or need to do something and you are able to do it, then you have power to whatever extent you are able to do as you will. This is often called the "*power to*" do something. The reason that I refer to "actors" and use the pronoun "it" is because we have to be able to see actors not merely as persons but also as organizations.[1] With regards to organizations, we can refer to a form of *social* power that occurs wherever multiple actors cooperate to increase their power—"many hands make light work" as the old saying goes. This is one thing that human social organizations, whether formal or informal, represent. People often cooperate to move a couch because two people can exercise more power than only one alone. It is not any different for building pickup trucks, making whiskey, farming, or educating students. It's pretty much that way for all human activity even where it isn't obvious. Myths about heroic

---

[1] It is worth noting that Weber—and many other sociologists—may not approve. The only things in the world capable of action are conscious persons. Organizations are merely abstractions—a way of referring to the activities of multiple persons. This is a long-standing ontological problem for the social sciences and I am not going to get distracted by it here. Suffice it to say that in a technical, empirical sense all actors have to be corporeal persons. However, formal organizations are *programs for action* that, once established, exist independently of the particular actors that occupy offices at any given moment.

individualism in US culture aside, humans beings are social creatures and are really only capable of doing what they do by virtue of a social context and coordinated collective actions that make it possible—in other words, by virtue of social organization. Thus we want to be able to think about organizations as tools for *collective power* that provide actors the *power to* accomplish things that they would find more difficult or impossible to do otherwise.

In the study of power in the social sciences, it is much more common to be concerned with what is called "*power over*," as in some actors having power over other actors. So one of the most typical definitions given of social power is that it is the ability of an actor to realize its will, *even if other actors resist*. This power over other actors is called *distributive power*. It is called distributive because power is distributed—not all hold it equally and some have more than others. *Collective power implies distributive power* because for collective power to work, activities have to be coordinated and the coordination implies that people submit to an organizational plan, even if an ad hoc and informal one. Bureaucracy is just such a plan, but as we have seen much more formalized than other ways of organizing human activity. Within formal organizations, distributive power in a bureaucracy is, of course, formalized in the hierarchy of authority and in the rules that define action.

Distributive power does not necessarily imply that some actors are getting over on other actors in the sense that they wield their power for selfish gain or according to self-serving whim, and at the expense of order-takers. For one thing, in the pure form of bureaucracy, everyone is under the rules and thus subject to power. Power is in the rules themselves, not in the persons. Furthermore, the distribution and hierarchy of authority is supposed to be functional—geared toward the goals of the organization—and justified by technical criteria. To the extent that collective action can be coordinated so that the goals of an organization are met, it can certainly be the case that all involved are meeting their own interests and gaining benefit. Of course, this does not mean that distributive power *can't* operate according to principles of selfish gain or whim where some benefit at the expense of other. Indeed, this is very often the case. But the mere existence of distributive power does not imply that. For example, most people do not stop at red lights and then go on to curse politicians for their self-serving behavior even though things like traffic lights are implemented and enforced by the state. Similarly, you don't curse your friend for telling you to grab the left side of the couch while they grab the right. These do represent distributive power, even if they don't match the image of some actors controlling other people for their own benefit.

Given their codification in written rules that transcend the situated decision-making of whatever actors happen to be involved, bureaucracies function as very well defined and very stable power structures in both the collective and distributive sense. As Weber himself wrote:

> ...*bureaucracy was and is a power instrument of the first order for one who controls the bureaucratic apparatus. Under otherwise equal conditions, rationally organized and directed action is superior to every kind of collective behavior and also social action opposing it. Where administration has been completely bureaucratized, the resulting system of domination is practically indestructible*[2]

---

[2]Weber [1922] 1978: 987.

Accustomed as we are to thinking of persons as the primary actors of society, the relative rigidity and stability of formal organizations as things that structure social power is often overlooked. But it is crucial. Formal organizations direct and limit what office holders do. That is, organizations control people rather than vice versa. And by design the bureaucratic form permits for continuity by defining courses of action around offices with assigned duties rather than around what the persons involved at any given time happen to decide to do. Formal organizations are thus very stable kinds of power relations that transcend persons in terms of the exercise of power. Do note that I am still referring to things in ideal typical terms, but we are just starting here and will consider variations later.

Consider a couple of common complaints that people have about those who sit in positions of organizational power. Politicians, we are told, are famous for making promises to people and then not keeping them. Surely sometimes this may just be because they are unscrupulous and will lie to get their way. But consider the fact that political office does not simply bestow upon people the power to do whatever they wish. The powers of all politicians are limited by the rules as well as by competing political interests. Perhaps it is merely the case that politicians are often promising to do things that they are not capable of achieving given the powers of their office. Similarly, corporate leaders are often decried for being "greedy," as if removing greed from persons would mean that corporate organizations would no longer be expected to produce the highest possible profits. Inside of the boundaries of ethical and legal considerations (ideally), maximizing returns for the owners of a corporation (shareholders) is the primary obligation of a business. As such, working to that end comes to be the primary duty of corporate leadership—whether they are personally "greedy" or not. Not everything about these matters can be explained away by organizational obligations and restraints. Politicians surely do knowingly mislead people at times and corporate leaders very well may be greedy and will sometimes do unethical and illegal things out of greed. But it is important to know that this does not explain everything either. Often what we're seeing in terms of what persons do or do not do is symptomatic of the functioning of formal organizations.

The most important point to recognize, as Weber did long ago, is that social power does not fundamentally lie with persons, but with organizational structures. Those structures, by design, are more powerful than the people who occupy the offices within the structures. And an integral part of organizations is that they are designed to perpetuate themselves. As such, we have created a world with highly stable formalized power structures that persist even as the individuals come and go. This is one key point for the *power structures* view.

Social Power Resources: IEMP

Given that social power is the ability of an actor to get its way even despite resistance, how is it that this can be done? If we started to make a list we could probably make a very long one. But almost anything that we could put on the list can be grouped fairly simply according to a relatively small number of social power resources. Though the specifics can be discussed in slightly different ways by social scientists that study social power, for the most part virtually all discuss power according to what Sociologist Michael Mann has simplified as an *IEMP model*. The "I" stands for *Ideological* power; the "E" for *Economic* power, the "M" for *Military* power, and the "P" for *Political* power (see Figure 2.1). It is important to note that this is an ideal type. None of these kinds of power resources exist or are held independently of the others. It is also worthy to note that it closely mirrors another ideal type of Weber's where he described the basis for social stratification as having to do with *Class* (the E), *Status* (the I), and *Party* (the M and P) resources.

Ideological power is basically about the ability to control ideas—how people think about and understand the world, themselves, and others. Human beings are symbolic creatures who act toward things in the world on the basis of the meanings that they have for them. The ability to control or influence meanings is thus power over the premises upon which people act. This involves not only morality (the sense of right and wrong), but also understandings of reality (knowledge of true and false). If, for example, people believe that poverty is the result of personal failures on the part of those who are poor, they will be less inclined to act toward poor populations as people who should be helped by others. Their beliefs about the reasons for poverty say that people must help themselves. (The rest, I guess, is up to God.) The orientation toward assistance for the poor would be very different if one understands poverty to be the result of structural issues in the economy, rather than of personal failings. What is believed to be true by people matters a lot in how they act in the world. If we move to matters of morality, one might believe that righteous people assist the poor no matter what, but the correct type of assistance would vary quite a bit according to whether or not one still sees poverty as a matter of personal failings. Perhaps more obvious now than ever, many of our contemporary disagreements regarding matters of politics and economics are underlain by disagreements regarding basic facts and values. Thus, the ability to manipulate those beliefs is an important basis for social power.

In his *Class/Status/Party (CSP)* ideal type, Weber was discussing the positions of individual actors in a social setting, and the ideological dimension

FIGURE 2.1   **Social Power Resources: IEMP**

	Type of Power	Definition	Organizational types
I	Ideological/Cultural Power	Control of ideas, both in terms of fact and value	Universities, Media Organizations, Think Tanks, Churches (and virtually all other organizations)
E	Economic Power	Control of productive resources for meeting material needs	Business organizations / Corporations
M	Military Power	Ability to enforce will via sheer physical coercion	Military and Police Forces
P	Political Power	Ability to make the rules and adjudicate	Government, Government Agencies, Political Parties

corresponds to the status dimension. Status is a cultural judgment of ones "social honor" as Weber called it, or what we would frequently just call reputation these days. This is a matter of cultural values and morality in that some actors are held in higher esteem than others as measured by social values. Someone like Steve Jobs who started Apple, and Larry Flynt founder of *Hustler* magazine are both entrepreneurs who founded successful businesses and became quite wealthy. Larry Flynt, however, would not carry the same *status* as Steve Jobs.

The *Economic* basis of power is generally more obvious and more often thought of as power. Some actors can get other actors to do what they want them to do because they hold goods or services or some other manner of resource that others need or want. It can include a lot of different things. Rent is paid to people who own buildings. People who own land can raise agricultural products for sale. You can cut firewood from your land and sell it to your neighbor. People may only go to work because they need to get paid. While at work people will follow orders for the same reasons. If you have developed some form of specialized skill or work experience that others need, often called *human capital*, you can sell that. In Weber's ideal type, this was the *class* dimension of social power. Operating as he was at the level of the relative positions of specific actors he defined ones class as a *market position*. It is basically based on what an actor has to sell or trade. Most college students these days report that they are going to college to improve their chances of a getting a good job. In other words, they are trying to earn a credential that will improve their market position beyond what a high school diploma would provide.

We can discuss the M and P together as the *Political* dimension of power. Sometimes people make the mistake of assuming that social power is only about politics. But the political dimension is only one among the others. In simplest form, it is the ability to make and enforce the rules. In general, the making of the rules is represented by the P and enforcement comes under the M. So you don't have to think about the Military dimension as only including formal militaries. It boils down to the ability to use sheer force. In the end, for thinking about it as a dimension of power, that's pretty much it—the legitimate right to use force in a given territory. To many readers this isn't the first thing that comes to mind, but when you strip things down to the bare essentials, that is where you end up. If you fail to perform your duties at work or violate the rules of your workplace you can get fired, suspended, or demoted. But if you fail to perform your duties for the state (e.g., jury duty) or violate the rules of the state, then agents of the state can kidnap (arrest) you, physically bind you, and imprison you. Your employer is not allowed to do that. It's true that if you violate a rule at work that *also* violates a rule of the state (such as stealing from your employer), then you can get arrested. But even then agents of the state have to do it. Your employer cannot. But the police aren't going to come get you if you're late for work for the third time this month, and your employer can neither arrest you for it, nor have you arrested. All they can do is dock your pay and/or suspend or fire you.

In contemporary times it is frequently the case that there is a political system that exercises authority over actors in a territory without a great deal of appeal to force and the use of force. This is where the political system is considered by its constituents to be legitimate. *Legitimacy* is about whether or not people accept power over them and thus is nothing other than a special form of Ideological power carried by state organizations, although the question of legitimacy applies to all actors who exercise power. In cases where political organizations of the state carry legitimacy, those organizations generally maintain control over official Military organizations in the form of its actual armed forces and other enforcement agencies such as police. So M is often under the authority P in terms of power. However, this situation can always break down, as one would find in instances of military *coup d'état* where militaries take control of government. So while militaries are ideally under control of a legitimate political system, for questions of social power one can never ignore those who actually control weapons whether under political control at any particular time or not.

Wherever you find people talking about issues of social power, whether inside of the social sciences or not, you will always find the discussions of power conceptualized according to these resources, whether or not those talking about it realize it or use precisely this same terminology. All issues of power from day to day interpersonal relations to global international relations can be conceptualized in this way. It all just comes down to how you can get others to do what you want them to do. One way is to pay them (E). Another way is to force them (P & M). Yet another way is to *make them believe that they should do and/or want to do* what it is that you want them to do (I). When parents want their kids eat their vegetables they often start with ideology—convincing a child that it is good for them. If that doesn't work there is always the control of material rewards, such as dessert. Then when push comes to shove, there is the old "go to your room!" imprisonment response. When the US government wants another state or global actor to do something or to stop behaving in a way defined as deviant, it often starts with ideas—diplomacy, negotiations, shaming, and blaming. If that doesn't bring another actor into line, the next move is often economic sanctions such as trade restrictions or full embargos. When all of that fails, there are several P/M routes including international rule making organizations such as the World Trade Organization, and then of course there is always the actual military option. So in one way or another, regardless of the social arena, when we are talking about social power we are looking at the dynamics among these basic power resources.

Strictly speaking, ideological control is always the most efficient if you want power to operate smoothly. Its maintenance is relatively cheap and effective by comparison to other strategies. It operates very quietly and smoothly, normally doesn't even look like power, and is generally not even felt as such. Order-takers, in fact, may follow orders with great fervor and enthusiasm, as people do when they follow *charismatic leaders*. If ideological control is weak the next best form of control tends to be economic. It is generally more expensive and harder to administer than ideological power, but material reward does tend to make for willing participants. But it generally just doesn't work as well as ideological power even in gaining compliance, and it carries larger costs. If neither of those forms work, then one can appeal to formal rules and their enforcement, but this kind of power now gets very expensive and is difficult to maintain. If legitimacy is lost and the only thing left is sheer force then the situation is especially bad for those who would attempt to wield power. In fact, it indicates that they are not actually all that powerful. Truly powerful actors never have to turn to enforcement because those under them willingly go a long with the orders. In other words, the most effective forms of social power often do not look like the exercise of social power at all.

It is important to be able to take this classification of power resources as ideal typical. That is, they don't exist independently of each other in neat little boxes. Rather they are completely intertwined, and often highly correlated. In bringing up *legitimacy* for a political system, for example, the ideological and political dimensions are immediately blurred since legitimacy is ultimately found in the beliefs of the ruled. Anyone who pays any attention to matters of politics or economics is also well aware that economic power can be converted to political power, and that political and military actors need access to economic resources.

Note that many people do not think of power as multidimensional because many do think of power only in its overt form of rulemaking and enforcement—in terms of P & M. Economists, for example, don't tend to think of market economies as arenas of power because all of the actors in it are assumed to engage in the actions voluntarily. This works well in textbooks and certain specific contexts, but in the realm of practical reality this assumption misses a lot. People's choices are frequently highly constrained by many things including uneven access to economic resources. It also misses the fact that modern economic theory, in making such assumptions, is part of what provides significant ideological support for existing economic arrangements and inequalities of power. So always keep in mind that Political/Military resources are only one way that social actors get other social actors to do what they want them to, and will always be intertwined with Ideological and Economic power resources. Just because the latter forms are more invisible does not mean that they aren't forms of power.

Social Power and Formal Organizations

The important point for our present purposes is that over the last 200 years or so, the major sources of social power have become increasingly concentrated in formally rationalized systems. As we will see in Part II, starting with the organizational revolution, most of our major industries in the United States came to be dominated by *oligopolies* (or sometimes *monopolies*), a situation where an industry is controlled by only one (*mono-*) or only a small number (*oligo-*) of companies. The US auto industry, for example, quickly came to be dominated by "the big three" of Ford, General Motors, and Chrysler. Railroads companies, of which there were initially hundreds in the nineteenth century, were consolidated under the control of just a few companies at the turn of the twentieth century. The Standard Oil Trust came to virtually monopolize the early oil industry, while US Steel dominated the steel industry. In industry after industry economic activity came to be dominated by small numbers of companies. While the extent of concentrated industry control has waxed and waned some over the course of time, and whole new industrial sectors have appeared, the situation is now just global. Older industries like oil and gas, metals, and autos continue with oligopolistic structures. And the same pattern seems to emerge every time new industries emerge. So we also find oligopolies in computers and software, smart phone manufacturing and wireless service, and mass media. The global economy is not a nice game of kids setting up a lemonade stand on the corner. It is one of giant multinational corporations operating in highly concentrated industries.

Similarly political and military power is concentrated in very large governmental and military organizations. States and militaries have frequently concentrated power around the globe and at all different times and places over history, yet their growth in size and scope is a hallmark of the modern (perhaps now postmodern) period in the West. In addition, wherever democratic and parliamentary political institutions are in place, the battle over their control takes place via other organizations, the most prominent of which are political parties. To be sure, there have been large P/M empires in the past, and some have been very large with many of the vestiges of bureaucracies. But their presence was still geographically limited to particular regions. We are at the first point in human history where the formal organization of state and military control covers the entire globe and its entire population. Furthermore, the existing system of nation-states along with their militaries is tied up tightly to the dynamics of the global economy.

Ideological power tends to be a bit more dispersed, but is heavily organizational nonetheless. Media corporations are some of the most central ideology producers as are such things as churches, universities, and think tanks. Wherever people provide windows on the world and interpretations of what is occurring in it, and wherever one finds attempts to instill or manipulate morality one is looking at operations in the realm of ideological power. It is about organizations battling over the nature and content of truth and morality. In this regard, since organizations of any kind need legitimacy, all are engaged at some level in the production and forwarding of ideas and perceptions, even if it is merely limited to how the organization is viewed by others.

Thus we live in an age when the primary resources for social power are concentrated in large, formally rationalized systems. This should come as no surprise after looking at the general rationalization thesis. Formal rationality grows and spreads to encompass more and more of social life to the point that society becomes the iron cage of rationality. Thus it stands to reason that basic power resources in a society are similarly rationalized and come under the control of large administrative hierarchies. The end result is not only power concentrated in organizations but also even further concentrated in the top positions of those organizations.

Robert Michels and the Iron Law of Oligarchy

At about the time that Weber was raising concerns about the rise of formal rationality, a young associate of his named Robert Michels was throwing a bit more fuel on the fire. Michels was a social scientist and active for a while in Germany's Social Democratic Party (SDP) which was a socialist workers' party. Contrary to popular legend in the United States, socialism is contrary to capitalism, but not contrary to democracy. In fact, those with socialist orientations tend to be adamantly democratic at the same time. To grossly oversimplify for the sake of brevity, socialists just can't figure out why anyone would want democratically run political systems, but not have democratically run economic systems. Thus, as its name implies, the German SDP political platform thoroughly espoused democratic ideals. Yet, Michels was bothered by the fact that the party organization itself did not seem to run itself democratically. It was, rather, largely controlled by a small elite in top leadership positions in ways that frequently did not reflect the interests of the party membership or its stated ideals.

The common sense approach to explaining this kind of inconsistency between professed values and actual actions would be to individualize and moralize. We would blame the persons in the party leadership and perhaps others for being hypocrites. If we cared at all, we might furthermore demand their removal and replacement with others who might act more virtuously and remain true to the membership and the organization's values. This is what people in the United States are doing every time they locate issues of politics in the actual persons who currently occupy an office. People tend to believe that political issues can be fixed by replacing the current "bad" persons with new "good" ones. It is possible that Michels had such thoughts, but he was also a social scientist with a close relationship to Max Weber. So what he did, instead of merely yelling about "bad apples," was to do an intensive study of the administrative operation of political parties to see how they worked. Out of that came his now famous 1911 book called *Political Parties* in which he outlined what is called the *iron law of oligarchy.*

In simplest summary form, the iron law of oligarchy is that any large organization, regardless of its stated principles, will inevitably end up being controlled by a relatively small, self-perpetuating elite. (If you break down the term *oligarchy,* it is made up of: *oligo-* which means few and *-archy* which refers to ruling, and thus rule by the few.) That small elite strata in the leadership positions of the organization will end up taking on distinctively different orientations from the mass constituents of the organization, and will act for the benefit of the organization, even if this leads to straying from its original purposes and the interests of the constituents. The idea of acting for the benefit of the organization regardless of what it means for being true to principles is an important one. Organizations, by the way they are structured, develop what are now called *structural interests*. These are the needs of the organizational structure itself, which shape group interests and power relations in the organization. If the needs of the organization are not cared for, then the organization may not survive at all. Thus organizational survival itself will generally come above all else, and can easily result in what has been dubbed called *organizational drift*, which is largely about the straying from officially stated principles, processes and procedures. Rather than being rationally planned means to accomplish stated ends, organizations can be seen as drifting along through time driven largely by their own survival. For this reason, it doesn't really matter much which actual persons end up in leadership positions within organizations. Whoever they are, their outlooks, interests, and actions will be generated by the structural needs of the organization itself. The tendency toward oligarchy is a seen to be a universal tendency in organizations. It isn't a decision that people make. "*Who says organization says oligarchy,*" Michels declared.[3]

The main starting point for the logic of Michels' argument is the simple difficulty involved in having large groups of people make and implement decisions. If everyone is involved, and everyone needs a say, and everything has to be voted on all of the time, then it becomes very difficult, or even impossible to get anything done. This is, of course, is among the reasons that large scale democracies are largely representative rather than direct. If anything is to get done, then delegation of decision-making and implementation of action is inevitable. This is the case even where there is a strong democratic purpose and spirit in an organization. If organizations remain

---

[3]Michels [1911] 1962: 365. We will have a more complete account of things like structural interests and organizational drift in Chapter 8.

relatively small and their activities relatively simple, then it can remain possible for the leadership of organizations to remain accountable to the will of the constituents. But small and simple has not been the story of our last couple of hundred years.

Much of Michels' focus was on labor parties and unions which were in the process of ballooning in size right along with the growth in size of businesses (which we will discuss further in Part II). As such, the size of these organizations was increasing along with the complexity of their activities. This complexity is important. The running of an organization itself easily becomes a difficult and full-time job for those delegated to carry authority, and those jobs increasingly require various kinds of technical expertise in management, law, accounting, and so forth. This sets in motion a whole host of things that result in the inevitability of self-perpetuating oligarchy that ends up working foremost on behalf of an organization's own survival and power rather than on whatever its principles are.

For one thing, since the leadership positions become the full time occupations for the leaders, it becomes the source of their salaries, benefits, and prestige. As such, organizational survival becomes a matter of personal survival. Furthermore, the business of the organization comes to take up their full attention and subtly shapes their values and their views on the world in ways that are quite different from the constituency. Leaders of a blue-collar labor union, for example, cease to be blue-collar workers. Instead they become white-collar office workers who do very different kinds of work than the people that they are supposed to represent. They don't spend their time on the shop floor with other workers, but in company board rooms and political offices where they associate with other organizational elites of business and government. What ends up becoming most important to them is how well the organization itself does—how secure it is, and how powerful it is. This is how their bread is buttered, but can easily *appear to be* what *is* in the best interests of their constituents, even if their activities tend to depart from the stated or initial goals of the organization. They quickly find that stability and security for the organization tends to mean playing the game with other powerful leaders. You negotiate and strike bargains and make compromises, all of which aim toward the production of the stability of the *status quo*.

The complexity of the work of is done by organizational leadership feeds right into this. Organizational leaders need to end up with some manner of expertise with regards to matters of law and accounting. They need to become effective orators and professional writers. Michels observed, in fact, that various training programs had emerged in many places for providing specialized training to party and union leaders thus producing something of an elite professional class within the working class. But it's not merely about formal technical training either. There is a lot of tacit knowledge that comes from being involved in elite circles. The leaders become "insiders" in larger games of power, learning how the wheels get greased and how bargains are struck. It is not easy business running a large organization. This is a large part of the reason that oligarchies become self-perpetuating. New leaders are selected and groomed—or socialized—into these complex roles. In other words, regardless of what an organization was formed to do, organizational leadership will end up being oriented toward the flows of power in a larger interorganizational system. As part and parcel of this process, the mass membership of the organization has to give up on being able keep a watchful eye over the actions of the leadership.

There are too many things to pay attention to, and too many things that remain unknown. The complexity of much of the organization's activities transcends to ability of the membership to know about and understand.

Surely though, one must think, even a light amount of surveillance must keep organizational leaders in line with the wishes and values of the masses. If the leadership strays too far the membership must be able to resist and keep the organization in line with the ultimate program. It rarely comes to this, however, because the constituents of the organization will generally have neither the inclination nor ability to stage any kind of collective response to the oligarchic conditions. The organizational leadership controls the organizational resources and is able to shape the understandings that people have of it. They control the agenda for organizational activities and the official communications channels of the organization. They explain what the organization is doing, what is going on in it, and why. In fact, the membership frequently looks to organizational leadership to do just that. And even if they see things wrong and want to stage some manner of resistance it is generally fairly easy to paint them as uninformed reactionaries and dissidents who don't understand the practical reality of things. But even more to the point, the constituents, *en masse*, have no organizational base from which to make a challenge for power. There is little way to formulate and advance alternative, critical assessments of organizational leadership nor any way to produce an alternative. Regardless of what might be behind the scenes, formal organizations tend to develop a front face that explains to its constituents and outside observers that it is doing exactly what it is supposed to. Ironically, the only way that the masses could challenge the organizational leadership is by building a new organization—at which point the same processes are put into motion. For Michels' the results of his analysis are clear. Thus his conclusion (noted above) that *"Who says organization says oligarchy."* It doesn't matter what the intentions or wishes of people are. The dynamics don't reside inside of the heads of persons or their intentions. They reside in the dynamics of organizing itself.

The larger issue that goes beyond the narrow subject matter of understanding power in formal organizations lies in Michels' more general main point in the book which is that mass democracy is actually impossible. In order for masses of people to engage in coordinated and concerted collection action they require formal organizations. In other words, mass democracy requires organizations. Yet, formal organizations make true democracy impossible. It is a classic catch-22. The point is not that the formal trappings of democracy can't exist. Obviously they do. Many political systems and organizations have representatives and voting and input mechanisms and so forth. The formal trappings of democracy amount to part of what keeps oligarchic power structures in place because appeals to democratic principles are an important means of maintaining legitimacy for the organization and its leaders. But for Michels, all of that is largely illusion. Whatever the values of an organization happen to be, these serve largely as symbolic tools used rhetorically to whip up the emotions of the masses. Mass democracy was sure to turn politics into *demagoguery*, or forms of political activity where support is sought by making appeals to population sentiment, beliefs, and prejudices. And so it has.

Of course, Michels' argument was about mass membership organizations where power is not *supposed* to be concentrated. Many types of organizations, such as business corporations, have power concentrated at the top of administrative hierarchies by design. This doesn't mean that the same basic processes don't apply. It just means that a small number of elite are expected to be in control and to operate on behalf of the wellbeing of the organization itself.

As with Weber's description of bureaucracy and rationalization, it is best to take Michels' analysis of oligarchy as an ideal typical description of the tendencies of large organizations. The issue of power and control in organizations is very complicated and any dogmatic clinging to Michels' conclusions is unwarranted. There is a lot of variation in organizations—in how they operate, how power actually works, and in what kinds of things can increase or decrease tendencies toward oligarchy. For now we can simply note that regardless of what an organization is supposed to do or what it is supposed to be like or what the people in it say that it is or will be, there are very strong tendencies toward power becoming concentrated in a relatively small, self-perpetuating elite, and this will frequently be accompanied by a disconnect between stated principles and goals and actual actions.

Power Elite Interpretations of Power

Once we have the picture of social power being concentrated in large organizations, and then add the observation that power in large organizations tends to be concentrated in elites at the top, then you arrive at the roots of *power elite* conceptions of social power. Among the first observers to make this view prominent was mid-twentieth-century sociologist C. Wright Mills. As Mills explains, the world is certainly full of important forms of social organization such as family, church, or school. But the twentieth century, especially in the United States, saw an unprecedented growth in the size and power of just a few institutional sectors of society: the state, the military, and industry. As Mills wrote in the 1950s:

> *The economy—once a great scatter of small productive units in autonomous balance—has become dominated by two or three hundred giant corporations, administratively and politically interrelated...The political order, once a decentralized set of several dozen states with a weak spinal cord, has become a centralized, executive establishment... The military order, once a slim establishment in a context of distrust fed by state militia, has become the largest and most expensive feature of government...*[4]

Very importantly for Mills, these forms of power are not separate and distinct. As the various organizations have grown larger in terms of their size, complexity and power, they have also grown in their interdependence with each other. The large corporations cannot do without the support and assistance of the state. The state cannot do without the wealth generated by corporate revenues. The military cannot function and fund itself without the state, nor can it meet its material needs without industry. These three dominant sectors of society are thoroughly dependent upon each other and become more and more interconnected and coordinated.

The size and complexity of these organizations increases the tendencies toward oligarchic control, while the coordination needs bring top decision

---

[4]Mills, 1956: 7.

makers into tighter and tighter linkages with each other. So sitting at the top of the organizations in these sectors of society is an interlocked network of economic, political, and military elites. They also move relatively easily between different organizational sectors. Elites from economic organizations can hop to political organizations and *vice versa*. It is worth mention that the US president (top political position) at the time Mills was writing the book was Dwight D. Eisenhower, formerly a top 5 star Army general (top military position). It is the elites in these organizations that make the serious decisions that affect everything from the day to day activities of individuals up through decisions about worldwide military conflicts.

Perhaps the most crucial thing is that the power elite must be seen through a bureaucratic logic. While Mills' was quite interested in the characteristics of the persons involved, the structures of power are not actually made up of persons, but of the top positions in these organizations. As such, changing power in society is not about changing out the actual persons who sit at the top of the organizations. The persons can come and go, but the organizational positions remain and carry with them the demands—and powers—of the position. For this reason, leadership can turn over at any point time, but even with new leadership the operations of power tend to remain about the same. The organizational machinery remains set to accomplish business as usual on a day to day basis—that is how it is designed. And organizational dynamics shape new occupants in the same way that they shaped the past ones. They demand performance of duties as the primary focus of the occupant, and those duties are centered on the well-being of the organizations that they are expected to serve. They shape the occupants understanding of the world and shape interpretations in light of what is best for the organization itself.

Although the important issue is the structure of the positions themselves, this does not mean that nothing can be said of the persons that occupy the offices. They do make up relatively identifiable networks of people who tend to travel in the same professional and social circles. They not only find themselves frequently working together, but also tend to see one another socially, have links from the same universities and even prep schools, belong to the same social clubs, go to weddings of each other's children and so on. It is not as distinctive as a definable club with membership, but more of a set of partly formal and partly informal overlapping networks that mingle both work and personal relations. Thus the mind shaping properties of the organizational positions are reinforced by a background of informal network activity.

At present, it is likely that no one has done more since Mills to document the kinds of social networks that underlie elites than has sociologist G. William Domhoff whose work on power elite research has been ongoing since the 1960s. Despite operating explicitly in the tradition of Mills, Domhoff distances himself a bit from Mills in arguing that, while there is a distinctive power elite structure involving multiple kinds of organizations, the United States is thoroughly a class dominated system of power. Calling it class dominated simply means that the real flow of power in the United States goes through economic organizations rather than political, military, or cultural ones. Domhoff is not saying that state and military institutions are not very large and very powerful in the United States. He is merely saying that the driving force behind their activities is rooted in the needs, interests, and power of economic actors more than anyone else. In other words, there is really a chief pinnacle of power in the United States, and it is found in economic organizations which dominate the power structures.

The main reasons for this are rooted in history and have to do with the fact that as the United States developed through its colonial period and into independence there were no large, strongly entrenched power networks in place. There was, for instance, no large Catholic Church organization as there was in Europe. Nor was there an old aristocracy, founded as it was in Europe based on an alliance between the Church and land owners. Both the state and military in the United States were rather small and weak until well into the twentieth century. Thus, there were no other forms of power in place to counter or challenge the power of concentrated wealth. In other words, the United States was heavily decentralized in terms of IMP sources of power. But, partly because of this, it did eventually develop highly concentrated forms of E power. The concentration of the other forms followed behind this, but economic power remains the center-pin.

A full review of even just Domhoff's career in developing his class domination version of power elite theory could take up a full book of its own, and is beyond the scope of what I can do or need to do here. Suffice it to say for now that the details can get very complex and those interested can begin with the sources and suggested readings listed at the end of the chapter. But there has been a bit of resurgence of attention of late as the economy, and economic organizations have become more and more globalized. C. Wright Mills, writing in the wake of World War II was observing and writing with regards to a power elite in the United States. This stood to reason because at this time the United States was the world's premier super-power on all of the IEMP dimensions. This situation has since shifted, but not necessarily in ways that made social power more dispersed, and it may be that the level of analysis is shifting from the national power structure of the United States to the possibility of a—still emerging—global power structure.

A Global Power Elite?

To emphasize the point that formal organizations provide for highly stable forms of power arrangements should not lead one to believe that there is anything static or unchanging about it. The world that C. Wright Mills wrote about does not really exist any longer in the form it had at the time of the writing of the *Power Elite*. The particular nexus of state-military-corporate relations that he observed in the United States was arguably at its zenith at that time. But as we will review in Part II the basic situation changed quite a bit starting by the early 1970s. The root changes have to do with the extent to which corporate activity is increasingly global. The post-World War II period in which Mills wrote was one in which US companies were dominant over the whole of the globe and faced little competition. But starting by around the beginning of the 1970s, they faced increasing competition from other areas of the globe, and we are now in a period, not where a relatively small number of companies dominate a US economy, but where a relatively small number of multinational companies dominate in a global economy.

Of late, there has thus been a resurgence of power elite research attending to the global situation, and, consistent with Domhoff's emphasis on class power, at the core of the dynamics is the rise of what is sometimes called a *transnational capitalist class* (TCC). The most systematic documentation of the existence of a global power elite (GPE) has likely come from political sociologist Peter Phillips in his 2018 book called *Giants: The Global Power Elite*. In it he does provides an analysis of the main actors that is easily sorted out by its IEMP organizational features. The "giants" in the title refers to the globe's largest 17 transnational investment corporations which serve as the primary coordinating organizations (the E). The "Managers" (as Phillips calls them) are the directors of those 17 companies and make key financial decisions in the global economy. In political terms, they are tied, not to state organizations but to similarly global nongovernmental organizations (NGOs) such as World Economic Forum and Council on Foreign relations. These are called the "Facilitators," and act as policy shaping centers for states and other organizations (e.g., the International Monetary Fund) aimed at allowing capital to flow freely according to the needs and wishes of the managers. (This is largely I, but with the goal of influencing P.) The "Protectors" exist as various kinds of military and intelligence agencies that help to pave the way and provide security where opposition is faced in the form of resistant state actions or popular movements (the M/P). Finally, he refers to the "Ideologists" (obviously the I) which is represented by corporate media organizations that frame out a picture global capitalism to be not only inevitable but also beneficial. Thus in the end, even despite changes since the time of the writings of the likes of Michels and Mills, there is still an underlying architecture to social power relations that has arguably expanded to cover the globe.

Pluralist Interpretations of Power

Pluralism is probably closer to the standard picture of power offered up in the mainstream of the United States. It is assumed in most public debate and dialog and is taught or implied in standard textbook versions of civics, political science and economics, whether in secondary schools or in higher education. Its basic imagery is rooted in the tradition of *Classical Liberalism* which emphasizes the political and economic liberties of all individuals, and descends from those Enlightenment ideas that I brought up early on in this chapter. The term Classical Liberalism is often used to distinguish this more comprehensive body of thought from the contemporary use of the word "liberal" in politicized contexts. In Classical Liberal thought, for example, virtually everyone in the United States, "liberal" and "conservative" alike, counts as a "Liberal." To get past the confusion, note that the word liberal shares the same root as other words like *liberty* or *liberation*. All of these words are just from the Latin *liber* which means "free." So Liberalism is just "freedom-ism." Classical Liberalism emerged as a philosophy of political economy, largely in Europe and the United States through the eighteenth and nineteenth centuries. Its origins were a critical reaction to the old aristocratic order of Europe that dominated throughout the Middle Ages. During that period there was a belief in a natural inequality among people in that only some people—those of aristocratic blood—were capable of the wise and responsible exercise of power. This was most commonly justified by religious thought where the aristocratic order was seen to be sanctioned by the Judeo-Christian God. The idea was that people were not free, but were beholden to a hierarchical social order that all the way up to God himself. Thus the Medieval social order was rooted in a melding of political (P) and religious (I) power.

Classical Liberalism emerged from the Enlightenment as part of an intellectual movement to fundamentally overturn these ideas. The central thing is to reject any manner of belief in natural inequality among people, at least in terms of our fundamental capacities to use reason and rationality. All people are declared to possess the capacity to use reason which means that they are perfectly capable of making decisions for themselves. They don't need some purportedly "superior" person to give them orders of provide direction. Thus we find an emphasis on all of the values we celebrate with regards to democracy, equality, and self-determination. We operate with representative political institutions and those are ruled by the people rather than vice versa. An integral part of that is our emphasis on basic civil rights and individual freedoms regarding things like speech, the press, assembly, and religion. Similarly, we operate with market economies where freedom is the same. In market economies, everyone is free to do as they will as a buyer and seller of goods and services (within the confines of the law, of course). To the extent that anyone is in a position of power over someone else in the economy, this is merely a matter of their own choice. You are not required, by law or by God or anything else to submit to someone else's power over you because you are always free to do something else. If we are talking about an employment relation, you are free to quit whatever job you have and thus not be subject to those orders. If you don't want to take orders from anyone else at work, then you never have to because instead of getting a job you can simply work for yourself instead. You are free—politically and economically.

In political terms, it's a little bit different because there are all sorts of rules that you are required to follow and/or fail to violate. Here you don't have much personal choice other than "love it or leave it," I suppose. *However*, you do have as much right as anyone else to participate in the rule and policy making. If you don't like rules or think that some are missing, then it is on you get moving and exercise your rights to speak out about it and act to influence the political system. Given all of this, the logic is that social power is widely dispersed among the populace rather than highly concentrated only in some places in society.

Generally speaking, for the pluralist power is not perfectly distributed, in the sense that there is any manner of complete equality among actors. But it is seen to be widely distributed nonetheless. The world is full of a multitude of different kinds of interest groups with varying amounts of power. The state itself is seen as something like the referee and sometimes a vehicle for these competing power interests. But even then the key thing is that competition for power remains. The world of social power for the pluralist resembles the picture of markets as told by economists. There are plenty of interests and actors that take them up and these compete for power to see that their interests are met. There may or may not be overlap between different kinds of interests but those will likely be in the form of dynamic alliances and coalitions that come together and fall apart at various times. No one set of actors or interests truly dominate. Rather there is a constant quasi-market for power.

Obviously economic and governmental actors wield quite a bit of power. But unlike for power elite theorists, there are all manner of other kinds of interest groups that are able to check that power and often get their way. Some common observations have to do with the success of things like the ability of labor unions to arise and check the power of business, itself requiring cooperation of governmental actors. Similarly things like civil rights and environmental movements in the United States during the 1960s and 1970s are offered up as ways that power is a battle among the many rather than the few, and that ordinary people can get together and get in the game. Thus concerted actions by various coalitions of citizens, and general public sentiment and opinion matters a great deal. Given Liberal political institutions operating with representative democracies, governmental actors are always beholden at least to some extent by their constituents. They cannot survive in office by solely attending to the needs and wants of only a corporate elite.

Furthermore, unlike for elite theorists, economic organizations are seen to be too narrowly centered on their own particular interests, and so frequently in competition and conflict with each other that they rarely, if ever, form a unified basis for exercising dominating power. In addition, like governmental organizations, they have to yield to the general public, especially the general public as consumers. In economic theory corporate actors can't rule, but are ruled by the power of the consumer pocketbook. They are taken to be at the mercy of the masses because they have no choice but to meet our demands in the market place. Thus, whether in the political or economic arenas, the masses actually rule the elite who are obligated to do their bidding.

Power elite theorists do not deny that there is a pluralist nature to a great deal of political activity. It's quite obvious that contemporary politics is full of noise regarding many different issues and that many different groups have their interests represented. So for the power elite thinker there is no argument regarding whether or not politics isn't a lively place with many different kinds of interests and many different winners and losers in various respects. It's just that the day to day business-as-usual politics that fills TV screens and daily news outlets is relatively insignificant in terms of the most crucial and far reaching power decisions. Going back to Mills, this is generally accommodated this by arguing that power structures have three basic levels. The top level is the relatively tight power elite that dominates in making the most important national and international decisions on things like foreign policy, military strategies, and monetary policies. These are things that people are often not even aware is going on, largely because they are distracted by what is called the *middle levels of power*. This is the level that people generally see as "politics," and is where pluralist ideas would be applicable. It is the world of political parties, special interest groups, social movements, and normal congressional activity. So this is where pluralism matters, but for elite theorists not nearly as much as pluralist ideas would have it. Finally there is a bottom level which is basically the masses that are unorganized and impotent, save for the ability to sometimes influence the middle levels via electoral processes. At the lowest level the electoral masses are obsessed with the middle level stalemate and distracted by popular culture. For the likes of Mills, it is this middle and bottom level activity that people tend to mistake for the operations of political power. In the end, what it does is actually insulate the activities of power elites from too much scrutiny or even notice.

Paying Attention to Variability—and Organizations

The purpose of this chapter is not to attempt to clear up questions of how power really works. It is all still a matter of contention among political scientists and sociologists, and the subject is well worth exploring. I point the reader to the sources and suggestions for further reading at the end of the chapter. For our purposes, I will round out this rather brief and incomplete treatment of the question of power with a final set of similarly brief and incomplete notes about how one may want to think about these things in the context of organizational sociology. The first key point, and the main purpose of the chapter, is to explain that, even for most versions of pluralism, regardless of all else *social power is organizational*. For elite theories, this point should already be obvious from the foregoing in this chapter, but it also significantly applies even in pluralistic arguments.

While pluralist arguments do often put a good deal of weight on electoral processes so that something like the "general public" and "public opinion" (the unorganized "masses") can be seen as important, generally more significant is attention to coalitions of people engaged in what are called *social movements*. The study of social movements is basically about the question of how it is that people outside of elite centers of power manage to get things done, and the central aspect of successful social movements are called *social movement organizations (SMOs)*. Without an organization, masses of people don't have a way of coordinating for sustained collective action. This is the reason that, according to Michels, a small elite can always dominate the masses of an organization. Elites are well organized, while the masses are not. Surely the growth of electronic communications technologies has made it easier to generate various kinds of "moments" of collective action such as protests. And it is obvious that those can sometimes be important in terms of influencing what formal organizations do. But just as Weber initially pointed out with regards to bureaucracy, there is nothing like setting out a structure of regularly defined activities with persons assigned to various roles to coordinate actions toward the accomplishment of particular goals. Thus the success of things like labor, civil rights, or environmental movements are the successes of social movement *organizations*, such as the AFL-CIO which is an umbrella organization of labor unions, the *National Association for the Advancement of Colored People (NAACP)* which is focused on civil rights issues, or the *Sierra Club* or *National Resources Defense Council (NRDC)* for environmental issues.

The second key point is to always be attentive to variability. Despite my references to organizations creating well defined and stable power structures, there is no static situation with regards to the dynamics of social power. Rather than thinking about power as *either* a matter of elite interests *or* of more pluralistic competition, it is sensible to see the state of affairs in flux along a continuum. Given a formally rationalized world, organizations will continue be central to issues of social power. But just how concentrated power is, and in what kinds of organizations is subject to variability. There are, for example, quite a few different variations on what counts as pluralism, sometimes now grouped under the term *neopluralism*. Among these is what is often called *elite pluralism* or, similarly *biased pluralism*. These conceptions take power as pluralistic, but not as equally distributed across the population. Rather large variations in the social power of citizen groups are built upon underlying social inequalities, and, generally speaking, wealthier and more organized segments of a population speak the loudest. Despite the pluralist label, something like biased pluralism lands quite close to power elite theories. For example, in an influential paper on "Testing Theories of American Politics," political scientists Martin Gilens and Benjamin Page note:

> *The central point that emerges from our research is that economic elites and organized groups representing business interests have*

substantial independent impacts on U.S. government policy, while mass-based interest groups and average citizens have little or no independent influence. Our results provide substantial support for theories of Economic-Elite Domination and for theories of Biased Pluralism[5]

But even then, it is useful to avoid searching for the "correct" final position or label in this regard as organizational dynamics are always in flux. As we will discuss in Part II, for example, we actually started the twentieth century in the United States with a situation of intensely concentrated economic power as wielded by the growth of massive industrial businesses. In your high school textbooks this was the basis for what would have been called *The Gilded Age*, and included the rise of the *robber baron* capitalist. At the time, the US government was actually quite small and weak, and it was clear that economic organizations dominated society (though not without a fight as we will see later). The large labor forces of people, who worked for these new giant enterprises, while not small, were even weaker. By comparison to increasingly organized sources of economic power, industrial workers were the disorganized majority.

It is quite plausible to argue that *as compared to* that early twentieth-century situation, later points in history saw significant changes. By the middle of the twentieth century when C. Wright Mills wrote, both the US government and military had grown, especially due to the two World Wars. Relatedly, workers had gained the right to organize as labor unions to press for their rights, and these developments tempered, at least somewhat, the concentrated power of business organizations. Furthermore, labor unions, along with the expansion of white-collar work to staff the growth of large bureaucracies, created a large new middle class in the United States. In an influential pluralist treatment of power in the United States, political scientist Jeffrey Berry, in his 1999 book *The New Liberalism: The Rising Power of Citizen Groups*, argued that this was a significant part of what underlay the successes seen in social movements oriented toward such things as civil rights, environmental issues, and consumer protection that were witnessed starting in the 1960s and up through the 1990s. The rise to middle class status was an important basis upon which various citizen coalitions have been able to have enough resources (largely time and money) to participate in social and political issues forming the basis for various social movements. Thus, *as compared to* the first part of the twentieth century, the power of business organizations during the middle, and possibly into the late part of the twentieth century was arguably less than it was at the turn of the twentieth century.

And the situation remains in flux. For example, organizational sociologist Mark Mizruchi in a 2013 book, tellingly named *The Fracturing of the American Corporate Elite* argued that the US corporate elite, while rather unified in many respects for much of the twentieth century, fragmented in the period after about the year 1990. The full story is complicated, but a central part of it involved organizational change. A significant portion of the unity of business elites for much of the twentieth century came through *interlocking directorates* which is a situation where people sit on the board of directors of multiple

---

[5]Gilens and Page (2014: 565). This point is not lost on G. William Domhoff either (see, 2020: 7).

companies. For much of the twentieth century commercial banks were at the center of those interlocking directorates as central hubs. A typical bank would have directors who were also directors of large companies in multiple other industries, and thus corporate board meetings were central to producing and maintaining unity and coordination of business elites across the entire economy. However, beginning in the 1980s, Mizruchi argues, commercial banks lost their central importance, largely owing to alternative means of accessing capital. When this occurred, interlocking declined and a significant portion of corporate elite unity went with it. The idea is that corporate elites are now quite disunified and largely pursuing their own narrow interests. As such, the power elite as observed by Mills is now gone, and the situation is left more pluralistic than it was for much of the twentieth century.

But the story is never simple. In the same year that Mizruchi published a reappraisal of Mills' *Power Elite* (2017), sociologist Joshua Murray published a near simultaneous paper providing evidence that, even as US based interlock networks may have thinned out, the extent of transnational interlocks has been increasing. Thus the basis for corporate unity has shifted and the end result, he argues, is that ties among corporate actors are actually denser overall and the corporate elite is becoming more and more a global elite. This is, of course, consistent with the *global power elite* arguments such as those of Peter Phillips, noted above.

Furthermore, in his ongoing work, G. William Domhoff has continued to argue, and provide evidence for the assertion that power continues to revolve around the interests of unified corporate elites. Domhoff's focus on what brings corporate class interests together and gives them voice does include interlocking boards of directors, but in addition a much broader *policy planning network (PPN)*. The PPN is largely made up of not-for-profit, NGOs, frequently funded by corporations and wealthy individuals (whose wealth is rooted in corporate ownership or control on one way or another), and heavily populated by corporate executives. These organizations include policy discussion groups such as the Business Roundtable (which is purely an association of corporate CEOs), the Committee for Economic Development (the Trustees of which are all corporate executives), and the Chamber of Commerce, along with various *think tanks* such as the American Enterprise Institute, Council on Foreign Relations, and Brookings Institution. The preferences of the *corporate community*, as it is often called, make their way into government policy by way of things like lobbying, the provision of "expert" testimony in Congressional proceedings, and by having people move back and forth between the PPN and top advisory posts in the government.

In any case, as I noted, one brief introductory chapter cannot offer conclusions that settle arguments regarding how it is that power operates. It is an ongoing matter of investigation and dispute in the social sciences that has taken on a new significance as the globalization of the political economy continues. However, social power does remain significantly a matter of the concentration of IEMP resources by formal organizations, though just how concentrated is variable and open to question at any given time. But formally rationalized systems have strong centralizing tendencies which will always leave important questions to ask regarding the relative power of formal organizations and of their elites.

SOURCES AND FURTHER READING

The **IEMP** power framework was defined as such by **Michael Mann**:

- Mann, Michael. 1986. *The Sources of Social Power, Vol 1: A history of power from the beginning to AD 1760.* New York, NY: Cambridge University Press. (See Chapter 1. This was adopted by Domhoff, see below).

- Weber's "class/status/party" predecessor can be found on pp. 926–929 in: Weber, Max. [1922] 1978. *Economy and Society: An Outline of Interpretive Sociology.* Edited by Guenther Roth & Claus Wittich. Berkeley, CA: University of California Press.

Michels **iron law of oligarchy**:

- Robert Michels. [1911] 1962. *Political Parties: A Sociological Study of the Oligarchical Tendencies of Modern Democracy.* Trans. Eden and Cedar Paul. New York, NY: Free Press.

- The concept of the iron law remains a matter of discussion, whether because it is found useful (Drochon, 2020) or to challenge its status as a "law" (Diefenbach, 2019):

  o Thomas Diefenbach. 2019. "Why Michels' 'iron law of oligarchy' is not an iron law – and how democratic organisations can stay 'oligarchy-free.'" *Organization Studies* 40: 545–62.

  o Hugo Drochon. 2020. "Robert Michels, the iron law of oligarchy and dynamic democracy." *Constellations* 27: 185–98.

Discussion of the **power elite** literature typically begins with **C. Wright Mills'** classic (1959). And noted, the tradition has been most earnestly carried on by **G. William Domhoff**:

- C. Wright Mills. 1956. *The Power Elite.* New York, NY: Oxford University Press.

- G. William Domhoff:

  o Keeps an updated list of publications here: https://whorulesamerica.ucsc.edu/domhoff_bibliography.html

  o His initial classic was (1967). *Who Rules America?* Englewood Cliffs, NJ: Prentice-Hall.

  o As of this writing his most recent includes:

    o 2020. *The Corporate Rich and the Power Elite in the Twentieth Century: How They Won and Why Labor and Liberals Lost.* Abingdon, UK: Routledge.

    o 2018. *Studying the Power Elite: Fifty Years of Who Rules America?* Abingdon, UK: Routledge.

  o In addition, he maintains and extensive website revolving around the ongoing work regarding *Who Rules America*: https://whorulesamerica.ucsc.edu/

On the **global power elite** the possibility of a **transnational capitalist class**:

- Phillips, Peter. 2018. *Giants: The Global Power Elite.* New York, NY: Seven Stories Press.

- See also, Carroll, William K. 2010. *The Making of a Transnational Capitalist Class: Corporate Power in the Twenty-First Century*. New York, NY: Zed Books.

- And Murray (2017 – below).

On **pluralism:**

- The classic work on pluralism produced largely as a rebuttal to Mills' *Power Elite*:

  ○ Dahl, Robert A. 1961. *Who Governs? Democracy and Power in an American City*. New Haven, CN: Yale University Press.

- For an overview of **neopluralism** see: Andrew S. McFarland. 2007. "Neopluralism." *Annual Review of Political Science* 10:45–66.

- On **biased pluralism**: Gilens, Martin and Benjamin Page. 2014. "Testing theories of American politics: Elites, interest groups, and average citizens." *Perspectives on Politics* 12: 564–81.

- On **Berry's** argument regarding increased pluralism: Berry, Jeffrey M. 1999. *The New Liberalism: The Rising Power of Citizen Groups*. Washington, DC: Brookings Institution Press.

On the question of the fracturing of the corporate elite:

- Mizruchi, Mark. 2013. *The Fracturing of the American Corporate Elite*. Cambridge, MA: Harvard University Press.

- ———. 2017. "The Power Elite in Historical Context: A Reevaluation of Mills's Thesis, Then and Now." *Theory and Society* 46: 95–116.

- Murray, Joshua. 2017. "Interlock Globally, Act Domestically: Corporate Political Unity in the 21st Century." *American Journal of Sociology* 122: 1617–63.

- See also Carroll (2010), above.

Other General References

- Henry Mintzberg. 1983. *Power in and Around Organizations*. Englewood Cliffs, NJ: Prentice-Hall.

- Weber, Max. [1922] 1978. *Economy and Society: An Outline of Interpretive Sociology*. Edited by Guenther Roth & Claus Wittich. Berkeley, CA: University of California Press.

Organizations and Inequality

In a famous old, yet timeless book called *The Sociological Imagination* the sociologist C. Wright Mills provided an inspirational piece of writing on what he called *the promise* of developing a sociological imagination. The core of the promise is the ability to grasp what he called the *intersections between biography and history*.[1] The biography part is about the lives of individual persons. It's about you and about me, and anyone else that inhabits the planet. We each have our own biographies—our actual lived experiences in life including our thoughts, feelings, values, and activities. But all of those biographies, of course, take place within the much larger context of the flow of human history. We are born at particular places and times into a set of existing social circumstances. Those social circumstances are not random but have structures to them that transcend, and significantly shape the biographies of the specific individuals of the time. It was the promise of sociology to understand all of that—the existing structures, how they came to be as they are, how they are changing, along with the actual persons and their experiences in given times and places.

Here is one very direct and simple way to think about this: the fact that you are reading this right now owes a lot more to the flow of history than it does to anything that is special about you or your character or your own biography. For one thing, it presumes the existence of written language and widespread literacy. Apparently you can read. For much of human history there were not even systems of written language, and even once there were, reading and writing were not common skills. Most people reading this are probably also in a college or University in the United States. A mere 50–60 years ago most of you would not have been in a college or University. That is especially true of women and people of color, but certainly of many white males as well. The fact that you are currently in a college or university also owes a lot more to large scale social changes (history) than it does to anything about your own biography. Not too long ago many of the males would have gone straight to a job after high school. Middle class white females would not have gone to a paid job at all, except for the few who went to things like teaching and nursing. Step back a mere 150 years and most people didn't obtain any formal schooling at all.

---

[1] Mills ([1959] 2000). See pp. 3–13.

The reasons for these kinds of changes in educational biographies are varied and complex, but they do go right along with the organizational revolution. Formal organizations need people schooled, at minimum, in the "three r's" of reading, 'riting, and 'rithmetic. Thus we find that the growth and spread of formal rationality coincides with the establishment of compulsory educational systems. It quickly came to be the case that some level of formal schooling provided a *credential* that was required for entry into many occupations. As organizations, the economy, technology and the like have grown in complexity, the needs for higher level skills have continually boosted the basic educational credentials required. By the middle of the twentieth century a high school diploma was a cherished marker giving one a decent market position. By about the 1970s, changes in occupational structures and an ample supply of people with high school diplomas started to lead to more and more people going on to seek college degrees which became the new high school diploma as a marker of technical competence. At this point in time more and more college students are now looking toward graduate school because the supply of people with Bachelor's degrees is too high, so you know that you need to distinguish yourself from all of those Bachelor's degrees. Meanwhile, along the way people refer to this process, not as a process of getting an education, but one of getting the "piece of paper." The piece of paper is the credential, and is now what makes the world go 'round for you in your daily life. If you are going to be able to support yourself, and have basic security in life such as a decent income, health insurance and retirement benefits, your piece of paper is a ticket into the organization from which many of you will (hopefully) procure these things in return for your labor.

In the end, if we shift our focus from that of overall macro-structures of power in Chapter 2 down to the level of biographies, it pays to realize that your own ability to have any power—your ability to realize your own will—is also significantly a question of organizations. If organizations control power resources, then the ability of individuals to access these depends on how their own characteristics mesh with those of the structures of formal organizations. Organizations condition our *life chances* as Max Weber called them.

Agency and Structure in Life Chances

While the details vary a great deal, all societies contain social inequality—generally referred to as *social stratification*. Stratification refers to layering. In social terms it refers to the layering of people roughly according to their social power along the lines of the ability to access and control IEMP resources as introduced in Chapter 2. Power involves the ability of an actor to get its way, and includes both the *power to* do things and possibly some degree of *power over* others. The amount of control that people have is, of course, variable. Some actors have more and some less and that is what stratification is about. At the individual level, this is most often thought of in economic terms. Some people are very wealthy. Others are very poor. Most, of course, are somewhere in between, although that varies by time and place. But stratification almost always means more than just access to economic resources as it also involves questions of cultural *status* and the ability to influence formal rules, policies, and procedures of organizations. This is Weber's *class, status, party* ideal type introduced in Chapter 2 that is mirrored by the IEMP framework.

For much of its first century, Sociology is seen to have been largely pre-occupied with the focus on economic stratification according to social class. However, in recent decades the scope has been expanded, and it has now become the norm to discuss stratification in terms of *class, race,* and *gender,* although there are many other "slices" that can be made as well. The importance of expanding the scope beyond matters of social class alone, which is heavily focused on variable economic positions, is that there are many other bases of stratification that can operate independently of, yet also *intersect* with matters of class. The race and gender distinctions that we make among people are matters of cultural meanings and thus represent *status* distinctions in Weberian terms. And those status distinctions matter for people's life chances. One of the reasons that concerns about race and gender made such a late appearance in formal sociology is that women and people of color were long excluded from the ability to fully participate in educational and knowledge production activities. It wasn't for a lack of people who were paying attention to such issues, it was for a lack of *inclusion* in participating in the organizations that build and pass on knowledge.

Some manner of stratification is found in all human societies, though the extent and bases for it vary significantly. So formal organizations certainly do not originate stratification, nor do they account for everything in terms of the dynamics of stratification. But they are now central to shaping social stratification structures and have to be understood to fully grasp contemporary social inequalities. As was already discussed, formal organizations concentrate control over economic resources, but they obviously distribute those resources as well. Formal organizations are where people get much of the important stuff of stratification in the form of wages, benefits, and occupational prestige. So understanding life chances is very much about understanding where and how people end up landing where they do in relation to organizational structures.

Generally speaking in Western cultures, although especially so in the United States, concern with people's life chances tends to focus heavily if not completely on the biography side of things. The general idea is that we live in what is largely a *meritocracy* so that where people end up in life depends upon what they themselves achieve. This includes things like the choices that you make such as whether or not to go to college and what to major in. It also tends to include any kinds of things that might be considered "natural" talents, such as whether or not things like math or science come easily to you. And finally, perhaps the key focus is often on how hard you work and the kinds of work experience you build up for yourself. In social science terms, your natural affinity for certain kinds of things and the educational and work experiences that you build up are called your *human capital* and it is this which determines where you end up in life. Your human capital is the basis for your *market position.*

But most people are also aware—though much more vaguely so—that this is only one half of the equation. Some of my readers may be entry level business students, and they may be majoring in business because their parents told them to so that they could "get a good job." Even if you are more interested in something like Sociology, Art, or Theater, you may have been dissuaded from majoring in such things because the perception is that it won't connect you to a good job. I know that I had to go through it twice—once when I majored in Sociology as an undergraduate, and then yet again when I went on to graduate school in Sociology. "That's fine, but how are you going to get a job with that?" was a common question.[2] What people are not articulating very well is that there is also a structural side of this equation, and this is generally called a *labor market*.

Organizational Structures, Segmented Labor Markets, and Class Inequality

A labor market is exactly what it sounds like—an economic market for human labor. If you're not a social scientist that might not bring anything too concrete to mind, but it's simple. There are markets for cars, for instance. Auto companies offer of a *supply* of cars with various kinds of characteristics which they are trying to match up to various kinds and levels of *demand* in the car market. In labor markets workers represent the labor supply, and in trying to build up various kinds of human capital they are trying to match themselves up to various kinds and levels of demand among employers. Employers are the consumers of labor. The reason that people might tell you not to major in things like Sociology or Art is that they believe that you will be building up kinds of human capital for which there is not very high demand—no one will want to buy your labor power. If you recall Max Weber's ideal typical definition of "Class" from Chapter 2, we would say that your human capital does not put you in a very good *market position*.

So even those who tend to emphasize human capital are generally aware that there is also a labor market structure, although this is given little articulation. This is where organizational studies is very helpful because labor market conditions are heavily shaped by organizational structures. Organizations create and concentrate social power resources, and individuals gain access to those resources through those things called "jobs." As arranged in typical hierarchical form, they thus provide people variable access to the power resources wherein, generally speaking, access is greater as one moves upward. In other words, labor market structures are mapped to organizational structures, and we can think of that as occurring in two different ways. First, inside of organizations there are *internal labor markets* that are related to the organization's structures and functions. Internal labor markets have to do with how people might be able to move around to different jobs inside of the organization. In keeping with a career ladder logic, the typical idea is to be able to move upward in the hierarchies to jobs that command more authority and better pay and benefits. Second, internal labor markets are linked to *external labor markets*, which generally just means the rest of the labor market as a whole. Obviously people not only sometimes change jobs within organizations, but might also change jobs by moving to a different organization. Similarly, when an organization needs to fill a position, it might find someone who is already in the organization (internal labor market), or it might look to fill the position from outside of the organization (external labor market).

Labor markets are not a free-for-all, but can be seen as having stratified divisions with them. In terms of internal labor markets, consider the old legend about people who "start out in the mailroom" and, through sheer

---

[2]For any reader who is a nervous Sociology major, the American Sociological Association does a lot of work on that and I'd encourage you to visit https://www.asanet.org/careers/careers-sociology

determination and effort, work their way all the way up "to the top" to become the Chief Executive Officer (CEO). Well, I suppose that might happen if the organization in question is the postal service or a similar shipping business. But what if it's a car company? If you start out in the mailroom, then the human capital that you build will be useful for handling, sorting, and distributing mail. But it won't be of much use for designing, building, marketing, or selling cars. I am not going to tell you that the mailroom stories have never happened or that they can never happen. But it's just not really how it generally works. Traditionally, the career ladders that lead to the top are those that center on the organization's core functions. And in business organizations it tends to be those directly related to making the money such as sales, marketing, and finance. Most other career ladders on the inside stop short of the top. Given organizational structure if you start out in the mailroom, then the highest you are likely to go is to manager of the mailroom regardless of how ambitious and hardworking you are.

Organizations can be quite full of these little mini-hierarchies, which you can think of as *segments* within the hierarchy, and a great deal of where you land in the end is as heavily conditioned by organizational structure as by your human capital. If you are a software engineer who takes an entry level position in a software company, this is quite a bit different from being a software engineer who takes an entry level position in an energy company. In the software company, you will be what is called a *line worker* because you will be doing software work for a company whose main product is software development. You will also be building up human capital that much more plausibly leads all the way to the top. But in an energy company, you will be a *staff worker*. Staff workers don't perform the primary functions of the organizations, but offer support functions instead. You will still be building human capital, but it won't be human capital that relates to the main functions of the organization. Thus, even if you advance along some career ladder, you are likely to eventually bump up against a ceiling that reflects an intersection of your human capital with organizational structure.

Segmentation and Dual Labor Markets

While above I introduced the idea of *segments* applying to internal labor markets (which it does), the term is more often associated with theory and research regarding overall *labor market segmentation. Segmented labor market theory (SLMT)* originally grew, starting in the late 1960s and early 1970s, as a critique of standard economic analyses of labor markets which did not provide any good explanation for observations of persistent divisions among workers along the lines of such things as gender and race. In typical economics terms, inequality will largely be explained simply by variations in human capital relative to demand for labor. Whether one is male/female or of color/not of color doesn't matter, and companies that discriminate on such bases should be at a competitive disadvantage in not hiring purely on the sole basis of their capabilities. As such, it would not predict persistent divisions among groups of people, or if we started with some, they should decline over time as the market for human capital works its magic. But the data on inequality persistently say otherwise.

The most prominent approach to SLMT is called *dual labor market theory* which sees labor markets as being divided into two main segments: a *primary labor market* and a *secondary labor market*. The primary labor market is full of what are generally thought of as "good jobs"—those with relatively high levels of pay, benefits, job security, and opportunities for growth and advancement. The secondary labor market is where the "bad jobs" are with, on average, poor levels of pay, benefits, and job security. They also tend to be *dead end jobs* meaning that there is little opportunity for advancement, whether under one employer or by moving to other employers within the labor market. The reason that people are so often encouraged to go get a college degree is related to this. A college degree is often your best chance at a ticket into the primary segment of the labor market. The idea is that without the degree you're likely to end up serving coffee or digging ditches for a living.

Of course, any strict dualistic notion of labor markets will generally over-simplify things and perhaps also make them seem like they are static. But they are always changing and more complicated than that. So take the dual labor market image as something of an *ideal type* that can be useful as a baseline starting point for understanding labor market conditions. Getting a handle on the specifics means taking a look at what is going on in terms of organizational structures, particularly those of business organizations. We will get an expanded story and more context for this in Part II or the book, but for the most part conceptualizations of what is happening in terms of segmented labor markets has been most strongly conditioned by major shifts in how capitalist business organizations have operated over the course of the twentieth century.

The Mid-Twentieth-Century Model of Dualization and Class Structure

Dual labor market theory emerged, largely from labor economists, during the 1970s which by most accounts was a different period of capitalism than the one we're in now. At that time, one of the most common ways to define labor market segmentation was to add a distinction inside of the primary labor market between and *independent primary labor market* and a *subordinate primary labor market*. The idea was that there were basically two ways of securing a spot in the primary labor market: high education and skill (*independent*) or union representation (*subordinate*). While much of the primary labor market involved relatively high level, professional and white-collar occupations—doctors, lawyers, accountants, college professors (!), and so on—where human capital is key, there were also large segments of the labor force in relatively unskilled or semi-skilled work where human capital isn't as important. These could be either blue-collar, manufacturing-style jobs or lower level white-collar work, and are frequently the same kinds of jobs that you find in the secondary labor market. The skills and abilities needed to do the work are not so rare or hard to acquire, so if supply and demand for human capital was all that governed work, then what leaves some of these labor market locations in the primary market? The answer was that it was usually labor unions.

Unions are organizations that do many things, but the basic principle is that they provide a way for workers in particular industries to exercise some control over the labor supply. If the credentials needed to acquire a particular job are not terribly rare or hard to acquire, this frequently leaves the supply of labor quite high. Under these conditions, if workers negotiate for working conditions on an individual by individual basis, they are put in competition with one another putting downward pressure on wages. But if an organization representing the masses of workers (a labor union), can do the negotiating then workers aren't played off against each other but are basically negotiating together. So if that can be done, then demands for decent pay, benefits, job security, and so on are easier to establish and maintain. Thus the thing that makes the difference between the subordinate primary and secondary markets is organizational—do workers have a union organization to represent their interests to the employing organization? Or do they have to operate as lone individuals where requests for better terms of employment can easily be met by employers explaining that they can easily just hire someone else? Unions stand between individuals and employers, making such things more difficult.

We can call this three-segment model of the *independent primary/ subordinate primary/secondary markets* something like the "mid-twentieth century" model that emerged out of the organizational revolution. As Weber noted, and as we will see Part II, the center of the rise of the iron cage was the growth in size of business corporations and, with that, greatly increased centralization of control over most major industrial sectors of the economy. This is frequently referred to as a *shift from competitive to monopoly capitalism,* although it is more accurate to say oligopolistic capitalism for most segments of industry. This is to say that in many sectors of the economy, such as rail transportation, steel and oil, business organizations grew to such immense sizes that they would operate over the entirety of the country with few (if an oligopoly) or no (if a monopoly) real competitors. It was these organizational changes that created segmented labor market structures.

The growth in the size of these businesses is what created both sub-segments of the primary labor market. On the one hand, the size of their operations created an awful lot for an organization to manage, and far too much for any single person or even small group of people "at the top" to oversee and manage themselves. This created a lot of "office work"—white-collar tasks like purchasing, sales, accounting, legal services, and management of personnel. These are tasks that do often require relatively high levels of education and/or training and this is largely what produces the independent primary labor market. The expansion of bureaucracy meant the expansion of professional and managerial white-collar office work.

I'll just call the white-collar work the tasks that have to do with running the show, and then there is "the show" itself. That is, all of the people actually doing the business of the organization such as running trains, assembling cars, or rolling out steel. This—eventually—becomes the subordinate primary labor market, and that story gets a little more complicated.

The centralization of business activities in a few very large businesses centralizes control over vast portions of a labor market. The more that business is concentrated, the fewer employers there are. At the same time, the growth in size was very much about growth in the *scale* of production which often involved more and more work becoming mechanized. The flip side of the mechanization of work is frequently called the *deskilling of labor* because whatever skills were needed to do various tasks are now embedded in machines. Thus the human capital that gave a lot of people a foothold in blue-collar labor markets became obsolete. The concentration of demand for labor, and widespread deskilling tips the power balance in labor markets in favor of employers. There are fewer buyers of labor, so if you don't like your job or working conditions there are frequently not many (or any) other choices. At the same time, because of deskilling, you are now interchangeable with that many more other people. Thus, under these conditions employers now have an easier time controlling the terms of employment. This resulted in the kinds of poor work conditions that you've heard of historically—poor wages and working conditions; low levels of job security; the widespread use (and abuse) or child labor; and so on. These conditions created decades of serious labor unrest and conflict during the late nineteenth and early twentieth century and provided the basis for the rise of labor unions which—eventually—became the organizational leverage for workers to be able to demand and secure those "good job" characteristics found in the primary labor market.[3] This growth of both the independent and subordinate primary labor markets is what produced the famous large *middle class* of the United States. A middle class that has since been significantly eroded as we will see below.

The general reasoning that explains why the secondary market persisted is that many kinds of economic activity, and thus many jobs, remained outside of industries that had been consolidated under large oligopolistic enterprises. Centralized oligopolies tended to arise in industries that could rely on very stable mass markets, and those that were *capital-intensive* rather than *labor-intensive*. We'll get more on this later, but for now, in capital-intensive industries you can increase the amounts of what you produce largely by investments in things like equipment and machinery, while in labor-intensive industries production increases can only be done by also adding more labor. So sectors of the economy with less stable forms of demand for labor, and where tasks were more difficult to mechanize tended to remain under competitive capitalism. It is there that businesses tend to remain smaller, more precarious, and often dependent on larger companies. Their labor forces remain more fragmented, and thus unionization was more difficult to establish. This gives the economy what is known as a *core-periphery* structure. There was a core of very large and powerful companies operating under conditions of monopoly capital and with unionized labor forces (once unions were in place). And a periphery of smaller, weaker, and more precarious business activities under conditions of competitive capitalism with nonunionized labor forces. Stratification among organizations is thus strongly tied to stratification among individuals.

So in sum, both labor markets as we know them, and their particular structures during the middle part of the twentieth century were largely created by organizational conditions. In many industries, business organizations changed in form. They grew large white-collar labor forces that provided the basis for growth of the independent primary labor market, and large blue-collar and lower level white-collar labor forces that, once represented by labor unions, yielded the subordinate primary market. Wage work that remained outside of either of these conditions is where one found secondary labor market conditions. This basic structure largely persisted up until about the 1970s when major economic changes took place, and with that, shifts in organizational structures.

---

[3]The struggle for workers to gain full rights to union representation was a rather long and ugly chapter of US history, and is the reason that we have a holiday called *Labor Day*. It is beyond my scope here to cover that, but you would do well to learn of the history.

The Post-1970s and Dualization and Class Structure

We will cover this more in depth in Part II, but the situation changed radically beginning in the 1970s. The large oligopolistic firms that had dominated many industries for so long were faced with a series of crises, including what is often called a *competitiveness crisis* spurred increasing competition from companies outside of the United States. Foreign companies were producing goods that were both higher in quality and frequently lower in costs, and US businesses didn't seem able to adapt. Large US companies had set themselves up to operate in standardized fashion in large and stable mass markets, which worked pretty well as long as there was little to no real competition. But once things were shaken up the general assessment is that they found themselves too inflexible to move, and had to become much more flexible and reduce their operating costs. The changes that flowed out of this have now created major shifts in the dual labor market structure.

The short story is that the 1970s began a period of the disappearance of the subordinate primary labor market, along with great shake-ups even in the independent primary market. The heart of the subordinate primary market was the old unionized blue-collar working class. The iconic image was that of automobile workers. If you worked for Ford in the middle of the twentieth century you very well may have worked in a relatively low-skilled job on an assembly line, but the United Auto Workers labor union helped ensure that you had job security, opportunity for advancement, decent pay, health and retirement benefits, and so on. But the competitiveness crisis, across many industries, led to slower job growth as well as the loss of jobs as companies stumbled in the face of competition.

Other than the lack of job generation, and sometimes job loss, there were major changes to the old style of doing business. We met up with the term McDonaldization in Chapter 1, and here we can borrow another catchy label from organizational sociologist Gerald Davis: *Nikefication*.[4] Nike is an athletics apparel company, of course, best known for its footwear. But unlike the way a company like Ford would have operated, Nike doesn't actually make any of its products. It has a corporate headquarters in Oregon, and the only thing that happens there is the design and marketing of apparel. All of its production work—the actual physical creation of its shoes and the like—is done by subcontractors. That is, Nike hires other companies to actually make its stuff, and those companies are most often in places like Southeast Asia for the simple reason that labor costs in Southeast Asia were quite low as compared to a place like the United States. This process of leaving or moving tasks outside of a company (and frequently outside of a country) is called *outsourcing*. This (along with ever-increasing mechanization and automation) has contributed greatly to the decline of manufacturing jobs in the United States and the shift toward more and more service jobs.

In the old-style of doing business that dominated starting around the turn of the twentieth century up until about the 1970s a typical company would generally do most of its tasks itself. The classic exemplar early on is probably the Ford Motor Company which would certainly design and market its autos, but also made the autos, and most of what went into them, often starting at raw materials. In the middle of the twentieth century the people who produced your Ford auto would have been unionized employees of Ford in the

---

[4]See Davis (2016), esp. Ch. 6.

United States, and thus had jobs in the subordinate primary labor market. The people who assembled your Nike shoes were not employees of the Nike Company, not unionized, and not in the United States. While many companies, such as Ford, didn't do full Nikefication they did move to much heavier reliance on cheaper labor by outsourcing for various parts and services, and where production was still done by the company, production facilities were frequently moved out of the United States to places with cheaper, nonunionized labor. If you think of the economy in terms of a core-periphery imagery, noted above, a lot of what was in the core was basically tossed out into the periphery and what was now a more and more globalized periphery. This led to large reductions in subordinate primary sector jobs, and thus the shrinking of labor unions which, at this point, are mere shadows of their former selves. It has also destabilized many areas of even the independent primary labor market to the point that those typical career ladders creating internal labor markets, discussed above, are frequently not relevant any longer.

Meanwhile, the secondary sector of jobs in nonunionized, low level work still exists and has expanded along with the growth of part-time, temporary, and *contingent labor*. A good portion of this is now captured by the term *gig economy* which, in keeping with using exemplar company names, Gerald Davis has dubbed *Uberization*.[5] If you work in the gig economy, you don't get a job and have an employer. You get *tasks*, and you perform them as a self-employed subcontractor. Uber drivers don't work for Uber as employees. They are just registered in a software platform that may send a task their way when someone logs in and needs a ride. Gig work is not new, but by most accounts is now proliferating and good deal of discussion regarding labor market segmentation has shifted to focus on a new form of *dualization*. While the primary/secondary distinction remains relevant, a lot of attention is being given to the distinction, largely in secondary labor markets, between traditional and nontraditional work arrangements. Here the interest is in a new stark split in labor markets between *insiders* and *outsiders*. *Insiders* still have some manner of traditional employment arrangement—they have "jobs." *Outsiders* are in the gig economy as temporary and contingent workers who are put on "tasks" rather than having a regular job.

All of these are the reasons that it has become so much more important than in the past to earn a Bachelor's degree, if not more than that. If you were born in the early to middle part of the twentieth century, you could still do quite well with only very basic levels of education.[6] It was important that you could read and write and do basic math, for example. But good, stable jobs could be had in many blue-collar industries and middle level service occupations without having to go on for a college degree. And even though it was better to be represented by a union, the prevalence and power of unions still helped to boost worker well-being even in nonunionized areas of the economy.

But if you were born in the last quarter of the twentieth century, or early twenty-first, then you generally need to shoot for the primary sector of the labor market which often means that you need advanced educational credentials as an entry ticket. Not many want to land in the secondary segment of the labor market, and then certainly not as an outsider. To go back to C. Wright Mills' language, "history" has significantly shaped the "biography" of the average worker. The structures of business organizations over time have

---

[5]See Davis (2016), esp. Ch. 14.
[6]Though perhaps mostly if you were white and male. See below.

given rise to distinctive structures in labor markets. It is those structures that people need to be able to "read" and navigate.

Organizational Change, the Shrinking Middle Class, and Income Polarization

Thus we come to what is largely an organizational understanding of structural issues that underlie both the *shrinking of the middle class* and increasing degrees of *income polarization*. Bureaucratic business organizations grew and spread throughout the first part of the twentieth century, leading to both an increase in demand for professional service work, and the growth of labor unions. These two things created a large stable middle class. In the post-1970s period business organizations changed form and many of those middle class occupations were tossed out to the secondary sector of the labor market. One direct symptom of that has been increasing shares of income going to top wage earners with falling shares at the bottom (see Figure 3.1).

Here is one useful way to visualize it: Expanding upon imagery from sociologist C. Wright Mills, economist Bennett Harrison has argued that the basic shape of social stratification structures since the late nineteenth century can be divided into three main periods conceptualized as simple shapes. In the early period of industrialization the stratification structure looked somewhat like a *pyramid*, with a narrow top and very large and fat bottom, although I'll say that it more easily visualized as a chocolate chip. At the very top, of course, are mostly owners of growing industrial businesses. There relatively narrow middle is made up of the small numbers of support staff including supervisors and foremen, accountants, and attorneys and the like along with the "old" middle class of small business merchants, professionals, artisans, and so on. The very fat bottom is made up of the industrial working classes.

With the growth of layers of bureaucracy populated by white-collar management and the rise of labor unions we got the creation a *new middle class*, as contrasted with an *old middle class* composed of small business owners and independent white-collar professionals. Thus the class structure came to

FIGURE 3.1   **Income Shares (%) of Top 20% versus Bottom 80%**

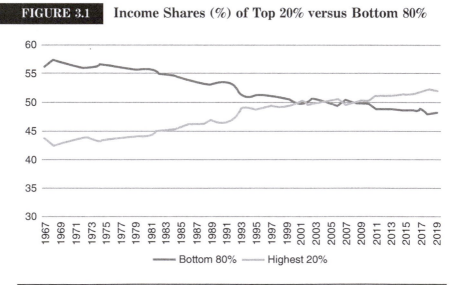

Source: U.S. Census Bureau: https://www.census.gov/library/publications/2020/demo/p60-270.html, 3/12/21

FIGURE 3.2 The Pyramid, Diamond, and Hourglass Class Structures

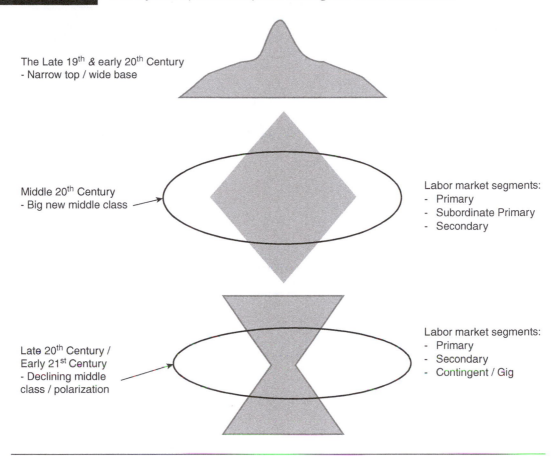

The Late 19th & early 20th Century
- Narrow top / wide base

Middle 20th Century
- Big new middle class

Labor market segments:
- Primary
- Subordinate Primary
- Secondary

Late 20th Century /
Early 21st Century
- Declining middle
class / polarization

Labor market segments:
- Primary
- Secondary
- Contingent / Gig

resemble a *diamond* more than a pyramid. Its top (rich) and bottom (poor) are both relatively small and pointed with a large swollen middle. But then the post-1970s era degraded the middle of the diamond, intensified the difference between the primary and secondary segments of labor markets, increased the amount of contingent labor, and the class structure shifted its shape to that of an *hourglass* (see Figure 3.2). Ours becomes a world divided between players at the top of the hourglass that move things and themselves around the economy like a chess board, and masses of undifferentiated labor in the secondary labor market—now all over the globe—at the bottom of the hour glass. Thus class structures in industrial and now postindustrial societies have been significantly shaped by processes of organizational change. Yet, a focus on class structures alone tells only part of a story of the structuring of social inequalities.

Intersections: Gender, Race, and Ethnicity

Much of the foregoing story with regards to the growth and fall of a middle class as conditioned by labor market structures can be said to apply predominantly to white males, and even then only to some of them. While things have been changing quite a bit, especially since the last part of the twentieth century, the ability to enter an independent or subordinate primary market labor market segment was not equally open to all. This was especially so for the independent primary market, partly because it frequently required relatively advanced educational credentials. And even though things have changed with regards to the position of women and racial and ethnic minorities, a great deal of inequality persists along these divides. There is a persistent *gender wage gap* that, while shrank in the last half of the twentieth century, remains independently of things like levels of education and occupation (see Figures 3.3–3.5). This does, however, intersect with racial and ethnic status as, for

FIGURE 3.3   Median Earnings for Full-Time Workers by Sex, 1970–2019

Source: U.S. Census Bureau: https://www.census.gov/data/tables/time-series/demo/income-poverty/historical-income-people.html, 3/13/2021

FIGURE 3.4   Median Earnings by Sex and Educational Level, 2019

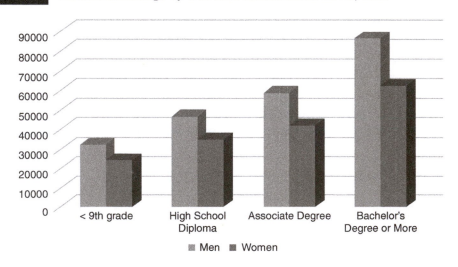

Source: U.S. Census Bureau: https://www.census.gov/data/tables/time-series/demo/income-poverty/historical-income-people.html, 3/13/2021

| **FIGURE 3.5** | **Median Weekly Earnings by Sex and, Selected Occupations 2020** |

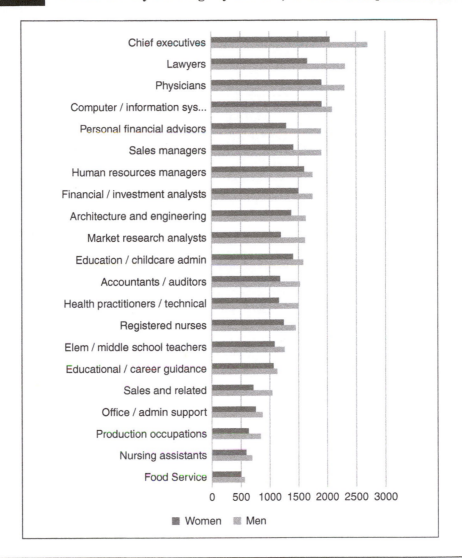

Source: U.S. Bureau of Labor Statistics: https://www.bls.gov/cps/cpsaat39.htm, 2/17/21

example, median earnings of black and Hispanic workers are lower than those of white women, although the gender wage gap does persist *within* racial and ethnic categories (see Figure 3.6). While these inequalities were even larger and more intense if one goes back to the turn of the twentieth century and much of importance has changed since then, many echoes of the past remain alive and well. Thus we need to put our conversation about changing class structures in touch with their *intersections* with cross-cutting bases of inequality such as gender, race, and ethnicity.

Formal organizations do not originate social power disparities between men and women or people of different ethnicities, nor are they the origins of things such as sexism, racism, and discrimination. However, they can—and often do—significantly channel and even amplify these disparities. This can be quite purposeful and stem from outright forms of discrimination. But it can also

FIGURE 3.6   **Median Weekly Earnings by Race/Gender, 2020**

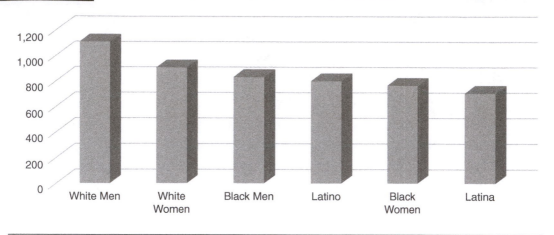

Source: U.S. Bureau of Labor Statistics: https://www.bls.gov/cps/cpsaat37.htm, 3/12/21

stem from structural processes that don't actually require distinct acts of discrimination. In certain respects, we might even think of formal organizational structures, because they are supposed to be based the principle of technical competence, as a means by which these social divisions among people can be, so to speak, "laundered." That is, organizations can sometimes help to maintain, increase, and otherwise solidify underlying forms of inequality, but then make the inequalities appear to be the outcome of legitimate, merit-based processes.

It is worth noting that in the logic of economics, over the long haul it is not possible for organizations, especially business organizations, to discriminate or otherwise participate in the maintenance of gender or race based forms of inequality on this very principle of technical competence. Organizations that favor particular gender or racial/ethnic characteristics—the right "kind" of person—rather than technical competence—the *best and most qualified* person—will be at a competitive disadvantage. As we will see, however, that is an in principle argument that only works under the assumption that markets are near perfect and the only things that shape organizations. It also requires turning a blind eye to various institutionalized aspects of society that systematically shape variations in opportunities for building human capital.

Race and Ethnicity

The term "race" refers to distinctions that get made among people based on physical characteristics, with skin color being the most prominent one. "Ethnicity" generally refers to cultural differences among people in terms of things like language, traditions and customs, styles of dress, diet and so forth. In either case, we are looking at divisions among people rooted in culture in the sense that these categories are socially constructed. That is to say, particular kinds of differences between people have to be selected and treated as meaningful. Because it is defined by biological characteristics, many people think of race as "natural" rather than socially constructed. But while, biologically speaking, people obviously vary in physical characteristics, we don't come in discrete categories of racial groups. To the extent that we do see people as coming in discrete racial categories, this is a matter of selection and the attribution of meaning, and it is the same with cultural variations among people that are thought of as ethnicity. Formal organizations don't explain the origins of racial and ethnic divisions. However, they do become entangled with them in various ways, and have actually exploited them.

As we will see later, the particular path that the organizational revolution took was very strongly influenced by the way that the process of industrialization played out in the United States. From the very beginnings of European settlement in North America, chronic labor shortages for the development of natural resources and thus the economy were apparent. One of the primary ways that labor shortages were met was with migration. There was, of course, the *forced migration* of Africans during the slave trade. This was integral to the rise of what many would call the roots of industrialization which were found in the creation of the factory system for textile production because it was helped significantly by plentiful and cheap cotton created by the forced labor of Africans.

There were also various large waves of migration to the United States from about the middle of the nineteenth century into the early twentieth century, a period known as the *Age of Mass Migration* (often dated from 1850 to 1920). This was significantly spurred by the growth of industrialization that lies at the center of which was the organizational revolution. It was truly an era of open borders (at least for immigrants from Europe) as new arrivals were welcomed (at least by some) as they bolstered the labor force. These waves of migration were more voluntary than forced, although they were often spurred by people fleeing poor economic conditions in their home countries. The most famous example is likely of waves of Irish immigration that were generated by the mid-century potato famine, but that was just one wave among many. By the turn of the twentieth century, the bulk of them were coming from Central, Southern, and Eastern Europe. The key here is that we're talking about populations of people who were often migrating because they were relatively destitute and looking for work. As such, incoming immigrants provided sources of very cheap labor. They weren't slaves in the technical sense, but they were frequently poor and desperate enough to accept whatever working conditions were put upon them. In fact, early on in the industrial period it was common to refer to wage work as *wage slavery*.

The Early Ethnic Immigrant Situation

With regards to the Age of Mass Migration, there is no easy way to characterize the experience, as there was a good deal of diversity over time among arriving immigrants, among geographic locales, and employment strategies. However, generally speaking, how well they fared in labor markets had to do with, among other things, whether they arrived as skilled or unskilled workers, just how destitute they were, and—very importantly—just how different they were from the dominant white culture. Many immigrants from Northern European countries such as England or Germany, for example, often came as skilled workers and were not so culturally distant from the dominant culture. Other immigrant groups, such as the Irish and Italians faced more difficulties, including some fairly intense forms of discrimination.

Despite the fact that most nineteenth and early twentieth-century immigrants were from Europe and would now largely be grouped together as "white," the differences between the groups, and from the dominant white Protestant culture were obvious and salient to people. New immigrants faced serious forms of discrimination from the dominant white population, and, as new waves of immigrants arrived, from earlier more established ethnic groups. However, one potential unifying factor was often finding themselves in the same lowly kinds of jobs with poor working conditions, pay, and job security. As industrial organizations became larger and increasingly mechanized this helped to contribute to making the labor force more homogenous with regards to work experience, and spurred the growth of interest in labor unions as a basis for collective action.

In the tradition of *labor process theory* interpretations of labor market segmentation, this is precisely one of the main reasons that labor markets came to be segmented in the first place. *Labor process theory* begins from the position that the primary logic behind organizational structures is not efficiency of operations. Rather, structures are oriented specifically toward the control of labor. In the employment relationship a worker gives over a certain amount of time and work capacity to an employer. Employers need to be able to maximize the actual amount of work that is gotten in the given time, while returning as little of the value that was produced to workers as possible. The more that employers can control workers, the more value they can get from their work time and the lower they can keep wages and/or other benefits. This is relatively easy when there are very large workforces of quite poor and desperate people, and the result tended to be quite harsh working conditions for very low pay. But to the extent that this results in labor unity and militancy it upsets that balance of power. One response on the part of employers was to purposely introduce divisions among jobs inside of the organization in order to divide workers and set them in competition with each other. As the labor process theory goes, this was even the case for the bureaucratic career ladders in the white-collar hierarchies. The promise of advancement up the ladders gives an incentive to commit to the organization, while competition with others for promotions and raises discourages worker unification.

But the existing social divisions among people on the basis of race and ethnicity, and gender could be exploited as well. Particular labor market segments would frequently be kept homogenous according to ethnic groupings (and gender as well). In this way different immigrant groups were set to compete with other workers for jobs, not merely as individuals, but as members of ethnic minorities. Hence ethnic divisions were used, but also enhanced and maintained. Generally speaking, the newest and thus generally most desperate immigrant groups would be relegated to the worst jobs—those that we would now say are in the secondary labor market. The homogeneity by group and hierarchy made it possible to use threats that members of other, poorer, and more desperate ethnic groups could always replace existing workers if they didn't want to accept labor conditions. All of this helped in keeping the labor force divided among itself, and was often a tool for keeping downward pressure on wages. Keeping workers focused on their competition with and distrust of each other makes collective action and unionization among workers more difficult. Thus, ethnic divisions were explicitly exploited, and frequently heightened by employment practices.

However, segmentation according to ethnic group doesn't mean that there was a static situation where immigrants always remained at the bottom. At least with regards to many of the European-based immigrant groups, there was a pattern over time where they would "move up" social class ladders over time. This would often occur, not to individual persons in their own work careers, but to populations over time. First generation immigrants would enter the country and be provided jobs only at the bottom of the ladder. This meant older, more established groups were bumped upward. The children of immigrants would have improved chances for additional reasons. One is that, with the expansion of formalized public education early in the century, there were better chances of achieving some level of formal schooling. Another reason is that, the cultural differences that make ethnicities apparent, such as language, dress, and diet, frequently become diminished among children of immigrants (although this is variable). The children of immigrants were thus more likely to be able to *assimilate* to the dominant US culture—which means to drop many of the markers of their cultural origins and adopt those of the dominant US culture. And, by the time the native born children of immigrants are ready to enter the labor force, there was often a newer, more impoverished population of immigrants that could be relegated to those spots at the bottom. This process of moving up the ladder over generations is referred to as *intergenerational mobility,* where the idea is that each generation is a little better off than their parents. The general process of *social mobility*—that of moving across levels of social stratification, is often seen as something that individuals do according to their human capital and their efforts. But much social mobility is structural and intergenerational rather than individual.

This (albeit oversimplified picture) describes the situation and patterns for immigrant groups from Europe. The situation was quite different for other groups. Chinese labor, for example, was integral to building the trans-continental railroad. But these Chinese workers were not allowed to bring their families or become citizens, and in 1882 the Chinese Exclusion Act cut off Chinese immigration in any case. Similarly, labor shortages during World War II were addressed with the Bracero program which allowed Mexican workers to enter the United States, but only as "guest workers." The work was restricted to low-level, unskilled jobs, very frequently in agriculture, and residency in the United States was only temporary. When the work was done, they were supposed to return to Mexico. Some symbolic markers of race and ethnic divisions—especially those tied to physical appearance—are seemingly more powerful than others. In the US experience, the most powerful, it seems, continues to be skin color as the story of the African American population of the United States is the most distinctive of all.

The African American Context

We obviously need to start with the legacy of slavery, and the fact that people of African descent were restricted from full participation in US society, including the labor force, even by law until well into the twentieth century. Historically speaking the bulk of the African American population lived in the South of the United States which was largely agricultural. Most of the industrializing, and thus most the new industrial wealth creation, was being done in the North. Whatever wealth was generated in the South was largely from agricultural and related products, but that obviously landed in the hands of wealthy, white, Southern land owners. Even with the official abolishment of slavery at the end of the Civil War, things didn't change very much. The southern United States remained largely rural and agricultural, and the work lives of many former slaves and descendants of slaves stayed much the same as they were. Men tended to work as sharecroppers on the same lands owned by their former owners and women both as agricultural workers and in domestic service to wealthier whites. Any freed slaves or their descendants who found other forms of employment, once again, tended to get relegated to the most menial and low skill forms of work. Educational opportunities were highly restricted although small numbers of African Americans in the South did benefit from the growth of all-black schools including colleges and universities. This did help to create a small middle and professional class for African Americans as preachers and teachers and the like, but for the bulk of the population in the South the need for work on the farm forestalled whatever desires for education may have existed.

It continues to be a long road, but what helped to change the early situation for many African Americans were World Wars I and II, some degree of change in terms of racism, and a cluster of organizational factors having to do with governmental organizations and labor unions. The two world wars created labor shortages in the industrial North. World War I thus spurred the beginnings of what is called *The Great Migration* in which people of African descent began moving out of the agricultural south northward to find jobs in industrial cities. So oddly, despite the fact that African Americans are one of the oldest ethnic groups in the United States they were actually new arrivals with regards to the patterns of immigration waves discussed above. Thus they were, as was the norm, also relegated to the lowest level jobs in the North. For women this meant the same kinds of low level service occupations connected to domestic tasks—cooking and cleaning and such. For men it was the low level, unskilled, manual industrial jobs if any of those could be had at all.

Racism was intense and worse for African Americans than other ethnic groups, and this was exploited by employers in the same ways as noted above. European based ethnicities were favored and given preference, including for more secure, lucrative, and higher level jobs. Where there were substantial populations of African Americans in need of work, their presence was used to threaten existing employed workers with replacement. In fact, African American workers were frequently used as *strike breakers*—meaning that they were brought into workplaces where existing workers had gone on strike. Needless to say, this does not help matters with regards to racist attitudes on the part of other workers. Thus the position of African Americans moving north during The Great Migration was similar to first generation incoming immigrants from Europe, but worse. This includes that fact that the patterns of intergenerational upward mobility didn't occur in the same way. The children of white European immigrants can lose their cultural markers of status such as language and dress. The same cannot be said of skin color, and attempts to rid the world of this kind of racism are quite obviously ongoing.

One thing that helped the position of black migrants in terms of industrial jobs, at least a little bit, was a period of increased restrictions on immigration to the United States. The Immigration Act of 1924 established strict and small quotas on European immigrants, thus shrinking the populations of people competing for industrial jobs. Whatever boost that may have provided, however, was short-lived as the Great Depression affected black workers more than any other population. Being kept at the bottom of the racial/ethnic hierarchy black workers tended to be the first to be laid off or fired, and then had to compete with unemployed members of white ethnic groups to be rehired—a dynamic that often gets called *last hired, first fired*. If anything "helpful" could be said to have come out of the Great Depression for black workers, it would have be the *eventual* emergence of The New Deal under Franklin Roosevelt.

Governmental Organizations and Labor Unions

For one thing, the 1935 *Wagner Act* (a.k.a. *The National Labor Relations Act*) gave legal legitimacy to labor unions in the United States and established the *National Labor Relations Board (NLRB)* to oversee workers' rights and ensure fair labor practices. All by itself, this might not have helped because there was also plenty of racism among labor unions. Many would not accept black workers at all. However, 1936 saw the founding of the Congress of Industrial Organizations (CIO), a federation of industrial labor unions, which explicitly rejected segregation by race or any other characteristic. While not overly common in labor unions of the time, apparently at least some union leaders did realize that things like discrimination kept workers divided and hurt unionization over the long run. Thus an opening was formed for the acceptance of some black workers into some industrial labor unions. This was the time of the emergence of the subordinate primary labor market, and thus also the time that at least some black workers were able to enter it.

These changes all ran headlong into World War II which created an even greater demand for industrial labor than had World War I, along with a greater need for cooperation rather than conflict between industrial organizations and their workers. Given the huge war-time production needs President Roosevelt issued an executive order that banned all forms of discrimination in any organizations—whether businesses or unions—that were involved in war related production. The order also established a *Fair Employment Practice Committee (FEPC)* to oversee it. It is these events that we might say begins to establish something that resembles a true black middle working class, although one would not say that white and black middle classes were on their way toward integration or the decline of the importance of race. Racial segregation, racism, and discrimination obviously persist even now. Yet this combination of governmental and labor union change did create a pathway to the subordinate primary labor market for some.

Another aspect of the New Deal that improved the fortunes of many black workers was the great expansion of public sector employment. The New Deal represented a vast expansion of federal level agencies and activities. Historically speaking, black workers had always faced fewer barriers in public sector employment than in the private sector, and at a time when the federal government was both expanding and (at least formally) explicitly rejecting discrimination on the basis of race, this opened up yet another set of opportunities. In the post-World War II years, the growth of opportunities related to the public sector probably contributed more than anything else to black upward social mobility, initially more for black women, but eventually for black men as well.

In the decades following World War II these same trends continued, and with the civil rights movement (recall the importance of *social movement organizations* to social change as noted in Chapter 2) and legislation such as the 1963 *Equal Pay Act* and 1964 *Civil Rights Act*, discrimination was basically outlawed by federal law. On the human capital side, schools were becoming integrated, and opportunities expanded in terms of access to opportunities for higher education as well. These were coupled with more proactive measures such as the establishment of affirmative action programs which are not designed to merely prevent discrimination, but to take active steps to ensure the inclusion of minorities. Thus, the period from the 1960s and into the 1970s represented a particularly important period of black upward social mobility in US history.

Continuing Challenges

Since then, however, progress has remained choppy and slow, and there have been some important setbacks. For one thing, this thread of history ran into the 1970s competitiveness crisis outlined above. Just as a blue-collar black middle class of unionized industrial workers was getting established, the subordinate primary labor market upon which it depended entered a period of decline as did the labor unions that helped to create it. Many of the conditions faced by African Americans in today's urban areas can be traced to this period of time. The growth of black populations in industrial cities of the North was related to the growth of industrial jobs, and those provided for their well-being. But once those jobs moved elsewhere, there wasn't anything there to replace them. People who were better off were often able to relocate themselves to places where jobs could be found. But lower-income people are often not able to do this and are stuck in places devoid of good employment opportunities which, of course, has the effect of rendering human capital characteristics irrelevant. This kind of situation is known as *structural unemployment*, and forms the basis for what is called a *spatial mismatch hypothesis* in which unemployment and poverty are literally explained in terms of geography. Those in need of jobs live in places that have relatively few opportunities, and have few if any reasonable means of traveling to geographically distant workplaces.

Then there are other issues that continue. Certainly racism and discrimination obviously still matter. And black workers are still more likely to end up being funneled toward more peripheral kinds of jobs in secondary labor markets. But many of these things occur at the intersections of racialized thinking and organizational structure. Ironically, some of the things that were intended to help blacks in terms of employment opportunities may have actually hurt, or at least not helped as much as some believe. For example, the federal efforts in the 1960s and 1970s which did help increase opportunities for racial minorities, coupled with expansion of higher educational opportunities produced a significant cohort of black managers that entered into the previously all-white ranks of many US corporations. At the same time, things like affirmative action and equal employment opportunity mandates actually created new labor market segments—positions in organizations that were meant to administer and oversee such efforts. Positions like these are called *racialized jobs* which means that they are, whether by cultural assumptions, existing structural patterns, or by specific design, tied to matters of race. In a very well-known study, for example, organizational sociologist Sharon Collins documented that those in this early wave of young and promising black managers were often offered these kinds of positions. It did not appear to be out of any purposeful attempt to marginalize anyone. Rather, they were considered to be important jobs, and these men were generally offered excellent terms with regards to salary, prestige, and benefits.

However, the end result of this was frequently stagnation in terms of the ability of these black managers in racialized jobs to advance up career ladders. The issue here becomes one of how organizational structure and human capital intersect. It is a version of the "mailroom problem," discussed above. In terms of developing skills and experience that contribute directly to a company's bottom line—like sales, marketing, or finance—the oversight of hiring practices or the management of community relations just doesn't cut it. The ladders that many young black managers climbed onto simply don't go to the top. Thus, at least this kind of *glass ceiling* (an invisible barrier to advancement) is to be found in organizational structure. It is worth noting that the situation can be quite similar for women, who often end up on part of the ladders that have to do with human resources management—the administration of payroll and benefit functions and the like. They're often quite good positions with stability, good pay, and benefits. But the top rung of the ladder does not lead to the executive suites.

In addition to challenges in both the white-collar and blue-collar private sectors, the prospects for black workers in the public sector have also been harmed. Many public sector jobs are, of course, dependent upon political changes such as the expansion and contraction of governmental organizations. In general, the period from about Franklin Roosevelt's New Deal through Lyndon Johnson's Great Society of the 1960s was a period of government expansion, and thus employment opportunities that greatly helped both black men and women. Furthermore, especially with the 1960s expansion, many of those positions were *racialized* as they were connected to government efforts to reduce racial inequalities and assist what were often predominantly black populations. That trend, however, largely reversed in the 1980s with large government cutbacks under the Reagan administration, cutbacks that did disproportionately affect black government workers.

In attempting to highlight the importance of organizational changes in helping to shape racial and ethnic inequalities, the intent is not to try to suggest that things like racism and discrimination don't matter. They obviously do matter, but all by themselves are insufficient for full understanding and attention to organizational dynamics helps a great deal. The same logic also applies when it comes to questions of gender stratification where the intersection of long-standing social and cultural divisions interacts with organizational dynamics to shape the position of women in society relative to men.

Gender Inequality

There are distinct similarities in the ways that racial/ethnic and gender inequalities are shaped by cultural elements in relation to organizational dynamics, but there are also distinct differences. While racial and ethnic minority groups have been, generally speaking, lower down in class hierarchies relative to dominant whites, there have always been women distributed throughout from top to bottom. Of course, historically speaking this was normally by virtue of attachment to men, especially at the middle through higher class levels. It is only relatively recently that women have become independent actors in terms of economic, political, and cultural activity. Even to this day, the custom of having a bride's father walk his daughter down the wedding aisle to the groom is a leftover from a ceremonial logic that emphasized the transfer of property and authority from one man to another. So while women could be found at the top of class hierarchies, they were always still under men in terms of power. And like with cultural ideas regarding race and ethnicity, *patriarchal* (male-rule) assumptions and attitudes have fed into formal organizations, shaped them, and have been shaped by them.

When "Women's Work" Stopped Being "Work"

The organizational revolution has intersected with gender issues in quite a few important and interesting ways. We can start with a simple, but strange observation. If you take what is considered to be the traditional model of a "housewife," this points to a person who does not engage in *paid* work in the labor force. Rather the housewife is someone who stays home and takes care of the home and the children. Ever since working for wages became the norm, there is thus an idea that the traditional housewife "does not work." Now, I've never been a full-time stay-at-home parent, but as a guy who has spent significant amounts of time on home and childcare myself, I can tell you that the belief that stay-at-home parents "don't work" is a very strange one. It's actually rather insulting. Anyone who has ever stayed home to take care of the household and the children knows that it represents a ton of "work." And thinking of it as somehow "not working" is historically new, quite unusual, and completely tied to the organizational revolution.

We could say more loosely that it came with the Industrial Revolution, or perhaps just "industrialization." But there is nothing too specific about these processes that require this new way of thinking and acting. In fact, a good deal of early factory work, especially in the textile industry was done by women and children. Rather it is tied to the rise of bureaucratic organizational characteristics—that as a condition of employment, one's full working capacity belongs to the organization, and that there is a strict separation between one's personal life and their employment position. Working as someone else's employee for pay was not a normal thing to do in the United States throughout the nineteenth century. That was something only very poor and desperate people (such as ethnic immigrants) had to do. As noted above, working for wages which now seems so normal was often called *wage slavery* and carried a stigma along with it, not unlike the stigma attached to reliance on food stamps or other forms of public assistance these days. A great deal of work was agricultural, but even where it wasn't people's work was still generally centered on the home. There was typically a division of labor based on gender, but women's labor was still considered to be essential labor. The work of both men and women was known to be essential to the maintenance of home and family. It was formal work organizations that created a stark separation between "work" and "home."

Home was culturally transformed into a place of rest and leisure rather than of work. But rest and leisure for whom? The idea obviously requires a male centered perspective as it was a place of rest and leisure for working men. But certainly not for the women. This is perhaps the real kicker. In the traditional male bread-winner/female housewife model, women had to work through the day on home and children. They then had to continue working to make sure that their husbands were cared for after a "hard day's work." In other words, unlike their husbands who put their feet up after work, women had to work a *second shift*. The *Second Shift* term was popularized in a 1989 book of that title by sociologist Arlie Hochschild. It wasn't actually about the housewife at the turn of the twentieth century. Rather it was about how in the late twentieth-century women, even if they are full-time workers and bread-winners themselves, still bear the brunt of handling household labor.

These patterns do represent echoes of historical gendered assumptions that cannot be attributed merely to formal organizations. There is a long standing idea that the *public sphere* of such things as political life and forms of economic activity outside of the home are the domain of men, while the *private sphere* of what takes place in and around the home is the domain of women. This is generally referred to as the *ideology of separate spheres*. Thus, once the primary economic activities of the production and distribution of goods and services became something that takes place outside of the home, "work" came to be understood as paid employment outside of the home. As such this ideology of separate spheres helped to assure that a strong line came to be drawn between the proper place of men and women in the economy, and created the idea that women who stay at home "don't work." This intensified the extent to which women were seen as mere dependents of men, and helped to reinforce a secondary social status for women. So while the formal organization of work and of government did not create this division, it did amplify it.

Intersections with Class

Of course, the world is not nearly as simple as all of the women stayed at home "not working" while all of the men went to work. In fact, we can say that the iconic breadwinner/homemaker model of marriage and work most easily describes many middle and upper class white couples. Poor women frequently did participate in paid employment as a matter of necessity, and much of the time this also meant that they were members of ethnic minorities. We will hear some about this later in Chapter 5, but when large textile factories started to operate in the United States they were frequently "manned" by poor immigrant laborers and much of the time women and children. Culturally speaking this was not a stretch because textile work was something that women and children traditionally did in the home setting. There is ample evidence to suggest that in many occupations, if women were deemed capable of doing the necessary work, they were preferred as employees because they tend to work for less and be less militant and easier to control than men. This was indicative of much of women's paid work at the time. Basically they were accepted only into jobs in the secondary labor market such as low level manufacturing and service jobs, such as domestic laborers (e.g., maids) for wealthier people. And, as with the exploitation of race and ethnic divisions, labor process theorists argue that sex segregation was purposeful as part of attempts to maintain divisions among workers.

For unmarried women from the middle classes, there did tend to be more options, though with those opportunities often being tied to the ability to access formal schooling. As I noted at the beginning of the chapter, the growth of bureaucratic organizations helped spur the growth of formal schooling, and the importance of educational credentials as part of human capital for entry into better segments of the labor market. Thus there was an expansion of the population of people who were completing high school, and many of those, including women, were finding employment in the expanding ranks of office workers. Opportunities were still limited, however, as certain lines of work quickly became highly segregated by gender, and, in keeping with the ideology of separate spheres, even in wage work women remained seen as best in service to men. This we find the birth of the quintessential "secretary"—a person to take dictations, type up and file documents, handle messages for the (virtually always male) bosses, and so forth. Since access to these office jobs was frequently dependent on having obtained some manner of formal educational credential, women entering office work at this point tended to be white and from relatively well-off families. Poorer families often needed their children out in the labor force rather than in school, so access to education was not within the realm of possibility for all.

For the proportionally small number of women (more likely to be middle to upper class) who went beyond high school to college and professional training programs, opportunities for professional work were better, but still generally limited. Again, in keeping with the notion of the separate spheres, if women were going on to higher education and some manner of professional career it was likely into one of what are called the *caring professions*. This includes things like nursing, teaching, and social work—occupations where you care for other people. So in other words, up and down the entire class hierarchy, if and when women went to work for pay they largely went to work doing jobs that are an extension of those things already considered to be the domain of women—things like textile work and domestic service, looking after men's needs, and taking care of people. And in keeping with the general cultural devaluation of the female domain, areas of work dominated by women generally remained a notch (or more) below occupations dominated by males in terms of income and prestige.

The Continuing Echoes

While things did change a great deal over the course of the twentieth and into the twenty-first century, the echoes of all of this remain stamped into economic life and culture in many ways. Overall *gender segregation* remains quite high in the labor market, meaning that many occupations remain dominated by men or by women rather than being integrated. To this day over 90% of executive secretaries and administrative assistants remain female, and the same applies to other traditionally female labor force roles in such things as nursing, preschool and kindergarten teaching, and childcare work. One of the ways to track the overall level of segregation in labor markets is what is called a *dissimilarity* or *gender segregation index*. This is one number that indicates the proportion of women/men who would have to change occupations to achieve complete occupational integration by gender. Expressed as a percentage, this number hovered in the mid to high 60% level through most of the twentieth century, began a noticeable fall starting around 1970, but then largely stagnated and remained at 42% as of 2018.[7] A lot of this is because of a fairly large number of highly segregated occupations. Those dominated by women have been dubbed *pink-collar* jobs as a contrast to blue- or white-collar jobs (see Figure 3.7). Many of these pink-collar areas are secondary labor market jobs, and thus sometimes referred to as *female ghettoes*. But even regardless of the labor market segment, female dominated occupations as compared to comparable male dominated occupations overall bring lower wages. And if women tend to start to enter new occupational locations that were previously dominated by men, it tends to place a downward pressure on wages.

This is certainly reflected in the long-standing *gender wage gap* (see Figures 3.3 and 3.5), and even as women have been much more likely to earn

---

[7]England et al., 2020: 6991.

FIGURE 3.7   Occupations 90% or More Female, 2020

Occupation	% Female
Preschool/kindergarten teachers	99.8
Medical records specialists	97.6
Dental assistants	94.6
Speech-language pathologists	94.1
Medical secretaries / admin assts	93.7
Childcare workers	93.5
Secretaries / admin assts	93.1
Exec secretaries / admin assts	92.9
Compensation / benefits mgrs	92.9
Dietitians and nutritionists	92.8
Dental hygienists	92.7
Audiologists	92.3
Home health aides	91.3
Psychiatric technicians	90.6

Source: U.S. Bureau of Labor Statistics data https://www.bls.gov/cps/cpsaat39.htm, 2/17/21

advanced degrees and pursue high level, prestigious work, the wage gap remains regardless. At the same time women remain underrepresented at the highest levels of political and business organizations. While some of the reasons for this can be explained in typical human capital terms (see below), much of it cannot and this there may exist a *glass ceiling*—or, basically an invisible barrier that seems to prevent women from being able to continue to advance to the highest levels of organizations.

Things such as segregation, the wage gap, and lack of advancement relative to men is often explained away as matters of choice and human capital. So while it remains the case that professions like nursing and elementary and secondary teaching in the United States are disproportionately female (typical pink-collar jobs), no one literally forces women to choose those paths. They could, perhaps, just as well decide to become engineers or computer programmers. But it is possible to emphasize the notion of choice too much as it is here that we run into the echoes of the separate spheres. Cultural ideas about gender and gender roles have changed quite a lot, especially since about the 1960s. But we are still saturated by gendered ideas and those are communicated very powerfully throughout our lifetimes by parents and grandparents, peers, teachers, professors, the media, and so on. Many people operate with deeply ingrained assumptions regarding what is expected of or appropriate for people to "choose" to do based on gender, and these are internalized by both men and women.

Furthermore, given the historical marginalization of women, many occupations and work places are dominated by male values steeped in cultural assumptions about masculinity. This will be intensified in occupations historically dominated by men. One example that has been much discussed recently is the extent to which *geek culture* is prevalent in the computing industry and may account for the continued low representation of women in the industry. The notion of geek culture goes well beyond the computing or related industries as it is more often than not seen to be rooted in subcultures of people who are fans of things like science fiction, comic books, and related video games. But the culture significantly involves computing as well. Geek culture is known for its *toxic masculinity* in which masculine values such as strength and dominance are overtly and aggressively portrayed, frequently with the help of the use of sexist and homophobic behaviors. The pervasiveness of geek culture in the computing industry has been put forward frequently as one of the reasons for continued low female representation.

As another echo of the past, women remain much more likely than men to organize their work lives around childbearing and child care, so they are more likely to leave the labor force while caring for children or at least scale back on paid work to accommodate family responsibilities. Imagine some young couple who met in college while both earning degrees in accounting. After college they marry and both take entry level jobs at major accounting firms. After five years, the woman becomes pregnant and they decide that she will stop working temporarily to take care of the child. Perhaps she remains out of the labor force or perhaps she picks up a little bit of part time work doing the books for a local construction company just to help with the bills. Meanwhile the husband remains in his regular job. Now fast-forward five years. The child is ready to go off to kindergarten, so the woman decides to go back to regular, full-time paid work. Well, now they both have the same educational background and professional skills, but the husband has five more years of experience and has possibly earned raises and promotions along the way. It is unlikely, then, that they will be earning the same thing or be at the same level in the organizational hierarchy.

In this regard, women face tensions and conflicts that men do not. Take for example what has been named the organizational concept of the *ideal worker*. This concept was first introduced by feminist scholar Joan Acker in 1990 landmark journal article called "Hierarchies, Jobs, and Bodies: A Theory of Gendered Organizations," and it continues to shape how people understand gender stratification in work organizations. The simple story of the ideal worker is that it is someone who can and will devote their full-time energy and attention to their work without distraction or interference. Work is a calling or a vocation, and the ideal worker is ambitious, hardworking, competitive, rational, and committed to the job above all else. But women face a conflicting "ideal"—that of the *ideal mother*. The ideal mother is completely devoted to children and family life. And it is not just men who hold this ideal. Women do as well. Ambitious males can devote themselves to their careers and live up to the ideal worker, but at the same time be seen as meeting their family obligations by being a good breadwinner. Meanwhile women are just stuck either having to choose—and thus failing at one or the other of these ideals—or trying to juggle both sets of conflicting demands. And because this conflict applies most strongly to women, this *family–work conflict* (*FWC*) is seen to be a problem for women, but not for men.

The *FWC* story is now well known, but even trying to address it on behalf of women can have detrimental effects. The typical means of addressing the *FWC* is through introducing options for flexible work arrangements. But these don't seem to help in terms of keeping female workers with children from falling behind. What they seem to do instead is just grease the skids so to speak, providing formal means for women to cut back on work obligations. Thus women who accept flexibility arrangements do keep working, but are then faced with a stigma that further degrades their position in both internal and external labor markets.

It is hard to consider this as anything other than an intersection between cultural ideals and the logic that dominates formal organizations. The rationalized bureaucratic form is built on ideas and values that many feminist scholars argue are gendered at their very core, and built significantly around principles of operation that match up to the experience of males and values associated with masculinity. Rather than taking the notion of the *ideal worker* for granted, perhaps we might wonder how organizations might be different if they were originally built with the needs of women in mind, rather than of men. Why is it, one might wonder, that the entire notion of a rationalized bureaucracy doesn't include the assumptions that people—male or female—have homes and family members to tend to? This, of course, contributes to how and why women so frequently end up in the lower ranks of organizations and in secondary areas of the labor market. We will see later (Chapter 7) that this idea of an organization owning one's entire working attention and capacity was quite explicit among those building early industrial work organizations that set the template for the organizational revolution. Furthermore, it was not only explicit but also a rather new way of thinking about work, and the ability to accomplish it was significantly related to the ideology of separate spheres. Organizations could expect ideal workers because someone else was taking care of home and family.

The feminist idea is that if organizations were built by, around, and for the experience of women they would be very different, and many of these have been constructed. They operate a lot like anti-bureaucracies, emphasizing things like equality over hierarchy, participatory forms of leadership, the lack of strict divisions of labor and segregation or work tasks, and low levels of formalization of tasks. They also include explicit recognition that issues of people's personal lives and emotional selves are not only valid, but also important. For reasons that we will consider later, this style of organizing can often be difficult to maintain although often not likely because it produces any problems of efficiency.

Gender stratification is complicated, and it obviously involves a great deal more than organizations and their structures and associated labor markets. Patriarchal culture and social structures were not initiated by the organizational revolution. However, many of the current manifestations of gender inequalities, including their stubborn persistence even in the face of long-standing efforts to eliminate them have been directly conditioned by the rise and spread of the iron cage.

Conclusion

The foregoing all just represents a glimpse of the issues involved in social stratification. The study of stratification is an important area of Sociology in and of itself with entire texts dedicated to introducing it. One can also find entire texts dedicated purely to gender issues and others dedicated to those of race and ethnicity. It is all worthy of further attention. And formal organizations and their structures certainly cannot explain everything about stratification. However, they are at least one necessary component of any good understanding of the dynamics of social stratification since the turn of the twentieth century. In language from sociologist Joan Acker that is commonly used these days, organizations consist of *inequality regimes* "defined as loosely interrelated practices, processes, actions, and meanings that result in and maintain class, gender, and racial inequalities within particular organizations."[8] Their divisions of labor and hierarchies make up central aspects of the occupational system which, for most, is their link to accessing, at the very least economic and cultural power resources. With regards to matters that are more strictly behavioral or cultural in nature, such as racism, sexism, and discrimination, organizations frequently remain important to how those things are shaped and channeled. Formal organizations, in other words, are central to shaping variable *life chances*.

SOURCES AND FURTHER READING

On **segmented labor markets:**

- Among the earliest to define **dual labor markets:**

  o Doeringer, Peter B., and Michael J. Piore. 1971. *Internal Labor Markets and Manpower Analysis.* Lexington, MA: D.C. Heath and Company.

- For foundational work defining I've called the **Mid-twentieth Century Model** of market segmentation see:

  o First defined (as far as I know) in Reich, Michael, David M. Gordon, and Richard C. Edwards. 1973. "Dual Labor Markets: A Theory of Labor Market Segmentation." *American Economic Review* 63: 359–65.

  o For a full and later development: Edwards, Richard C. 1979. *Contested Terrain: The Transformation of the Workplace in the Twentieth Century.* New York, NY: Basic Books.

  o These arguments also provide the **labor process theory** interpretations of dual labor markets.

- On the **Post-1970s Dualization, good jobs/bad jobs, insiders/outsiders** and the **gig economy,** see, for example:

  o Adamson, Maria and Ian Roper. 2019. "'Good' Jobs and 'Bad' Jobs: Contemplating Job Quality in Different Contexts." *Work, Employment, and Society* 33(4): 551–9 (This is a Foreword to a full special issue of *WES* on good jobs/bad jobs).

  o Davis, Gerald F. 2016. *The Vanishing American Corporation: Navigating the Hazards of a New Economy.* Oakland, CA: Berrett-Koehler Publishers, Inc. (For **Nikefication** and **Uberization**).

  o Hudson, Kenneth. 2007. "The New Labor Market Segmentation: Labor Market Dualism in the New Economy." *Social Science Research* 36: 286–312.

  o Kalleberg, Arne L. 2011. *Good Jobs, Bad Jobs: The Rise of Polarized and Precarious Employment Systems in the United States, 1970s to 2000s.* New York, NY: Russell Sage Foundation.

---

[8]Acker (2006), p. 443.

○ Nicolaisen, Heidi, Hanne Kavli, and Ragnhild Steen Jensen. 2019. *Dualisation of Part-Time Work: The Development of Labour Market Insiders and Outsiders.* Chicago, IL: Policy Press/University of Chicago Press.

○ Schwander, Hanna. 2019. "Labor Market Dualization and Insider–Outsider Divides: Why This New Conflict Matters." *Political Studies Review* 17:14–29.

On the visualization of class structures as shapes:

• Harrison, Bennett. 1994. *Lean and Mean: The Changing Landscape of Corporate Power in the Age of Flexibility.* New York, NY: Basic Books. (Specifically discussed, p. 29.)

• Mills, C. Wright. 1956. *The Power Elite.* New York, NY: Oxford University Press. (The *pyramid* and *diamond* reference is on page 148. This was before the age of the *hourglass*.)

On the **new middle class**: This concept goes all the way back to the beginnings at the turn of the twentieth century, but it is a shifting target as the term keeps getting re-appropriated. My use here was a reference back to the early uses with regards to the "bulging middle" that brought the diamond shaped class structure. It was *mostly* begun in the context of Marxian theory regarding class polarization and how the growth of bureaucracies and their ballooning white-collar ranks threw a wrench in the works. But the emergence of unions and stabilization of a good deal of blue-collar work figured in too.

• C. Wright Mills addressed both of these aspects of shifting class status:

○ Mills, C. Wright. 1948. *The New Men of Power: America's Labor Leaders.* New York, NY: Harcourt, Brace. (Although this was more about labor leaders than unions, *per se.*)

○ ———. [1951] 1973. *White Collar: The American Middle Classes.* New York, NY: Oxford University Press.

• For a basic review, especially in the context of the roots in Marxian thought, see:

○ Burris, Val. 1986. "The Discovery of the New Middle Class." *Theory and Society* 15: 317–49.

On **race/ethnicity** and **gender**: This entire subject matter intersects strongly with the related area of the *Sociology of Work and Occupations*, and I borrowed some valuable organizing ideas from:

• Sweet, Stephen and Peter Meiksins. 2017. *Changing Contours of Work: Jobs and Opportunities in the New Economy.* Washington, DC: Sage.

On general dynamics of ethnicity during the **Age of Mass Migration**:

• Abramitzky, Ran and Leah Boustan. 2017. "Immigration in American Economic History." *Journal of Economic Literature* 55: 1311–45.

• Catron, Peter. 2016. "Made in America? Immigrant Occupational Mobility in the First Half of the Twentieth Century." *American Journal of Sociology* 122: 325–78.

• Portes, Alejandro and Rubén G. Rumbaut. 2014. *Immigrant America: A Portrait,* 4th *Ed.* Oakland, CA: University of California Press. See especially, Ch. 1.

- Restifo, Salvatore J., Vincent J. Roscigno, and Zhenchao Qian. "Segmented Assimilation, Split Labor Markets, and Racial/Ethnic Inequality: The Case of Early-Twentieth-Century New York." *American Sociological Review* 78: 897–924.

With regards to **African Americans**:

- Collins, Sharon. 1983. "The Making of the Black Middle Class." *Social Problems* 30: 369–82.

- ———. 1997. *Black Corporate Executives: The Making and Breaking of a Black Middle Class.* Philadelphia, PA: Temple University Press.

- ———. 1997. "Black Mobility in White Corporations: Up the Corporate Ladder but Out on a Limb." *Social Problems* 44: 55–67.

- Katz, Michael B., Mark J. Stern, and Jamie J. Fader. 2005. "The New African American Inequality." *The Journal of American History* 92: 75–108.

- Ndoboa, André, Alice Faure, Jeanne Boisselier, and Stella Giannaki. 2018. "The Ethno-Racial Segmentation Jobs: The Impacts Of The Occupational Stereotypes On Hiring Decisions." *The Journal of Social Psychology* 158: 663–79.

- Nkomo, Stella M. and Akram Al Ariss. 2014. "The Historical Origins Of Ethnic (White) Privilege In US Organizations." *Journal of Managerial Psychology.* 29: 389–404.

- Parks, Virginia. 2011. "Revisiting Shibboleths of Race and Urban Economy: Black Employment in Manufacturing and the Public Sector Compared, Chicago 1950–2000." *International Journal of Urban and Regional Research.* 35: 110–29.

- Wingfield, Adia Harvey and Renée Skeete Alston. 2014. "Maintaining Hierarchies in Predominantly White Organizations: A Theory of Racial Tasks." *American Behavioral Scientist.* 58: 274–87.

- Zieger, Robert H. 2007. *For Jobs and Freedom: Race and Labor in America since 1865.* Lexington, KY: The University Press of Kentucky.

With regards to **Gender**:

- Acker, Joan. 1990. "Hierarchies, Jobs, Bodies: A Theory of Gendered Organizations." *Gender and Society* 4: 139–58.

- ———. 2006. "Inequality Regimes: Gender, Class, and Race in Organizations." *Gender and Society* 20: 441–64.

- Alfrey, Lauren and France Winddance Twine. 2017. "Gender-Fluid Geek Girls: Negotiating Inequality Regimes in the Tech Industry." *Gender and Society* 31: 28–50.

- Boris, Eileen and Carolyn Herbst Lewis. 2006. "Caregiving and Wage-Earning: A Historical Perspective on Work And Family." Chapter 4 in *The Work and Family Handbook: Multi-Disciplinary Perspectives and Approaches*, edited by Marcie Pitt-Catsouphes, Ellen Ernst Kossek, and Stephen Sweet. New York, NY: Taylor & Francis Group.

- Bourgault, Sophie. 2017. "Prolegomena to a Caring Bureaucracy." *European Journal of Women's Studies.* 24: 202–17.

- Brumley, Krista M. 2014. "The Gendered Ideal Worker Narrative: Professional Women's and Men's Work Experiences in the New Economy at

Mexican Company." *Gender & Society* 28: 799–823.

England, Paula, Andrew Levine, and Emma Mishel. 2020. "Progress Toward Gender Inequality in the United States has Slowed or Stalled." *Proceedings of the National Academy of Sciences* 117: 6990–7.

Ferguson, Kathy. 1984. *The Feminist Case against Bureaucracy.* Philadelphia, PA: Temple University Press.

Gorman, Elizabeth H. and Sarah Mosseri. 2019. "How Organizational Characteristics Shape Gender Difference and Inequality at Work." *Sociology Compass* 13: e12660.

Healy, Geraldine, Ahu Tatli, Gulce Ipek, Mustafa Özturk, Cathrine Seierstad, and Tessa Wright. 2019. "In the Steps of Joan Acker: A Journey in Researching Inequality Regimes and Intersectional Inequalities." *Gender, Work, and Organization* 26: 1749–62.

Hochschild, Arlie. 1989. *The Second Shift: Working Families and the Revolution at Home.* New York, NY: Penguin Books.

Padavic, Irene, Robin J. Ely, and Erin M. Reid. 2020. "Explaining the Persistence of Gender Inequality: The Work–family Narrative as a Social Defense against the 24/7 Work Culture." *Administrative Science Quarterly* 65: 61–111.

Scheepers, Ella and Ishtar Lakhani. 2020. "Caution! Feminists at Work: Building Organisations from the Inside Out." *Gender & Development* 28: 117–33.

Wynn, Alison T., and Shelley J. Correll. 2018. "Puncturing the Pipeline: Do Technology Companies Alienate Women in Recruiting Sessions?" *Social Studies of Science* 48: 149–64.

Forging the Society of Organizations

In Part I we looked at some of the most important contours of "Our Society of Organizations." The first step was to catch on to the extent to which our lives and social patterns are encased in *formal rationality*, and to recognize that Max Weber was largely correct in foreseeing the continued spread of the *iron cage*. We then considered some important aspects of what this means in terms of how social power operates at both the macro levels of social *power structures* and the micro levels of the *life chances* of persons. There is no single and necessary way to think about it all, but the picture can easily be seen to not match up terribly well with what we might think the ideal ought to be. We live in a culture that is largely shaped by assumptions born of the Enlightenment where human action is a matter of reasoned persons making informed decisions. In keeping with this we frequently celebrate our economic and political arrangements that are derived from this. Our market economies and participatory political process are supposed to create equality of opportunity and leave social power broadly dispersed through the population, although certainly allowing for some variations as it stems from individual achievements. Instead we learn that more and more of social action is formally rationalized rather than being based in the exercise of reasoned decision-making; that social power has been highly concentrated, economically, politically, and culturally; and that individual achievement is frequently hemmed in by organizational structures.

In Part II, we're going to ask a big question—possibly the biggest of questions: "Could things have been otherwise?" Could social power have been less concentrated, and could people's lives have been shaped more by local and personal things than by the impersonal and self-serving needs of large formal organizations? Could we be in a society dominated more by *substantive rationality* and less by formal rationality? Though judgments about this will vary, the current state of affairs wasn't "natural" or inevitable or necessary. The center of our story will be the consideration of *the rise of "big business."* This will mean learning of the rise of the modern *corporation* as a new kind of social actor in the world that exists in the legal system right alongside of regular people. And it will mean learning of the establishment of very large, rationalized, hierarchical management structures throughout the economy—the classic Weberian bureaucracy as it colonized the business world. Business organizations will be the center of our story because—well—mostly because the rise of BIG business *is* the center of the story. While the world would undoubtedly contain quite a bit of formal rationalization regardless of changes in the form of business, especially in matters of the military and political administration, the form that businesses took at around the turn of the twentieth century was the catalyst for a great deal of the organizational revolution.

We'll start in Chapter 4 with what can be loosely called the "efficiency" argument for the rise of big business organizations. This will largely come from business historian Alfred Chandler whose accounts tend to be the most well known and are often uncritically accepted. It is the kind of argument that more or less says that it was all rather inevitable because it was the most efficient way for the economy to develop, and that it was all for the best in any case. Chapter 5 will offer an alternative perspective, the bulk of which will come from seeing the rise of big business as being driven by various actors in the explicit interest of concentrating economic, and relatedly, political and cultural power. These two chapters will largely be focused on the roots—basically the turn of the twentieth century. In Chapter 6 we'll zoom ahead to the last part of the twentieth and early twenty-first century and the question of whether or not all of this concern about the *iron cage* is now outdated. Very important shifts in the global economy can be seen to have resulted in the walking back of the central elements of the organizational society to the point that we might no longer be in one. At its center, then, will be the question of the *fall of big business*. The core vocabulary for this story will involve a common historical narrative that the dominant mode of business has gone from *markets* (much of the nineteenth century and prior), to *hierarchies* (late nineteenth century to about 1970), and now to *networks* (post-1970s). A couple of important threads that hold it all together are that (A) it centers on changes to organizational forms, especially as rooted in business organizations but with relevance to other kinds of organizations and (B) many of the same logics are used to examine the rise of big business as are used to examine the question of whether it has fallen.

The Rise of Bureaucracy and the Question of Efficiency

Bureaucracy, *per se*, is not new. If you were to ask historians or archaeologists, they might point you to places like ancient Sumeria (second millennium BCE) or Egypt (first millennium BCE) where the identification of bureaucratic principles can be found without too much trouble. In terms of present existence, perhaps the world's oldest continually operating bureaucracy is the Catholic Church which dates back to the Roman Empire, and continues to operate with plenty of bureaucracy. But none of these things deliver to us the direct roots of today's society of organizations (keeping in mind that we have yet to question whether or not we still are in a society of organizations). The ancient empires like Sumeria and Egypt came and went. And while the Catholic Church was an all-pervasive institution throughout Europe during the Middle Ages and remains important in some respects, it is not central to what has given today's world its shape. Today's organizational society took shape through the nineteenth century (though in ways that have roots going back through the Middle Ages), and is basically synonymous with the rise of *industrial society* (and now *postindustrial society*, though that is part of where things can get fuzzy in terms of whether we are beyond a society of organizations. Flip ahead to Chapter 6 if you just can't wait).

If you asked people these days about the existence of very large and powerful bureaucratic organizations, it is likely that "government" would immediately come to mind. In other words, the "P" from our IEMP power framework from Chapter 2. And it's true that, historically speaking, the growth of centralized governments and their associated military organizations are the most likely places to find bureaucratic development. One of Weber's references in the development of his ideal type was the Prussian state of his time, and we'll learn later that the Prussian military served as an inspiration for early builders of bureaucratic practices in business organizations. But if government bureaucracy was so central to bringing about the world we inhabit, then why would the focus so often be on the development of industry? Industry is about the economy and, much more so than the state, lies at the center of the coming of the society of organizations. This was, of course, an important aspect of Weber's story – that one of the prime movers of the bureaucratic impulse was the coming of capitalism. In capitalism, the goal of economic production is basically just to take some amount of capital and turn it into more capital – or in more familiar terms, to make profits. The upsides of bureaucratic organization in this regard are the predictability and calculability, but especially the potential for efficiency. As we saw in Chapter 1, Weber took efficiency as a primary reason for the growth and spread of bureaucracy. And this is nowhere more important than in a market economy, as economists are happy to remind everyone.

The rise of industrial society would often lead one to think of the Industrial Revolution. That is the famous one in all of the history books, often dated at something like the middle of the eighteenth century through the early to middle part of the nineteenth century. But there is a lesser discussed *second industrial revolution* that took place right around the turn of the twentieth century. In US history books it coincides with the period usually referred to as *The Gilded Age*, and "stars" the *robber barons* of the turn of the twentieth century such as J.P. Morgan, John D. Rockefeller, Cornelius Vanderbilt, and so on. This was a period of intensive industrialization, the heart of the organizational revolution, and those robber barons were important in creating it. The industrial revolution is normally described with a focus on technological changes in how goods and services are produced and transported. The key thing was the introduction of the use of nonanimal energy sources (such as wood, coal, and other fossil fuels) to run newly developing machineries for production and transportation. The second industrial revolution is certainly a story of industrial machinery. But it is even more a story about human social organization because it is where large scale industrial machinery got tied up with very large human organizations. And it happened somewhat suddenly. It's always tricky (impossible, really) to put specific dates on these things, but let's just say the revolutionary period was from the end of the Civil War in 1865 to roughly about 1920. In the space of only about 60 years formal rationalization went from the exception to the rule in human social action, and has been spreading ever since.

The central changes, of course, were to how the economy of the United States was organized, though similar developments were taking place in at least some parts of Europe. Directly on the heels of that came the growth and further bureaucratization of government, the rise of large labor unions, the establishment of compulsory public educational systems, and so forth. Furthermore, these changes were not confined to the United States, but soon affected all industrializing countries, whether capitalist or not. In short, the second industrial revolution was about the rise of *big business*, largely in the US, and lies directly at the core of the organizational revolution. Do note that the term "big business" has no precise or exact meaning. It is and will remain a fuzzy target. Things like big government, big labor unions, and mass public education followed rapidly from it. And if you recall the lessons of Chapter 1, then you know that the spread of formal rationality has not slowed. In this chapter we review what is likely the dominant understanding for how and why this came about—an *efficiency* argument.

"Big Business" and the Emergence of *Managerial Capitalism*

The typical business of the middle of the nineteenth century and prior was a *small business*. It was very specialized in its functions, focusing only on a single or small number of products or services, serving a limited geographic area, and operating in *proprietary* form. A *proprietor* is just the owner of a business, so to operate in *proprietary form* is to say that there is a person—or

| FIGURE 4.1 | **Summary Characteristics of the Managerial Revolution** |

Size of Businesses: Businesses went from small, single function, local operations to large, multifunction operations operating over regions and the entire country and the globe
Vertical Integration: Putting multiple stages of business operations in the same company
Horizontal Integration: basically when competitors end up in the same company.
Monopolies/Oligopolies: one or only a small number of businesses dominate entire industries
Conglomeration: the same company owns product lines in different industries (though didn't generally become common until after World War II).
The Corporate Form and Capital Requirements: Businesses can exist as entities that are legally separate from their owners and managers. It was a useful tool for accumulating financing.
Separation of Ownership from Control/Managerial Revolution: a great deal of economic activity is consciously coordinated by corporate managers rather than by business owners and the *invisible hand* of the law of supply and demand

perhaps a family—that started the business and both owns and manages it on a day to day basis. But the story of the second industrial revolution represented a fairly dramatic shift where businesses went big and changed form. They took on many different functions related to the production and distribution of goods and services, dealt in multiple different product lines, started operating over entire regions, then the entirety of the United States, and even the globe, and largely shifted from *proprietary* to *corporate* form (see Figure 4.1 for a summary).

Growth in Business Size

There is no single business characteristic to point to with regards to "bigness," but no matter how one wants to measure it—by number of employees, numbers of functions, products, or organizational divisions, the value of assets held, production and sales volumes, and so on—businesses became very large, and went from serving local or regional markets to national and then global markets. One can find very large work organizations around in the course of human history, such as those that went into Egyptian pyramid construction and the like. But the turn of the century is where bigness became the standard mode of operation for much of the economy. So much of the economy was swallowed up by big businesses that this also coincides with the period of time that working for wages was becoming normalized. Recall that wage work was commonly called *wage slavery*, and people avoided it when they could. But by the middle of the twentieth century, and to this day, the idea that most people work as employees at the direction of others became the norm.

To take a few examples, business historian Alfred Chandler, borrowing language from economist Alfred S. Eichner, referred to the arrival of the *megacorp*. For Chandler the first *megacorp* in the United States was the

Pennsylvania Railroad. In the 1880s, at a time when a "big" industrial business might have had assets valued at around $1 million, the value of the Pennsylvania grew to $400 million. It owned or controlled as many miles of railroad track as could be found in all of Prussia. Furthermore, by about 1890 it employed around 100,000 people, growing to over 200,000 by about 1910.[1] As one point of comparison, with the exception of the period of the Spanish-American War of 1898, the Pennsylvania's labor force was far larger than the entire US military. Perhaps the world's first Amazon.com was the Sears, Roebuck & Company which, operating through old-fashioned snail-mail ordering and shipping, was processing 100,000 orders per day from all over the country—more than a typical local merchant would fill in an entire lifetime.[2] And it wasn't just growth in terms of assets, employees, or business volume, but also in terms of business functions. Whereas older, traditional, small businesses would have specialized in only one or a few functions, the newly emerging format was one of performing multiple functions in the same company—generally referred to as *vertical integration*.

Vertical Integration

In order to get a handle on what *vertical integration* means picture any product with which you are familiar and imagine how it makes it way from raw materials through to finished form on the store shelves. You need to start someplace with raw materials. Raw materials need to be extracted or harvested or whatever, processed, packed, and distributed. They then have to be accepted and transformed/processed, often multiple times. Any particular product, of course, will have multiple raw material streams. Take your basic old-fashioned wood pencil. Its typical components include the wood, the graphite core (the "lead"), the rubber eraser, the metal ferrule that holds the eraser, and the paint or other coating applied to the pencil. (We'll leave aside packaging for the moment just for simplicity.) Each of those components represent their own "streams" of raw materials and each of those streams represents yet another whole set of products such as equipment for cutting and milling trees, chemical plants for the production of paints, various kinds of transportation equipment, packaging methods, and the like. These days, the whole collection of things that go into putting out a product of some kind, from raw materials on through final point of sale, are referred to as *supply chains* or *value chains*. The supply chain language is probably obvious. The *value chain* language comes from the idea that at each stage of the process economic value is being added into the final product. A tree standing in the woods isn't worth very much in a pencil business. But once it is cut down and prepared for transport, economic value has now been added to it.

Let's say that you will start your own brand of pencils to sell. To imagine what *vertical integration* amounts to, just ask yourself how many of these different things you will deal with inside of your own company. Full vertical integration means that you will do it all. At one end of the supply chain your company owns such things as forests and tree harvesting equipment for the wood, and mines and mining equipment for extracting graphite and metal ores, and so forth. You would also own rail cars or trucks or ships (or all of the

---

[1]Chandler, 1977: 151–155.
[2]Chandler, 1990: 61–62.

above) for transporting the raw materials. In the middle you will have production facilities for processing, finishing and marrying all of the materials together into pencils that get packed up for shipping. All the way at the opposite end from the raw materials your company would have advertising and sales teams for getting the finished products out to market. All along the way, you will also need to maintain labor forces to do whatever work hasn't been embedded in machines. In general, the more of these things that you do inside of your own company, the more vertically integrated is your company. You don't necessarily have to do them all because you can instead *outsource* many of the business functions in a number of ways. You could just buy your pencil blanks and graphite and paint and erasers and eraser ferrules, and have them assembled at your factory. You could also then just sell to a separate wholesaling business, or hire advertising and sales companies to get the pencils out to market. In this case you would be much less vertically integrated than if you did all of these things inside of your own company. So always take vertical integration to be a matter of degree.

One of the reasons that the Pennsylvania Railroad, noted above, became so large was because of the extent of vertical integration in the railroad industry. Railroads have a lot of supply needs such as timber and steel for rails and cars and other equipment and coal for powering locomotives. They also manage a lot of functions such as scheduling, ticketing for passengers and for freight, operating, repairing, and maintaining rail equipment and so forth. Historically speaking these different functions would have been performed by different businesses in the transportation industry, but the railroads ended up putting most of it under the same company. The Pennsylvania, for example, owned coal mining properties, interests in steel production, and was invested heavily in the famous Pullman Palace Car Company famous for making luxury passenger cars. The Baltimore and Ohio Railroad actually preferred to build its own cars in-house, and also went so far as to build a chain of hotels along its rail lines (although the latter is more a form of *conglomeration*, defined below).[3] One of the more famous examples of vertically integrated companies from the early twentieth century was that of the Ford Motor Company. Ford is mostly famous for streamlining the assembly of cars on a moving assembly line, but the company also owned mining and timbering operations, ships and a railroad, produced its own glass, steel, and so forth. Ford's goal was to not have to rely on any suppliers at all and have everything about autos produced within the same company and under his direction.

While vertical integration is normally discussed with regards to business organizations, there is no need to limit it to that. Virtually all other organizations have to make the same kinds of decisions. Most organizations, public or private, for example, use paper. Few of them make their own, and simply buy it from paper supply companies instead. But it is not, in principle, impossible for an organization to decide to make its own paper—or, as is commonly the case, just buy an existing paper company.

Horizontal Integration and Oligopoly

Another business practice that became common and contributed to growth in organizational size is called *horizontal integration*. Horizontal integration is

---

[3]Chandler, 1977: 151–155.

what happens when different organizations that supply the same kinds of goods or services merge together in some way. It often happens when one company purchases another company, though there are also various kinds of agreements such as cartels and trusts than can horizontally integrate an industry. In the case of your pencil company, you would horizontally integrate if you bought one of your competitors, and then owned two pencil brands. Many companies that you know of today represent the results of horizontal integration. Though some of the brands have now been abandoned or sold back off, General Motors Corporation owns or owned vehicles branded as GMC, Chevrolet, Oldsmobile, Buick, Pontiac, and Cadillac among others over the years. Exxon and Mobil used to be separate energy companies but merged back in 1999 to become the ExxonMobil Corporation. When you go to the grocery store to buy cereal, you might think that all of the choices point to a large number of competing cereal companies. However, if you started to actually look at the fine print on the boxes you would find very few cereal companies. Kellogg, General Mills, and Post account for most of the US cold cereal market.

The first large waves of horizontal integration occurred during the turn of the century as part and parcel of the second industrial revolution. Once again to return to the Pennsylvania Railroad, it did not become so large and control so much rail track by building it all. Its growth came largely from either buying or leasing the assets of other existing regional rail lines. The frequent result of horizontal integration was that economic control in many major industries became highly concentrated in *oligopolies* where only a few companies control most of the market for particular goods and services, or, less commonly, *monopolies* where a single company controls an entire market. The most famous case was probably that of John Rockefeller's Standard Oil Company which, through various forms of alliances, combinations, and buy-outs controlled 90% of oil refining in the United States in the last part of the nineteenth century. The case of Standard Oil also illustrates the fact that many companies were engaged in both vertical and horizontal integration. At the beginning, the company was only an oil refiner, but then expanded to include all aspects of production, transportation, distribution, marketing, and sales.

While oligopolies were commonly formed through horizontal integration, there were cases where the growth pattern in certain industries sometimes left no room for many competitors from the start. In the late 1880s, the Singer Manufacturing Company, maker of the famous Singer sewing machines, was supplying 75% of the sewing machines, not just to the United States, but to the world. However, this was largely attributable to the fact that the company pioneered mass production techniques, including the use of standardized, interchangeable parts rather than through horizontal integration.[4]

All of this industry concentration lies at the roots of the emergence of the *power elite structures* outline in Chapter 2 and also marks the *shift from competitive to monopoly capitalism* that was noted back in Chapter 3. Typical nineteenth-century businesses were small, didn't control very much of their markets, except sometimes on a very small and local scale, and thus generally operated in a competitive business environment. Up to this point, economic power was rather widely dispersed. While technically few industries became

---

[4]Chandler, 1990: 66.

controlled by literal monopolies, industry concentration even in oligopolistic form means far less competition—or, as I will discuss later, far less "market."

Conglomeration

While not an overly common practice until much later in the twentieth century (after World War II), another business practice that contributed to bigness and market concentration is called *conglomeration*, where a company branches out into completely different product lines. If you go to the grocery store or someplace similar and buy anything in the world of personal care or cleaning aids from toothpaste to dish soap to hemorrhoid creams, there's a good chance that you'd end up with a Procter & Gamble product. The furnace that heats your house may very well carry the brand name Carrier, while the plane you took to your cousin's wedding last year may have been powered by a Pratt Whitney jet engine. Both of these brands were once owned by United Technologies Corporation (UTC), although aspects of that changed when UTC merged with Raytheon in early 2020 to become an even larger "Raytheon Technologies Inc." If you watch the business news you will see that this kind of thing still occurs all of the time—which means anything I might write here in terms of who owns what might have changed by the time you're reading this. What hasn't changed for the last century is that a lot of important economic activity involves companies doing a lot of buying and selling of other companies. As we will see in Chapter 6, conglomeration has fallen out of favor as a business practice by comparison to its post-War heyday, but plenty of very large and powerful conglomerates remain.

The Rise of the Corporate Form of Business

It is hard to imagine how all of this could have happened without the legal invention of a new kind of business actor—the *corporation*. A corporation is created by people on paper as a legal actor that is separate from themselves. Under law it has the status of an actual human in that it can do things like own property, borrow money, have a bank account, write checks, and produce and sell goods and services. But in real form it does only exist on paper as a set of legal documents. Specific, corporeal people start corporations, own corporations (though normally only small fractions of them), and act as legally designated officers to carry out the functions of the corporation. But the people carrying out the functions are technically employees of the corporation. The business itself remains a separate legal entity.

It wasn't always the case, but at this point, pretty much anyone can easily start a corporation, and by simple number most of them are tiny. Imagine that you are Jane Doe, a plumber, and that you want to go into business for yourself. It is unlikely that you would do business as (*DBA*) yourself. Rather, you would set up a company legally separate from yourself to do business. It might end up being called JD Enterprises, Inc. ("Inc." is short for "incorporated.") When someone hires you to do a plumbing job they do not really hire you—Jane Doe the person—they hire your company: JD Enterprises, Inc. When you go to the work site and work on the plumbing, you—Jane Doe the person—are actually there as an employee of your own company. When the work is finished, the bill does not come from you and payment is not made to you. Rather your company sends the bill and collects the payment. In order for you to be able to pay *your* personal bills, you have probably set yourself up with a salary to be paid to you by your company. In that case, money is paid out of the bank account registered to JD Enterprises, Inc. and into your personal bank account, registered to Jane Doe.

One of the things that business people find handy about this set-up is a principle called *limited liability*. If you make a mistake on a plumbing job or have some manner of parts failure and the customer's house gets flooded, the "person" who is legally responsible for that is your company. The customer can seek damages from your company, but not from you personally. So let's say a plumbing mistake results in a law suit which produces a debt too large for the company to repay. The customer's lawyers can try to go after your company's assets (vehicles, tools and other equipment, any real estate the company might own, and so on). However, they cannot come after your personal assets, such as you own home, personal bank accounts, or vehicles registered to you rather than to the company.

Another important thing that is tied to both the creation of a separate legal entity and limited liability is that it is easier for multiple people to pool their resources together. Starting a business (or buying an existing one) can be quite expensive, so multiple people can put their resources together. Limited liability means that the most that you can lose is whatever your initial investment was, so it helps people be more willing to take risks and thus successful new businesses. Having the separate legal entity means that one single person doesn't have to be the one to take on all of the financial responsibility, and it makes it harder for participants to cheat because everyone has access to the company books. So if you wanted to expand your plumbing company, but needed the financing to do so, you could always go to the bank and have the company apply for a loan. Or you might be able to find someone who is willing to invest money. The way that would work is that they give you a chunk of money and in return you give them a percentage of the business. You would now have a *shareholder*—someone who owns a *share* of the business. This ability to take on investors was crucial to business growth because all of that vertical and horizontal integration and conglomeration and such is very expensive. Big business comes with big *capital requirements* and is rarely within reach of individuals as owners. But even if one person or family could finance such things it would be a lot of eggs to put in one basket.

While very small business corporations, like your imaginary JD Enterprises, are numerous, most of those are also rather insignificant in the grand scheme of things. Economies these days are dominated by very large business corporations that have quite different form. You're familiar with many of these—ExxonMobil, Citibank, Ford Motor Company, Microsoft, Google, Amazon, Wal-Mart, and so on. Though they might sometimes still be privately held, these kinds of corporations are often *publicly traded* on stock markets and have many stockholders because most anyone (with enough money) can buy shares if they want to. Generally speaking, stockholders (i.e., the owners) play no direct role in the business. They had nothing to do with starting it, and don't participate in running it, although their shares do provide them with a right to vote on certain matters of company activity. The people who are directly involved, and who run the business on a regular basis are hired managers. You may have heard of the typical titles used at the highest management levels such as CEO (Chief Executive Officer), CFO (Chief Financial Officer), COO (Chief Operations Officer), and the like. Those top positions, of course, are the peaks of internal hierarchies in bureaucratically defined organizations.[5]

The Separation of Ownership From Control and the Managerial Revolution

The situation where some people own a business, while other people manage it is called the *separation of ownership from control* and this brings us to yet another revolution reference—that of *the managerial revolution*. While there is a lot of variability across particular businesses, the foregoing changes to business forms are part of one integrated package. Among the important ways that businesses grew dramatically in size were vertical and horizontal integration along with conglomeration. And it is unlikely that is all could have occurred on the scale that it did without the rise of the publicly traded corporation, which provided the ability to pool together finance capital, and to control companies by only owning portions of them. In short, businesses got to be very large and very complex. Combined with the dispersion of ownership, this necessitated having hierarchies of professional managers to run business operations. These managers may, and frequently do, own some of the stock in the companies they work for (so they might be among the owners) but it isn't their ownership that gives them control. Some might be people who did establish the company, or relatives of those who did. But even then they are still paid employees much like everyone else in the organization. For economic historian Alfred Chandler, whose argument about the causes of these changes we will consider shortly, this change in management was actually the key feature of the second industrial revolution because what was crucial wasn't technological change, but organizational change. And it brought us to a whole new era of capitalism that involved a major shift in economic logic whereby the *invisible hand* of the market was replaced by the *visible hand* of management. In order to pick up on many aspects of the coming story and clarify let's pause a minute and review the notion of economic markets and the invisible hand.

Adam Smith and the Invisible Hand

If you've never heard of Adam Smith (which would be weird), then you should know that the world you inhabit is awash in his ideas. Smith was actually a Scottish Moral Philosopher, but back in 1776 published his famous book *The Wealth of Nations* put him in history books as the father of the discipline of economics. An economy is a system for the production and distribution of goods and services, so all societies obviously have them. People need stuff—like food, clothing, water, medical care, and car insurance. Descending down from Adam Smith, the dominant idea in the discipline of economics is that the best way to produce and distribute everything is through free markets. In a market economy the way that you get these things is through exchanging things with other actors. If you need shoes then you go and buy them from the store. The purchase is an exchange of one thing for

---

[5]Do note that there are many different legal forms that a corporation might take, and a typical incorporated small business operates in a very different legal form from a typical publicly traded corporation. We don't need the details here, but for a simple overview of typical types of corporations under US law see https://www.sba.gov/business-guide/launch-your-business/choose-business-structure.

another, and these days it is usually mediated by money. You get your money to do this because you, or someone who is supporting you, is also out there in the economy providing some good or service that other people are buying from them. So maybe you are a baker. You sell your bread and take the money to go buy shoes from the shoe maker who is taking her money to buy a hat from the mad hatter who is taking his money from that exchange and giving it to you for bread. So that's how the world goes 'round. Everyone exchanges goods and services so that everyone's needs are met.

Growing out of the second industrial revolution, what most people now "supply" in the market is their labor power. This is called having a job. You supply your labor power in the market place in exchange for this stuff called money which is just generic exchange value. So people aren't exchanging bread for hats. From your point of view as a market actor, your exchange of labor power for wages in the form of money is on the *supply side*—you are supplying your labor. You then take your money out into the market to buy your bread and hats. This is the *demand side*—you need or want things like bread and hats.

What Adam Smith is famous for is not the idea of a market economy because the exchange of goods has frequently been part of what humans do. Rather, what Adam Smith argued is that if you want to make everyone as happy and healthy and wealthy and wise as possible then you should have *free markets* what is now generally called *laissez-faire* markets.[6] *Laissez-faire* is French and basically just translates to "leave to do"—leave market actors to do as they will. In a free market, every single person gets to do whatever he or she wishes with regards to the economy. You may produce and sell whatever you wish. If you don't wish to directly produce and sell any particular kinds of goods or services, then you can try to get someone else to hire you as an employee, and get your money that way. In that case, recall that you are still a supplier—of labor power.

In a *laissez-faire* market you may also consume whatever you wish which includes the right to *not* consume things that you don't want. In other words, free markets are actually somewhat anarchic within some basic bounds. Markets do require basic sets of rules in order to function, and there frequently are at least some limitations on what can be produced and distributed and consumed and so forth. The question of what, if anything, should be regulated and to what extent takes up a good deal of political attention in systems of political economy. But, but by and large, what is bought and sold and produced and consumed is not dictated by any set of plans. No one is in control. Perhaps you've never thought of it that way, but that's what it amounts to. No one is in charge. There are basic ground rules, but people are not ordered to supply or demand anything. Everyone does whatever he or she wishes. The contrast is to a *command economy* where supply and demand are planned under some manner of authority.

When you think about the somewhat anarchic nature of *laissez-faire* markets, it doesn't sound like it could somehow add up to the best way for everyone to be healthy, wealthy, and wise. On the face of it, it might seem like it would make a mess. But that's where the famous *law of supply and demand*

---

[6]This can be disputed since Smith himself didn't use the term and also thought that purely free markets would lead to collusion among businesses. There is no need for us to clear that up here. See McLean (2006).

comes in. The world is full of people that have needs and desires. The needs and desires create *demands* for certain things. Hungry people need bread. Cold people need coats. People with wet feet might want shoes. You might want a new gaming system. If the economy is left open for free action, then any kind of demand that people have creates an *incentive* for other people to *supply* it. If there is a bread shortage and you know how (or are willing to learn how) to make bread, then you can start producing bread and have something that others need. When you have something that someone else needs, that someone else will be willing to give you something for it. These days that typically means they'll pay you for it, so in simple terms, if you can supply an unmet demand in the world then you can make money. That's the center pin around which the entire system operates—allowing people to pursue their own rational self-interest.

What the *law of supply and demand* will do is make sure that pretty much everything that is needed is produced, in pretty much the correct amounts, at the level of quality that people want, and at prices that they are willing to pay. The mechanisms for this are those basic incentives for gain coupled with market *competition*. If there is an unmet demand, whether from low quantity or unacceptable quality, then there is incentive to supply it. Of course, if everyone now rushes into a market to supply it, we might now risk over production and that can happen briefly but, if markets are left alone to work their magic, the situation will eventually correct itself. Given an oversupply, prices will fall. This takes away the incentive for new suppliers to enter the market, and produces higher competition among existing suppliers in which it is likely that only some will survive. The ones that survive will be the ones supplying the stuff that best meets consumer demands in terms of price and quality. When prices are low and goods are plentiful, consumers can afford to be picky. So any oversupply will correct itself just as an undersupply will. And so it goes. Given a whole bunch of people allowed to do as they will in terms of buying and selling stuff, all needs get optimally met in a self-correcting economic system. Automatic triggers kick in to fix problems where things aren't supplied appropriately, regardless of whether it's too little stuff, too much stuff, or not the right stuff. This is the famous *law of supply and demand* which is the *invisible hand* that regulates a market economy. Especially, although not exclusively, among economists, this remains the best and most efficient was for an economy to operate.

From the Invisible to the Visible Hand

So now we can return to Chandler's use of the term *visible hand* that gave title to his 1977 book on the subject: *The Visible Hand: The Managerial Revolution in American Business*. The visible hand in the growth of large businesses is the hand of management. Any business organization actually removes a certain number of things from the market depending on how vertically and hierarchically integrated things are. If your pencil company only assembles various pencil parts that were purchased from suppliers, and if it subcontracts out to other companies for advertising and sales services, then a lot more is left in markets than if you had gone to full vertical integration. Inside of a fully vertically integrated pencil company, supply and demand throughout the supply chain are controlled by decisions of management—the visible hand. Similarly, horizontal integration produces a situation where there is less competition for supply, so fewer things are left in the market. Thus, in the lingo of the organizational studies field, the managerial revolution represented a shift *from markets to hierarchies* where the hierarchy part is a reference to formal organizational management hierarchies. The way that people throw around the term "market economy" these days would suggest that there is just a binary opposition where an economic system is either a market system or it isn't. But it is really much better to start thinking of economies as having *more or less* market in them. In the case of the United States, and most of the rest of the industrialized world, the pre-twentieth-century economy had much more market in it than it does now. And, as we'll consider in Chapter 6, very well might have a lot more market in it now than it did in, say, 1950.

The markets and hierarchies language is about how economic relationships are organized, though in a more general sense it is about any kinds of social relations. In markets social relations work according to free exchange, and in hierarchies they work according to the giving and taking of orders. Partly because of economic and organizational changes that we will consider later in Chapter 5, we will be adding reference to an additional organizing logic that is generally called *community*. The last time that my neighbor's lawn mower broke down, he came to borrow mine. Note that I said he came to *borrow* it. He didn't come to rent it. Furthermore, I did not suggest or demand that he pay me any rent to use it. The same logic obviously applies to borrowing a cup of sugar or helping someone move the furniture. These are very common things for neighbors or friends or family members—or even strangers sometimes—to do with and for one another. These kinds of actions do represent the exchange of goods and services, but not through the logic of either market or hierarchy. Any of these things are also available on the market, and can be implemented within hierarchy. My neighbor could pay someone to fix his mower, rent or buy a new one, go to the store to buy a cup of sugar, or hire someone to help him move furniture. It is similar among family within my own household or among any neighbors and friends. There are plenty of goods and services that are exchanged outside of markets or hierarchies. It just works on the basis of old fashioned friendliness and reciprocal trust and favors.[7]

Community relations can be conceptualized and described as markets, but they are quite different. In fact, the typical way for humans to live over the last 200,000 years has been neither markets nor hierarchies, but has instead been communities. These are ideal-type distinctions, so that doesn't mean pure community with no hierarchy or market characteristics. It just means that neither markets nor hierarchies were the primary organizing principles for social life. Throughout the nineteenth century in the United States very large proportions of the population made their living neither by taking orders from others (hierarchy) nor from participation in a full, money-based market economy. There was a lot of self-sufficiency and a lot of community. In some respects the period of the nineteenth century can be seen as marked by a shift to an increasing importance of markets, followed by a rather sudden spurt of hierarchy—the managerial revolution—that ushered in the society of organizations. It is that which we now seek to understand. Why the sudden shift to hierarchy?

---

[7]This stuff about favors can easily be thought of in terms of exchange/market activity as well and has been in various scholarly traditions such as *exchange theory*. That is beyond our present scope. But see Cropanzano et. al. (2017).

Alfred Chandler's Efficiency Argument

The most popular, widely known, and widely accepted (usually uncritically) argument for how and why the managerial revolution occurred comes from economic historian Alfred Chandler. At the center of the entire story was the building of the railroads in the United States, and to some extent the related telegraph. Chandler dubs the railroads the first modern business enterprises which he says can be very simply defined as having two characteristics: (1) they have many different operating units; and (2) they are managed by hierarchies of professional, salaried managers. These characteristics were largely necessitated by the nature of railroads as technological systems. Building them required vastly more capital than prior business enterprises, and they thus normally ended up with many stockholders. And both building and running them were highly complex requiring many different forms of technical expertise, along with the constant coordination of a multitude of different functions, from running trains and scheduling traffic to track bed and equipment maintenance to handing and accounting for all of the transactions involved for passengers and freight business. They were monumental undertakings, and having them run by their multitude of shareholders and/or people without technical competence would not be possible.

Given both the capital and technical requirements of the roads, railroad companies became the pioneers of modern methods of corporate finance and of the institution of the bureaucratic form which, with one elaboration, matched up pretty well with the Weberian ideal type. The one elaboration was in also pioneering the *multidivisional form* of organization, now usually abbreviated as the *M-form*. In the M-form a single business enterprise actually operates a whole lot more like a collection of separate businesses under the umbrella of a central corporate office. The corporate office puts out the overall planning and direction, but does not involve itself with the daily running of operations. The day-to-day operations are left to divisions that work like quasi-independent businesses. The ideal typical depiction of an organizational chart that I included in Chapter 1 (see Figure 1.1) was a depiction of what is now called the *U-form*, short for *unitary form*. For simplicity sake, if you convert an organizational chart to the image of a triangle (to represent hierarchy), visualization of the M-form is presented in Figures 4.2 and 4.3.

The full historical development of the railroads was long and complex, and many would have operated in the U-form. But, especially during the last part of the nineteenth century, there was a major period of horizontal integration where the common form became multidivisional. This particular organizational strategy is actually a major tool for the process of integration whether horizontal or vertical. As such, it became a dominant bureaucratic form for big business though the course of the twentieth century—or at least the first three-quarters of it since, as we'll see in Chapter 6, some changes have taken place.

Thus the rail industry became the first centralized, bureaucratic, corporate, and oligopolistic industry, but it then provided the literal conduit that allowed the rest of the industrial economy to follow suit. Many industrial production technologies of the time had the *potential* to allow for what we came to known as true *mass production* on a national and international scale. But what would be the point of mass producing a warehouse full of goods if you couldn't reliably move them to markets, or do *mass distribution*? What would be the

FIGURE 4.2   Picturing the Bureaucracy Like a Triangle in *Unitary Form (U-Form)*

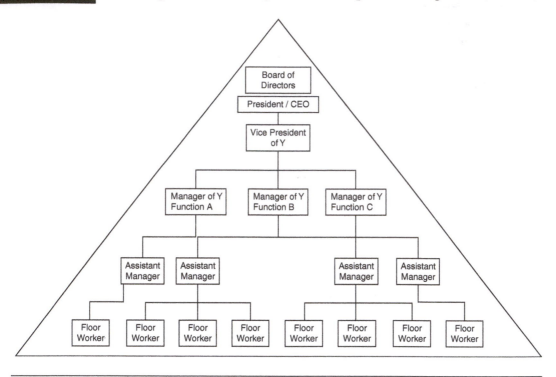

FIGURE 4.3   The *Multidivisional Form (M-Form)* is Like Organizations Inside of Organizations

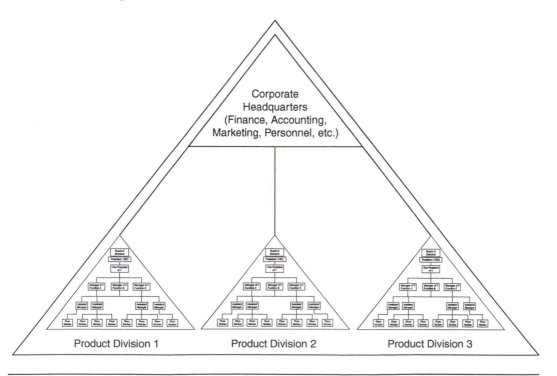

point of investing large amounts of capital in industrial machinery if you can't be certain about reliable supplies of raw materials? And without the ability to quickly communicate at a distance, it would not be truly possible to efficiently operate on anything but a very local scale. Transportation technologies such as railroads and steamships—but especially railroads—made it possible to more quickly, reliably, and efficiently move large quantities of goods, regardless of the point in the supply chain. Communications technology in the form of the telegraph and later the telephone (and now the internet) allowed better means of coordinating things all along the supply chain from raw materials supply through to production and then distribution of goods.

But even here all of that technology, all by itself, still only produces a *potential* for mass production and mass distribution. Just making a lot of stuff does not a successful business make. The question is who can squeeze the most of the large capital investments required to engage in large scale industrial production? So obviously people have to make it happen by making sure that the massive flows of materials from raw materials through finished goods are reliably guided through the whole chain. As Chandler wrote: "...scale is only a technological characteristic. The economies of scale...are organizational. Such economies depend on knowledge, skills, and teamwork—on the human organization essential to exploit the potential of technological processes."[8]

This is where the classic bureaucratic form enters. The role of the hierarchies of salaried managers with various specialized forms of expertise is to coordinate and manage all of the various functions in the most efficient ways possible. At the highest level you have a general manager—often called a President or Chief Executive Officer (CEO)—to oversee the entire enterprise. But there is too much to worry about and manage and pay attention to. So under the general manager you put other managers in charge of specialized functions such as purchasing, production, sales, finance, and distribution (the *division of labor*). Under each of those general managers there are generally further subdivisions, such as regional distribution managers under a central distribution manager. These are the *middle management* levels. These kinds of functions are called *line* functions in an organization as they are directly involved in getting the product to market. To line functions, we also add *staff* functions. Staff positions are support positions. They aren't directly involved in getting out the product, but help to manage the organization by providing such services as accounting, personnel management, public relations, legal services, and so forth. Industrial technologies allowed for certain things to happen, but the key to the success of big businesses was their organizational *strategy and structure* (as Chandler's first book proclaimed in its title).[9]

Chandler noted that very large, vertically integrated businesses started appearing at about the same time in both the United States and Europe, and were concentrated in the same kinds of industries, although US businesses were by far the leaders in most respects. According to Chandler's analysis, the growth in size normally happened in about the same pattern as well. First, a company would *integrate forward* and not only mass produce things, but also market, distribute, and sell them. After moving forward toward final marketing and sales they would *integrate backward* in the direction of supply acquisition and transportation. Despite the fact that the spatial imagery here

---

[8]Chandler, 1984: 482.
[9]Chandler, 1962.

is "forward" and "backward," this is vertical integration. The "vertical" imagery comes from the notion of hierarchy. All of these functions are going under the same hierarchy. The forward and backward is relative to the final point of sale, as in backwards toward raw materials or forward toward the market. (Sorry for the confusion. I didn't invent the terminology. If you want to be more confused, know that sometimes references are also made to *upstream* vs. *downstream* processes where up is backward toward raw materials and down if forward toward sales.)

Generally vertical integration would be followed by international expansion where the company would begin to operate outside of the United States. This is among reasons that the same patterns found in the United States also started to appear around the globe. US business practices and growth at the turn of the twentieth century set the basic mold for the contemporary global economy. The next expansion stage was generally horizontal integration followed by conglomeration to varying degrees. Throughout this process, according to Chandler, the emergence of *oligopoly* is inevitable and natural. With the growth in the scale of production, fewer and fewer companies are needed to meet demand. The careful management of new technologies of mass production means that companies could go from providing goods or services for a single town, city, or region to being able to supply to an entire nation and later even the globe. Competition among businesses all with increasing scale brings periods of overproduction and markets will correct for overproduction by sending smaller and/or weaker businesses out of the market or having them absorbed by stronger companies as part of horizontal integration. Obviously these stages are offered as ideal typical rather than precisely descriptive for any and all cases, but there you have most of the elements of the managerial revolution.

The key thing that the expansive industries had in common is that they were *capital intensive* rather than *labor intensive*. In labor intensive industries, the only way to produce more stuff is to add more labor and more equipment. Construction provides an example of a labor intensive industry. In capital intensive industries you can greatly increase production through expansion of production technologies and intensively integrated organization of the production process itself. Initially the capital intensive industries that became consolidated included things like steel, rubber, petroleum products, textiles, tobacco, and many different kinds of prepackaged food items. Yet part of the march of formal rationalization has been the persistent transformation of what were historically labor-intensive industries into capital intensive ones. Agriculture used to be a highly labor intensive industry and many aspects of it, such as some forms of fruit harvesting, still are. But many aspects of agriculture have now become highly capital intensive, and most of the food on a typical plate these days in industrialized nations comes from some manner of *factory farming*. Systematic and automated (to varying degrees) socio-technical systems have been replacing old-fashioned craft knowledge and human labor for a long time now.

According to Chandler, the central driver for how industries get organized revolves around the question of economic efficiency. In capital intensive production and distribution, there are very real competitive advantages that come with size alone, as long as things are well managed. The advantages come from what are called *economies of scale*. In simplest terms, economy of scale means you can turn out lots of stuff inexpensively, and the more stuff you can turn out the cheaper it is to do it in terms of costs per unit produced. This occurs because any business has certain *fixed costs* that go into its operation. These are costs, such as land, buildings and machinery, that you are going to need to build or buy whether you produce one thing or 1 million things. So let's say that you start your pencil business and you have to spend 1 million dollars just to get the land, building, and machinery. If you do that and produce one pencil, then you have to sell it for 1 million dollars just to break even on fixed costs. But if you produce 1 million pencils, you now only need to charge $1 per pencil to break even on the fixed costs. Therein lies the advantage that comes from ramping up the scale of production—you want to spread your fixed costs over as many units of production as possible.

The above example and calculation are, of course, oversimplified as there are other costs that are not fixed—those are *variable costs*. Labor and utilities, for example, are costs that increase as production increases. That is why you didn't tend to find the same business growth patterns in labor intensive industries. Simply producing more stuff—increasing scale—is not what brings costs down. It's producing more per unit of fixed cost—the *economy of scale*.

This also implies that the advantages to be found in economies of scale frequently increase as the scale increases. So bigger is better, but only if the entire enterprise is well-managed so as to maximize *capacity utilization*. If the number of units that you produce is the key to lowering costs, then you can't afford to have anything getting in the way of maximum *throughput*, as it is called. If, for instance, your pencil labeling machine is down 20% of the time because there is a bottle neck after the milling station, then you're losing a lot of value. You're paying for all of the capital regardless of whether you're producing the maximum possible amount; so anytime the stuff isn't working to make the products, it's actually costing you money and raising the cost of the products that you do produce. So to truly take advantage of the capabilities of mass production technologies, total coordination from beginning to end is required. In other words, you need to ensure *efficiency, predictability,* and *calculability* through careful management. There are many conditions under which this is very unlikely to happen reliably or quickly enough by market mechanisms of supply and demand. It frequently has to be *made to happen*—by directive of management.

So far this is primarily about the production or supply end, but similar kinds of changes were occurring in certain aspects of distribution and sales where supply meets demand. The turn of the twentieth century not only saw the rise of mass producers, but also the rise of mass retailers, such as Sears Roebuck which was something of the Amazon of the turn of the twentieth century. For mass retailers, the same kinds of efficiency principles apply except that here the key term is *economy of scope*. If it is economy of scale that allows a company to *produce* a lot of the same goods cheaply, it is economy of scope that can allow a company to *sell* a lot of goods cheaply. Economy of scope has to do with spreading fixed costs, not across many units of the same product, but across many different products. You might be able to start a successful company that manufactures wooden pencils, but you are unlikely to get very far with a store that only sells pencils. Rather, your pencils are likely to end up on the shelf at WalMart with many other kinds of school, office, or stationary supplies. Sellers, like producers, have fixed costs. Here the goal is to pack as many different products as possible into the location—to spread your fixed costs across as many different units as possible. The principle is the same in both economies of scale and scope. So around the turn of the twentieth century the world ended up with many mass producers taking advantage of economies of scale, but also started to end up with many mass retailers taking advantage of economies of scope. The most famous of these mass retailers today are companies like Wal-Mart and Target stores, or online retailers like Amazon.

But do note that economies of scope don't only apply in terms of sale, but can also apply in terms of production. For a good deal of early industrial production it wouldn't have applied because many production technologies were single purpose and could only produce one product. But this is highly variable. In industries like oil refining, other chemicals, and pharmaceuticals multiple products could be produced with the same fixed assets, so producers could benefit from both economies of scale and scope. And as we'll see in Chapter 6, one of the things that contributed to changing business organizations during the last part of the twentieth century was the increased development and use of industrial production technologies that were multipurpose, increasing the number of industries in which economy of scope is important.

Returning to the question of mass retailers, if you think about all of the different kinds of things that are sold by mass retailers, it becomes obvious that forward integration didn't go all the way to *point of sale (POS)* retail sales for many large companies. For Chandler, whether a producer will integrate all the way forward to final retail POS is explained by the same efficiency principles. As a general rule, retailers won't serve a producer as well as it can serve itself. In the retail context, any product is just one among many and it doesn't matter to a retailer which brand of pencil a customer buys so long as they buy some pencils. Multiple product retailers also have little in the way of specialized expertise with regards to a product. So given minimal commitment and expertise on the part of sellers, wherever a manufacturer could achieve a minimum efficient scale in terms of sales they would integrate fully to POS. This kind of thing was most common where products were relatively expensive and complex thus requiring informed and dedicated sales and service teams that were loyal to the particular company's products. It was products such as automobiles, sewing machines, and other large consumer goods that were likely to end up with their own retail locations vertically integrated into the company.

In either case, Chandler's argument comes down to one simple principle and it is not very different from Weber's explanation for the growth and spread and persistence of large organizations: *efficiency*. Large organizations grew and integrated and took on the classic Weberian bureaucratic form because that form was the most efficient way to utilize technologies of mass production and distribution. Underlying that is the mostly taken-for-granted assumption that the organization of the entire economy and the best form for the units within it to take are driven by economic market dynamics. Certain kinds of technologies made mass production, mass distribution, and thus mass production possible. There was a ton of money to be made there, and thus it drew entrepreneurial effort. The ensuing competition drove all companies to seek the most efficient form which was that of the vertically and horizontally integrated firm under the professional direction of a hierarchy of professional managers. Those that failed to implement the optimal organizational strategies and structures were driven out of the market—or absorbed as a part of horizontal integration. In other words, the world got the best possible thing. From now on we will call

Chandler's argument an *efficiency argument* for explaining the rise of the iron cage. It might also get called a *technology* argument since technology is the key foundation of the changes, although Chandler's emphasis was always on the coordinating role of management. As such, organizational sociologist Charles Perrow (who we meet again in the next chapter) has called it a *strategy and structure* argument after Chandler's famous 1962 book title. While Chandler's argument remains the most widely accepted, there is plenty of reason and evidence with which to question it, and we will take up the most common critiques and counterarguments in the next chapter.

We will also revisit Chandler's arguments again in Chapter 6 where we find that in the latter part of the twentieth century the integrated business form came to be seen as decidedly *inefficient*. The efficient business of today isn't vertically integrated and is certainly not a conglomerate. Rather it is highly focused and specialized. For at least some observers, this doesn't indicate any serious flaws in Chandler's initial analyses. Rather, it just means that his arguments needed to be supplemented to account for the changing times which is another matter that we consider later in Chapter 6.

SOURCES AND FURTHER READING

- While Weber acknowledged the establishment of **early bureaucracies** such as in **Egypt**, it didn't take up much of his attention. For a "long" view that largely centers on the case of **Sumeria**, and roots bureaucratization in administrative political needs that come with urbanization see:

  o Schott, Richard L. 2000. "The Origins of Bureaucracy: An Anthropological Perspective." *International Journal of Public Administration* 23: 53–78.

- Most of what appears in this chapter is drawn in one way or another from various accounts by Alfred Chandler whose works are voluminous. The following are the most relevant:

  o Chandler, Alfred D. 1962. *Strategy and Structure: Chapters in the History of the American Industrial Enterprise.* Cambridge, MA: MIT Press.

    o Chandler's second book which was predominantly a case study of Du Pont, General Motors, Standard Oil, and Sears Roebuck all of which implemented the *M-Form* structure which followed from strategic problems face by the organizations.

  o ——. 1977. *The Visible Hand: The Managerial Revolution in American Business.* Cambridge, MA: Belknap Press of Harvard University Press.

    o The title here rather speaks for itself. This book won the 1978 Pulitzer Prize for history, and does develop the main story of the rise of big business and thus transformation of the economy. Part I describes traditional businesses (pre-1850s). Part II is mostly focused on the development of the railroads as the crucial development both technologically and organizationally. The remainder of the book (Parts III–V) elaborates upon processes of vertical and horizontal integration throughout capital intensive industries.

o ———. 1984. "The Emergence of Managerial Capitalism." *The Business History Review* 58: 473–503.

   o Chandler's books are long and rich in detail. This paper contains a "nutshell" account of many aspects of the argument, including the typical sequences of organizational development and brief comparisons to Britain, Germany, and Japan.

o ———. 1990. *Scale and Scope: The Dynamics of Industrial Capitalism.* Cambridge, MA: Harvard University Press.

   o This book opens with a basic summary of the emergence of managerial capitalism as laid out prior, especially in *The Visible Hand* (Part I). It then develops a detailed comparison of its development in the United States (Part II), Great Britain (Part III), and Germany (Part IV), including the reasons that it was fastest and most extensive in the United States.

- Chandler's use of the term **megacorp** is attributed to:

   o Eichner, Alfred. 1976. *The Megacorp and Oligopoly: Micro Foundations of Macro Dynamics.* London: Cambridge University Press.

- It's not hard to find accounts or copies of Adam Smith's *The Wealth of Nations*. The one I have on my shelf:

   o Smith, Adam. [1776] 2004. *The Wealth of Nations*. Edited by C. J. Bullock with and Introduction by Prasannan Parthasarathi. New York, NY: Barnes and Noble, Inc.

   o For a discussion on the question of Smith and *laissez-faire* see especially Chapter 6 in:

      o McLean, Iain. 2006. *Adam Smith, Radical and Egalitarian: An Interpretation for the 21st Century.* Edinburgh University Press.

- On the question of **market/hierarchy/ community** more will be discussed in the next two chapters. But for an early discussion of these as ideal-typical forms of organizing relations that adds the community dimension see:

   o Adler, Paul S. 2001. "Market, Hierarchy, and Trust: The Knowledge Economy and the Future of Capitalism." *Organization Science* 12: 215–34.

- For a reasonably recent review of *exchange theory* see:

   o Cropanzano, Russell, Erica L. Anthony, Shanna R. Daniels, and Alison V. Hall. 2017. "Social Exchange Theory: A Critical Review with Theoretical Remedies." *The Academy of Management Annals* 11: 479–516.

The Rise of Bureaucracy and the Question of Power

Chandler's arguments have been widely accepted and do stand as the standard interpretation of the rise of large business corporations, at least outside of many corners of organizational sociology and many areas of history. In the next chapter, we will see that some have found the need to modify it all a bit given what has unfolded more recently with regards to business structures. But the ideas fit well with a lot of events, and fit especially well with the taken-for-granted ideas of our times that business forms and activities are driven by competition for efficiency as it plays out in the context of market economies. And it is generally taken to have been all for the best, in any case.

Throughout the latter part of the nineteenth and into the early twentieth century, the United States experienced rapid population growth, especially by way of immigration. And since most immigrants were arriving at port cities such as Philadelphia and New York, and many were fleeing poor economic conditions and poverty in their home countries, much of the population growth was in urban areas. Adding to urban growth was also an increased flow of population into cities from rural areas. This means a lot of demand for jobs and for the goods and services that the proceeds from work might be able to purchase. There were technologies available that had the potential to both put people to work, regardless of their level of skill, and to meet those demands. As such, the market responded by delivering to the world exactly what was needed, and then some.

The large businesses that grew up not only met the demands of a constantly growing population, but also created immense wealth and plentiful goods and services. The class of salaried managers that grew up to build and maintain and run these organizational wells of wealth were only doing that—designing the tools needed for the society to function well and efficiently meet the needs of its people. At the most general level, the large integrated form under the visible hand of management is what gave the United States its industrial dominance through much of the twentieth century and brought us into the modern age. This is an often unstated undercurrent that runs through popular, celebratory accounts of the rise of big business during the *Gilded Age*, and on into the *Progressive Era (GAPE)*. Big business arose because it was the most efficient and functional thing for society at the time, and it really was all for the best.

But, of course, everything about the GAPE was not all motherhood and warm apple pie. No one denies that the coming of big business also created very large negative effects—*negative externalities* (see below), as they are called—and these are frequently discussed in historical treatments of the period. The massive growth in wealth was not widely distributed. Rather, in a society initially in pursuit of equality and democracy, we ended up with highly concentrated economic, political, and cultural power (a primary subject of Chapter 2). For broad swaths of the US population big business meant the loss of economic opportunity whether in terms of the ability to own and operate businesses or in terms of the ability to practice various skilled trades. In direct relation to that, the enormous concentrations of wealth were in part created through the maintenance of rather harsh forms of labor exploitation—the deskilling and dehumanization of work through ever-increasing formal rationalization of work processes; harsh, unsafe, and unhealthy working conditions; long working hours; poor pay and job security; the use of child labor; and the enhancement of racial, ethnic, and gender divisions. Those growing urban areas thus also became home to overcrowded and unsanitary slums of concentrated poverty. Corruption and waste, including of public goods, were enormous particularly in the building of the railroads. And it wasn't only economic waste, but also ecological harm both in terms of the use (and sometimes using up) of natural resources and production of waste. Despite widespread awareness that not all was well and good, the downsides are frequently recognized and then promptly swept back under the rug as growing pains or the inevitable price of "progress."

Many of these growing pains are also often taken to belong to that period of history, but many of these things are still with us. While the rise of labor unions and a stronger state, among other things, eventually did some mitigation of the extent of social inequality, that has since gone by the wayside to the point that many observers now say that we are in a new Gilded Age, a point that we will visit in Chapter 6. Labor unions and a stronger state also helped to reduce some of the issues of the abuse and exploitation of labor (such as child labor and minimum age laws), but we have already seen that many aspects of the secondary labor market still carry the marks of the early period of the second industrial revolution. Furthermore, if you look outside of the United States in peripheral nations of the globe you can still find relatively unregulated working conditions that echo the worst of times early on in the US. Ecological degradation obviously remains a very serious issue and so forth. While all of these issues are certainly complex, many of them still bear the stamp of the effects of the big business form.

One salient question that has been raised is whether or not things could have been different. Could we have had many of the benefits that came with industrialization and modernization, but have avoided or at least mitigated the costs? This is not the kind of question that can be answered definitively. We have no way to turn back time for a do-over and try it out a different way. Our "sample size" will always remain one. But we can go back to the time and rethink what happened and how it happened. Quite a few scholars have done so and it is possible to give a very different account of how and why big business arose and took the form that it did. Analyses that most strongly challenge Chandler are basically power arguments. In this case, the rise of big business was not functional or efficient or necessary. These organizations were specifically built by people with economic power explicitly to further grow their own economic power. Along the way, this required modification to the legal system to allow particular kinds of organizational mechanisms that make the concentration of control over economic power resources easier and easier. The goal wasn't to be the best competitors in economic markets by being the most efficient. It was to control markets so that you can control competition. This makes plenty of sense. Businesses hate competition. It makes it harder to make money by keeping prices lower than they might be otherwise, and also means there is money being made by others that could be made by you. What very large vertically and horizontally integrated companies do is minimize, or even eliminate outside challenges by internalizing them so that they can be controlled. What you *externalize* are as many costs as possible which helps to account for an appreciable proportion of the "growing pains." Market control with the externalization of costs creates the appearance of efficiency, but only in a very narrow sense—it's very efficient for those in control.

By these accounts, Chandler's problems were many including that he largely ignored the downsides of the growth of big business in favor of marveling at the increased productivity which leaves us with a very narrow view of efficiency; he really only studied businesses that fit his model rather than contextualizing those in a broader view of existing organizational forms; and he was rather selective about what aspects of organizational activity were studied. Taking these things into account, it is possible to argue that things could have been different. There were successful alternative business models that could have brought the "goods" and likely would have come with fewer "bads." Our first stop will be on broadening our thinking about the question of efficiency.

Efficient for What? And for Whom?

In simple terms, efficiency is just the least cost means to a given end. On its face it seems like efficiency questions should be questions of fact and subject to straightforward calculation. But they are actually value questions because it is quite crucial to ask about what the ends are, who is able to set them, and who benefits. In other words, to call something efficient, we really first have to be able to answer at least two questions: *efficient for what?* and *efficient for whom?*

Efficiency is an important concern in many respects for people but in concrete and technical form is often a central and explicit focus of attention for people like business managers, economists, and engineers. In these cases, the specific ends can be made quite precise and also generally made to be quantitative. If you're an engineer who designs air conditioning units, for example, there isn't much question about the goal. The job of an air conditioner is to produce and distribute cold air. There is a standard unit of measure for how much cooling is produced by an air conditioner called a British Thermal Unit (BTU). It is fully possible to measure (1) the cooling capacity expressed in BTUs and (2) the amount of energy, such as electricity, that it takes to produce a BTU. If you compare a bunch of air conditioners on these measurements, then efficiency determination is easy—it's whichever unit produces the most cooling for the least energy.

It's the same in economics and business. The goal is to bring a product or service X to a market for the least cost. The precision of measurement here can get a little bit fuzzier at times, but it is a normal part of doing business and in the study of economics to calculate costs of production, and try to find ways to reduce them. Reduction in production costs per unit of a good or service is taken to be gains in efficiency. This is Chandler's taken-for-granted bar for efficiency—that the most efficient form of business operation is that which delivers the lowest possible cost per unit produced. That, of course, was delivered via economies of scale and scope which, as he argued necessitated the large, integrated business form under the visible hand of bureaucratic management. This narrow view answers the question of *efficient for what?*

On the question of *efficient for whom*, the conventional view is similarly narrow because it involves costs incurred by and paid by the business under question. By extension this can make it efficient for consumers of the good or service under question. This is, of course, integral to the whole story in the standard logic of economics and management. Consumers want affordable goods and services which is the ultimate driver behind the need for businesses to increase their efficiencies. When that it accomplished, then everyone wins. The businesses that are best at providing for the needs and desires of consumers thrive and consumers get what they want. The problem with this narrow view is the fact that it is virtually never the case that all costs are taken into account. Rather many of them can be *externalized*.

Externalities

Most readers will be accustomed to thinking about things in terms of their pros and cons. Economists and business people do it all of the time in thinking about things in terms of *costs and benefits*—the basic center pin of rational decision-making. The benefits are the pros and the costs are the cons, and decision-makers maximize on pros and minimize on cons. But for economists, this is only one category of costs and benefits. Another category of pros and cons is referred to as *externalities*. Strictly speaking externalities are in the same family as *unintended consequences*, but they can also be intended, particularly with regard to costs. Externality is an odd word, but the logic goes like this: the costs and benefits that were taken into account (intended/ anticipated consequences) are *internal* to the decision-making that produces particular courses of action. But there very well be other consequences that were not taken into account, and so those were *external* to the decision-making.[1] Those other consequences might represent benefits or costs so externalities can be either *positive* or *negative*. No one enrolls in a college or university in order to pump up local businesses in a college town. However, it is one of the things often regarded as a *positive externality*. And no one enrolls at a college or university to help create traffic problems for a college town. But this is often regarded as a *negative externality*.

I think that it is fair to say that economists and business people, and certainly Chandler, tend to pay a lot more attention to positive externalities and a lot less attention to negative externalities than do sociologists. And so it might be with thinking about the particular form that the rise of mass production and mass consumption took. The big business model is credited with providing for the global industrial dominance of the United States, and with bringing people all of the comforts and advantages of "modern" life—cheap and readily available clothes and electricity and cars and gasoline for powering them and radios and televisions and so on. One is often led to think that if it

---

[1] For economists the discussion is normally about parties engaged in a market transaction where their exchanges produce effects on third parties who weren't involved in (or "internal" to) the transaction. There is no need to limit it to what happens in transactions. Even individual human actions create externalities.

wasn't for "big business" we'd still all be farming by hand and animal, making our own clothes from animal skins and hand-spun wool, relieving ourselves in an outdoor outhouse, and cleaning our clothes down at the river by beating them with rocks. While negative externalities are recognized, they also tend to be recognized and then promptly swept back under the rug in the face of so much "progress." Economies of scale and the business model that brought them are largely celebrated, as they were by Chandler. There are various famous phrases that express the benefits. "A rising tide lifts all boats." "What's good for General Motors is good for the country." They are ideas that express the positive externalities in which everyone benefits. Economies of scale bring positive externalities of scale.

Negative Externalities of Scale

But we might do well to dwell on the negative externalities for a while and wonder whether *economies of scale* might not bring about negative *externalities of scale*.[2] I'm borrowing this turn of phrase from environmental sociologists Adam Driscoll and Bob Edwards who described the *vertical* and *horizontal integration* of the pork industry in North Carolina which occurred through the 1980s and 1990s.[3] This does shift our historical context from the turn of the twentieth century to the latter part of the century. But the phrase is telling, the case is particularly illustrative, and it helps to clarify the fact that much about the big business blueprint remains in place, so I will describe it at some length.

Prior to the 1980s, hogs (the source of pork, of course) were raised on small family farms geographically dispersed throughout the state. It was a *small business/proprietary capitalism* kind of a model with a lot of *market* to it, and so operated in a format that Chandler described as being common through the first part of the nineteenth century. As of 1982, there were over 26,000 hog farms throughout North Carolina with a hog population of about 2 million. The small farmers sold hogs to a network of small, independent slaughterhouses who turned around and sold the meat to wholesalers. At that time, small farms were highly diversified and hogs were only one of the things that independent farmers would produce for market. Herd sizes were relatively small and the farm locations were spread throughout the state. The food sources for the hogs were highly varied including waste products from other aspects of farming operations (e.g., unsaleable parts of crop plants). Hog waste was well within what the local soils could absorb and was often used to fertilize crops. As such, hog production was quite decentralized, and went on with few to no negative externalities especially in ecological terms which was the primary, though not sole, focus of Driscoll and Edwards.

However, through the latter part of the 1980s and into the 1990s, the entire industry was restructured via both *horizontal* and *vertical integration.* At the center of it, originally, were just two companies. One was Murphy Family Farms which introduced a method of contract farming that changed the methods of raising hogs from "farms to factories" as the title of Driscoll and Edwards' paper tells us. In contract farming, farmers don't own hogs. Rather they just raise them and are paid by the pound of meat. The company that

---

[2]This is not to be confused with the much more common term *scale externalities* which involves a different context and will be explained in Chapter 6.
[3]Driscoll and Edwards, 2015.

owns the hogs can, by contract, specify how they are to be raised and the preferred method is by using what are called Concentrated Animal Feeding Operations (CAFOs) which are specifically designed to take advantage of *economies of scale*. They are highly capital intensive, and simply built to maximize *throughput*—or the highest total amount of hog meat possible given the facilities. They are called feeding operations because that is the entire focus. The goal is just to get the animals to market weight as quickly as possible, so they are simply fed and kept from illness as much as possible and that is all. The animals are kept in a series of buildings according to stage of growth and left largely immobile in a grid work of pens. The pens are just about exactly large enough to fit the animals once they've grown to move to the next production stage or to market weight. To make this possible, to speed the gaining of weight, and to produce fattier meat they are generally fed a diet of purchased corn. In order to take care of the inevitable problems of over-crowding, such as diseases and insect infestations, antibiotics and pesticides are added into the mix.

In addition to the introduction of antibiotics and pesticides, there is also the issue of hog waste. Hogs produce more waste than people, and being confined indoors in buildings with thousands of hogs produces an awful lot of waste. The floors of the buildings are of a slat design that allows the waste to fall through, and it is periodically flushed out of the buildings. Inevitably, the waste will also include other things, such as afterbirth, and residual antibiotics and pesticides. With this many hogs in such a small geographic space, far more waste is produced than can be absorbed by the surrounding ecology. So the waste is simple stored in "waste lagoons"—basically just a big pit in the ground that acts as a giant storage puddle of waste. For the most part, the waste is left to sit to evaporate and be processed by bacteria. But when the lagoons get too full, the waste is pumped out onto a spray field. The spray field is not meant to grow anything of value because it is planted with things that can most quickly use up all of the nitrogen and phosphorous in the waste.

This infusion of a capital-intensive and continuous flow factory farming process certainly increased the production of pork at the same time that it horizontally integrated the pork production industry into a classic oligopoly. Between 1982 and 1997, the number of hogs in North Carolina had gone from about 2 million to 10 million (about a 400% increase), while the number of hog farming operations had fallen from over 25,000 to a little under 5,000 (about an 81% decrease). While the hog population then leveled off at about 10 million going into the 2000s, the number of farming operations continued to fall to around 2,300 by 2006. But even this didn't mean 2,300 independent operations because most of the operations were contract farms where the contracts were held by just three companies (Murphy Family Farms, Brown's of Carolina, and Carroll's Foods.) Additionally, of those contract operations that were left, even if any of the older family farms had converted to be among them, they would have been those that were the largest as larger size was favored by the con-tractors. The contracting companies have minimum herd sizes, so smaller farmers in North Carolina were simply squeezed out of participating in the market for hogs.

Yet further consolidation and integration of the industry was to come. Smithfield Foods had already horizontally integrated pork slaughtering and processing and accounted for 95% of North Carolina's hog processing by the middle of the 1990s. It then moved on to vertically integrating the industry.

During a steep downturn in pork prices in the late 1990s, the contracting companies saw very large losses, while Smithfield reaped the benefits. Using the proceeds from windfall profits, between 1998 and 2000, Smithfield proceeded to buy all three of those now-struggling contract companies. So, in essence, by the year 2000, one company controlled almost all pork production in North Carolina, from production through processing, packaging, and branding.

This mass production of pork is, of course, celebrated in many corners, yet came with massive negative externalities—or, as Driscoll and Edwards put it, *externalities of scale*. The market model of smaller dispersed farms produced few, if any, negative externalities in environmental terms, and left the economic benefits that came from pork production widely dispersed. CAFO farms are now massive polluters of both air and water largely because, with the growth in the size of farms and their fall in number, production became geographically concentrated in the counties of eastern North Carolina. The largest air pollution effects are generally fairly localized in the areas adjacent to the farms where people find both degraded air quality and, as a result declines in property values. But water pollution, while also a local threat, impacts much broader geography. The eastern coastal plain of North Carolina is particularly prone to flooding events, especially from hurricanes and tropical storms. On multiple occasions this has led to the overflow and sometimes complete failure of waste lagoons. All of that hog manure, along with the excess antibiotics, pesticides, and whatever else has landed in the lagoons, is distributed by floodwaters. A good deal of it ends up in North Carolina's waterways where it is transported to coastal areas and, ultimately, into the Atlantic Ocean. All of these things represent aspects of the costs of CAFO pork production, but they are costs that do not appear on the company's books or in the final prices of the product. They are *externalized*.

One could think that people might put up with such things if it was largely beneficial to the people of North Carolina or the coastal plains—if the benefits were widely dispersed and outweighed the costs. But on the whole this has not been the case. The reorganization of the industry saw the displacement of networks of small businesses, largely by one massive corporate organization. Many small family farms were simply run out of business by the contracting system. What were once widely dispersed profits through the industry were centralized by Smithfield which was a company headquartered in Virginia (and later came to be owned by a multinational corporation headquartered in Hong Kong). In terms of employment, given the capital-intensive labor of the contract farms, those don't provide very much employment. The bulk of pork industry employment is in the slaughterhouses which are largely secondary labor market jobs often occupied by cheap immigrant labor. One can certainly call contemporary CAFO meat production *efficient* in a narrow economic and technological sense. A lot of pork gets produced very cheaply. One can also call it highly *efficient* for Smithfield, and those who like cheap pork products. But if our ends are broader, and we were to worry about things like maintaining robust economic opportunity, healthy local communities, and environmental sustainability, perhaps they're not so efficient.

This particular story is not isolated. Rather the roots of these dynamics run deep, and hold a central place in one of the most influential and comprehensive perspectives in the sociological study of our environmental relations called the *Treadmill of Production (TOP)*.

The Roots of the *Treadmill of Production (TOP)*

As initially laid out by environmental sociologist Allan Schnaiberg in a 1980 book called *The Environment: From Surplus to Scarcity*, the *treadmill of production (TOP)* theory largely applies to the post–World War II period which saw significant increases in automation of work throughout much of the economy as well as increasing environmental degradation. However, the roots of the processes identified by Schnaiberg were being discussed as far back as Karl Marx in the nineteenth century, and can easily be observed in the context of the rise of big business in the United States. (We will return to that time period shortly, after this illustrative detour to the more recent.)

The key issues in TOP theory are as follows. Given the explosion of scientific and technological development (the birth of what's called "Big Science") during World War II along with the expansion of industrial production, we saw an increased premium on finding technological innovations to speed up production—in other words, increasing capital-intensivity. Speeding up production necessarily speeds up resource extraction, energy use, and waste production. As a matter of economic production, this is all presumably done to meet human needs and increasing *productivity* is seen as *progress*. It remains a central focus in economic thinking. However, even while larger extractions are taken from the ecology, capital-intensive production is actually *less efficient* at meeting human needs because most humans, by now, meet their needs by working for wages. Increased reliance on non-human labor means that more natural resources are extracted and more waste produced without the returns going to human workers because more and more work is done by technologies.

Thus, rather than everyone being better off, substantial portions of the labor force suffer ill-effects due to economic dislocations and job losses. This certainly occurs as a direct result of technologies replacing human labor and/ or *deskilling* labor, but also by various forms of *capital mobility* where companies seek out cheap labor sources for whatever labor needs remain. For certain times and industries this may have meant moving operations from the industrial north where labor unions were well established to the more agricultural south with less unionization and cheaper labor. It can also mean moving operations outside of the US entirely where there is even much cheaper labor, and frequently much less regulatory protection for labor and environment. The exception with regards to workers applies largely to jobs in the primary labor market among those engaged in management and finance, and the like, along with those involved in continual development and implementation of new technologies. (This was all briefly described in Chapter 3 and we will revisit it again more in depth in Chapter 6.) Thus, the benefits of increased productivity accrue to corporate managers, shareholders, and other financiers (e.g., lending institutions), while the bulk of the costs falls on workers, their local communities and the environment which absorb the *negative externalities*. In fact, it is fair to say that business models that best externalize costs are often the ones that fare the best in terms of competition.

Furthermore, the dynamics are completely self-feeding, and accelerate over time. Because the technologies of production represent *sunk costs*—or basically money that is already spent—they have to be utilized at full capacity. When capital is not generating revenues, far worse than merely producing no value, it is actually accruing losses. This was crucial to Chandler's logic. Sunk costs are generally fixed costs and it is, of course, the key responsibility of management to keep the wheels greased and maximize on *capacity utilization* in order to maximize on *throughput*. It is important to note that this pressure to both pay for and generate revenue out of your sunk costs is on *regardless of levels of actual demand*. In organizational terms, these investments generate *structural interests* for the organization that has invested in them. The typical actor operating on by this logic is a corporate entity where the need to consistently show profitability to shareholders and creditors is integral to survival. As such, economic actors can't stop running but generally only manage to keep up with each other. Everyone runs faster and faster, but stays in the same relative place, thus the treadmill of production imagery. Because the driving dynamics occur regardless of levels of demand, demand needs to be manufactured in one way or another whether via advertising strategies in existing markets or by searching out new markets.

While the ramp up of these dynamics in the post–World War II period was certainly important, and did greatly accelerate the speed of the TOP, it is also not too difficult to observe all of these processes getting their start at the turn of the twentieth century. The building of railroads and steamships, production of automobiles, telephones, radios, and so on do represent huge increases in natural resource extraction. If you look at something like fossil fuel use in the US, coal started its takeoff in the latter part of the nineteenth century, and petroleum and natural gas use took off soon after that. The corporate form of business, as we know it, along with the Wall Street institutions that helped coordinate the huge capital needs, and make those incessant demands for *return on investment* were largely in place by the turn of the twentieth century. With scale production, overproduction was common and handled by both horizontal integration, which allows greater control over output and pricing, and vertical integration, where whole company divisions are dedicated to marketing and sales—*so that the volume of sales might keep pace with the new volume of production* as Chandler succinctly put it.[4] Class polarization at the turn of the twentieth century was more intense in some ways, and the drive to *deskill* and displace labor through the use of new technology was ever-present, as was the search for cheaper labor. As we saw in Chapter 3, around the turn of the twentieth century cheap labor came from *labor mobility*—meaning workers geographically relocating themselves in the search for paid work (immigration). One thing that was different about the post–World War II period was the increasing likelihood of *capital mobility*—that is, businesses became more likely to roam around looking for places to set up shop near sources of cheap labor. The consistent speed-up and reliability of transportation and communications technologies certainly help to smooth the distribution of goods and services. But it's also quite good at allowing capital to move around and ultimately provides another route by which costs can be externalized.

The point here is not to criticize or argue with the TOP perspective for focus on the post-W W II period. It's just to say that if there was some critical moment in US history when all of the elements that go into the treadmill were put in place, it was the turn of the twentieth century even if things did accelerate after World War II. And to finally come back to the main point—*the question of efficiency*—it may just be that narrow conceptions of efficiency oversimplify our ability to think about it. *Efficient for whom?* and *Efficient for what?* need to be asked. There is no question that the twentieth century is a period during which economies of scale brought levels of material abundance

---

[4]Chandler, 1990, p. 8.

to incredibly high levels by comparison to the past, although not without strings attached. But without the rise of big business and the managerial revolution, would we still all be farming by hand and animal, making our own clothes from animal skins and hand-spun wool, relieving ourselves in an outdoor outhouse, and cleaning our clothes down at the river by beating them with rocks? Or could we have our cake and eat it too? Could we have had economic growth and vibrancy with fewer negative externalities?

Alternative Paths?

In the logic of economics, if economic markets are largely allowed to operate in *laissez-faire* form then the inevitable outcome will be that business operations and transactions will take their most efficient form over time. This will be a never-ending process as competition will ensure that attempts at increasing efficiency will be constant, and those businesses and processes that achieve it the best will be the only ones that survive. And at around the turn of the century, US markets were relatively *laissez-faire*. While the first economic regulatory agencies of the federal government were beginning to appear by the end of the nineteenth century (the Interstate Commerce Commission was the first in 1887 in response to abuses by railroad corporations), they were not very numerous, large, or powerful. As such, the logic would be that the shape that things took was rather inevitable. Chandler operated with these assumptions, as do most economists so the question of alternative paths tends to not be asked. But it has been asked by other social scientists and historians. We have already raised the question of whether people might operate with concepts of efficiency that are too narrow. So we can now raise the question of whether or not alternative business models may have been viable and able to operate well in terms of narrow economic efficiencies, but while also bringing fewer negative consequences for workers, communities, and for the environment.

Unfortunately, it is not possible to answer the question definitively in any social scientific way because we only have one "case" and nothing to compare it to. In other words, all we have was the historical path that was taken, so "maybe this could have been" remains a "maybe." Even so, we do have ways of asking and answering questions about the viable alternatives. First, rather than assuming that history is driven by some manner of natural law (such as supply and demand), we can think about history as being *path-dependent*. This just means that there are frequently forks in the road where societies or certain aspects of them such as their economies could have gone left, but went right instead. But you have to imagine this as something like a train route—once a fork is taken, it becomes difficult or impossible to go backward and take some other path. Second, you assume that even if there are any "natural laws" that operate to influence historical paths, there is always a great deal of complexity in terms of how things happen. Simple appeals to the efficiency of markets can greatly oversimplify. So you have to actually dig into history and recover things that may have been lost. Chandler certainly dug into history. His accounts of the dynamics of the managerial revolution are nothing if not rich with historical detail. However, did take the narrow view of efficacy, and also explained the success of big business only by focusing on how successful businesses became successful. This form of investigation comes with blinders.

Quite a few people in various disciplines have gone back to the time period of the managerial revolution and questioned Chandler's interpretations of how and why things took the path of hierarchy. One of these was organizational sociologist

Charles Perrow—the same person who gave us the *society of organizations* phrase. His 2002 book called *Organizing America: Wealth, Power, and the Origins of Corporate Capitalism* provides a reevaluation and critique of various kinds of efficiency arguments, including, most prominently, Chandler. Drawing from a range of historical and sociological work Charles Perrow did build up a picture of viable alternatives to the path of hierarchy, and they weren't hypothetical. Rather they are on the historical record. In order to get there, we'll have to expand our vocabulary of *market* and *hierarchy* to include *networks*.

Markets, Hierarchy, Community, and Networks

As we've already learned, the language of markets and hierarchies is about alternative ways of ordering and coordinating our relations with each other, especially in terms of economics. In markets it's all about supply and demand and prices. When we interact with others, it's on the basis of spot contracts and trading on the basis of what we can supply and what we demand, and our relations last for as long as our exchanges. If we have no reason to exchange with others, then there are no simply relations. In hierarchy, it's about order-giving and order-taking. The movement of goods and services occur by managerial plans, dictates, and standardized rules (bureaucracy).

But there are other forms of coordinating our interactions with each other, including our economic relations, and these are frequently referred to as principles of *community*. By the principles of *community*, our economic relations are neither coordinated by price, nor by order-giving and order-taking. Rather, it is just done on the basis of interpersonal relations. It's like when you ask your friend to help you move a couch. You could find a moving company and negotiate a price for a service, or you could make yourself into a company, hire an employee or two and tell them what to do with the couch and when. Instead, we just usually ask a friend for help. No money changes hands and no one is a formal superior or inferior in terms of giving or taking orders.

In discussions of the managerial revolution it is common to say that the US economy went from markets in the nineteenth century to hierarchy by the turn of the twentieth century. What this misses is the fact that a substantial chunk of economic activity in the nineteenth century was not organized by either market or hierarchy, but more by community. A great deal of organizing was on the basis of family relations and local community ties, although one does need to take all of this as ideal typical. The ideas of market, hierarchy, and community are pure types. Actual societies generally contain a mix. For example, family and community relations do contain hierarchy, such as where parents hold authority over children, although most often on the basis of informal and traditional practices rather than formal rules. And in the nineteenth-century US, one would be able to observe a great deal more being done via market relations in urban areas than rural, yet rural marketplaces would not be uncommon although the interactions might often look more like barter than precise pricing. If we feed some notion of community into observing the operations of formal businesses, then we can see that there are forms of business relations that—in the well-known title of a paper by sociologist Walter Powell—are "neither market nor hierarchy,"[5] but instead take the form of *networks*. While the title was catchy, it is likely best not to take networks as an alternative to markets or

---

[5]Powell, 1990.

hierarchy. Rather they're a bit of both of those things with a bunch of "community" mixed in. What the market and hierarchy logics both lack is a sense of what's called the *social embeddedness* of economic interactions. This is to say that in the real world of economic interactions, whether in a market context or a bureaucratic context (ordering by rational exchanges or by authority), we're still talking about humans and human relations that are not merely guided by rational calculations of cost benefit or by rule following. Rather we frequently have to operate with fuzzier stuff like social norms, values, trust, and interpersonal commitments in order to understand economic relations.

If we think about supply chains (introduced in Chapter 4) for a minute, we can make this clear. If your pencil company remains in market form, then you go shopping for suppliers every time you need a new shipment of raw materials. If you decide you don't want to go shopping every time and just want to have more stable and predictable relations down the supply chain over time, we already know that you can vertically integrate and thus shift relations to hierarchy. However, there is another option which is to establish regular, long-term relationships with various suppliers. Surely in the process of constantly procuring raw materials for your business you have "gotten to know" various suppliers and what they are like. There are likely to be some that you trust more than others in terms of things like reliability and predictability, fairness in pricing, and willingness to go out of their way to meet your needs. As such, a great deal of your procurement won't actually look very much like pure market transactions. But it won't be hierarchy either. It will contain much more intangible things like long-term relations of trust, mutual respect, and reciprocity. In Powell's words, a lot of economic relations look "more like a marriage than a one-night stand."[6]

In the next chapter we will come back to Powell (among others) and learn that by many accounts the network form of business has largely displaced hierarchy as the dominant mode of doing business. Thus, in "grand narrative" terms there is a story about how the dominant form of business has evolved from markets in the nineteenth century to hierarchy between the turn of the twentieth century and the 1970s, and then to networks in the post-1970s period. By this account, operating businesses in network form is the newest and latest thing, widely regarded as superior to vertical integration. However, if one does go back to the period of the managerial revolution when hierarchies emerged as dominant, it seems that it is fairly easy to find that the network form was already quite common and viable. Furthermore, there is good reason to believe that it did come with fewer and smaller negative externalities. There are multiple sources that we could appeal to in order to see alternative forms of organizing industry, but Perrow's *Organizing America* (noted above) provide a concise way to think about it.

Hierarchies and Networks in Nineteenth-Century US Textiles[7]

The Real First "Modern Business?"—Toward Hierarchy

Alfred Chandler referred to the railroads as the first modern business enterprises. They handled multiple business functions in the same company,

---

[6]Powell, 1990, p. 301.
[7]This description is drawn directly from Perrow, 2002, Ch. 4.

operated in different locations, were coordinated and controlled by extensive managerial hierarchies, and perfected the corporate form and associated means of modern finance. Alternatively, Charles Perrow has argued that all the hallmarks of the "the first modern business" could be found earlier in one particular business model in the textile industry. The mass production of textiles was one of the core aspects of change during the industrial revolution, and somewhat synonymous with the rise of the factory system itself. This was certainly the case in the United States although the mass production of textiles began quite a bit earlier in Great Britain. In the United States, the most famous example of early factory-style mass production is likely that of the Lowell mills of Lowell, Massachusetts. It is often seen as the first seeds of the rise of industrialization and mass production. As such, it might not be a surprise that one can also find most of the characteristics of the managerial revolution there too.

The entrepreneurs involved were called the Boston Associates who set up a corporation called the Boston Manufacturing Company in order to do business complete with the separation of ownership from control. Lowell was not their first place or only place of business, but was their most highly developed one where they bought up land along the Merrimack River north of Boston and built, not just a textile factory, but an entire town. Their first was built in Waltham, MA and thus the production system that they developed is often called the *Waltham* or *Lowell-Waltham system*. In order to raise enough funds for such an enterprise, they became one of the earliest companies to offer stocks for public sale. Profits from the company operations in their mill towns thus, just as with hog production in North Carolina, went to far off places rather than to local people or families, and the profits were substantial. Furthermore the business was fully vertically integrated. The water-powered factory buildings that they constructed took in raw cotton on the top floor and transformed it in a series of planned stages upon its descent so that finished cloth emerged at the bottom where it was loaded onto company barges and sent down river to market. They were horizontally integrated in the sense that they used their capital to establish multiple mill sites in many areas of New England. Their existence also depended on having a large available labor force, and therein lies another story that ties into questions about the characteristics of the labor force.

Their business and technological strategy of building large vertically integrated mills meant that they wanted to be able control the best areas of the river for running their machinery. The investments in the mill buildings and equipment meant very high fixed costs, so ensuring maximum throughput was critical and this meant reliance on a predictable and steady supply of flowing river water. The only way to have such control was to buy their property in rural areas, but the problem in rural areas is that there is no available labor force. In order to solve this problem, they recruited young, unmarried "farm girls"—"the Lowell girls" as they came to be called—from the surrounding area who could use their wages to help out their family and/or to build up a dowry. This is why the towns had to be built, and they were planned as very nice little communities with supervised boarding houses for the workers, a church (which the young women were required to attend), and educational and cultural activities. Both living and working conditions had to be kept quite palatable because the women were not *wage dependent* and could always return home if they wished. The entire model was very paternalistic as the company needed to conform to standard norms of the time. At least, this was all the case for the early "benign phase" as Perrow called it, beginning in the early 1820s. The working hours were long and the work tedious, but wages were relatively good as compared to what the women could earn elsewhere.

By the 1840s, a much more *wage-dependent* labor force in the form of Irish immigrants began arriving in Lowell. At this point began what Perrow dubbed the "exploitative phase." The young farm maidens were not dependent on wages and could always go back home. The new immigrant arrivals were wage dependent, had nowhere else to go, and working and living conditions subsequently went downhill. As Perrow put it:

> *No longer concerned with attracting a labor supply, labor policies changed and exploitation grew. Wages were cut in times of exemplary profits, the blacklist was intensified, there were steady speedups, and the boarding houses deteriorated.*[8]

Furthermore, Perrow goes on to emphasize the exploitation of social divisions in the labor force, in this case based on gender and ethnicity. The *mill girls* (as they were often called), regardless of how competent or skilled they became, would never be raised to supervisory positions. Those were strictly held by males. And when Irish immigrants arrived, they were offered only the lowest positions and often kept segregated from native workers.

The explanation that Perrow offers for all of this is not that the Boston Associates were mean people. It is that this is what one should expect from the way that business was organized—i.e. that this was generated by the *structural interests* of the Boston Manufacturing Company. It was set up as a corporation with absentee owners. The stockholders didn't live in the mill towns, and the purpose of investing is solely to see a return on their investments. There is thus always pressure on those actually operating the business to produce consistently high returns for shareholders. As far as the organization of actual production was concerned, the mills were geared toward standardized mass production using largely unskilled labor. With a large, wage-dependent labor force, the most straightforward way to provide sustained returns on investment would be to keep expenses as low as possible. Thus, you do what you can to keep labor costs down, including the avoidance of spending too awfully much on maintaining good conditions in the town. The strategies aren't driven by what is best for the community or workers or the like, but by what is best for the company.

By today's standards the operations of the Boston Associates were very small, and while there was quite a bit of industry dominance in the market for cheap, standardized textiles, the Boston Associates activities didn't create any serious consolidation of economic control of many aspects of the economy. However, what Perrow sees in it is most of the hallmarks of our turn of the twentieth-century shift to hierarchy—very large capital needs provided for by the corporate form; the separation of ownership from control with operations being overseen by managers; reliance on mechanization rather than skilled labor; vertically and horizontally integrated mass production of standardized goods; and the production of negative externalities, although that, it seems, may be dependent on the nature of the labor force. It is

---

[8]Perrow, 2002, p. 71. (Blacklisting is where different employers share information about "troublesome" workers. It is a way that companies cooperate to limit worker mobility in labor markets).

ultimately a question of power. The Lowell–Waltham model is widely discussed and most frequently celebrated as part of the seeds of the industrialization of the United States. But Perrow goes on to discuss a very different
industry model for textiles during the nineteenth century that has gotten less
attention. It was one that operated more in a network form rather than
hierarchy. And it did "deliver the goods" so to speak, but also came with
fewer and smaller negative externalities.

Toward Networks With the Philadelphia Model[9]

Far lesser noticed (or even invisible) in standard history books was another
area important to nineteenth-century textile production that was found in the
city of Philadelphia. Early on in the nineteenth century the Philadelphia area
had seen the arrival of some mass production textile mills that showed many of
the characteristics seen in the Lowell mills. But through the latter half of the
nineteenth century, running parallel to the exploitative phase in Lowell, the
dominant form of textile production was quite different. Perrow's account of
this was largely drawn from historian Philip Scranton's 1983 book on the
subject called *Proprietary Capitalism*. Scranton is among the historians who
have contributed a great deal to documenting potential alternative paths, or
what has been called *the "other side" of the Second Industrial Revolution*.[10]

As of 1880, there was a textile labor force of some 55,000 workers in
Philadelphia that contained a mixture of skilled, semi-skilled, and unskilled
labor. That was about the same size of the labor force employed under the
Boston Associates across their many mill towns. However, in Philadelphia,
there was not only one company doing all of the employment. Rather, there
were 849 companies, operating in proprietary rather than corporate form,
and with only one-third of the capital investment of the Boston Associates.[11]
It was a vibrant industry that came with what many might say are significant
advantages as compared to the Lowell model.

The Lowell mills were geared toward the production of cheap and highly
standardized cotton cloth. In fact, that is all they could produce because that is
all their production system was designed to do. Being vertically integrated
means that everything is connected to everything else, so even if improvements were made to certain aspects of the system, they still have to stick to the
same mold. They could not, for example, shift over to wool or do much if any
variation in terms of thread counts or weaving patterns, or the like. Up until
computers and robotics, this was frequently a very important limitation of
mass production machinery. It generally isn't very flexible. As we'll see in the
next chapter, lack of flexibility is taken to be the Achilles heel of the large,
integrated business form. In Philadelphia, one could find the mass production
of cheap and standardized cotton cloth, but one could also easily find a large
variety of products often of greater quality. What was present in Philadelphia
would today be called a *flexible production* or *flexible specialization* model in
that the businesses and workers in the industry could shift quite rapidly
between different kinds of products given changes in demand or supply chains.
The key is that those hundreds of companies were generally small and
specialized, operated in proprietary form, frequently relied on skilled labor

---

[9]Perrow, 2002, p. 81.
[10]Scranton, 1997,p. 3.
[11]Perrow, 2002, pp. 82–82.

rather than unskilled labor, and depended on exchanges with each other. Work space and production technologies would frequently be leased rather than owned. The same could be done with production technologies. Thus sunk costs were far lower. In the Lowell model, if demand for what they were producing declined, there was nothing they could do about it except try to increase demand—the treadmill of production strategy. But in Philadelphia, you could far more easily drop what you were producing and shift to something else along with shifts in consumer demand.

Thus we're talking about companies that are not strongly bound by the *structural interests* of an organizational form. Proprietary in form, they do not have to answer to outside investors purely on the basis of return on investment. With low capital investments, they aren't tied down by their sunk costs. And all of it came with fewer and smaller negative externalities. Given a reliance on skilled labor, and the large number of companies, workers—even if they were wage dependent—would have maintained some flexibility and choice and thus some independence. The degree to which wealth produced by the industry is concentrated is considerably less which also corresponds to a lower degree of concentration in political power. The employers are not absentee owners but live in roughly in the same areas of the city as their workers. As such, it seems that the basic infrastructure in the small firm production areas of the city was well kept.

One striking story involves the differences in response between the owners of the Lowell mills and at least some of the Philadelphia mills at the start of the Civil War when the supply of cotton from the South was cut off. In Lowell, the directors of the company shut down production and sold their existing inventory of raw cotton at exorbitant prices. They thus saw huge profits even while unemployment in the city soared and the community suffered. What did they care? They didn't live there. In Philadelphia, several mill owners formed militias of their male employees who went off to fight the war, even while their employers continued to pay the men their regular wages. As Perrow was fond of saying, the characteristics of organizations that are built matter.

Thus we have two different models in the same industry for how economic relations were organized, and thus even how social relations are shaped and how wealth and power are distributed. Perrow indicates that the network model found in Philadelphia often appears to be an exception to markets or to emerging forms of hierarchy at the time. But he notes that the logic is actually quite traditional having basically descended from the English model of non-corporate, flexible production woolen industries that predated the rise of a large textile industry in the United States. In fact, it has now become common to recognize that the Philadelphia model was the norm in many industries and these kinds of areas with concentrated firms that operate in the same industry are known as *industrial districts*. This was the backdrop against which Perrow was writing. The time that it became common to recognize and discuss such things is relatively recent and sparked by what many see as a return to this form in the post-1970s period which we will explore in Chapter 6.

Cementing the Hierarchy Path

So if there was an alternative path available, then the question remains as to why hierarchy became the dominant form. As already noted, in the logic of economists, including many economic historians like Chandler, it must have been because it was the most competitive form for business to take in efficiency terms. If you can outdo the competition on cost and quality, then you inevitably win. Yet, anyone who has ever tried to run a business knows that the surest route to success is to just not have any competition at all. So if it is possible to eliminate competition, wouldn't you try?

To pick up the last threads regarding Perrow's interpretation of hierarchy versus market models in the textile industry, he indicates that the most likely explanation for an industry taking the form of hierarchy in New England and network in Philadelphia was simply the degree to which capital (basically business financing) was able to be concentrated. Apparently, banks in Pennsylvania were heavily regulated to encourage investment in transportation infrastructure (e.g., railroads and canals), and those with capital to invest had quite diverse places to do it. So textile businesses tended to be funded by individual entrepreneurs without the corporate pooling of capital from multiple sources, which generally translated to smaller and more specialized businesses. In Massachusetts, banking was relatively unregulated and there was nothing that encouraged more diversified investments and thus nothing to stop capital concentration. According to market control arguments, this is pretty much all it takes—the ability to put together large amounts of investment capital so that you can buy suppliers and customers and competitors, or otherwise be the only game in town. The crucial tool for doing this was (and is still) the corporate form of business, and we'll now take a deeper dive into that.

Liberating the Corporate Form

As noted in Chapter 4, a corporation is a legal actor that exists only on paper, and is legally separate and distinct from the people who start it, own it, or manage it. At this point, it is quite easy for anyone to start a corporation by basically paying some fees and filing some paperwork, but that wasn't always the case. Prior to and then still through much of the nineteenth century, the potential founders of a corporation had to petition the state legislature to form a corporation. Each corporation thus had its own specific piece of legislation, called a *charter*, that was written to establish and define it. Since these were established by unique pieces of legislation, there isn't a way to precisely specify their characteristics, but generally speaking, the charters came with some strict limitations, most of which fell by the wayside through the nineteenth century. Charters were generally only granted if the corporation's purposes served not only the private good of the owners, but also some kind of public good. So, for example, chartered companies were generally formed for early transportation projects such as bridges and canals because the expense of those projects required different people to combine their capital. The owners were certainly expected to profit, but much of the public was also supposed to benefit from improved transportation. "We want to make a ton of money for ourselves" was simply not enough. This principle also came with the provision that public representatives sat on corporate boards so as to provide accountability in terms of that public good.

Generally speaking, chartered companies were also only allowed to partake in business activities that were specified in the charter. If your charter was to build a bridge over a river, then your company couldn't go on to also start digging a canal next to the river. For that you'd need a separate charter. Nor could it go on to build other bridges. As part of this, a chartered company could not buy another chartered company, nor could the company own any stock in other companies. If the corporation behaved badly, the charter could be revoked. Finally, the corporation's lifespan was specified. It was only allowed to remain doing business for a particular period of time, and if its owners wanted to continue, they had to return to the legislature for approval. In the most general sense, chartered corporations were not legal persons with the same kinds of legal rights as you and me. The only things we really had in common were liability for harms done (although this varied) and mortality.

These kinds of limitations would make the skin of today's boards, management, and investors' skin crawl. At this point, you can establish a corporation by simple registration and paying some fees; it does not need to serve anyone but its owners; carries no need for public representation; has an unlimited lifespan and is not limited in its functions; can own any property it likes, including other corporations; and its owners are free from liability for harms created by the company's operations. So why were all of the limitations and conditions in place historically? In simple terms, it was fear of the ability to concentrate economic power. The chartering system came down to the US through British law. Charters were a way for the state (P power) to limit the concentration of economic (E) power. As far as the context of the post-revolutionary United States goes, our culture of political-economy is founded upon a fear of concentrated power. These days this is normally only thought of and discussed in terms of limiting the power of the state (thus, for example, a system of checks and balances), but throughout the nineteenth century, the fear of concentrated economic power was just as salient. In fact, during the nineteenth century, corporate businesses were seen as the opposite of "free enterprise" rather than examples of it. That distinction has long since disappeared. We have not lost our fear of political power concentration, but many have apparently lost fear of economic concentrations of power, the most important tool of which is the present corporate form containing few, if any limits on their size and functions.

The normal interpretation for why such limits were dismantled would be functional—that in making it easier for people to invest money in various kinds of ventures, we free up entrepreneurial activity and grease the wheels of economic development. But this ignores a lot, including the fact that there was quite a bit of entrepreneurialism and economic development both via charters, and outside of a corporate form of any kind. What Perrow describes is a sustained effort over the course of the nineteenth century by moneyed interests to get rid of the kinds of barriers that were in place through Supreme Court's decisions and changes to state incorporation laws, some of which were achieved through outright bribery. Throughout the nineteenth century, if you want to imagine who lawyers and judges were, then you just have to think about who would be likely to go to law school. The answer, of course, would be children of the wealthy. From the colonial days and well into the early nineteenth century, a good deal of those with law degrees came from a relatively small number of elite families and from a relatively small number of elite law schools. And when they went to practice law, it was often to practice business law in the interests of the family's business interests. In Perrow's account, they created a "legal revolution that launched organizations."[12]

The requirement of public representation on charted corporations went by the wayside in 1819 in the Supreme Court case of *Dartmouth College v. Woodward* in which the Court ruled that Dartmouth College was a private

---

[12]Perrow, 2002, p. 31.

entity and its board of trustees should be free from trustees appointed by the state. This effectively removed any legal requirement of public oversight or obligation to serve the public good, greatly limiting the ability to establish any public controls. Further limits came in that same year in the *McCulloch v. Maryland* case where the Court basically declared the supremacy of federal-level law over state-level law. Oddly, the case was actually about whether or not the state of Maryland could tax a branch of a federal bank in the state. The court ruled that it could not impose such a tax, but the broader importance was that federal law became the supreme law of the land so that states could not enact laws that contradicted those at the federal level. One reason that this is fateful is because laws governing incorporation are made at the state level. If an organization wants some particular legal right (such as getting rid of public representatives), then it doesn't need to worry about laws in all of the states. With federal supremacy, changes at the federal level would suffice and the US Supreme Court could now become something of a one-stop shop for court rulings favorable to corporate interests or needs. In essence, corporations were turned into private entities that could be granted the same rights as private citizens and with limitations on the ability to regulate them.

This is not the place to provide an entire review of court cases as the history of corporate law is long and complex (see suggested readings). But generally speaking, the nineteenth century saw uneven though consistent movement toward providing more and more rights and powers to corporate entities, often limiting the rights of private citizens, including workers. At the same time it was becoming easier and easier to form a corporation that included rights of limited liability as a matter of course. Along the way, outside of court cases state laws regarding incorporation were changing in many important ways. With regard to financial obligations, New York had a version of a limited liability law on its books as early as 1811, though it was at first only for manufacturing companies. As of 1837, Connecticut started allowing incorporation merely by registration rather than by the need to seek a legislative charter. (This is generally how it works now. You fill out the paperwork, pay some fees, and "poof" you've created a new legal person.) This one is a very big domino. Combined with the 1819 Dartmouth decision, it meant that any group of people could combine assets, take on the legal form of the corporation for their own private benefit, and not face many of the limitations of charters. And while there was no simple and immediate rush to pass similar laws in other states, more liberal (meaning "free") laws of incorporation in some states do put competitive pressure on other states to follow suit in order to attract economic activity. There comes to be a competitive market geared toward granting corporations more and more rights.

As far as the main line of our story is concerned, the most fateful legal changes came from those that allowed *holding companies* by allowing corporations to own shares of other corporations. A holding company is a corporation that doesn't actually do anything...other than own other companies. What it represents is basically a tool for relatively easy vertical and horizontal integration. The ability of companies to buy shares in other companies provides a relatively cheap way to control those other companies because significant control of a company's board and major decisions can sometimes be had by controlling even small percentages of its stock.[13] Recall that the typical chartered corporation was not allowed to own stock in other corporations, and even as many of the limitations on chartered corporations were eased, the prohibition on owning stock in other companies held on for a long time. In 1853, largely by way of bribery, the Pennsylvania Railroad (PARR) was able to get the legal right to own other rail lines added to its state charter. This ability to buy up or control other railroads aided in the PARR becoming not only the largest railroad in the US by the early 1880s, but actually the biggest corporation in the world. A main turning point here for the overall economy, however, was in the late 1880s when New Jersey liberalized its corporate laws to allow this right for any business incorporated in the state of New Jersey. Not surprisingly, New Jersey subsequently saw a rush of incorporation in the state, particularly among the largest corporations of the time. It became, for example, the corporate headquarters of Standard Oil during the period of its consolidation of the oil industry, but that is only one of the most famous cases in a widespread rush toward oligopoly and monopoly.

There is no specific "moment" when corporations had become what they are today. In fact, it is still always open to change as the legal system changes. But suffice it to say that by the end of the 1880s, it was relatively easy to establish a corporation as a legal person with the ability to pool capital from many different sources; limited liability for management and investors; the right to operate only for its own benefit regardless of the public good; and the ability to control other companies simply by way of partial stock ownership. These are core elements of center pin of the organizational revolution that was in the making.

The Importance of the Railroads

Regardless of whose arguments are being made, the railroads lie very directly at the root of the organizational revolution. As noted, Chandler called them "the first modern business enterprise," in addition to explaining how crucial they were as a form of transportation. Perrow calls them "the *second* big business" because, as outlined above, he argued that all of the ingredients were present with the textile mills of the Boston Associates. But there is no dispute regarding their practical importance in allowing the growth of big business across much of the economy. At the start of the twentieth century, the US was a vast "unsettled" territory by the standards of the European-based people who were in the process of spreading throughout the territory. (Whether it was considered "unsettled" by the native populations is not a road we will go down here.) Transportation was a serious issue. To the extent that there were "roads" they were often a lot more like muddy, rutted paths. The best way of getting around long distances was by water routes, but those can be tricky to navigate, especially in the winter with regards to the North, or during periods of foul weather, flooding, or drought. And other than some limited ability to build some canals, their routes were not subject to human design or control. So even with good navigation conditions, there was very limited choice with regards to destination. The railroads represented reliable, all weather

---

[13]The actual percentage of stock required for a *controlling interest*, as it is called, is actually quite fuzzy and does depend on many things, such as the presence of other large shareholders and whether or not all outstanding shares of a company are voting shares. But regardless of all else, owning any amount over 50% of voting stock does provide a controlling interest.

transportation that can generally be built wherever you'd like them to go. They had huge freight capacity by comparison to other means of transport (and still do), even while they greatly reduced travel times for both people and cargo. They provided the potential for exactly the kind of efficiency, predictability, and calculability of transportation that is afforded by formal rationalization. They also generated a lot of demand for mass production as consumers themselves. Building and running a railroad requires vast quantities of things like steel, glass, wood, rubber, and so forth. In all practical senses, they were indispensable in terms of industrialization in the US and directly spurred some of the growth of mass production simply to fulfill their own supply needs.

But the dynamics of the story go well beyond their practical capabilities. They were crucial to the legal changes to corporate law discussed (albeit briefly) above, especially in terms of the bribery that assisted in legal changes and court rulings. They were also the center pin of the building of our system of modern finance complete with active stock markets, investment houses, and lending institutions which also benefit from the liberalization of corporate laws. And, just as importantly, they perfected the bureaucratic form of organization which came to be widely emulated by the big businesses that were to follow, and later by all forms of organizations. If the second industrial revolution were seen as an explosion, the railroads were the fuel and the fuse.

The Full Development of the Bureaucratic Form

Running a railroad is a complicated thing, although the complexity will obviously vary with the size and complexity of the lines that are operated as well as the kinds of things carried. As a technology, a good deal of standardization is required. For example, the track gauge (the width of the rails) has to be kept standardized along entire lines, while the cars and locomotives need to be built to those specifications so that they can all actually ride on the tracks. Letting rail layers or car builders make their own choices there won't do because if it all isn't built to strict, standardized specifications, it just won't work at all. In terms of operations, strict control of the running of trains will be needed as well. Rail lines aren't like roads that carry autos. Trains can only ride on the rails. You can't just "pull over" to let another vehicle by or to avoid colliding with one that is headed your way. There needs to be strict control over scheduling as well as *standard operating procedures* should things go wrong, such as breakdowns or other scheduling glitches. There are also a lot of different functions that have to be undertaken and coordinated. There are the people on the lines that operate the trains. Then you have train stations to run. There is a lot of purchasing to be done (or management of supply chains if vertically integrated). You need to have all of the equipment maintained and repaired and to deal with customers, whether those are passengers or shippers of cargo. It is no surprise then that the railroads were at the forefront of the perfection of bureaucratic control—control at a distance by pre-established routines, rules, and procedures.

While it might not truly be the world's first organizational chart, Chandler bestowed the honor on that of the New York and Erie Railroad created by its superintendent Daniel McCallum in 1854.[14] It may come as no surprise that the chart bore a striking resemblance to a regional train line looking like a tree

---

[14]Chandler, 1988.

with various branches that represented a schematic map for the rail lines (see Figure 5.1). The fully mature form that we would recognize today was developed by the Pennsylvania Railroad while on its way to being the largest corporation in the world. It set up main authority in a central corporate office

FIGURE 5.1   The First Organizational Chart

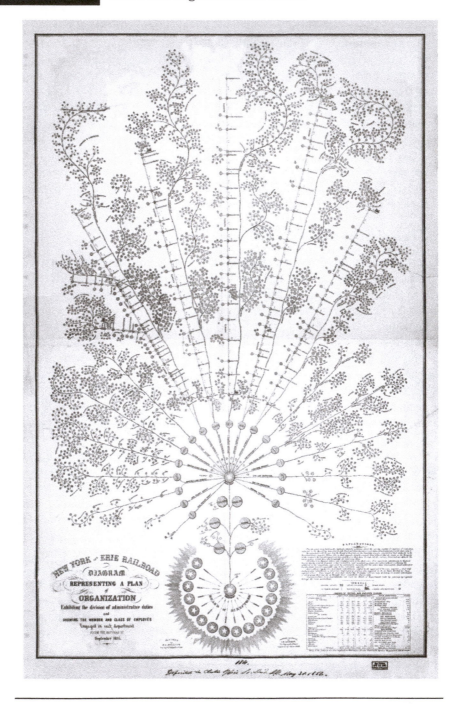

Source: Daniel McCallum & George Holt Henshaw, 1855, Public domain, via Wikimedia Commons.

that was not involved in day-to-day operational activities. Rather, it coordinated by sending orders down the line, while requiring regular reports of activities back up to the central office. It is control by information which is not a "new" thing just because of the emergence of electronic information technologies. It was set up with separate organizational divisions by track section, which—nicely enough—allows easily adding on more and more purchased railroads in the event of horizontal integration. The company developed the full-blown employee "manual" that specified all of the tasks and responsibilities according to organizational position including detailed schedule tables with instructions for how to handle contingencies. If we wanted an exemplar for Weber's ideal type put into practice—task specialization, clear hierarchies of authority and formalization—the PARR form would do nicely. As it turns out, this bureaucratic form was widely copied by other railroads and later in other industries where large, integrated firms came to dominate. As Perrow notes:

> *Bureaucratic control is indirect control through rules, regulations, and reports. The railroads were probably the first to develop these unobtrusive, inexpensive, pervasive, and impersonal control devices, the best elites have ever discovered. It is a virtually unmarked turning point in humankind's history.*[15]

In other words, whatever might be said of bureaucratic efficiency in terms of dollars and cents, it should also include a mention that it is an efficient means for concentrating social power. It is a great tool for "big business" in more ways than one.

Capital Needs and Modern Finance

Building a railroad is no picnic. It is very difficult and very expensive. For quite a while many people were skeptical that they could be made to work at all, whether in technical or economic terms. There were basic practical engineering issues such as whether smooth steel wheels could actually pull any weight on smooth steel rails, and especially uphill. But there were also major questions about whether or not the costs could ever be recovered and put a rail venture into profitability. But regardless, there was a lot of interest in having rail lines built, not only on the part of businesses who sought to benefit from the reliable transportation, but also on the part of governments as an important aspect of infrastructure for general economic development. But early on in initial rail development, entrepreneurs were frequently shy about undertaking the huge risks, and governments, whether at the state- or local-level, generally did not have the organizational capacity to do it. Thus a lot of the earliest rail lines in the US became publicly funded, but privately operated ventures, although some state lines were built as well. But herein lies the importance of so many of the elements of the corporate form. If corporations as legal persons independent of their owners, allowing widespread stock ownership with limited liability for investors could exist, then it becomes easier to raise private capital as well as public. Private capital was often preferred for the simple reason that public funds often come with strings

---

[15]Perrow, 2002, p. 163.

attached, but public support in various forms was ample. The dynamics of the private financing, however, are what lay at the center of the story.

The center of the private finance story lies, as it continues to, in the corporate financing system of New York centered around the famous Wall Street institutions—the New York Stock Exchange's (NYSE) stock and bond markets, investment banks, and brokerage houses. The institutions were initially nurtured by the government, more as bond markets to raise funds for the needs of government. Whereas stocks give you partial ownership of a company, bonds are basically loans. If you buy one, you are, in essence, providing a loan to the bond issuer who will pay you back at a fixed amount of interest after a particular period of time. Wall Street institutions became the clearing houses for certifying and buying and selling the bonds. As an aspect of infrastructure development, railroads were obtaining financing through this system, as had canals and turnpikes prior to that. Unlike today when you can buy stocks in companies operating in most sectors of the economy, that wasn't the case up until after the Civil War. The operations of Wall Street finance were largely limited to financing for state operations and for infrastructure needs, even if those were being undertaken by private companies.

While the railroad industry and many of the railroads that were built has a very bumpy history, a great deal of money was being made both in terms of building and running them (although possibly more in building them) and investment capital poured in, particularly after the Civil War. For various reasons, the War greatly intensified the amount of finance capital being concentrated in New York. The costs of the War were enormous and the Union government put out gigantic bond issues. In fact, they were so large that they couldn't all be sold initially. One of the early bankers central to the emerging system of finance was Jay Cooke, sometimes called the "financier of the Civil War" because he developed a system for mass marketing government bonds to the general public. The introduction of the stock ticker, made possible by the telegraph, made information about stocks and bonds available nationally. All of this meant that even people who were not wealthy, and not around any major financial centers could easily become investors. As such, more and more of the available capital in the entire country could easily make its way to New York financial institutions. But it was not only flowing in from the United States, but also from European investors.

Coupled with the legal tools such as limited liability, the ability of corporations to own stock in other corporations, and the corresponding legality of holding companies, the widely available capital made it possible to use various tactics to consolidate (horizontally and sometimes vertically integrate) entire industries into those oligopolies we encountered in Chapter 4. In Chandler's eyes, this was always done to achieve the efficiencies associated with economies of scale. But there is good reason to doubt that. One of Perrow's important sources was sociologist William G. Roy's book *Socializing Capital*.[16] In it he takes a second look at one of Chandler's favorite cases—that of the American Tobacco Company (ATC).

The ATC was founded by James B. Duke in 1890 out of a consolidation of his family's tobacco company with four competitors. For Chandler, the key to the story was the introduction of automatic rolling machines for pre-rolled

---

[16]Roy, 1997. The following will be drawn from his discussion of the tobacco industry, pp. 223–239.

cigarettes which did greatly increase the efficiency of rolling cigarettes. However, it seemed that the consolidation wasn't driven by any efficiency needs or requirements. The five companies that went into it were already an oligopoly accounting for about 90% of the US market for cigarettes. The industry was competitive, but all of the companies were profitable. Roy notes that "[i]t was difficult to see any compelling economic logic in this action other than the benefits of windfall corporate capital and monopoly profits."[17] Like so many other corporations of the time, it took advantage of New Jersey's liberal laws, formed itself as a holding company and issued $25 million in stocks, even while the company's total assets were estimated to be worth only $ 4 million. The other $21 million was kept on the company books as what is called *goodwill* value—intangible assets such as brand reputation, existing customer base and the control of particular patents.

Despite controlling about 90% of the cigarette market and having exclusive control of two of the top rolling machine technologies, the company still had trouble maintaining market share in the face of competition from smaller companies. But attempts to maintain and regain market share weren't driven by the pursuit of superior efficiency, but largely by the ability to wield superior economic power via their access to corporate capital. It would, for example, target markets where competitors were and sell below its actual costs, something smaller, independent companies wouldn't be able to do for long. It would use its size to make exclusive contracts with wholesalers and use various means to gain control of tobacco supplies to cut off competitors supply chain links. And where it could sufficiently weaken competitors, it would then buy them out even if it didn't intend to continue that company's operations. The point was simply to use superior economic power, not to be better than the competition, but to simply eliminate it. This has been a major business strategy ever since the legal tools of the corporation and the corporate finance system were solidified at the end of the nineteenth century. Up until about the 1890s, these kinds of business activities applied much more in the railroad industry than in any others, but there was one particular historical episode during which this model spread throughout vast portions of the entire US economy.

The Great Merger Movement

The large amounts of capital flowing to New York financial institutions through the latter half of the nineteenth century largely went into railroads. The intense growth went on to create various periods of boom and bust which had the effect of creating economic depressions. Today these periods of overinvestment are commonly called "bubbles," and they do burst. Major ones that can be attributed to the overbuilding and speculation in railroads occurred in 1857, 1873, and 1893. And this became the thing that very directly laid the path for widespread consolidation of control across major industries in the US—for the organizational revolution itself. During the bursting of a bubble, what happens is that many companies get into serious financial trouble. (It usually gets started by a major company or more failing and that has cascading effects that lead to further failures.) Some fail entirely, but many are "bailed out" often by being bought out at a discount by investors or other

---

[17]Roy, 1997, p. 228.

companies in the industry with greater capital reserves. While, as the case of ATC shows, depressions aren't necessarily required for consolidation activities, depressions tend to make it much more widespread. Indeed acquisitions and consolidations in the railroad industry were common regardless, and in fact, prior to the 1880s, few companies or industries aside from the railroads were involved in the corporate system of finance.

The most fateful depression that would change all of this was a particularly harsh one that began in 1893. It resulted in what came to be called *The Great Merger Movement* which went from approximately 1894–1904 (Figure 5.2). In Perrow's words:

> *the now-centralized capital markets needed someplace to invest other than in railroad consolidation...Money poured instead into the mining and manufacturing industries, so fast that in five short years (1898–1903) more than half of the book value of all manufacturing capital was incorporated, the aggregate value of listed stocks and bonds going from $1 to $7 billion. The firms were made giant by consolidating the assets of several firms in the same industry and market...By 1904 most of the giant firms that would remain giant until the present (after further mergers in some cases, of course) were formed, in a vast intoxication with market control and oligopoly. As a result, very big organizations were to be our lot and to determine our fate.[18]*

FIGURE 5.2   The Great Merger Movement

- 1895–1904: Over 1,800 companies disappeared into mergers / consolidations and 75% of those into mergers of 5 or more firms.

- Most of the large companies that dominated the 20th century founded here...

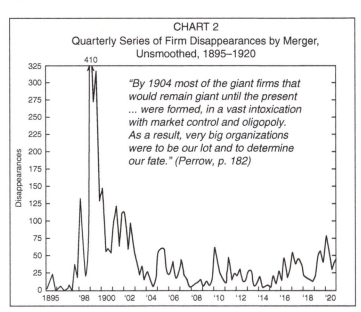

CHART 2
Quarterly Series of Firm Disappearances by Merger, Unsmoothed, 1895–1920

"By 1904 most of the giant firms that would remain giant until the present ... were formed, in a vast intoxication with market control and oligopoly. As a result, very big organizations were to be our lot and to determine our fate." (Perrow, p. 182)

Source: Ralph L. Nelson, Merger Movements in American University, 1895–1956. Princeton, NJ: Princeton University Press, pg. 33.

---

[18]Perrow, 2002, p. 182.

While the economy was well on its way to being transformed from market (or network) to hierarchy, this is literally a one decade period of time during which a major switch was flipped. In the railroad industry, 700 railroad companies went bankrupt between 1875 and 1897, and were consolidated (horizontally integrated) to become six major entities[19] by the turn of the twentieth century. During the great merger movement, over 1,800 companies were swallowed up in consolidations and most of those were large ones accounting for multiple companies at once. While a full story of what occurred during this period is quite complex and involves many people, the famous robber barons of the era, such as J. P. Morgan, Jay Gould, and John D. Rockefeller, were central figures who were actively and purposefully trying to reorganize the entire US economy along monopolistic and oligopolistic lines with themselves at the center of control. It is, after all, easier to make money if you can have very large markets, and don't really have to compete with other companies. This was the very sudden appearance of widespread oligopoly across many industries, and it was not generated by the quest for *efficiency*, unless one means in the very narrow senses discussed above. It was more like widespread business weaknesses, coupled with highly centralized control over investment capital, and quite liberal laws of incorporation.

Summary

To question Chandler's interpretation of the reasons for the rise of big business is not to question the importance of *economies of scale* in contributing to the vast economic growth of the United States through the twentieth century. Very large business operations, necessarily operating in bureaucratic form for coordination needs, can absolutely produce various kinds of narrow economic efficiencies. But it does not follow that this was all for the best or that it was an inevitable historical path. Here I have raised three general issues in that regard. First is to broaden our ideas regarding what we are after when we seek efficiency. The question "efficient for what and for whom?" should always be asked, and the answers aren't so simple if serious attention is given to externalities. Second, I have reviewed the very real possibility that a vibrant, dynamic economy could have been had in different form, but with far fewer and smaller negative externalities. On this latter note, however, the lesser ability to externalize costs would not allow mass consumption to become what it did. This does not necessarily mean that goods might not be plentiful and cheap. But many of them couldn't be as cheap simply because more of the true costs of production (such as environmental and labor costs) would be factored into the price of goods. Third, we have seen that, even if narrow economic efficiencies were gained by the coming of big business, they don't seem to explain jut *why* it happened. There is ample evidence to suggest that hierarchy came from a desire to build organizational capabilities and forms that were geared toward using financial power to control markets—rather than try to compete in them effectively. All of these provide for a very different orientation to the reasons behind the organizational revolution than one that would be gleaned from Chandler. But perhaps a better reason to question Chandler is that after about the 1970s,

---

[19]The term "entities" is necessarily vague largely because at the time the form that combinations of businesses could take was still in flux.

it seemed to be that large, bureaucratic, integrated businesses that were praised for their efficiency were decidedly *inefficient* even in narrow economic terms. The new efficient form? *Networks*—oddly, the alternative path not taken. So we move on to this next part of the story in Chapter 6.

SOURCES AND FURTHER READING

This chapter is thoroughly inspired by a book by organizational sociologist Charles Perrow:

- Perrow, Charles. 2002. *Organizing America: Wealth, Power, and the Origins of Corporate Capitalism*. Princeton, NJ: Princeton University Press.

This book is pretty long in the tooth by now, but also among the broadest treatments of theoretical accounts of the rise of big business. It synthesized a great deal regarding approaches to both organizations, generally speaking, and the managerial revolution. It also said much of what needs to be said regarding how economic power rather than efficiency has shaped dominant business forms. The chapter is not, however, any manner of summary of the book's overall argument. While a reasonably short book (228 pages, not including Appendix or notes), it addresses a very broad range of business history that is far too dense to be summarized in the space of one chapter of an introductory book. For those interested, Chapter 7 "Summary and Conclusions" does provide a reasonable overview of the general story of the book. I have also not provided a full account of alternative theories here, but Perrow does offer a brief summary in the Appendix.

- On **externalities of scale**: Perrow never uses the term but it is thoroughly implied in his account, and in similar form in consideration of *normal accidents* which we will encounter in Chapter 10. Generally speaking, the idea is that virtually all activities include both positive and negative externalities. But the smaller and more decentralized the organizations, the smaller are the negative externalities. Although the issue of negative externalities is raised throughout the book, it was one among many ancillary issues and I simply supplemented it with a source that took it as an explicit focus and, as far as I know, coined the phrase. For that account see:

  - Driscoll, Adam, and Bob Edwards. 2015. "From Farms to Factories: The Social and Environmental Consequences of Industrial Swine Production in North Carolina." In *Twenty Lessons in Environmental Sociology*, 209–30, edited by Kenneth A. Gould and Tammy L. Lewis. New York, NY: Oxford University Press.

  - The **Treadmill of Production (TOP)** is one of the central orienting frameworks in the Sociology of Environment/Environmental Sociology. On its origins see:

    - Schnaiberg, Allan. 1980. *The Environment: From Surplus to Scarcity*. New York, NY: Oxford University Press.

    - For a brief overview of TOP, later reflections, and assessment see: Gould, Kenneth A., David N. Pellow, and Allan Schnaiberg. 2004. "Interrogating The Treadmill of Production: Everything You Wanted to Know About the Treadmill but Were Afraid to Ask." *Organization & Environment* 17: 296–316.

- Generally speaking, **environmental issues** have not loomed large in historical treatments of the **Gilded Age/ Progressive Era (GAPE)**, but that has been changing. See, e.g.:

  - Johnson, Benjamin. 2017. "Environment: Nature, Conservation, and the Progressive State." Chapter 6 in *A Companion to the Gilded Age and Progressive Era*, First Edition. Edited by Christopher McKnight Nichols and Nancy C. Unger. Hoboken, NJ: John Wiley & Sons, Inc.

- **Alfred Chandler's stark admission that demand has to be created to meet whatever can be supplied** is in: Chandler, Alfred D. 1990. *Scale and Scope: The Dynamics of Industrial Capitalism*. Cambridge, MA: Harvard University Press.

- Perrow's contrast of the **Lowell Model** and **Philadelphia Model** of textile industries is drawn from multiple sources. Accounts of the Lowell-Waltham are not hard to find. Scranton (1983) was the key to the account of the Philadelphia model.

  - Dalzell, Robert F. 1987. *Enterprising Elite: The Boston Associates and the World They Made*. Cambridge, MA: Harvard University Press.

  - Dublin, Thomas. 1979. *Women at Work: The Transformation of Work and Community in Lowell, Massachusetts, 1826–1860*. New York, NY: Columbia University Press.

  - Gitelman, H. M. 1967. "The Waltham System and the Coming of the Irish." *Labor History* 8: 227–53.

  - Gumus-Dawes, Zehra. 2000. "Forsaken Paths: The Organization of the American Textile Industry in the Nineteenth Century." Ph.D. diss., Sociology Department, Yale University.

  - Scranton, Philip. 1983. *Proprietary Capitalism: The Textile Manufacturers at Philadelphia, 1800–1885*. New York, NY: Cambridge University Press.

    - Scranton is a historian who has been instrumental in documenting alternative forms of nineteenth century industry, calling it **"the 'other side' of the Second Industrial Revolution."** That particular phrase appears in the introduction of a book (p. 3) not cited in Perrow: Scranton, Philip. 1997. *Endless Novelty: Specialty Production and American Industrialization, 1865-1925*. Princeton, NJ: Princeton University Press.

    - If we fast-forward to Chapter 6, the **Philadelphia Model** would be seen as operating in **network** form which can be said to be **neither market nor hierarchy**. The reference there is from:

      - Powell, Walter W. 1990. "Neither Market nor Hierarchy: Network Forms of Organization." *Research on Organizational Behavior*. 12: 295-336.

- Perrow's account of **railroads** and their effects on transforming organizations and the economy is similarly drawn from multiple sources. Of the following, Roy (1997), Berk (1994) and Dobbin (1994) were most directly engaged in critiques of efficiency interpretations.

  - Berk, Gerald. 1994. *Alternative Tracks: The Constitution of American Industrial Order, 1865–1917*. Baltimore, MD: Johns Hopkins University Press.

○ Chandler, Alfred Dupont, Jr. 1965. *The Railroads: The Nation's First Big Business*. New York, NY: Harcourt Brace and World.

○ ———. 1977. *The Visible Hand: The Managerial Revolution in American Business*. Cambridge, MA: Harvard University Press.

○ Dobbin, Frank. 1994. *Forging Industrial Policy: The United States, Britain, and France in the Railway Age*. New York, NY: Cambridge University Press.

○ Goodrich, Carter. 1960. *Government Promotion of American Canals and Railroads, 1800–1890*. New York, NY: Columbia University Press.

○ Hartz, Louis. 1948. *Economic History and Democratic Thought: Pennsylvania, 1776–1860*. Cambridge, MA: Harvard University Press.

○ Roy, William G. 1997. *Socializing Capital: The Rise of the Large Industrial Corporation in America*. Princeton, NJ: Princeton University Press.

○ Schivelbusch, Wolfgang. 1986. *The Railway Journey: The Industrialization and Perception of Time and Space in the Nineteenth Century*. Berkeley, CA: University of California Press.

○ Chandler's discussion of the **first organizational chart** (for the **New York and Erie Railroad**): Chandler, Alfred D., Jr. 1988. "Origins of the Organization Chart." *Harvard Business Review*. 66: 156–157.

○ The **graphic in Figure 5.2** illustrating **the Great Merger Movement** did not appear in Perrow (2002). It is from p. 33 of: Nelson, Ralph L. 1959. *Merger Movements in American Industry, 1895-1956*. National Bureau of Economic Research Number 66, General Series. Princeton, NJ: Princeton University Press. Out of print. Full text pdf is available here: https://www.nber.org/books-and-chapters/merger-movements-american-industry-1895-1956

The Fall of Big Business?

It may very well be that one of the best reasons to question Chandler's interpretation of the rise of large business organizations is that by the time his famous *Visible Hand* book was published in 1977 big business in the United States was in big trouble. The 1970s saw a long drawn out period of economic crisis that extended into the early 1980s and, generally speaking, US companies did not fare well. It was during this period that it started to look like the big business model was not all that efficient after-all, and the dominant form of economic relations shifted yet again. So it is now common to say that the form of business in the United States moved *from markets* in the nineteenth century, *to hierarchy* (big business) in the period from the early twentieth century to about 1970, and then to *networks* in the post-1970s period to the present. This tends to be the mainstream economics and business story, anyway. It will lead us to question Alfred Chandler some more, but also Charles Perrow's idea of the *society of organizations*, that I myself have adopted, along with the argument that we are stuck on the path of hierarchy. By now, it is possible to argue that 1970s period marked "the end of the society of organizations," as organizational sociologist Gerald Davis[1] put it.

The 1970s Economic and Competitiveness Crisis

In the immediate post–World War II period it is probably fair to say that US businesses had it relatively easy. The United States had emerged from the war with greatly ramped up industrial production capacity, while other parts of the industrial or industrializing world were left in a bit of disarray from the ravages of the war. With major industries operating as oligopolies and without any serious forms of global competition, the United States reached its heights of prosperity. It was a period of US global dominance in terms of all social power resources—IEM and P. But starting by about the mid-1960s, the situation had begun to change. Foreign industrial and industrializing economies were getting back on their feet, and US businesses started to face increased competition. What is likely even worse is that many of the foreign goods coming into the United States seemed to be of higher quality, while at the same time lower in price. The most notable industries in which this occurred were the auto and

---

[1]Davis, 2009b.

electronics industries, where Japanese companies in particular were producing higher quality goods at lower prices.

This helped to stall out US economic growth and the early part of the 1970s saw two economic recessions with accompanying increases in levels of unemployment. Much of that unemployment was in the areas hardest hit by foreign competition—manufacturing. This was the beginning of the decline in size of the US *subordinate primary labor market* along with the labor unions that were an integral part of it. The troubles were compounded by an oil crisis that began in 1973. Arab members of the Organization of Petroleum Exporting Countries (OPEC) imposed an embargo on oil exports to any country that was lending to support to Israel in its 1973 war with Egypt, including most notably the US. Oil prices shot up and US consumers experienced shortages that extended to the gas pump to the point that gasoline rationing was introduced. You had to wait in long lines to buy gas, and rationing meant there were only certain times that you were allowed to buy it. Some days were even number days, and you could buy gas if your license plate ended in an even number. The other days, of course, were the odd number days. High gas prices and gasoline shortages just gave an extra boost to demand for cars from Japanese companies, most notably Toyota and Honda. US auto companies had specialized in relatively large and powerful "gas guzzling" cars, while Honda and Toyota were marketing small and fuel efficient cars. This certainly didn't help the US auto industry.

Stagnant economic growth with very high oil prices produced a previously unheard of phenomenon that was dubbed *stagflation*—economic stagnation combined with inflation. At the time economists would not have believed it could happen. When an economy stagnates and/or goes into recession, unemployment rises. Rising unemployment suppresses demand for goods and services, and thus inflationary pressures are very low. However, in this case high oil prices were largely behind growing prices because oil is such an integral aspect of everything in an economy. It is not only necessary as an energy and raw material source for many kinds of production and distribution, but it is also an important product in its own right. The US economy was in turmoil and this period of history would fundamentally change it. At the center of those changes would be changes, once again, in how US businesses organize.

All by itself a period of economic stagnation might not have been so bad, but with more competition in markets, consumers have more choice. Their tastes can change more rapidly. They can seek out better quality goods, and ones that are less generic and standardized. The speed of technological change was increased, at least partly because of the increases in competition, as was the speed of transportation and communication. The boat was rocked, and it seemed that US companies couldn't get moving fast enough to change with the times. This is not too surprising if you know anything about large, bureaucratic organizations. Vertically and horizontally integrated hierarchies are great at doing the same things over and over again—efficiently (in the narrow sense), predictably, and reliably. But this only works when your environment remains predictable and stable. Once your environment becomes *turbulent*, and you need to adapt and innovate to change with the times, big and bureaucratic is a hindrance. The old traditional model would no longer do, and so this period is seen to be another major turning point for business organizations that has gone on to affect how other organizations (e.g., government) operate as well.

When it comes to characterizing what changed and how, therein we run into some different interpretations. By many accounts we entered a new age of economic organizations that is dominated by *network* principles, rather than either *market* or *hierarchy*. This is often called *Post-Fordism*, in contrast to *Fordism*—after Henry Ford, of course—which is a term frequently used as shorthand for describing fully vertically integrated mass production. This orientation tends to be more common among those who see economic forms as being driven by the best business practices in terms of competition and efficiency. In contrast, there are interpretations that have been called *Neo-Fordist*.[2] The neo- prefix just means new, so the idea is that the same old large business format still dominates everything, but just in new form. Things on the surface have changed, but beneath the surface the idea is that all of the negative aspects (negative externalities) of hierarchy have been intensified. The competing orientations mirror efficiency (Chapter 4) versus power (Chapter 5) arguments for understanding how organizations get their form.

Post-Fordism

To get the picture with Post-Fordism, it might be easiest to recall the discussion in Chapter 5 regarding the contrast that Charles Perrow described between the Lowell and Philadelphia models of textile production. In the Lowell mills all of the eggs are in one basket, so to speak. One business sinks a lot of capital into a very specific and vertically integrated way of producing goods and doing business for a mass market. Your *sunk costs* in this model are so high that it becomes very hard to change over to doing anything else. The Lowell model was built on the availability of cheap cotton (thanks to slave labor in the South), along with a standardized process for handling it, and large stable mass markets. And as long as all aspects of the system remained stable and standardized, it was able to efficiently turn out cheap cotton cloth. It all worked great as long as you can take in round pegs and stick them in round holes and then pump out round products—so to speak. But if any part of the system changed, nothing would work. Everything was connected to everything else, and significantly dictated by a rigid, expensive, and inflexible production system. Changing to square pegs (e.g., from cotton to wool) was not in the cards. As long as the round pegs keep rolling in, and the round products can be marketed, all is well and economies of scale are efficient.

These limitations were not present in the Philadelphia textile industry. Recall that it was dominated by smaller, more specialized businesses utilizing more skilled labor, developing fewer sunk costs, and faced with various options with regards to production technologies. This is why it could be called a *flexible production* model. If the incoming pegs went from round to square, it was comparatively easy to drop whatever you were doing and shift to something else. And it was still possible to do mass production of cheap goods for a mass market even if that meant teaming up—temporarily—with some of your competitors. But you didn't need to be married to that strategy, and could still easily shift to something else. As the conventional wisdom came to have it, US

---

[2]The terminology here is not entirely precise or institutionalized. The use of the term Post-Fordism is rather common, while Neo-Fordism not so much, and sometimes they are folded together. I am merely using it to make a distinction that will be clarified as the chapter unfolds.

businesses were basically operating in Lowell mode when they crashed into the 1970s economic turbulence. And when they needed to go from round to square pegs, and then maybe over to triangles and then to ovals, they couldn't easily do it. As such, what was needed was a whole change in the logic of doing business. Being large and integrated wasn't going to work because it meant that you couldn't easily adjust and adapt to changing technologies or changing consumer demands, especially when there were a growing number of competitors trying to do exactly that. US companies had lost their ability to *control markets*, and thus had to learn how to *compete* in them instead. But this requires becoming more flexible and adaptable which is not the specialty of large, integrated bureaucracies. So what started to be observed and actively advocated by economists and business consultants were new kinds of organizational forms that operated more in Philadelphia rather than Lowell mode.

Some Inspiration from the *Japanese Model*

As noted, one of the important reasons that traditional US companies were struggling was because of foreign competition and, especially in certain industries, the most prominent competitors were Japanese companies. And when US corporations and management scientists went to take a look at how these companies were doing business what they found was something that seemed quite different. It has gone by many names—the *Japanese Style of Management (JSM)*, *Toyotaism*, *The Toyota Production System (TPS)*, *Japanese Lean Production (JLP)*, or now, more generally, just *Lean Production (LP)*. The different terms can sometimes be used just depending on the context of the discussion whether focused mostly on production techniques (JLP or LP), or on the more general system of organizing and managing as coupled with production techniques (JSM or Toyotaism). The Toyota references are common because Toyota is seen to have been a foremost pioneer in lean production in the auto industry. For our purposes, it doesn't matter much which terms one uses. I'll generally just refer to *JSM* because the management and production technique aspects are inseparable. And by whatever name is used, it quickly became a common reference point, or guidepost, in the management sciences and many US industries.

For starters, Japanese industrial firms did not operate as *vertically integrated hierarchies*. Rather companies operated as members of *keiretsus*, which translates from Japanese as "headless combine." The *keiretsus* are business networks of companies that lie at different locations along supply chains in the case of *vertical keiretsus* or in different industries in the case of *horizontal kieretsus*. Thus they are akin to vertically integrated companies or conglomerates, but they operate a bit like mutual aid societies where technically independent companies operate cooperatively for collective success. Coordination of their activities is not done by the bureaucracy—the visible hand of management—but rather by continual communication, mutual consultation, and trust. In terms introduced in Chapter 5, their relations are all about business oriented toward markets, but they operate with a very strong dose of *community*.

On the inside of companies things were also done much differently from the US hierarchical style in that it also included a lot more community-style relations. The most studied companies were likely in the auto industry, partly because by the 1980s US automakers started to actively cooperate with

Japanese auto makers, and to copy the *JSM* in their own operations. Japanese auto companies certainly used versions of assembly lines with a great deal of automation which inevitably dictates a good deal to workers via formally rationalized processes. But the organization and management of work was much different. Most notably, workers operated in *self-managed work teams*, and those teams had a great deal of discretion over how their work was to get done. Indeed, built into the job was the idea that workers themselves *should* oversee how their tasks get done and to continually work out better ways to do it all. This is rooted in an overriding work philosophy called *kaizen* which translates to "improvement." More generally these days you will see reference to what are called *continuous improvement* philosophies. In formally rationalized business, the blueprint is laid out at the beginning by management and followed day after day after day by workers. In the JSM, today things should be done differently from yesterday—because it should be done *better* today than yesterday. And it is not management who leads this process. It is the workers in those self-managed work teams. Partly for this reason, workers were not prescribed highly narrow tasks but had multiple skills and could rotate to multiple different tasks in production. All team members knew how to do all of the tasks for their given area of operation. Thus, workers were skilled and able to control important aspects of their own work tasks. This shift in social organization was necessary to go along with technical aspects of Japanese car production.

The traditional Fordist style of mass production relied on single purpose machines. This meant, for example, that an auto assembly line could only produce one model of car. Just as with the Lowell mills, production lines were *inflexible*. Employees were also highly specialized, trained to do only one or a few tasks. This also meant separate personnel responsible for things like machine maintenance and changing out machines when production changes needed to be made. It was all very time consuming and costly to make changes. Toyota, as the organization generally seen as having first perfected *lean production*, was an early pioneer in adopting multipurpose machines which could be more easily changed to handle different production tasks. Production workers were trained not only to operate the machinery, but also to do machine maintenance and changing machine set-ups to alter what was being produced. This greatly reduced the time and costs involved in changing what was being made, along with that required for the upkeep of the equipment. Japanese auto companies *could* change from round to square pegs and with minimal time and cost. This is integral to *flexible production* (a.k.a. *flexible specialization, mass customization*). It is also inseparable from the need for teams of multiskilled workers, and thus flexibility was built into both the humans and the machines.

With increased responsibility over their work areas and relatively high skill levels came increased attention to product quality all along the way. In the Japanese system this is generally called *jidoka* which basically means automation that is overseen by human intelligence. A good deal of production would certainly be automated, but as skilled teams working in groups it would be up to the production workers to watch out for and flag any problems that occur during production. The goal is to always try to achieve *zero defects* in all aspects of production. Work teams can, in fact, stop a production line if things go awry so that things can be set back straight before defects get sent along down the line. This is generally said to be integral to the higher quality of goods that were being turned out by Japanese companies. This policy and practice of constant quality monitoring is now generally referred to as *Total Quality Management (TQM)*, a continuing staple of activities seen as crucial in best management practices.

Another important characteristic of the JSM is called *Just in Time (JIT)* production and inventory management. The idea is to have all facets of production perfectly coordinated so that whatever is needed along the way is provided in just the right quantities at just the right times and in just the right places. A typical mass production system operates with *buffers*—or extra stock—in terms of all of the things needed for production. Buffers provide assurance that production speed isn't affected by things like defective parts or slowdowns in other parts of the production system or supply chain. Buffered systems are often called *just-in-case* systems because things are kept around just in case they are needed. Lean production does away with this. This applies to both internal processes in terms of work flow across different areas, and also to the means of getting supplies to a work site. A Japanese car manufacturing plant, for example, did not maintain a large inventory warehouse full of buffers of needed parts. Rather it had a steady stream of deliveries with parts arriving from suppliers—ideally—*just in time* for them to be used. This is where operating in networks of companies becomes so important because you need to know that your suppliers and distributors are reliable and supportive of your own success. The visible hand of management coordinating systems by giving orders is replaced by visible teams of different businesses operating by mutual regard and active cooperation. Of course, with this kind of system in place glitches can occur which makes it all the more important that workers have the ability to stop production lines so that problems can be addressed.

What all of this amounts to is the ability to produce a wide variety of goods that are of high quality. But all of that variety and quality does not come with higher costs as one might suspect. The ultimate guiding principle is *muda*—minimizing costs by the elimination of waste: wasted time, wasted materials, wasted efforts, and so on. Without JIT inventory management you have to maintain costly extra facilities and equipment for warehousing, along with extra staff to manage inventory, so that took care of a lot of waste. Operating on a TQM basis means that quality inspection is constantly being done by production teams rather than after the fact by a separate staff of "quality inspectors." The latter strategy uses up a lot of time and money in the form of a separate staff and extra process. Traditional quality inspection also tended to be based only on a sampling of finished product, so it was normal for at least some number of defects to get by. TQM reduces defect rates and thus the associated losses, all without separate staff and inspection process. The fact that production workers deal with their own equipment maintenance and setups drops another set of separate and costly job designations for machine maintenance and changeovers. This also saves a great deal of time when changes do need to be made, and limits the downtimes associated with changeovers. That all adds up to much higher *capacity utilization*—or, simply maximizing the extent to which you achieve the highest possible level of output given whatever your theoretical capacity is. And it partly did so by using previously untapped capacities of labor—aspects of the *variable costs*. In other words, the JSM maximized efficiency (in the narrow economic sense of lowest cost per unit), and did so better than those Chandlerian bureaucracies.

In short, the way of the future for efficiency was not to be the large, vertically integrated bureaucracy with narrowly defined jobs, highly specific and formalized work procedures, and thus low to semi-skilled workers. The future would instead belong to more specialized companies, operating in cooperation with networks of buyers and suppliers with relatively low levels of strict, Weberian bureaucracy at the level of work on the shop floor, and a more highly skilled labor force that is granted some level of autonomy. These ideas emerging from the study of the JSM ended up running strongly parallel to other developments of the time in the study of industrial organization.

Some Inspiration from the "Rediscovery" of Industrial Districts

In the post-1970s period as big business was struggling, we started to see the emergence of new, vibrant, and growing industries that were operating in much different form. The most prominent was probably in the computing industry, where small startup businesses seemed to be producing much of the innovation and vibrancy for the industry. If you wanted to find some innovation, dynamism and vibrancy in the United States you wouldn't go visit Ford's River Rouge assembly line full, as it was, of vertical integration and bureaucratic controls. Rather, you'd go visit the Silicon Valley. The Silicon Valley is an area on the south side of the San Francisco Bay in California that has been a world-wide center for innovation in the information technology sector of the economy. It is certainly home base to a lot of now-industry giants such Facebook, Netflix, and Google, but it is well known as a place where a great deal of the IT innovation that we witness daily gets its start from small startup companies. In fact, many of those now-giant IT companies began as small startup companies—often from something like a garage or college dorm room—rather than from the research and development (R&D) labs of large corporate entities. And while the newer IT giants tend to be "giants" in terms of things like stock value or numbers of customers, they don't tend to be "giants" in the old way where they are vertically integrated and employ large labor forces.[3]

The businesses of the Silicon Valley tend to be quite specialized, working in specific aspects of computer software or various aspects of hardware. But it isn't just IT companies that you find in the Valley. One of the largest reasons that this region became the center for all of this activity is that it is where Stanford University is located, and Stanford researchers have been involved all along. In addition there are a host of other businesses that offer specialized support services for things like legal issues, marketing, accounting, and business consulting. It is a dense thicket of largely specialized companies that have expertise in and around the IT industry. This tends to both attract and to cultivate a large labor force of highly skilled workers in the IT industry. It is the kind of place where the future is being invented and developed.

At the same time that the Silicon Valley was gaining attention, Italian economists, most notably Giacomo Becattini, were reviving work done around the turn of the twentieth century by British economist Alfred Whitehead

---

[3]This does vary quite a bit. As of 2020 Apple, for example, had about 137,000 employees worldwide, and does quite a bit of vertical integration. But none of it rivals, for example, the old-style labor force sizes of degrees of vertical integration in the auto industry. It can also change frequently as companies may still decide to do things like buy up (or sell off) suppliers or assemblers and the like.

regarding what have come to be called *industrial districts*. Whitehead's work was based on standard industrial production models found at his time in nineteenth-century Britain, while Becattini's work was focused on ongoing changes in Italian industry, and the re-emergence of industrial districts there. Knowledge of this work outside of a relatively small number of Italian economists was initially limited by the fact that all of the work was published in Italian. However, in 1984, an associate of Becattini, US based political scientist Charles Sabel along with economist Michael Piore brought this work—and thus the notion of the industrial district—to international attention with the 1984 publication of their book *The Second Industrial Divide*.[4] Charles Perrow's description of the Philadelphia textile industry and his argument regarding potential alternative paths to hierarchy presented briefly in Chapter 5 drew quite a bit from this book. Soon after Piore and Sabel's work, Michael Porter of the Harvard Business School published another landmark book called *The Competitive Advantage of Nations*[5] which, while not specifically focused on industrial districts, solidified the attention of both economists and those in management studies on the idea of industrial districts as an old, but now becoming new again, alternative form of industry organization to the vertically integrated hierarchy. What I've given so far is obviously just a list of stuff that doesn't tell you much. For our purposes here we don't need (or have room for) a detailed literature review of the re-emergence of academic and business world attention to industrial districts. The important point is that it did occur and was very much inspired by people trying to come to grips with the crisis period of the 1970s and what could be done about it.

So what is an industrial district? Generally speaking it is a geographically identifiable area where the economy is dominated by a particular kind of industry, such as the IT industry in the contemporary Silicon Valley, or textiles in the Lancashire region of Britain which was crucial in the Industrial Revolution and described by Alfred Marshall. At its core is a dense population of *small to medium sized enterprises (SMEs)* that generally specialize in a particular aspect of the industry rather than being vertically integrated. They are typically set up to engage in flexible rather than mass production, and most will not be producing for a standard consumer market, but for other firms forward of them along the supply chain. Being specialized and flexible, there is a heavy reliance on skilled labor, so an industrial district tends to attract and to generate a concentrated pool of expertise in whatever the industry is. Furthermore, this tends to develop more and more strongly over time as the area comes to have a culture and atmosphere strongly tied to work in the industry. As such, these regions become centers of innovation. The concentration of particular kinds of knowledge, skills, and information sharing makes them a crucible for the cutting edge in terms of information about where the industry is headed in the future, and the latest forms of technologies. This frontiers of what is coming next are "in the air," so innovations are frequent and spread rapidly.

The relations among businesses in these areas tend to be both cooperative and competitive—the term *cooperative competition* is frequently applied. On the horizontal dimension, businesses that specialize in the same things do compete with each other, but can also cooperate. This can come in direct form by companies passing work back and forth between each other as

---

[4]Piore and Sabel, 1984.
[5]Porter, 1990.

contingencies might dictate, alliances where different capabilities might be shared, and in the formation and maintenance of local professional and trade associations set up to further the interests of the industry, profession, or trade. On the vertical dimension, since companies are specialized they rely on sub-contracting for needs outside of what they themselves do, but it tends not to operate in market form. Rather relations among businesses occur in networks of ongoing cooperative relations. There is generally a widespread sense of interdependence—an understanding that the success of each depends on the success of all, even despite the co-existence of competitive relations. Because of various forms of close cooperation, the results of vertical integration—economies of scale and efficiently produced goods and services—can be achieved by coordination among distinct firms at different locations along a supply chain without any visible hand of management to direct everything.

In addition to the organizations working directly in the industry, you also find a myriad of satellite organizations that offer support services. This includes, for instance, such things as financial, marketing, legal, and accounting functions where service providers are highly attuned to the issues and needs of the particular industry. They tend to be located near (or generate) research institutes and training centers, sometimes based in universities, which contributes both to innovation and the maintenance of a skilled labor force. The supportive infrastructure often extends to local governments that have a direct interest in the economic vitality of the region (as all governmental organizations do). Taken together, this kind of dense population of businesses and associated supporting structures operating in the same industry is frequently called *agglomeration*. The word itself simply means a large collection of different things, and is most useful for its contrast to vertical and horizontal integration. Agglomeration allows all of the different elements to add up to more than just the sum of the parts, producing what are called *scale externalities*.[6] The idea is that my having all of these businesses together with dense network relations among them, more value is produced than could be produced if they were all separate and operating along in something more like a market mode.

There is not a lot formal integration where all of these things are located in the same organization and controlled and coordinated by the visible hand of management. Nor are they coordinated by the invisible hand of the market. But there is a great deal of coordination provided by networking links. As far as our narrative of the moment goes, when accounts of the structure of industrial districts were hitting the front pages of business and organizational studies periodicals, the industrial districts looked far more like the Japanese *kieretsu* than the vertically integrated Fordist production model, and thus far more suited to handling the economic conditions of the time.

Some Push from Financial Markets[7]

A central part of the managerial revolution introduced in Chapter 4 had to do with how companies were controlled. Common sense ideas have it that companies are controlled by their founders and owners. But once companies grew to be large and complicated enterprises, the ownership became dispersed among many stockholders (whether the stocks are publicly traded or not) and

---

[6]Do not confuse this with *externalities of scale* introduced in Chapter 5 which are more associated with integration rather than agglomeration.

[7]This section owes a large debt to Davis, 2016, see especially Chapter 5.

control came to be the domain of professional managers who were more employees than owners. This was the *separation of ownership from control*, that characterized the age of "hierarchy"—an age where the stockholders of businesses were not actually all that relevant. Control lay instead with that visible hand of professional managers. But this situation of *corporate governance* largely came to an end right around the same time as all of these other changes.

You'll also recall from Chapter 4 that vertical and horizontal integration were followed by *conglomeration* as businesses would branch out into unrelated industries. This generally occurred by acquiring existing companies, and the post–World War II period, in particular the 1960s, was the high point of the growth of conglomerates. At that time, the dominant thinking was that conglomeration could produce various kinds of *synergies* among companies so that their combination could produce value that was greater than the sum of the parts—something similar to what one might see from agglomeration. (There were also very low interest rates which helped quite a bit with financing acquisitions.) Given the general prosperity of the post-War period there wasn't much to shake up this situation. But as the 1970s competitiveness crisis dragged on and large integrated firms struggled, the idea came to be that companies had pursued growth for its own sake, not because growth had made them economically efficient or competitive. One main reason to pursue growth rather than efficiency would have been the old one of increasing market control. But it was also directly to the benefit of company management as compensation (things like salaries and stock options) was often strongly tied to business size.

However, from the point of view of the company's owners—its shareholders—this would often be undesirable largely because of a thing called the *conglomerate discount*. It is frequently the case that financial markets tend to value diversified businesses that are all tied together under the same company as less valuable than what the value would be if all of the companies were separated to stand alone. In other words, even if some manner of conglomeration does produce synergies that create higher value, this doesn't mean that it gets reflected in stock prices. Quite the opposite. This made conglomerates attractive targets for *corporate takeovers*, where enough stock is purchased by some actor (business or individual) to gain control of the company. The conglomerate could then be broken up and its parts sold off, often for a hefty profit. In these instances, shareholders benefit while management suffers. The interests of owners and managers were are odds in this regard, but corporate management tended to have the upper hand in terms of corporate control. In Robert Michels' terms (Chapter 2), they were the organized minority (oligarchy), while shareholders were generally the disorganized majority. There were also federal level rules in place that both incentivized conglomeration and inhibited takeovers. But this changed starting in the 1980s.

First, the 1960s *conglomerate boom*—as it came to be called—is often seen as a response to anti-trust rules that were put in place by the Celler–Kefauver Act of 1950 which greatly limited the ability to do horizontal integration. So if growth was a goal (which it was, persistently, since the turn of the century), then it was done by acquiring companies outside of one's own industry. In addition, many states had laws that restricted hostile corporate takeovers. So there were incentives in place for conglomeration along with protection against takeovers in the event that companies held undervalued assets because of the conglomerate discount. But the anti-trust rules that limited horizontal mergers were relaxed by the Reagan administration early in the 1980s, and in 1982 the Supreme Court, in *Edgar v. MITE*, issued a ruling that struck down most of the state laws aimed at preventing takeovers. As such, the legal incentives and protections that encouraged conglomeration fell by the wayside. The result of this was a huge wave of corporate takeovers and horizontal mergers during the 1980s. In the eyes of the financial markets being integrated and diversified became a liability, signaling inefficiencies and undervalued assets. The new rule became that the best companies would be focused only on their most essential core functions, products, and/or services. The logic seemed to be that it is best to not be a jack of all trades rather than a master of one.

This push was only enhanced as there came to be a major shift in how corporations were controlled. Stockholders, of course, are not only individual persons. They are also other organizations, called *institutional investors*, which include such things as pension funds, mutual funds, and banks. In the context of the takeover wave of the 1980s shareholders were frequently the winners in acquisitions and mergers, while managers tended to resist them as they could easily lose control, status, compensation, or even their jobs. The rise of institutional investors meant that shareholders were no longer the disorganized minority (except for your everyday individuals who buy stock), and we entered an age of *shareholder activism* in which investors seek more and more control over how companies are managed.

For our purposes here, the most important shifts have to do with two things. First, there has always been a question about who or what large, publicly traded corporations are supposed to serve. Should they benefit all of the companies *stakeholders*, such as employees and the communities within which companies operate? Should they be of general social benefit (as the old-style chartered companies were)? During the period of the dominance of hierarchy, this was largely the idea. Corporations were supposed to be good citizens, and "what is good for GM is good for the country" (or was supposed to be) was how the old saying went. But with the rise of shareholder activism there was a strong shift to the idea that corporations should be about one thing, and one thing only—generating *shareholder value*. While this can mean several things, such as paying out strong, sustained dividends over time, the central focus tends to be stock price. Second, shareholders were able to gain more say in technical details about how companies are run including how it is that management (the "employees" of shareholders, after all) is compensated. Since share prices are so crucial, this meant tying executive compensation much more to stock prices rather than to business size. If you turn managers into shareholders, then the interests become aligned, and companies will be geared much more strongly to achieving the highest possible stock price.

Given everything else that had gone on, this didn't mean big, integrated (except, perhaps horizontally), and conglomerated. It largely meant becoming as lean as possible, meaning finding ways to produce healthy profits with the lowest costs which, in reality, translates to having as little done inside of the company as possible. In other words, it meant *Nikefication*,[8] first discussed in Chapter 3. Holding a lot of expensive assets and carrying large labor forces became liabilities in the eyes of investors, so there came to be a strong push to

---

[8]Davis, 2016: Chapter 6.

become small in terms of the assets and labor force that are carried by the company, and to become much more focused and specialized.

The Networked Company

If you take this shift in emphasis coming from the financial markets and filter that through all of the attention to things like the JSM and Industrial Districts, then you land at a major shift in thinking about the best way to organize a business (or anything else for that matter). A business should not try to do it all, but instead should only focus on its *core competencies*—that is, whatever it does best. Newly established companies should work that way, while the old integrated dinosaurs should spin off any of their divisions that do not relate to their core functions. Decide what you want to be—and be it. Supply chain needs should now be met, not by vertical integration, but by way of subcontracting arrangements. But given what was going on in terms of things like the Japanese model and the revival of interest in Industrial Districts, the prominent contracting strategy was not to be that one acquires things from the *market*.

While meeting your needs through market transactions certainly provides for a great deal of flexibility, it can also introduce a great deal of slop as inefficiencies are created by *transaction costs*. We will discuss transaction costs in more depth in Chapter 9, but for now simply note that any time you buy something the actual costs include more than just the price that you paid. You had to use time, for example, to arrange and complete the transaction. And perhaps what you received in return was not appropriate given whatever your actual needs are, or maybe you just got cheated. For Chandler this is among the reasons that hierarchy can sometimes be better than markets because then you can achieve purposeful coordination in one organization rather than operating with a multitude of contract negotiations among separate actors in the market. But integrating also weighs you down, and makes it harder to change, adapt, and innovate. So rather than relying on either market transactions or internalizing multiple functions, you establish various kinds of partnerships with other businesses in the form of long term relationships—in *networks*. Your partners remain separate companies, so there is no hierarchy (except whatever you institute inside of your own core). But it is not merely a market either because you don't go shopping for your needs but aim to build up long term relationships with your business partners in which you get to know one another's capabilities and establish long term relations of trust and reciprocity. Companies become interdependent over time, but without necessarily being tied under the same legal structure. As first introduced in Chapter 5, the building up of relations of familiarity, trust, and cooperation represents strong infusion of *community*.

Such arrangements can be more or less formalized. They might be based simply on hand-shake kinds of agreements that have no formal existence at all. They can also take the form of what are called *strategic alliances*, typically defined by what is called a *memorandum of understanding (MOU)*, or *memorandum of agreement (MOA)*. MOUs/MOAs put down the basic terms of an agreement in writing, but not in the form of a legally binding contract, and the organizations involved remain legally separate. Formal contracts can, of course, be drawn up but this occurs at the cost of decreasing the flexibility of all parties to the agreement. More formal arrangements that don't weigh down companies with extra assets can occur through *joint ventures (JVs)*. In a JV different organizations team up to share various capabilities, but do so by establishing a separate organization to house whatever the project or business activity is.

In doing business this way, there is still a lot of market activity going on as you will do a lot of buying and selling. And there can still be a good deal of hierarchy within companies. However, the idea is that what goes on here that makes it different is business relationships are really *"neither market nor hierarchy."*[9] Reducing the degree of hierarchy by not vertically integrating greatly increases everyone's flexibility, so you get the advantages of markets in terms of being flexible and adaptive. Markets are based on the spot transactions, and so are highly flexible. No one is locked into anything, so change and adaptability are easy. But transaction costs can be a problem, so relationships that get built with business partners are the things that minimize on transaction costs. You do give up some degree of flexibility and choice because you now have normative obligations to your partners. But you still maintain a great deal of flexibility relative to vertical integration, while gaining some of those advantages in terms of better coordination. And in the eyes of financial markets, where that is relevant, you can remain focused on your own specialty and as light as possible on assets and labor costs which just makes it easier to turn healthy profits.

But it is not merely in your overall business model where hierarchy should be reduced. It should also be reduced inside of your own organization. In turbulent environments where organizations have to be able to change quickly and adapt to new circumstances, a lot of bureaucracy won't do. Rather than relying on standardized rules and processes, it is far better to rely on skilled and knowledgeable people who can solve problems and come up with new ways of doing things, as illustrated by the JSM *kaizen* philosophy. This implies a good deal more consultation among people in an organization rather than order giving and order taking. And the information that is flowing around needs to be more horizontal than vertical. Bureaucratic hierarchies are said to too often create *silos* inside of the organization where people in different divisions don't know what is going on in others and this can create problems of information and coordination, especially in rapidly changing markets. So the idea is that organizational structures need to become less bureaucratic, run less by authority and more by mutual consultation. Work processes needed to be far less "McDonaldized" with more discretion and decision-making left in the hands of employees. In essence, network rather than hierarchy logic should dominate relations both inside and outside of an organization. Hierarchy, integration, and bureaucracy were now out.

The IT Boost

All of the foregoing was (and continues to be) helped along—or perhaps one might say rocketed along—by the development of computing and information technology (IT) because IT tools make coordination among various actors so much faster and easier. The most powerful aspect of this was the development of the globalized internet. Part of the reason that industrial districts can be so dynamic and vibrant is because of geography. Physical closeness provides for easy information sharing and collaboration because it is easy for people to get together. But the internet can often make geography quite irrelevant. To be

---

[9]This phrase is from the title of one of the more widely cited academic papers of the time by Powell, 1990.

sure, what it allows is not completely unique. The telegraph and soon after the telephone were also seen as a miracles of their time in terms of the diminished the importance of geography, providing different actors the ability to communicate and coordinate their activities without much regard for geography. Even the US postal service was seen as a bit miraculous, and the precursor to today's Amazons was the Sears Roebuck & Co. selling goods nationwide via paper catalog by mail order. So it's possible to see certain things about the internet age as being continuous with the past. But it also brought a radical transformative potential. In terms of the speed and complexity of information handling, and the ability of people to coordinate and collaborate without regards to location, todays' IT world is monumentally different. We can coordinate action in real time at locations all over the globe.

The Image of the Virtual Corporation

I'm going to violate the sensibilities of at least some in organizational studies by introducing the concept of the *virtual corporation* (a.k.a. *virtual firm* or *virtual organization*) by talking about a company that is assisted by new forms of information technology, but does not exist by virtue of them. I have a friend who runs a small construction company. He operates as a general contractor (GC) which means that he doesn't specialize in any specific aspects of construction, such as foundations or framing or plumbing or electrical work or so on. His company makes whole projects happen. They'll build you a deck or remodel your bathroom and kitchen, put an addition on your house or even build you a house. But it's a very small company. At any given time he has from two to four full time employees, occasionally with some part time workers mixed in. It's certainly not a big, publicly traded corporation, but just a small, local Limited Liability Company (LLC). The company recently did build a reasonably large house in the space of about six months. It was about 4,000–5,000 square feet with a price tag of something like three-quarters of a million dollars. And they built if from the ground up—all the way from excavation and foundation work through to the roof with all of the electrical and plumbing and HVAC and sheetrock and painting and so on. How, one might wonder, could a tiny company with just a few employees do all of that? Would they really be able to hold all of the assets (tools and equipment) needed for all aspects of the work? Could these few people possibly hold all of the necessary licensing to legally perform electrical, plumbing, and HVAC work? Or even have the time to get it all done within a reasonable timeframe?

The answer, of course, is that this isn't how it works. The company employees do have multiple forms of expertise and skill, to be sure. They do most of the carpentry, for example. And the company and its employees do own a fair quantity of various kinds of tools and equipment. But they certainly don't have enough of any of it to actually accomplish all aspects of the building trades. And this is often so even if the *project* is smaller than an entire house. We could be talking about a 500 square foot, $25,000 addition to a house, and it would still require things that lie outside of what the company can do in-house. The needs that can't be fulfilled by the company itself are, of course, met by sub-contractors. My friend knows many of the sub-contractors in the construction trades in our area and maintains relations with them. They all know each other and have each other's phone numbers and they all have "history." When he gets a *project*, such as whole house to build from soup to nuts, he becomes what is called a *lead firm* and enlists a temporary network of subcontracting firms. He does have to do something resembling "shopping" as one would in a market because in order for him to provide cost and time estimates on jobs, he needs cost and time estimates from his subcontractors. But he is not opening the Yellow Pages or going online to Angie's List and flying blind. He already knows all of these subcontractors, their technical capabilities, degree of reliability, what kinds of rates they charge, and so on. And it is the same with his suppliers of building materials. He is already very busy just keeping up with issues on various projects, putting together bids, meeting with clients and architects and building inspectors, and doing billing and the like. To also have to spend a lot time "shopping" and monitoring the quantity and quality of what he gets from suppliers would put things over the top.

Could he do some vertical integration, and add many of these things as regular parts of his company? Could he, for instance, hire a licensed electrician and plumber as employees? Sure, but in doing that the company now loses a lot of flexibility. In order to continue to maintain all of the assets and his labor force, he'd have to always be building full, and probably quite large, houses. He couldn't have a deck project going alongside of an addition alongside of a restaurant remodel. By being able to assemble just what is needed at any given time based on the current market for projects, he is able to change form and adapt very rapidly. His primary role through all of this is, once again, as the *lead firm* that assembles and coordinates all of the different activities along the way. In the case of a large project, such as an entire house, he puts and holds together what could be called the equivalent of a fully vertically integrated construction company. But it only lasts for as long that *this project* is ongoing, and then it disburses. It ceases to exist as an organization, and next week, for some other project, he can put together some other *virtual organization*.

These days, the image that I've just delivered is normally not what people mean when they refer to a *virtual corporation* (or *firm* or *organization* or *company*). More often than not, if one uses the term virtual it is a reference to something regarding cyberspace or other aspects of information technology (IT), but the actual meaning of the word is broader than that. It roughly just means not truly a thing, but might was well be the thing as you can't tell the difference in the effects. Thus a company can achieve the results of vertical integration without, in fact, existing in vertically integrated form. But the idea is almost always associated with IT because the notion of the *virtual corporation* came about as all of these Post-Fordist trends were running into the development and emergence of the internet. Among the most widely cited roots of the concept came from a 1993 *Business Week* article by then-executive editor John Byrne:

> The virtual corporation is a temporary network of independent companies—suppliers, customers, even erstwhile rivals—linked by information technology to share skills, costs, and access to one another's markets. It will have neither central office, nor organization chart. It will have no hierarchy, no vertical integration.[10]

Thus, if the term virtual corporation is being used, it normally does refer to internet enabled interactions among firms that, presumably, would not be possible otherwise. Yet, it also does pay to keep in mind that a lot of things

---

[10]Byrne, 1993: 99.

happening these days will be more quantitatively than qualitatively different. The virtual firm isn't new—but it has incredibly powerful new tools of communication and coordination that make it possible to put together virtual firms much more quickly and without regards to geography. My friend's options for subcontracting are largely limited to the immediate geographic area. But for many business purposes these days you can use the entire planet, and pick up and drop subcontractors just as quickly and easily across the globe as across town.

It is this convergence of the general move toward networked forms of business and the emergence of the internet that has been significant in producing the explosion of what Gerald Davis dubbed *Nikefication* (noted above and in Chapter 3). Recall that a company like Nike doesn't actually manufacture any of its products, and only does some of its own sales. It is primarily a design and marketing company—apparently its *core competency*. Most everything else that it needs, which certainly includes a great deal of manufacturing, is carried out by subcontractors, normally in low wage places. And the internet obviously makes it easy. Apparel designs and plans can be easily shipped around the globe at the speed of light. Business services can be picked up and dropped at will. And if Nike doesn't like the terms it is getting from subcontractors in, say, China, it can always shift its contracts to other subcontractors in, perhaps, Indonesia or Vietnam. Instantly. At the click of a mouse.

At this point in time, the internet allows one to go even farther than does Nike, and some people have. Why even design and market your products yourself? Why not contract out for those services as well. If you wanted to *you* could (try to) start a global sports apparel company right now with nothing but your internet enabled communications device and—probably—some manner of funding. Use a credit card. Or perhaps just *crowdfund* some financing by using any of the myriad of web sites that make this possible (e.g., Kickstarter, GoFundMe, Indiegogo). With some working capital you just have to start finding contractors. Find your design and marketing firms. They're all over the web. With that ready to go, find your suppliers, distributors, manufacturers, and perhaps just sell your stuff via Amazon. And/or, you can just have a sales and marketing company set up your own company website for doing sales. You can start what Davis called a *pop-up company*.[11] While there is always at least some degree of continuity with the past, we've come a long way from Henry Ford—and thus we are now in a new era. The one that came *after* Fordism—or, as you already know: *Post-Fordism*.

There is often a lot of optimism, excitement, and cheerleading for the Post-Fordist trends. The *new economy*, as it is sometimes called, is much more dynamic and innovative. Its flexibility and greater levels of innovation make it that much better at serving the needs of customers who are now able to be much more picky and, thus, much more uniquely satisfied than in our mass production past. Furthermore, now being global it allows much of the globe's population, historically excluded from the economic "progress" of the industrialized world to make it into the game. If you go back to the discussion in Chapter 5 regarding how history might have gone down a different path—toward an economy organized more in image of Industrial Districts rather than the Lowell mills and mill towns—we might have had a world with less concentrated wealth and

---

[11]Davis, 2016: 82.

power, and with fewer and smaller negative externalities. Perhaps we've actually made it there, albeit not as soon as we might have otherwise.

But there is plenty of dark side to Post-Fordism, and it may even be that dark sides are just as dark as those produced by the hierarchical form of the twentieth-century economy. Thus it is possible to tell the story in such a way that, beneath the surface of how this or that company, industry, or production process has emerged or has changed, is still the same old thing although in different form on its face. So one could say that we are now not in a period of Post-Fordism, but in a period of *Neo-Fordism*. It's *leaner*, to be sure in that many kinds of costs and waste have been reduced or eliminated. But it may also be *meaner*.

Neo-Fordism

Lean and mean is probably my favorite phrase for headlining a discussion of *Neo-Fordism*. It comes from the title of a 1994 book called *Lean and Mean: The Changing Landscape of Corporate Power in the Age of Flexibility*, by dissident economist Bennett Harrison. Along with his sometimes co-author, economist Barry Bluestone, he was among the most prominent critical voices throughout the period of the "leaning out" of US businesses. The dominating logic of the Post-Fordist discussion was that businesses changed form to become more efficient, and that meant becoming smaller, more focused and specialized, and less bureaucratic due to a higher reliance on skilled labor that is granted greater degrees of autonomy. There tended to be a celebration of a return to small business and entrepreneurship, which would also mean a decline in centralized economic power along with a general increase in economic opportunity. It sounds like a lot of "winning."

In *Lean and Mean* Harrison visits the central areas of discussion regarding Post-Fordism and does concur with the Post-Fordist idea that operating in networks is the new, dominant business form. However, beneath the surface of having multiple companies team up for projects without being in the same formal hierarchy, he saw the same old Fordist logic and dynamic of hierarchical control. It's just that it is now often *implicit hierarchy*, and operates by forms of control other than formal authority.

For example, in the JSM, described above, what one generally finds is a tiered structure of subcontractors that are *de facto* dependent on one powerful lead firm (such as Toyota) through *monopsony* power—a situation when there is only one buyer for companies, goods or services. (Or perhaps *oligopsony*, where there are only a few buyers.) While it is true that subcontractors might sometimes be supplying more companies than only a single lead firm, more often than not that lead firm accounts for so much of their business that they couldn't survive without them, so they are *de facto* under the control of the lead firm. And the tier system is quite hierarchical where suppliers at each tier are expected to manage the next tier down. The requirements for skilled labor also tend to drop as you move down tiers. Subcontractors performing the most complex and skilled tasks are located in the upper tiers, while the simplest, most labor intensive, and often unskilled labor is performed in the lowest tiers. It is these lower tiered contractors that can most easily be substituted, and thus are the least powerful. Thus these relationships, while they do take on a networked form, often rely on an *asymmetrical* dependence where the lead firm, in effect, does have power over the subcontractors. The industry is set up as what Harrison calls a *core and ring*, or *core and periphery*, structure—an imagery that we first encountered in Chapter 3 in the context of *labor market segmentation*.

As for the Silicon Valley, Harrison indicates that a closer look does not reveal a vast bubbling up of entrepreneurial spirit from small firms that provided the region with its origins and its character. Rather, the most significant dynamic in making the Silicon Valley what it became was the relationship between the US Government, especially the Department of Defense, and Stanford University. There was certainly a great deal of growth of *small to medium sized enterprises* (*SMEs*) in the 1980s, but much of that was pushed by venture capitalists looking to cash in on the next big thing rather than representing organic growth. In some respects, the growth of SMEs can be a form of outsourcing research and development activities in order to keep the associated costs and risks external to a company. And it was not just venture capital that got involved in financing the experimentation, but also global multinational companies, such as the giant Japanese multinationals Fujitsu and Kubota.

One might think that Hewlett-Packard (HP) provides a quintessential look at the Valley because it was started in a garage by Bill Hewlett and Dave Packard, both graduates of Stanford University. But HP was founded in the 1930s, early on in the hierarchy phase, and by the 1980s was a large multinational corporation engaged in its own acquisition activities in the Valley. It is not that no vestiges of the typical industrial district image could be found. But the character of the place largely does not, and never did, fit the typical pattern described in the literature on industrial districts. And where one did find the SME that has become successful, they might become one of the next giants, as HP did, and begin acquiring other companies. Or they become the next company that *gets acquired* by some larger entity. The small, innovative start-up strategy is often not to remain small and innovative, but to "get backed, get big, and get bought."[12]

This kind of pattern echoes what Harrison observed with regards to some of the dynamics inside of Italian industrial districts where the very success of SMEs make them attractive acquisitions for larger companies. For example, Harrison described the case of the Sasib Company of the Emilia-Romagna region of Italy. It was a medium sized firm (1,000 or so employees through the 1970s) that was one of the world's leading producers of tobacco packaging machinery operating in quintessential network form of SMEs in cooperative and competitive relations. It frequently operated as a lead firm for various contracts, and assembled whatever network of subcontractors was needed for a contract. But it would also sometimes act as subcontractor for some other lead firm. Its form of doing business, however, was changed when it was acquired by a holding company out of Milan, *Compagnie Industriali Riunite* (CIR), as part of CIR's more general strategy of going into the manufacture of food packaging machinery. Sasib soon ended up listed on the Milan stock exchange, later became a holding company itself, and then began to integrate by buying up many of its former business partners. The key factor involved was the same one that it has been since the rise of the corporate form and modern finance brought to us by US railroad companies—the availability to use ample capital to buy up suppliers, customers, and competitors.

---

[12]Entire business and consulting strategies exist for helping to do thing, including the "how to" advice books. I borrowed the phrase from Barrow, 2009.

In general for Harrison, a description of the global economy as moving toward being dominated by networks of small firms is simply a superficial reading because it is easy to observe the extent to which industries and their future directions are still a game of giant companies. This goes even for industries such as electronics where the image of the focused, innovative, and adaptive entrepreneurial firm should be ruling most of all. Against that notion he describes what came to be known as the "Grand Alliance" in the 1990s development of HDTV standards. In 1987 the Federal Communications Commission (FCC) put together an advisory committee to recommend standards for an HDTV system for the United States. Of the many proposals that were submitted, the possibilities came down to those proposed by three competing "teams," none of which represent small, entrepreneurial startups: AT&T allied with Zenith versus Philips, Sarnoff Labs, Thomson, and NBC versus General Instruments with MIT. But all of those organizations eventually threw in together to collaborate on a set of standards and split up the market for it among themselves. It was something like networked oligopolists becomes networked monopolists. So here we have a process instigated by the federal government and controlled and carried out by existing large corporations and research centers. And, while Harrison's analysis and this particular story are old, this is still not unusual across many industries. The speed and growing complexity of keeping up with changing times is real, and the networked form of business is now common as a way of being able to gain access to knowledge, capabilities, and markets. But we're often still seeing either collaborations among giants, or giants acquiring innovations by buying the companies that develop them.

Harrison's analysis is an old one, but not much about the central dynamics has changed. So, moving past Harrison's time and closer to the present, we can look at a company like Google which was a classic entrepreneurial Silicon Valley startup in 1998. But, of course, it grew to a near monopolistic internet search engine to the extent that "Google" emerged as a verb meaning to do an internet search. In 2015, it restructured itself and formed a separate company called Alphabet, Inc. which is now the parent company of Google and is one of the largest multinational conglomerates companies in the world. A main purpose of forming Alphabet, Inc. was to form a holding company for buying up smaller companies of which it now owns hundreds including, just to name a few (as of this writing), YouTube (video-sharing), Nest (smart-home products), FitBit (wearable fitness tracking), and Waze (mobile navigation application). What started as one of the World Wide Web's (WWW) most successful search engine companies has now morphed into a conglomerate getting into virtually all aspects of technology innovation and production, not by being innovative and developing things itself, but by waiting for others to do it and then buying them up with nothing other than access to large quantities of finance capital. *An old story by now, indeed.*

And it isn't just Google. Many aspects of the IT industry are controlled by just a few giants to the extent that there are shorthands for referring to them. The FAAGs, for example, refers to Facebook, Apple, Amazon, and Google. Or the "frightful five" which is the FAAGs with Microsoft added in. And while the IT industry is heavily concentrated—now globally—it isn't confined to that industry. Business professor Chris Carr has recently produced an entire book analyzing *Global Oligopoly*, as its title tells us. As just one way of summarizing, citing a 2016 report, he wrote

10% of the world's public companies generated 80% of all profits. Firms with more than $1bn revenue accounted for nearly 60% of total global revenues and 65% of market capitalization. [Mergers and acquisitions] were equivalent to about 3% of global GDP compared with 2% in 1990. Firms with over 250 employees accounted for over half of value-added in every country monitored by the Organization for Economic Cooperation and Development (OECD). In the USA, large companies created 58% of total employment; in Japan 47%; in the United Kingdom (UK) 46%; and in Germany 36%.[13]

And despite the fact that apparently some employment is being created by large companies, many of today's giants are only giant in terms of their economic power. The old industrial firms in railroads, steel, chemicals and the like were large in terms of economic power, but also in terms of the provision of employment. They needed large labor forces. But the newer giant IT and financial firms often have huge value with very few employees. As Carr noted, in 2016 Facebook's market capitalization per employee was $20.5 million as compared to $230,000 for General Motors[14]—which *used to be* the largest corporation in the world. This doesn't look very much like a widespread emergence of smaller businesses working in networks. Just leaner and meaner ones.

The idea here is not that bringing products and services to market has remained in vertically integrated form. The post-1970s shift to heavy reliance on subcontracting with business partners is not denied. But it doesn't look like the agglomerated industrial district of SMEs in cooperative and competitive relations along with more widespread opportunities for access to wealth and power. It looks like very large and powerful lead firms setting the pace and dictating terms to smaller and weaker ones. Thus we have the essence of what Harrison labeled *concentration without centralization*. As he aptly summarized at one point:

> *...the empirical evidence seems overwhelming that the evolving global system of joint ventures, supply chains, and strategic alliances in no sense constitutes a reversal—let alone a negation—of the 200-year-old tendency toward concentrated control within industrial capitalism, even if production activity is increasingly being decentralized and dispersed.[15]*

Businesses have become *leaner* in that they take on fewer things in house. But they have also become *meaner* in that everything has become potentially disposable, including workers.

Labor Market Dualization and Growing Inequality

We first encountered the effects of the decentralization and dispersion of production activity in Chapter 3 where I initially brought up Nikefication and referred to the post-1970s form of *labor market dualization*. The dominant focus in business and management circles when talking about leaning down to

---

[13]Carr, 2020: 5.

[14]Carr, 2020: 4.

[15]Harrison, 1994: p. 171.

concentrate only on core competencies has to do with things like how much more efficient, flexible, and innovative you can be if you specialize. And that very well may be true, at least some of the time. But if that was enough, and if the economic world was driven merely by the question of narrow economic efficiencies, then companies likely would have stayed smaller and more specialized all along. As Gerald Davis has observed with regards to Nikefi-cation, the strongest incentives to change for large companies may have come, not from better efficiencies, but from shareholder-value dominated financial markets which were heavily focused on *market capitalization* (a.k.a. *market cap*), itself heavily dependent on what it can show in terms of *return on assets (ROA)*. A company's market cap is just the total value of all shares of a company's stock, while the ROA is basically the ratio of profits to the total value of the assets a company holds. Higher profits with fewer assets translate to a higher ROA, which contributes to higher stock prices and thus a larger market cap. Leaving aside the language, all of this is pretty simple. What investors want to see is companies that are spending the least amount of money per dollar earned. What this amounts to is holding onto the things that make the real money, such as your brand recognition, while dropping things that don't bring a great deal to your *value chain*, such as routine manufacturing tasks. This just comes down to what kinds of things are easily replaced without hurting your ability to make sales.

All of that cutting companies down to their core competencies that became so fashionable and important beginning in the 1980s and 1990s often just meant cutting loose the lower skill, more menial, and labor intensive work. It was a quest to shed labor costs and hold as few assets as possible on your own books. It was, in other words, the *purposeful externalization* of costs. The exciting stories of small, focused, innovative and adaptive companies with skilled labor forces is largely a story, not of the emerging form of the US or global economy, but merely of dynamics occurring in the *independent primary labor market*. Between continued automation of various jobs and the growth of outsourcing, particularly to lower wage areas of the globe, the *subordinate primary labor market*, as you'll recall from Chapter 3, has been emaciated in the United States. It was this, as noted in Chapter 3 that produced new forms of *labor market dualization* where a stark line is drawn between the jobs in the core and the jobs in the periphery. Outside of jobs in the independent primary market, the movement is toward more and more unstable, part-time and contingent ("Uberized") labor.

But even life in the primary market isn't always so rosy. Widespread vertical de-integration has meant that the career ladders of old have largely evaporated. There just isn't that much vertical hierarchy to progress through. And the ease with which business functions can be picked up or dropped or sold now means that everyone should think of their employment situation as temporary. The idea is that all jobs should now just be seen as gigs.

And if you look at something like the lean production model that is supposed to require multiskilled, team-based workers in core lead firms, the story also isn't always so rosy either. It is easy to overestimate the extent to which self-managed teams with some fair degree of autonomy, control, and decision-making authority over their own work stations means having any *true* sense of autonomy, control, or independent decision-making. The overall production lines generally remain computer controlled where management sets the ulti-mate rules. The *kaizen* continuous improvement philosophy actually means that workers are required to invent their own schemes for formally rational-izing their own jobs. And over time, the goal of always just making things more and more efficient by shaving out all waste tends to create a work pace that simply becomes more and more hectic. Add in the glitches that can come from hiccups in JIT systems, and intense stress on production workers goes hand in hand with the lean production model. The team based system doesn't help and actually adds a level of complexity to corporate control wherein formal authority ends up mingled with intense peer pressure. If you happen to have a bad day or aren't keeping up for whatever reason, then the pressure comes down not only from management but also from your own co-workers. Furthermore, having all members of a team cross-trained (multiskilled) for all functions under the purview of the team, in point of fact, provides great flexibility for management in terms of keeping labor forces as small as possible. Someone called in sick? That's ok—you all know how to do that job. No need to bring in anyone else. *Lean and mean.*

The mid-twentieth-century period in which hierarchy dominated in business was a period of relative stability for many, particularly for the white middle classes. The constant economic and business flux of the post-1970s significantly eroded, if not completely destroyed that. It has been quite a while since Harrison outlined his leaner and meaner description, but the same dynamics, helped significantly by the ceaselessly increasing speed and capabilities of communications and transportation technologies, have, if anything, intensified. Businesses—or various parts of them—are rather like commodities bought and sold like so many pieces on a chess board. What currently counts as an "organization" becomes a moving target, except that the dynamics do still tend to flow around the dynamics of financial markets. The US and now global economy continues to be most significantly impacted by the centralized control of capital. The lineup of giants changes from time to time, but if any giants fall it's generally from challenges by other giants. And the new, innovative, and dynamic new fish either get eaten or become big fish themselves. Labor itself (corporeal humans and their communities) is just so much flotsam and jetsam—potential resources for the big fish, but mostly just awash in the much larger ebb and flow of largely finance-directed economic strategies.

Has the "Society of Organizations" Reached Its End?

On the basis of his analysis of the rise of shareholder activism, the shift toward an emphasis on shareholder value, and all of the attending changes in how businesses operate—particularly with regards to the relationship of workers to companies—organizational sociologist Gerald Davis has said so. In his 2009 book, he argues that we have now become a *society of investors*. We are no longer managed by jobs and careers as provided by business organizations rather, as his book's title proclaims, we are *Managed by the Markets*. If we want something more recent than 2009, the basic sentiments were echoed in a 2019 book by Nicholas Lemann called *Transaction Man: The Rise of the Deal and the Decline of the American Dream*. The *Transaction Man* title is a play on the title of a 1956 book by William Whyte called *Organization Man*. Whyte's book was written at the height of the period of hierarchy and was actually a rather critical appraisal of what the society of organizations had wrought for people, especially in the United States. If you take the Weberian picture of life in the *iron cage of rationality* and ask what that means at the level of everyday life, including how people's minds are shaped, this is a bit like what Whyte was doing. His backdrop was in thinking about a US culture that places great value and emphasis on individualism, hard work, initiative, and achievement. But he was looking at an organizational world that turned people into the nameless and faceless masses of order followers in an iron cage.

But the message of the likes of Davis and Lemann is that this age is now past. It is not that people managed to throw off the chains. It is that the chains were cut, and the dynamics of getting by in the world and establishing one's well-being, and with that the formation of self-identity now revolves around the logic of financial markets rather than around formally rationalized organizations. In other words, there was a time when the lives of individuals were basically swallowed by their conditions of employment. The large hierarchical corporate entity was a stable social institution providing an underlying fabric of order and stability, especially as tied to its relations with labor unions and governments. Financial and career stability, healthcare, work benefits, and retirement security came through membership in these organizations. In other words, the society of organizations.

But this is what changed in the post-1970s period. Corporations as social welfare providers for employees fell in the face of the competitiveness crisis, the rise of the shareholder value movement, and the ability of businesses to easily reconfigure themselves. At this point, things like financial stability, health, and retirement security are to be acquired through everyone's involvement in financial markets. The ultimate symbol of this, perhaps, lies in the widespread shift of retirement funds from pension funds managed by your employer to 401(k) retirement funds managed by *you* through a mutual fund. Unlike with pensions, a 401K provides no guarantees regarding the funds that you will have available for retirement. If the stock market does well, then you do well. If the stock market does poorly, then you lose out.

It is the same with your house which is generally one of—if not the—most important assets held by many people. If the real estate market does well, then you are building *equity* in your house (your house is worth more than what you owe), and you can then basically make "withdrawals" on your equity in the form of mortgage refinancing or home equity loans. But if the real estate market does poorly, then you can end up "under water" and owe more than your house is worth. (Some of this is what contributed to the famous financial crisis of 2008.) Thus we get the story that we are now a *society of investors* who are *managed by the markets* rather than by organizations. And that our self-identity and self-understanding shifted from "organization man" to "transaction man." The organizational landscape is now constantly shifting and offers no order and stability that we can count on for very long. And we are not nameless and faceless cogs following orders to contribute our small part to the success of some larger entity. Rather we are all buyers and sellers in a marketplace—a marketplace of minds and bodies as we search for our next paying gig, and of our money and other assets.

Or Is This the "New Society of Organizations"?

Since I opened the book with the idea that we are in a society of organizations, it's probably obvious that I am not so sure that we've hit the end of the society of organizations. But I am not alone. The concept is not a simple and unidimensional one, and includes a lot of things. It is fair to say, of course, that at least some of the dimensions are not the same as they used to be, especially those most important to Gerald Davis' argument. In particular, the large hierarchical corporation of the middle of the twentieth century when coupled with labor unions helped provide something of a large, stable security blanket for the US middle and upper-middle classes, complete with career ladders and fringe benefits. In the world of business, this has now largely gone by the wayside. But I think it is also fair to say that this issue is derivative of a larger one, which is about how power is distributed in society. Davis' backdrop was a "golden age" of the middle-twentieth century US era of relative organizational stability, and thus social stability. It was an age when the wealth and power centralizing tendencies of private corporations were reined in by other large organizations—largely governmental agencies and labor unions. It was an age of security and stability for many, but not an age of ideal levels of *social inclusion* as it is often put today.

Social inclusion is about the extent to which people are in a position to influence the conditions under which they live their own lives. This was closer to Charles Perrow's concerns in writing his 1991 paper on *"A Society of Organizations."*[16] Those concerns were more about the location and distribution of power and decision-making in society. Perrow's backdrop was more or less a nineteenth-century US which was still more a society of families, neighborhoods, and communities rather than of formal organizations. There's no naïve romanticizing about what kinds of inequalities did exist, but by comparison to the world delivered by the organizational revolution, wealth and power were far less concentrated. One would be hard pressed to describe the post-1970s period as one where the conditions under which people live their lives are now somehow closer to "home"—in families, neighborhoods, and communities. Especially with regards to the continued development and use of complex communications and computing capabilities which greatly accelerated automation and economic globalization, the ability of people to control the conditions under which they live their own lives has, if anything, declined. The tools of formal rationalization are more formidable than ever, an issue to which we will return in Chapter 7.

Furthermore, declaring the end of the society of organizations doesn't really provide a good way for thinking about the expanding secondary labor market or the related growth of social inequality. For one thing, the description of the mid-twentieth-century corporation as having provided for middle class growth and stability, for the most part, only applies to the experience of those in the primary labor market (whether independent or subordinate). And similarly, the notion of a society as organized around finance markets doesn't speak to the half of US households that don't have any holdings in the markets, or the 30–40% who, at any given time, don't own a home. We could just as well call it the society of the disposable worker.

But most importantly, the changes are still about organizational configurations and change. Recall that the difference between jobs in the subordinate primary and secondary labor markets is largely an organizational one—the question of whether or not there are labor unions to effectively press the interests of workers. And this, itself, requires the active cooperation of the state. Between automation and capital mobility, however, the old union stronghold jobs disappeared and with them the unions. The difference between the old full-time, high-paying, stable job at General Motors and the now more common part-time, low security, and low pay job at Wal-Mart (or the Dollar Store or Amazon or McDonald's or…) isn't that one is in the service industry and the other in manufacturing. It is the presence or absence of unionization that makes the difference. The relative absence of unions is also not for lack of

---

[16]Perrow, 1991.

trying but unions are constantly and actively resisted by employers (as they have been since the rise of large business organizations).

Here the state has been of no particular help, and has largely been coopted by the interests of employers. The business of politics and economics is completely intertwined regardless of what various proponents of *laissez-faire* economics may profess to want. Governments rely on the well-being of their domestic businesses for revenues and their own financial stability while businesses rely on governments for various kinds of protections (legal or even military), the maintenance of stable legal and monetary systems, many aspects of infrastructure (for things like energy, transportation, and communication), and the production of a generally favorable business climate. In the age of intense growing competition, states have not gotten "out of the way" but have only become more and more involved. They have no choice but to try to attract business activities and actively pursue strategies for domestic economic growth. Davis has referred to the emergence of *vendor states*,[17] where governments increasingly offer up "products" for sale on global markets such as the ability to incorporate with few strings attached. The necessity of increased state involvement has only been accelerated by a surge in *state capitalism*, whereby governments play a central role in directing economic activity, but do so as players in global markets. It's sort of like socialist governments participating in capitalism. The objective is to produce competitive goods and services for sale on markets, but under a good deal of, if not total, state direction. The most prominent of the state capitalist as I write is China, but there are plenty of countries practicing state capitalism to one degree or another including places like Russia, Saudi Arabia, and Singapore. At this point in time, global competitiveness for businesses and states alike require more and more cooperation among them. This is not really a story about the disappearance of the society or organizations. If anything it is just an intensification of it that continues to revolve around concentrated economic and political power just as it did during the rise of hierarchy at the turn of the twentieth century.

And this brings me to my heading reference to the "new society of organizations." If you look up this phrase it will almost certainly bring up a 1992 paper by the very influential management scientist Peter Drucker.[18] This was just a standard Post-Fordist proclamation that we have entered a period of constant competition and thus the constant need for change and innovation. The center of Drucker's new society of organizations was fundamentally to be knowledge as its application is the key to remaining abreast of all of that constant change and innovation. But my reference is borrowed from a more recent and much more Neo-Fordist account of the present status of the society of organizations by sociologists Tim Bartley, Matthew Soener and Carl Gershenson.[19] Their story is pretty straightforward and much of it will generally sound familiar by now. They argue that today's organizational society is different from that described in 1991 by Perrow in two important ways. First, has been the "dramatic dis-embedding" of persons (mainly workers) from organizations. This is largely a reference to Uberization and the like. Second is an intensification of *concentration without centralization* as borrowed from Bennett Harrison. They describe the equivalent of the notion

---

[17]Davis, 2009: Ch. 5.
[18]Drucker, 1992.
[19]Bartley et al., 2019.

of the core and ring structure, though, following language used by Perrow refer to smaller and weaker firms as *satellites*. As they write: "...the new society of organizations is crowded with satellites orbiting planets that have fewer inhabitants than before but still exert strong gravitational pulls."[20]

Those gravitational pulls operate more and more as *power at a distance* (as the title of their paper suggests). *Network distance* largely refers to that exercised by powerful lead firms over subcontracting firms, and often by monopsony power. *Governing at a distance* refers to the increasing importance of financial institutions, the emphasis on shareholder value, and the state's role in helping to foster it. This is very much related, of course, to the widespread disembedding of workers as businesses are beholden to the preferences of those in the world of finance which is now where some of the most concentrated power lies. *Algorithmic distance* is basically about the ever increasing development and employment of electronic IT capabilities. The ability to formally rationalize action—to direct, and especially monitor action via standardized rules and procedures (bureaucratic control) has certainly not gone by the way side. To the contrary, it is constantly intensified, a matter we will return to in Chapter 7.

I suppose that these things could be called "new" because of the more powerful means by which they now operate. But by the same respect exercising power via mono/oligopsony or mono/oligpoly power, the control of finance, and the ability to impose rules are also as old as the organizational revolution itself. There is no doubt that, *on the face of it*, the society that we inhabit today, and the organizations that populate it, are in many ways radically different from what they were through the early and middle part of the twentieth century. Perhaps the true pinnacle of the society of organizations, if we were to turn it into Weberian *ideal type*, was the period from about World War II up until the 1970s. Yet beneath the surface, it is also not hard to see many of the same old dynamics at play. And it is even harder to see the world as a place where the central dynamics are not about the exercise of power by large and powerful organizations. My readers may obviously develop their own particular takes on these ideas. As for me, I'll keep the book's theme as a society of organizations—one that's "leaner and meaner" than it was in the middle of the twentieth century.

SOURCES AND FURTHER READING

On the **Japanese System of Management/Lean Production:**

- Well known early descriptions that brought it to attention in the United States:

  o Cusumano, Michael A. 1988. "Manufacturing Innovation: Lessons from the Japanese Auto Industry." *Sloan Management Review* 30: 29–39.

  o Krafcik, John F. 1988. "Triumph of the Lean Production System." *Sloan Management Review* 30: 41–52.

  o Womack, James P., Daniel T. Jones, and Daniel Roos. 1990. *The Machine that Changed the World.* New York, NY: Rawson Associates.

---

[20]Ibid., p. 4.

- Some reasonably recent reviews:

  ○ Danese, Pamela, Valeria Manfé, and Pietro Romano. 2018. "A Systematic Literature Review on Recent Lean Research: State-of-the-art and Future Directions." *International Journal of Management Reviews* 20: 579–605.

  ○ Samuel, Donna, Pauline Found, and Sharon J. Williams. 2015. "How Did the Publication of the Book *The Machine that Changed the World* Change Management Thinking? Exploring 25 Years of Lean Literature." *International Journal of Operations & Production Management* 35: 1386–1407.

- On the **"Neo-Fordist"** character of the **JSM/LP**:

  ○ James R. Barker. 1993. "Tightening the Iron Cage: Concertive Control in Self-Managing Teams." *Administrative Science Quarterly* 38: 408–37.

  ○ Graham, Laurie. 1995. *On the Line at Subaru-Isuzu: The Japanese Model and the American Worker.* Ithaca, NY: Cornell University Press.

    ○ A briefer treatment evaluating the central aspects of lean production: Laurie Graham. 1993. "Inside a Japanese Transplant: A Critical Perspective." *Work and Occupations* 20: 147–73.

  ○ Huxley, Christopher. 2015. "Three Decades of Lean Production: Practice, Ideology, and Resistance." *International Journal of Sociology* 45: 133–51.

  ○ Rinehart, James, Christopher Huxley, and David Robertson. 1997. *Just Another Car Factory?: Lean Production and Its Discontents.* Ithaca, NY: Cornell University Press.

  ○ Stewart, Paul, Mike Richardson, Andy Danford, Ken Murphy, Tony Richardson, Vicki Wass, John Cooper, Tony Lewis, Gary Lindsay, Mick Whitley, John Fetherston, Steve Craig, Pat Doyle, and Terry Myles. 2009. *We Sell Our Time No More: Workers' Struggles Against Lean Production in the British Car Industry.* New York, NY: Pluto Press.

On the revival of interest in **Industrial Districts**:

- Becattini, G. 1991. "The Industrial District as a Creative Milieu." In *Industrial Change and Regional Development: the Transformation of New Industrial Spaces.* Edited by Georges Benko and Mick Dunford. New York, NY: Belhaven Press.

- Belussi, Fiorenza and Katia Caldari. 2009. "At The Origin of the Industrial District: Alfred Marshall and the Cambridge School." *Cambridge Journal of Economics* 33: 335–55.

- Marshall, Alfred. 1919. *Industry and Trade.* London: Macmillan.

- Piore, Michael. J. and Charles Sabel. 1984. *The Second Industrial Divide: Possibilities for Prosperity.* New York: Basic Books.

- Porter, Michael. 1990. *The Competitive Advantage of Nations.* New York, NY: The Free Press.

- Sabel, Charles and Jonathan Zeitlin. 1985. "Historical Alternatives to Mass Production: Politics, Markets and Technology in Nineteenth-Century Industrialization." *Past & Present* 108: 133–76.

With regards to networks, **push from finance markets, the "IT Boost"** (as I headed it), the virtual corporation, and the "end of the society of organizations":

- Byrne, John. 1993. "The Virtual Corporation." *Business Week* Feb 8, 98–102.

- The following by Gerald Davis were particularly influential:

  ○ Gerald, Davis F. 2009a. *Managed by the Markets: How Finance Reshaped America.* Oxford: Oxford University Press.

  ○ ———. 2009b. "The Rise and Fall of Finance and the End of the Society of Organizations." *Academy of Management Perspectives* 23: 27–44.

  ○ ———. 2016. *The Vanishing American Corporation.* Oakland, CA: Berrett-Koehler Publishers, Inc.

- Lemann, Nicholas. 2019. *Transaction Man: The Rise of the Deal and the Decline of the American Dream.* New York, NY: Farrar, Straus and Giroux.

  ○ The backdrop for this came from the very well known: Whyte, Jr, William H. 1956. *The Organization Man.* New York, NY: Simon and Schuster.

- Powell, Walter W. 1990. "Neither Market nor Hierarchy: Network Forms of Organization." *Research on Organizational Behavior* 12: 295–336.

With regards to **Neo-Fordism** and the question of the **"new society of organizations"**, see everything above on the Neo-Fordist character of the **JSM/LP**, and also:

- Barrow, Colin. 2009. *Get Backed, Get Big, Get Bought: Plan Your Start-Up with the End in Mind.* West Sussex: Capstone Publishing Ltd.

- Bartley, Tim, Matthew Soener, and Carl Gershenson. 2019. "Power at a Distance: Organizational Power Across Boundaries." *Sociology Compass* 13: e12737.

- Carr, Chris. 2020. *Global Oligopoly: A Key Idea for Business and Society.* New York, NY: Routledge.

- Drucker, Peter F. 1992. "The New Society of Organizations." *Harvard Business Review* 70: 95–104. *[Not an aspect of Neo-Fordist critique. I simply mentioned it in that context].*

- Harrison, Bennett. 1994. *Lean and Mean: The Changing Landscape of Corporate Power in the Age of Flexibility.* New York, NY: Basic Books.

- Perrow, Charles. 1991. "A Society of Organizations." *Theory and Society* 20: 725–62.

- ———. 2002. *Organizing America: Wealth, Power, and the Origins of Corporate Capitalism.* Princeton, NJ: Princeton University Press.

Analyzing Organizations

We started our journey by taking the point of view that societies are made of organizations rather than of people—that formal organizations are the most important actors in societies. This is a tricky claim because organizations don't actually exist as actual "things" in the world. They are mere abstractions that refer to various collections of things in the world—computers and buildings, filing cabinets, legal documents and employee manuals, and, of course, the actual people and their actions. The only things in the mix that can truly *act* are the humans. But to think of an organization as merely being what all of the people in it decide to do or have decided to do would be a mistake. We know, for example, that one of the central principles of formal organization is that rules and standards frequently tell people what to do, and sometimes in rather deterministic terms such as when expectations are built into technological form. (If you need a refresher, you can go back to the discussion in Chapter 1 regarding how fences represent rules.) We also know that organizations develop *structural interests* that can be quite distinct from the actors in the organization, and we know that it is easy for all manner of organizational processes to run the same way day after day even as different people come and go. To one extent or another, formal organizations are programs of action that, at least to a large extent, do have an existence distinct from the specific persons who are involved in those programs.

One might be thinking that it is still people who are in control because someone has to set out the programs. We can say that is just a matter of the exercise of *distributive power*, so organizations can be seen as tools built by people to control other people. There is obviously much to that. Recall from Chapter 5 that for Charles Perrow this is a central reason for creating bureaucracies in the first place. They are great control devices for elites. However, we're also going to go on to see that it is easy to overestimate just how much control is possible. Organizing is often highly complex, as are the humans that you are trying to discipline. For a myriad of reasons, even if you are able to find yourself "in charge" of an organization, this doesn't mean that you can make it or all of the people in it do what you want. In fact, going back to Robert Michels in Chapter 2, it is often the reverse. The structural interests of organizations often end up being what *makes you do what the organization wants*. We will also run into very practical problems having to do with our abilities to actually foresee all of the possible outcomes of our actions. People do have to invent organizations, and participate in them, and run them. But this doesn't necessarily mean that they are in control, or that we can understand everything according to individual decisions and actions. Organizations do structure action and can easily escape our control and produce unplanned, unanticipated, and sometimes disastrous outcomes.

PART

III

So for all of these reasons and more, even though organizations, as abstractions, cannot technically be actors we will still treat them as such. And since they remain central to all of social life, we want to be able to understand them as social entities. If you think of Psychology as the discipline that emerged to understand human persons and their behavior, then take *Organizational Studies*, of which the *Sociology of Organizations* is a part, as the discipline that seeks to understand organizations. Organizational Studies is a reasonably loose term for a very large interdiscipline consisting of people from the management sciences, psychology, political science, and sociology, among others. It is a very large and complex field, and one part of an introductory book cannot do it justice. But we can sketch out some foundations and contours that should help to act as a stepping stone for those who become interested in the field of study.

Everything that we have covered so far is in the mix. I started with Max Weber in Chapter 1, for example, who is one of the foundational figures in organizational studies, and we will shortly add some more foundational figures. Robert Michels and the issue of oligarchy, covered in Chapter 2, is (or at the very least should be) an obligatory stopping point for introductions to the field especially with regards to issues of power and control. The observation that organizational forms have very important impacts on stratification structures as discussed in Chapter 3 remains a central concern in a great deal of organizational research. And Part II on the question of markets, hierarchies, and networks is among the central meta-narratives for thinking about where we have been and where we are headed in organizational terms. Lurking in the background much of the time thus far has been an awful lot of what is called *Organizational Theory*. (You can find entire books and courses just on organizational theory.) Basically, there are very different ways of thinking about organizations, what they are, and how they operate. The discussion of the rise and possible fall of the large, bureaucratic business form is riddled with theoretical backdrop and differences in approaches, for example.

So Part III, which frequently structures entire introductions to the Sociology of Organizations, will be an introductory "tour" through approaches to organizational studies. Partly because the field is so vast and complex, and partly because the current state of things in organizational theory are in a state of flux because of the developments described in Chapter 6, there is no single, standardized way of summarizing the varying approaches. I will offer a starting foothold using an approach inspired by one of the better known ways of summarizing the various orientations that came from organizational sociologist Richard Scott.[1] It involves seeing organizations as *rational, natural/ human,* or *open systems*, which roughly emerged in a sequence over time in organizational studies. As with many other sets of categories, these should also be taken as ideal-typical rather than absolute.

To see organizations as *rational systems* (Chapter 7) is to see them as explicitly planned machine-like systems for accomplishing tasks as efficiently as possible. We already had a strong dose of this in Chapter 1 of the book with Max Weber, so I will remind you of that and then we will move on to just how deep the rabbit hole went and continues to go. This imagery will bring us very

---

[1]Scott, W. Richard. 2003. *Organizations: Rational, Natural, and Open Systems*, 5th Ed. Upper Saddle River, NJ: Prentice Hall. Also see W. Richard Scott and Gerald Davis. 2007. *Organizations and Organizing: Rational, Natural, and Open Systems Perspectives*. Upper Saddle River, NJ: Pearson/Prentice Hall, Inc.

much back in touch with the *second industrial revolution* and the organizational revolution itself.

To come to see organizations as *human* or *natural* systems (Chapter 8) is what happened when the engineers and managers trying to institute organizations as rational systems came to the realization that there are very strong limits on the extent to which human beings and social organization can be subjected to machine-like precision. The Weberian picture, so strongly delivered in Chapter 1, will get shaken to its core. But you have to remember, of course, that I explained that the Weberian description was an *ideal type*—only a pure conceptual model that is often a shadow of actual, observable reality.

To see organizations as *open systems* (Chapter 9), in simplest terms, is to see that organizations can't be studied as discrete entities in themselves. In rational and human systems terms, the focus is generally inward—on some specific organization and its processes and people and what is happening inside of it. But obviously organizations exist within complex *environments* where they have to deal with all sorts of things like suppliers and competitors and customers and regulatory agencies and so forth. At the extremes, organizations can actually disappear into a blur of their environmental relations.

We will see that organizational studies actually got its start with people trying to make organizations into rational systems. But there were a lot of bumps in the road and twists and turns along the way. The human systems approach emerged from some of those bumps and then the open systems approach partly emerged as organizations did become much blurrier as entities during the post-1970 shake-up period. What we will come to is that, of course, formal organizations are all of these things at once, but for various reasons they do represent, in one way or another, attempts at establishing rational systems. But this remains very difficult. The materials of Chapters 8 and 9 will present some of the reasons for this, and then Chapter 10 will be a direct examination of the limits that we face in trying to accomplish rational action. In Chapter 11, I'll use one tradition from organizational theory called *contingency theory* to provide a way to organize all of the different aspects of the varied approaches to organizational studies. There will be a lot of flotsam and jetsam along the way, but we will try to tie everything up into a comprehensible picture by the time we are done.

The Machine Organization

To see formal organizations as *Rational Systems* is largely to adopt the Weberian view of organizations that was introduced in Chapter 1. Organizations are basically means that are designed to accomplish specific goals. All of those aspects of the ideal typical bureaucracy as laid out by Weber—precise task specialization, hierarchy of authority, and formalization—are elements of organizations as means. (See Figures 1.1 and 1.2 for a quick refresher.) These are the things that make organizational activities efficient, predictable, and calculable in terms of achieving whatever the goals happen to be. The formally rationalized system is like a machine—a set way of running various activities that all fit together to accomplish the goals and can operate the same way day in and day out, even if the personnel happen to change.

The specific goals are not part of the ideal type because the goals vary a great deal. Formal organizations are merely means, and it is in organizing that goals get specified. For most any organization of reasonable size you can find formally stated goals in *mission statements* and sets of *goals and objectives* to specify the purposes of the organization. For any of my readers in a college course, you will very likely find that your course syllabus contains a statement of goals and objectives or something of that nature. If you check the formal documentation of your home department, it will very likely specify even loftier goals and objectives. In fact, you will find these stated for every division of the university organization as well as for the university itself.

While the terms *rational* and *rationality* can be seen to have very broad and ambiguous meanings, in this context it carries a very precise and narrow definition. To be rational is to make decisions regarding courses of action that will achieve your goals while maximizing your benefits and minimizing your costs. The goal might be as simple as you getting a cup of coffee when you get up in the morning. Getting the coffee is the goal or the *end*. The actions that you go through to end up with the coffee are the *means*. To be rational about getting a cup of coffee is to consider your available means and choose the one that maximizes your benefits and minimizes your costs. The rational actor is not one who will knowingly pay $2 for a cup of coffee that can easily be had for $1. Nor will the rational actor knowingly choose a course of action that will take extra time to produce the same result. Thus costs are not merely things that can be easily measured in monetary terms—money, time, energy, aggravation, and so on. All of these can be counted as costs.

As we've already learned, however, a great deal of formal organization isn't about the decision-making of persons. Rather it is about *formal rationality* where the bulk of the decisions are laid out beforehand in preplanned standards, routines, and procedures. This is the heart of the bureaucratic organization, and of the rational systems model. The idea is to produce collective power by coordinating the actions of many in predictable ways to achieve goals in the most *efficient* way. The *division of labor* specifies what all of the different tasks are and which specific offices are responsible for them, while the *hierarchy of authority* specifies which offices are responsible for ensuring that the various tasks are, in fact, done and done with maximum levels of competency. *Formalization* spells out and clarifies the division of labor and authority relations, and also records what *has been* done.

Recall that I refer to offices rather than persons because one important aspect of all of this is that organizations are made up of specialized tasks, rather than of people. If any of the particular persons who occupy an office decides to leave the organization or can't make it to work one day, this shouldn't matter as some other person (ideally with some level of appropriate *technical competency*, of course) steps into the office and carries out its functions. This is part of what makes them machine-like in their operations, and is responsible for all of that predictability. Formal organization can make people into standardized, interchangeable parts just like those of machines. Formal organizations are designed to be programs of action that are more reliable than persons because they are designed to control the persons. They are sets of instructions.

With that in mind, one should consider the utility of seeing the bureaucratic ideal type as more than merely *analogous* to pieces of physical machinery. Rather one can easily see them as the very same thing manifested in variable physical forms. A robot on an automobile assembly line is merely carrying out a set of instructions in the same way that a human assembly line worker would be, though often robots might be preferred because they are more precise, reliable, and predictable than persons. Technical controls *are* bureaucratic controls where the rules of social action have been built into the operations of physical machinery (Recall the discussion of the fence from Chapter 1). This is control on the input end, but the bureaucratic control is also exercised in terms of monitoring output. The results of tasks are counted, recorded, and reviewed in terms of *organizational performance*. In order to accommodate the collapse of the distinction between rules embedded in physical technical forms and merely in the normative written form, all we need to do is allow for variation in how strongly they dictate human action. A sign on the street that says "Cross at the crosswalk with the light" is a formal instruction for action, but is a much softer *determinant* of action than is a large fence and gate that make it difficult or impossible to do something else.

While it might not sit right at first to leave aside the distinction between machines and people (which is what this amounts to), it might pay to recognize that the development of ideas and strategies for organizations as rational systems were directly descendant from the development and engineering of technical devices themselves. The development and implementation of rational systems ideas for managing human action was integral to the organizational revolution, and was largely done from the reference point of engineers who were building large scale, mechanized, mass production systems. Vast portions of industrial work shifted to being done by machines rather than by people. Yet people still need to tend to the machines, and if the machine is to work then the people would need to become—in the famous old words of Karl Marx (among others)—*appendages to the machines*. Thus the humans in the systems can come to be seen as machines parts and treated like machine parts.

It is the rational systems model that goes along most with the *concentration of the means of administration* (see Chapter 2). At least in ideal typical form, rational organizations operate in highly centralized and top down fashion. *Organizational design* and monitoring are largely done higher up in the hierarchy by management. This was, of course, key for Alfred Chandler's understanding of what made big business work—those managerial hierarchies where people designed and monitored the overall program. The lower down the hierarchies you go, the more you find that people are merely carrying out orders. That is, instituting the Weberian bureaucracy removes decision-making from most people and concentrates it at the top of the organization. In Michels' words (Chapter 2), rational systems purposely institute the control of the many by the few, although it is also important to keep in mind that everyone is under the control of the rules to one degree or another.

Note, of course, that the time during which Weber was writing was exactly during the period of the organizational revolution. Weber was an observer of all of those organizational developments of the turn of the twentieth century, and that is what inspired his account of a world being turned into an *iron cage of formal rationality*. But Weber was not so much a participant in bringing it about, as much as an observer. We have already learned that rise of the large bureaucratic form was not necessarily natural or inevitable. That is, these kinds of organizations had to be purposefully designed and instituted, and in some respects this results in the birth of what is sometimes called the *management sciences*, and thus significant portions of what I have loosely called organizational studies. An important part of that is a sub-discipline that generally goes by the name *Organizational Design (OD)*. If we go back to the rise of the first very large business organizations, we find people who developed mass production and distribution machineries were also designing formal organizations according to the needs of the machines.

The Emergence and Institutionalization of *Classical Management Theory*

In terms of the early beginnings of rational systems thinking, Weber certainly looms large and is frequently recognized as a starting point for the sociology of organizations. But, he wasn't so much involved in the engineering or in trying to develop ideas about what *ought* to be the case in the normative sense as he was trying to make sense of the development of the "modern" world in the West. This is not the case for other people around at the time who were, quite purposefully, trying to devise the most efficient ways to organize. Around the turn of the twentieth century organizing was being made into a science of management. The ideas that emerged and developed as dominant during this period are frequently referred to a *Classical Management Theory (CMT)*, and while its origins come out of the growth of economic organizations, its influence spread throughout many parts of society even including even how to run a household. Uncertainty regarding how to characterize our current organizational world (see Chapter 6) notwithstanding, we continue to live in a world that is significantly shaped by the principles and concerns of CMT. As we will see in Chapter 9, these ideas are actually now deeply embedded cultural expectations. That is, it is widely assumed the organizations should operate according to the logic of rational systems.

The central concern of CMT was certainly efficiency. It was about overall efficiency of an organization in terms of performing whatever it was supposed to accomplish, but that included reaching all the way down to the smallest of work tasks such as the best way to stick a nut on a bolt or file a document. While a lot time and attention was given to the design and control of technologies of production, this inevitably means the need to design and control human actions to meld them efficiently to the machines. In this regard, the hallmark of CMT is often taken to be that it sees people merely as pieces of larger machineries, and operated with a highly simplified view of workers wherein people are largely assumed to be motivated by a desire for physical comfort and the highest possible material rewards (wages). Max Weber is often identified as a part of the birth of CMT, though he was much less a part of creating it than others. Among the most prominent, if not *the* most prominent figure involved in this was Frederick Winslow Taylor.

Frederick Winslow Taylor and *Scientific Management*

Frederick Winslow Taylor (1856–1915) is the central person in the development of a field of study and of practice known as *scientific management*. This can likely be called the first wave of organizational design consulting. Taylor was not a professional social scientist or management professional. Rather he began his work life as a machinist and later earned a degree in engineering. His main obsession in life was efficiency in work processes. At the turn of the twentieth century as large industrial companies were appearing throughout the economy, managing them and making them work smoothly was a problem. People simply didn't know how to do it, and it produced great efficiency problems. Taylor was one of the most prominent people to make work efficiency the central point of what he saw as a new science.

Like many engineers and business people Taylor didn't think very much of your average worker. I know that sounds odd and many might object to the statement. But from the point of view of getting things done in the best way, there is a common belief that, left to their own devices, workers tend to be a hindrance to establishing efficient work processes. One problem is that people are often assumed to be basically lazy. The idea was (and for many remains) that, given their choice, workers will sit around and do nothing all day in the hopes of still getting paid. If they are actually forced to do any work—whether by direct threats and surveillance, or the more unobtrusive method of measuring output—they are going to do it in the easiest way possible. One of the things that this means is that they will do it in as leisurely a manner as possible (i.e., slowly) without getting in trouble from their supervisors. Another thing it means is that they won't go through the extra work of changing how they do things or learning how to do things differently to make it more efficient. Remaining with old habits is the path of least resistance. As Taylor famously wrote: *hardly a competent workman can be found in a large establishment...who does not devote a considerable part of his time to studying just how slow he can work and still convince his employer that he is going at a good pace.*[1]

This laziness on the job was widely referred to as *soldiering*, and Taylor defined two kinds. The first is *natural soldiering*. Natural soldiering is that mentioned above. Given the opportunity to follow their own preferences people will avoid work as much as possible—*the natural instinct and tendency of men to take it easy,* as Taylor put it.[2] The second kind is *systematic soldiering*. Natural soldiering can apply in any kind of setting, but systematic soldiering is largely found in employment situations and is done by workers strategically and with forethought. For various reasons, workers basically cooperate with each other to control maximum levels of expected output. Even if people *could* work faster and get more done, they won't. Rather, in order to keep the pace of work leisurely and to make sure they keep themselves and others with work to do, they will cooperatively put a cap on output as a way of controlling the expectations of their bosses. This, of course, would be done informally and we will revisit such informal organizational realities in the next chapter.

A second problem that engineers and business people often find with the humans in a system is that they can be rather incompetent from the point of view of figuring out how to achieve maximum efficiency—from the point of view of systems engineering, in other words. At the turn of the twentieth century many work processes remained largely craft based. Skilled craftspeople were often responsible for planning and executing work, operating on the basis of rules of thumb and traditional forms of knowledge handed down by tradition in the various crafts. There was not a persistent idea, such as *continuous improvement philosophies* discussed in Chapter 6, that part of the work should involve finding more systematic and efficient methods for getting things done. But even if workers were explicitly ordered to devise ways to make their work more efficient, most would not be considered competent to do so.

Taylor held the common idea that people naturally have very different competencies. Some are very strong and not very bright and thus are well suited to do tedious and heavy manual labor, for example. Others might be very smart and good at, say, math but are not very strong. These people should probably be doing something with accounting rather than manual labor. What few, if any, workers would excel at would be the use of scientific methods to actually study work processes. This is where Taylor and his associates and followers come in. Taylor was sure that for any job, no matter how large or small, there was *one best way* to accomplish it. The "best" way, of course, was the one that produced the maximum amount of *productivity*—or the amount produced in a given interval of time. In other words, the maximum benefit for the least cost, a.k.a. the most efficient.

Because workplaces would inevitably be filled with so much laziness and incompetence, they would not be nearly as productive as they could potentially be unless counter-measures were taken. The counter-measures came in the form of *scientific management (a.k.a. Taylorism)*. Both words are meaningful here. To say *scientific* is to say that work tasks should not be governed by traditional rules of thumb or ad hoc arrangements, but by systematic scientific study. It is quite possible to carefully observe work processes of any kind,

---

[1]Taylor, 1911/1919: 21.
[2]Taylor, 1911/1919: 19.

analyze the kinds of things that have to get done to accomplish the tasks, and systematically discover the most efficient ways to do them. To say *management* is to say that it is this scientific knowledge that should guide how work is managed. This latter point means that managers, as the "smartest guys in the room," should take responsibility for discovering the most efficient work methods and processes and implementing them.

So Taylor's approach was to remove all responsibility and control over the planning of work from workers. The planning and organization of work processes was to be management's job. Managers (often by hiring Taylor or others as consultants) should analyze all of the work tasks and, by using scientific methods, discover the most efficient ways to do a job. The principle methods used were *time and motion studies*. Tasks were scrutinized and broken down to define all of the motions that were required to perform them. The motions would all be timed and continually adjusted and refined to reduce the time required to an absolute minimum—or optimal level of productivity. With all of the tasks clearly defined, highly detailed instruction cards were drawn up for every task, including the time that should be taken to do them down to the fraction of a second (see Figure 7.1). The next thing is to systematically assign specific workers to jobs to which they were best suited. Then workers are trained to do the tasks according to the detailed instruction cards, and work output is constantly monitored and measured to ensure appropriate levels of productivity and address deficits when and where they occurred.

If you stop and think about this for a moment, all of this provides the very definition of *formal rationality*. It is rational because it is geared toward the maximization of benefits while minimizing the costs (at least if by "benefits" we mean what is most efficient for the organization—always ask *efficient for what and for whom?*). And it is formal because the means to do this are laid out beforehand in standardized rules, routines, and procedures. Workers are actually forbidden to attempt to exercise any form of rationality of their own—*practical*, *theoretical*, or *substantive*. Their only job is to follow the rules. And if they did not follow the rules, Taylor's system was designed to detect that because the constant monitoring of output is integral to the system.

Scientific management is cold and calculating, reducing workers to mere cogs in the larger machinery of the workplace. If you think that this might not always go over so well with workers you would be right. But Taylor did have an answer for that. Recall that he was operating during the rise of the large corporations that produced those very large labor forces complete with the rise of mass worker unrest and the rise of labor unions. Taylor thought that his system could put an end to the adversarial relationship between employers and employees. Employers always want to get more time and effort and productivity from workers while giving less in terms of wages and other benefits. Workers want the opposite, and it appears to be a zero sum game. The arguments are about who gets how much of the pie. By increasing efficiency Taylorism promised to just make a bigger pie so that *everyone* got more. The idea was that this orientation could replace workplace conflict with cooperation. It was the responsibility of management to devise the appropriate ways of maximizing productivity which is ultimately the thing that makes the pie so much bigger. But they would have to realize that in order to get workers to cooperate, they needed to devise incentive schemes to go along with the program. In other words, wherever companies reorganize work and expand

FIGURE 7.1   **Scientific Management Instruction Card for Operation**

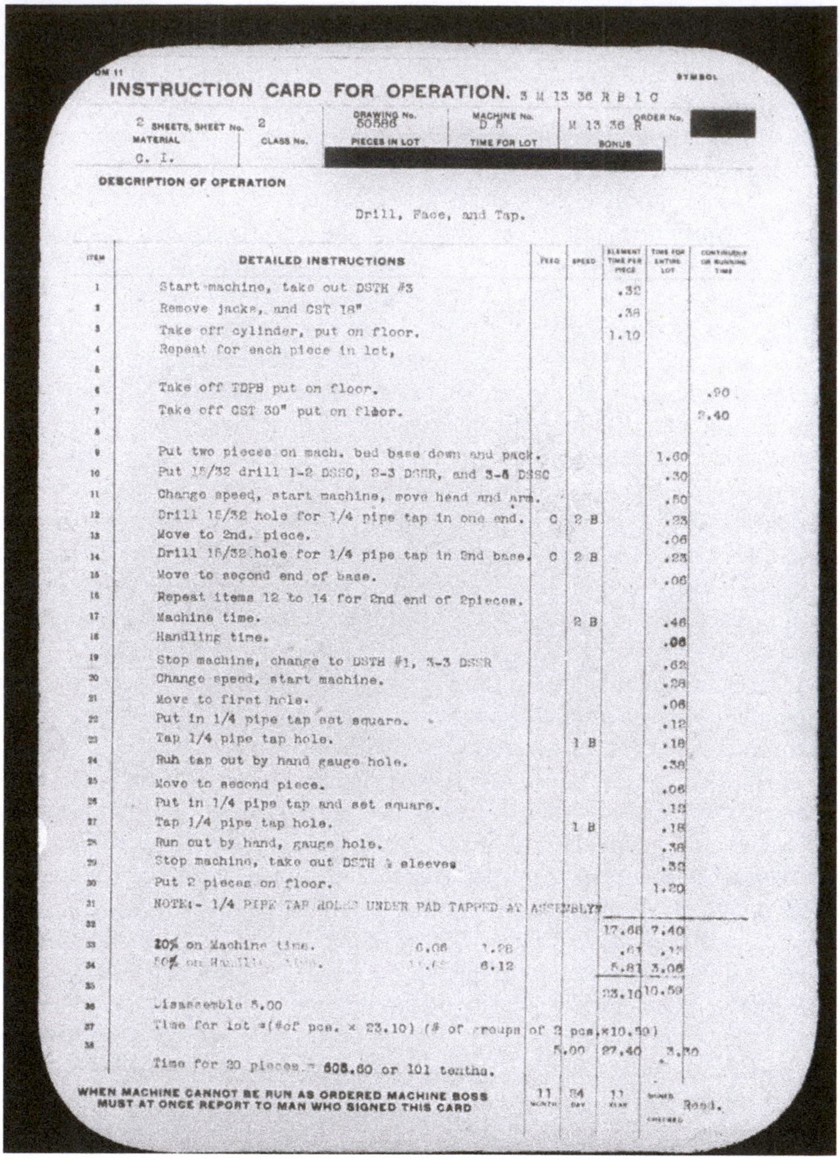

Source: Instruction Card for Operation, 1910 ca. Frederick W. Taylor Collection, SCW.001. Archives and Special Collections; Samuel C. Williams Library, Stevens Institute of Technology, Hoboken, NJ.

their profits, employers can't just keep all of that for themselves but have to give some of it back in the form of higher wages that act as incentives for going along with the program. This too was the constant subject of scientific study—experimentation with various pay schemes to find out what maximized worker productivity (see Figure 7.2). Employers should be happy because their profits are bigger nonetheless. And workers should also be happy because their wages would increase.

| FIGURE 7.2 | Charts of Effective Incentive Plans of Productivity |

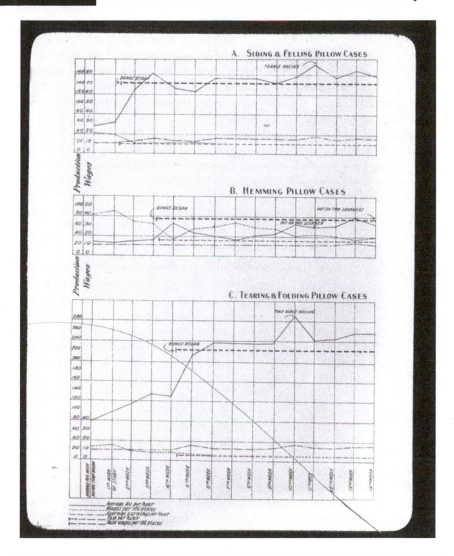

Source: Charts of Effective Incentive Plans of Productivity, 1910 ca. Frederick W. Taylor Collection, SCW.001. Archives and Special Collections; Samuel C. Williams Library, Stevens Institute of Technology, Hoboken, NJ.

In fact, Taylor thought of himself as a friend to workers because he believed that scientific management would greatly improve their lives. On the one hand, his methods would result in increased wages for workers because those would be tied to higher productivity. But it should also make their working lives easier. For one thing, the systematic selection of people to match their skills and abilities to tasks would mean that no one was stuck doing a job that they felt poorly by doing (whether mentally or physically). Another matter was that part of the systematic study of tasks was to learn about things like worker fatigue. Taylor is, for example, sometimes credited with providing the early roots for the present day study of *ergonomics*, a branch of applied science that tries to align the physical and mental health of workers with their work environments. Maximum productivity will require the ability to provide maximum effort while on work tasks, so the planning of jobs included not just telling people when to start work and what to do, but also when to rest and for how long. Finally, by assigning responsibility for work planning to management, Taylor saw this as a reduction of some of the labor that fell on the shoulders of workers. In other words, under traditional work systems the workers had to both plan and execute the work tasks. Now they would only be responsible for execution. Higher pay, greater physical and mental comfort, and a reduced workload. Who could argue?

Apparently plenty of people could argue. Taylor's consulting business gained a large number of customers, and at various times and places gains in productivity were realized. But probably just as common was worker resistance. He had started his zeal for reorganizing work around maximum productivity while the chief engineer at a steel plant in Philadelphia, and there he encountered extreme forms of resistance from those working under him. They did not appreciate having control removed from them, but also did not appreciate what often amounted to mere speed-ups of existing work processes. His efforts to reorganize work there were so antagonistic that he received death threats and ended up hiring body guards. Regardless of resistance, however, Taylorism spread broadly throughout US industries and beyond.

Running parallel to Taylor's efforts to redesign tasks in the name of efficiency was what many see as the origins of *high volume mass production (HVMP)* in Henry Ford's development of the automobile assembly line. The logic of the system Ford built is captured by the term *Fordism*, first introduced in Chapter 6.

Fordism

Henry Ford did not invent the automobile, nor did he "invent" the assembly line. In fact, no *one* invented either because that's rarely, if ever, how it works. Development is likely a far better term than invention because, generally speaking, new innovations are developed over time, and emerge from networks of people. The unfolding of things is much more about what's "in the air" than about individual geniuses suddenly hitting on something, yelling "eureka!" and then taking the world by storm. All of that aside, Ford did take assembly line principles and develop them (along with a lot of assistance from highly skilled craftsmen and engineers) in the automobile industry to the extreme. At the center of that was the development of the first version of an automobile that, because of Ford's production system, was affordable for everyday people to buy, operate, and even repair.

At the turn of the twentieth century cars were luxury items. They were generally built one at a time and in one place by having workers bring parts to a build site. So the cars sat in one place while workers moved various parts to the cars. In many cases all of the different parts were built by skilled craftspeople who were experts in particular trades. Wheels, for example, were made by people called wheelwrights. These were simply people who knew how to make wheels which is a particularly difficult skill. Others were metal or glass workers, all working to produce various parts of the cars. While general templates were in place, being custom built by hand meant that cars were each somewhat unique. They generally weren't made from precisely designed and machined interchangeable parts. There was no guarantee, for instance, that a part from one car would work on another. (It might, but there was no certainty about it.)

Given all of that custom craftwork by skilled workers, it took a long time to produce a car, and with all of that skilled labor time cars were very expensive which is why they were a luxury item. They also tended to be very difficult to operate and maintain, so if one wanted a car, one also frequently needed a chauffeur. For these reasons, they were largely affordable only to the very wealthy. This is what Henry Ford was intent on changing. He wanted to develop a car that was easy to operate, and to change the way that cars were made so that they were not so expensive. The goal was to increase efficiency to such an extent that even his own workers would be able to afford to buy one. There is some degree of uncertainty regarding just how much direct influence Frederick Taylor had on Henry Ford, especially given that Henry Ford denied any effect. But the logic and many of the methods were the same. There was, for example, ample use of time and motion study at Ford including constant experimentation with machinery and work layouts in order to develop the *one best way* to do all of the tasks that go into producing cars. There was also an awful lot of breaking tasks down into their most minute elements—a lot of *division of labor.*

But Ford's focus was different in important ways, and his ambitions grander. The scientific management movement was generally focused on particular work tasks. Once management (or Taylor and his consultants) figured out the one best way to do a task and to coordinate various tasks, written instructions were handed off to the workers so as to optimize their efficiency in performing those tasks. Formal rationality here takes the form of written rules and the focus is predominantly on the reorganization of existing work tasks. Henry Ford thought in terms of large-scale, integrated mechanized systems. This certainly means a focus on the specific tasks, but more importantly about how all of those tasks could be systematically broken down and then integrated and coordinated in such a way as to reduce all waste—wasted time, wasted movement, wasted energy, wasted material. His primary focus was also not on workers and how they should do things, but on machines and how they could be developed to do things rather than workers. Thus, rather than providing a lot of written instructions to a bunch of workers, Ford would build as much formal rationality into mechanical forms as possible. It might be said that workers were something of an afterthought to take up their positions as parts of the machinery for whatever tasks hadn't been automated yet. A lot of written bureaucracy wasn't really needed. The machines dictated how the work was to be done—or just did the work entirely.

One of Taylor's favorite stories to tell when giving lectures on his methods was of a workman named Schmidt whose job consisted of loading pig iron[3] into rail cars. As the story went, before Taylor came along Schmidt was loading 12 and a half tons of pig iron in a work day. After time and motion studies and a reorganization of the work process and layout, Schmidt was loading over 47 tons in the same workday. Henry Ford probably would have built a conveyor belt system instead. For our purposes, the question of the specific cross-influences or similarities and differences doesn't really matter all that much, and we can leave curiosity about it to historians.[4] In at least many

---

[3]Pig iron is just what you get after iron ore is originally smelted. It is basically globs of raw iron that then go into making steel.

[4]The take on this that I have just laid out was most directly influenced by historian David Hounshell, 1985, pp. 249–253. See also Paxton, 2012.

important respects, Ford and Taylor were both cut from the same cloth and very much represented the spirit of the age—rationalization and efficiency. They were central figures (though far from alone) in influencing those very systems of high volume mass production observed by Chandler.

Ford's mass production system was developed to produce his famous Model T car. This was the first mass produced car that became affordable to average working people, including even Ford's own employees (In one piece of enlightenment that many businesses could still use, workers in an economy are also consumers in an economy). The production system for the Model T was developed in steps over a number of years beginning around 1907. When the first Model T rolled out of production in 1908, it took about 12 hours to build one car, and it sold for about $900. By 1925 a new Model T rolled off the line about every 30 seconds and the price had come down to under $300. While many things contributed to this, at the core of it lay the basic Tayloristic principles or breaking all tasks down to their most basic components, and reducing the movement of workers to a minimum. Initial assembly line system development was done at Ford's Highland Park factory in Highland Park Michigan. The idea was not to set up work stations where each car would be built. It was to set up a whole chain of work stations where different aspects of building a car would take place. The goal was to set up a linear flow of materials and processes that worked their way through the factory where different stages of production were carried out.

Much attention was given to machine development and the arrangement of machines relative to each other given the sequence of tasks. Whatever tools or machines or materials were needed in a stage of production were placed exactly where they needed to be and when. And a great deal of specialized single purpose machinery was built. For example, there is a lot of very precise drilling of holes that goes into producing something like an engine. Rather than having a worker at milling machine that would be changed and adjusted for the size and placement of various holes (something that can be Taylorized as illustrated in Figure 7.1), there would be as many milling machines as needed to drill out each of the different kinds of holes. And those machines would be arranged in the correct order and layout for the smooth and continuous flow of materials through the factory—*continuous flow production*. All of the operations of all of the work areas, machining and assembly operations, and so forth were carefully timed and monitored to make sure that everything in the entire system remained coordinated just like clockwork. As we'll see more clearly below, it was not at all unlike today's *Just in Time (JIT)* systems discussed in Chapter 6. Wherever possible, various kinds of mechanical conveyor systems were used to transport materials and parts rather than humans. Mechanical conveyor systems are incredibly important tools for the coordination of different activities and might be the utmost symbol for the moving assembly line, which is often the thing most associated with Ford.

Rather than being a part of the design all along, going to the moving assembly line built up over several years starting in about 1913. At the outset of production at Highland Park, assembly workers generally operated at their own work stations and would assemble an entire part. Engines, for example, sat on work tables and a specific worker put together all of the parts that go into the engine. Inspired by many things in other industries, such as the way that tin cans were produced in a continuous flow mechanized system, and even how meat butchering worked (which was referred to by Ford as a *disassembly line*), Ford's engineers started to experiment with breaking tasks down even farther. It likely started with flywheel magnetos which are the things that create the spark for ignition. (If you don't know how gas engines work, they blow up compressed gasoline and air. The spark is what makes it blow up. No spark? No ignition, and a car doesn't run.) The flywheel magnetos were made up of quite a few parts that all had to be assembled—magnets, bolts, clamps, and so on. At a work station it took about 20 minutes to put one together. Experimentation with line assembly began, in very Tayloristic fashion, by breaking down all of the different steps involved in assembly, lining up the workers, and assigning to each worker only specific steps. When finished with his step a worker passed the magneto down the line to the next worker who would carry out his steps and so on. This did create some coordination issues because of the variable pace of workers. Some might work fast and others slow, so you get idleness in some places and bottlenecks in another. This was solved by setting up a chain system that moved the part down the line at a predetermined speed. This speeds up the slow-pokes, paces them better with fast folks, and best of all for management, provides control over the speed of the line. After about a year of experimenting and tweaking, the average time to assemble a flywheel magneto was down from 20 minutes to five. With the success in increasing efficiency with this line model, it was then developed in other assembly areas of the factory all the way through to final assembly of everything onto the chassis.

While this was all going on at the Highland Park site, Ford was busy building even bigger. In 1915 he bought 2000 acres of land along the Rouge River in Dearborn, Michigan and set his people to work building a fully integrated production facility that was meant to make virtually everything required for producing a Model T on site. The model was one of full *vertical integration*. Virtually everything from raw materials through to marketing and sales was done by his company. He owned iron mines, lumber mills, glass plants, his own railroad and ships for transporting goods, for example. All the way at the point of sale (POS), he licensed Ford car dealerships. Production moved to the new plant in the 1920s, and this is where a new Model T was rolling out of the works every thirty seconds, and his *economies of scale* brought the price of the car down to $300.

One of the more fateful things here for the organizational revolution is, just like with Taylor, how quickly his methods and practices spread throughout multiple industries. Ford was a bit of a renegade in many respects. One of them that was very important for the spread of continuous flow, mass production, was that he did not regard his systems as being a secret. It is typical in the business world to try to keep competitors from knowing how you do things, lest your ideas might be stolen and you lose whatever competitive edge you might have. But Ford was completely transparent and invited anyone, including even competitors, into his plants to see how things were done. Because of this, Fordist ideas and methods spread rapidly and became the standard in many industries. Of course, this might lead people to overestimate the influence of one person. Rational system building was certainly in the air, and not merely on the shop floor. The management of not just work processes, but also organizations themselves was simultaneously on its way to becoming a "science" in a much more general sense than that defined by Taylor or Ford.

Henri Fayol

People like Ford and Taylor were very much task oriented. They were "doers." Their thinking and activities took place, for lack of a better phrase, from the bottom up. Technical tasks need to be accomplished and you work to find the one best way in which to do them. Given that part of the strategy is to break the tasks down to highly specific and discrete components, this also requires organizing humans in order to map them onto the tasks. But there wasn't much thinking with regards to the humans beyond carefully matching physical and/or mental capabilities to tasks, and devising a system of incentives and punishments to make sure that they follow orders. In essence, Taylor and Ford's thinking was really about designing and running work processes rather than designing and running *organizations*. But the times were also certainly producing ideas about that.

The most famous early general theorist was probably a Frenchman named Henri Fayol (1841–1925). Fayol's concerns were also borne out of very practical issues of managing tasks *and people* as he was actually a civil engineer of mines and eventually head of a large French mining and steel operation. At the time it was one of France's largest enterprises with something in the neighborhood of 10,000 employees. Fayol drew upon his experience at the lead of this organization to lay out a general set of management principles in a famous 1916 book called *Administration Industrielle et Générale* (translated to English as *General and Industrial Administration*). It is always tricky to say what kind of thing counts as "the first" of its kind, but this is certainly among the first books in what is now called *management* or *administrative science*. In other words, this wasn't a book about how to set up mining or steel operations, but a book laying out general principles for setting up and running an organization full of people.

Most of his ideas will be very familiar to my reader by now. For instance, he defined five *functions of management*—that is, what management is supposed to do: Plan, Organize, Command, Coordinate, and Control. Sounds familiar. This was accompanied by a set of fourteen principles (see Figure 7.3) that are something like the first systematic ideas for how to do *organizational design*. Almost all of these probably could have been written by Max Weber had Weber's interests been *normative* ones of telling people what they *ought* to do. The *division of work* into specialized and clear tasks was one, for example. Another was the need for clear lines of authority that run from the top to the bottom of the organization (which he called *scalar chains*). These lines of authority should be such that it is clear to whom one reports (*unity of command*), and designed in such a way that no one is overwhelmed by having too many subordinates to manage (reasonable *spans of control*, as they're called).

Where Fayol provides some ideas that haven't already come to the fore through consideration of the likes of Weber and Taylor, is probably in thinking at least a bit more about the humans, and in ways that somewhat foreshadows ideas that we will encounter in Chapter 8. Fayol, like Taylor, knew that one of the most important things in organizing is to get buy-in from the human components of the system. You need to make sure that people have incentives to obey their orders and go along with the program. Taylor's methods were pretty simple—it's the *carrot and the stick* method of exercising power. On the one hand, you entice people with material rewards (the *carrot*—this is Economic control), and on the other hand you use threats and punishments (the *stick*—the equivalent of Political control). Fayol does not doubt this. One of his

FIGURE 7.3 **Henri Fayol's 14 Principles of Management**

Division of Work: Specialized workers are more efficient than those who are "jacks of all trades"
Authority & Responsibility: Higher ups need the authority to give orders, but also need to know that it comes with responsibility.
Discipline: Discipline has to be kept in organizations, but the methods for doing it can vary.
Unity of Command: Workers should have only one direct supervisor so that orders are clear and don't conflict.
Unity of Direction: Work groups with the same goals should work under one manager to make sure that action is coordinated.
Subordination of Individual Interests to the General Interest: The needs and interests of any of the individuals in an organization (including management) are less important than the needs and interests of the organization.
Remuneration: Worker satisfaction depends on fair pay-back in terms of good pay, but also other considerations
Centralization: Centralization of authority is needed for clarity and coordination, but decentralization is needed so workers can do their jobs. You have to find the right balance.
Scalar Chain: Authority is hierarchical and everyone should understand the chains of command.
Order: The workplace has to be kept in order in terms of cleanliness and the organization of materials.
Equity: Even-handed fairness on the part of management is important, along with basic understanding and consideration for workers.
Stability of Tenure of Personnel: Efforts should be made to create conditions that retain employees. The more that human capital is built up by job experience the better.
Initiative: Workers should be allowed at least some degree of freedom to take their own initiative as it provides people with satisfaction.
Esprit de Corps: (= "spirit of the body" or just "team spirit") Get people committed to the organization so that they want to do well in order to contribute to the success of the whole.

Source: Author's summary from Fayol, 1949, Chapter 4.

principles was *Discipline*, and another was *Equity* which in partly involved "fair remuneration" (fair pay). However, there was a more general current in Fayol's ideas that reflected a more complicated picture of humans. The principle that captures it most generally was the importance of building *Esprit des Corps*. This literally translates from French to "sprit of the body" but in this case, of course, it means spirit of the organization (or *corporation*. *Corp* means "body").

Fayol didn't see organizations as mere systems of interconnected machine-like parts, but as larger, organic wholes that included living and breathing humans. In simple terms, he thought it to be important for the people in it to identify with the organization. Thus another principle was *Stability of Tenure of Personnel*—what we would now just call *job security*. One of the things this does is merely technical as it allows consistent development of workers' capabilities (*human capital*), but it also signals a form of commitment by the organization to the well-being worker. Furthermore, part of the Equity principle was "kindness and justice." In other words, despite knowing that all aspects of an organizational system are basically cogs in a larger machinery, Fayol did recognize that the humans should not be treated merely as inanimate cogs. We will return to this idea in the next Chapter with ideas that more fully develop the view of organizations as *Human Systems*.

While the value of Fayol's thinking is frequently recognized in treatments of the development of classical management theory (CMT), its actual impact at the time he was writing is somewhat questionable. In a general sense, his ideas tended to get overshadowed by Taylorism. This may explain why CMT has always been associated with largely reducing workers to cogs. But this question is not of very great practical significance. Pulling out individuals from the flow of history tends to produce somewhat distorted pictures of things. Thinking about organizations as rational systems and trying to make them so came about as more of an explosion rather than a trickle here and there, and you don't find isolated individuals so much as ideas of engineering for efficiency coming to permeate culture. In the long run, the most important development may have been the establishment of business management as an institutionalized area of study in universities. People like Taylor, Ford, and Fayol make their living in actually building and running organizations. But other people were concurrently emerging who make their living by explicitly developing ideas about how to design and manage them. In other words, the organizational revolution is where we find the origins of what is now *organizational studies*.

The Institutionalization of Organizational Studies

The turn of the twentieth century was a busy time for rational systems building in many respects. We know that business organizations underwent dramatic changes and that this ushered in changes in how the economy operates, and with that, changes in the organization of work and employment. But it wasn't only business and economic changes, of course, as the changes reverberated throughout virtually all sectors of society. We have already seen, for example, that the growth of labor unions and large bureaucratic government, especially in the United States, was spurred by the externalities borne of new industrial enterprises. And it was also a time of transformation in educational institutions. The emerging industrial organizations needed some human capital development in the general population, and people needed human capital for many of the emerging jobs. So mass public education systems were close on the heels of big business and bureaucratization. As part and parcel, it was also a time of expansion and change in higher education. So, in fact, the period from roughly 1870–1910 has been called the *Age of the*

University. It was a period of expansion including the founding of new academic disciplines, departments, colleges, and schools within universities. The first Sociology department, for example, was established at the University of Kansas in 1892, and was soon followed by many others. The true emergence of organizational sociology would be some time in coming, but many other parts of organizational studies were emerging all around this time.

Political Science was also getting its institutional foothold as a formal discipline at the end of the nineteenth century. One major and important area of political science and organizational studies is called *Public Administration* which concerns itself primarily with the orderly and efficient operation of governmental organizations. The origins of this are often traced to an 1887 paper by (the not-as-of-then yet president) Woodrow Wilson called "The Study of Administration." It didn't read so much like a treatise in how to Taylorize tasks, manage personnel, or build *esprit des corps*, but it was a thoroughly rational systems orientation borne of the age. According to Wilson, the purpose of studying administration is *to discover, first, what government can properly and successfully do, and, secondly, how it can do these proper things with the utmost possible efficiency and at the least possible cost either of money or of energy.*[5] While an aspect of government, administration was to be removed from politics. He actually defined it as a field of business where policies are simply applied and carried out as efficiently as possible. Civil servants were to be very highly trained and dedicated to their tasks rather than any forms of personal or political agendas—in other words ideal typical bureaucratic participants. And the machine metaphor was explicit. As Wilson put it:

> *we must prepare better officials as the apparatus of government. If we are to put in new boilers and to mend the fires which drive our governmental machinery, we must not leave the old wheels and joints and valves and bands to creak and buzz and clatter on as best they may at bidding of the new force. We must put in new running parts wherever there is the least lack of strength or adjustment.*[6]

Government policy is the machine. Administrators are the machine parts.

Psychology was also getting into the game (as it seems that there few, if any, games that the psychologists do not get into). One specialty area of Psychology is called *Industrial and Organizational Psychology (I/O)*, and is nearly as old as Psychology itself. It is generally considered to be a branch of applied Psychology wherein the goal is use psychological principles to understand individuals *vis-à-vis* organizational structures and settings. The questions can very much be about how to design organizational structures and processes with knowledge of human psychology in mind—that is, how to build organizations that work well for and with people. However, the goal is often just as much about how to make sure that people are molded to the needs of organizations, and that is certainly where it started. The founding text for the field is frequently seen to have been *Psychology and Industrial Efficiency* published in 1910 by Hugo Münsterberg. Münsterberg, incidentally, studied with Wilhelm Wundt at the University of Leipzig. Wundt is widely regarded

---

[5]Wilson, 1887, p. 197.
[6]Wilson, 1887, p. 216.

(often along with William James at Harvard University) as having founded Psychology as a distinct discipline, which is why I've said that I/O is nearly as old as Psychology itself.

Daniel Wren, who has been a very influential historian of management thought clearly indicates that industrial psychology got its "ethics, scope, and direction" from scientific management, and quotes Münsterberg:

> We ask how we can find the men whose mental qualities make them best fitted for the work which they have to do; secondly, under what psychological conditions we can secure the greatest and most satisfactory output from every man; and finally how we can produce most completely the influences on human minds which are desired in the interests of business. In other words, we ask how to find the best possible work, and how to secure the best possible effects.[7]

In essence, Taylor and his followers were mechanical engineers trying to systematize and standardize work processes, and industrial psychologists were emerging as the complementary "human engineers" working on how to make sure that people fit themselves to the new systems.

Just a year after Münsterberg's, founding work, Walter Dill Scott (who also worked with Wundt) published his own early contribution to Industrial Psychology, and the title leaves little doubt as to his orientation: *Increasing Human Efficiency in Business: A Contribution to the Psychology of Business*. In addition to that he turned his psychological gaze to advertising, and thus is recognized as part of the founding of *Marketing* as a discipline and profession. He spent a lot of his career as a consultant to both industrial and military organizations. In the case of the former, he focused on both personnel selection and advertising, and in the latter on personnel selection. This was very much in line, of course, with Taylor's ideas of finding systematic ways to match people to tasks. In 1923 he published *Personnel Management: Principles, Practices, and Points of View* which was largely a mixture of Freudian psychology, the emerging field of industrial psychology, and Taylorism, and it became a very popular text both inside of business schools and out.

On the subject of university *business schools*, it may come as no surprise that their origins are found here as well. The famous Wharton School at the University of Pennsylvania was the first university business school in the United States, founded in 1881, although it only offered undergraduate programs. Harvard's business school was founded in 1908 and was the site of the world's first Masters of Business Administration (MBA). Thus was instituted during a flurry of other business school foundings right at the turn of the century, such as the Tuck School at Dartmouth (1900) and the Booth School at the University of Chicago (1898, originally the College of Commerce and Administration). While at the time it seemed to be rather unclear what it is that business schools are supposed to do and teach, Frederick Taylor loomed large. He regularly lectured at Harvard and his books *Shop Management* (1903) and *The Principles of Scientific Management (1911)* were highly influential and frequently identified as the world's first books in *management science*.

---

[7]Münsterberg, 1913, pp. 23–24, quoted in Wren, 2005, pp. 192–193.

Harlow Person who served as Dean at the Tuck school organized and hosted the first conference on scientific management in the United States and also served for a time as president of the *Taylor Society* (formerly *Society to Promote the Science of Management*). Person's idea was to take scientific management, not as a narrow vision of shop floor management, but more as an overall framing philosophy for all of management. This orientation is what fundamentally shaped what business schools and the management sciences became. Often thought of as most closely related to economics, it may be better to see the management sciences as much more akin to engineering.

In sociological terms the important observation here is that the rise of large industrial organizations at the turn of the twentieth century helped give birth to a science for designing and administering them. And this then provided the formation of ideas that fed back into the rationalization of the world. A great deal of the importance obviously lies in the development of the ideas alone, such as those of Fayol, Münsterberg, or Scott. But even more important was the rise of *organizations* that ensured the continual, systematic development of those ideas. The institutionalization of things like industrial psychology and management science in University colleges, schools, and departments, along with associated academic organizations ensures that there are people whose primary jobs are to develop ideas with regards to understanding management. So far more important that the specific names that have been memorialized in organizational and management history is that management as a professional discipline, in and of itself, has been central to the *iron cage*. The founding ideas, which are then the basis for future development all bear the hallmarks of a rational systems orientation. We might call this foundation of management science the rationalization of the rationalizers.

The Enduring Legacy of Taylorism and Fordism

There are ways of presenting organizational theory that make it appear to be the case that rational systems approaches to understanding organizations are old and have been surpassed. It was a way of thinking arose at the turn of the twentieth century, but the general idea is often that, as the study of organizations developed, rational systems models of organizations were replaced by newer models such as Human Systems (see Chapter 8) and then Open Systems (see Chapter 9). This is sometimes tied to historical changes in the challenges faced by organizations themselves. We will, for example, briefly revisit the 1970s crisis period in Chapter 9 as it coincides with the rise of open systems thinking. There is certainly some logic and utility to this conception as it does reflect changes in thinking and doing with regards to organizations. However, it is just as important to recognize that the rationalizing spirit and its methods continue to lie at the heart of most organizing and a good deal of the management sciences. As we'll see in Chapter 9, rationalization is actually a deeply ingrained cultural assumption that is expected of organizations. For that reason, among others, the purposeful development of formal systems, processes, and techniques for the coordination and control of human action to accomplish defined ends has not ceased.

The Continued March of Formal Rationality

If you back to Chapter 1, we started out by using Max Weber's ideal typical definition of bureaucracy and its connection to his larger *rationalization thesis*. The basic idea was that Weber was observing the growth and spread of large, rationalized systems at the turn of the twentieth century—the *organizational revolution* itself—and predicted their continued growth and spread. By extension, we visited Sociologist George Ritzer's relabeling this as a process of *McDonaldization* whereby he argued that the Taylor- and Ford-ization of human action and organizational processes has continued to spread, and now far beyond just the manufacture of goods which lay at the heart of the initial rationalization of society. It has entered into many service industries, as Ritzer described, so it is now both production of goods and services that are increasingly automated. But it is also further embedded into how goods and services are distributed and consumed. The kinds of tasks that have been automated have frequently been rather low level, and simple ones such as the installation of car parts, flipping of a burger, or grocery store checkouts. But the increasing development of *artificial intelligence* and *machine-learning (AI/ML)* technologies now has many predicting the displacement of humans from even relatively high level production and service work in such areas as marketing research, sales management, or chemical engineering. Those instruction cards that Frederick Taylor created to direct the work of human workers can now just be programmed into computers where the instructions are fed into increasingly automated machines and systems that do increasing amounts of work, while continuing to control whatever humans are left in the processes.

The first edition of Ritzer's book on McDonaldization was published in 1993 and many things have changed since then. One of the most significant things is that *electronic commerce* (a.k.a. *e-commerce*) was only in its infancy and has since become huge. So in more recent editions of the book, he posits the question of whether or not we should be talking instead about something like the *Amazon.comization* of society. Or, since Wal-Mart has continued to grow and expand, including both in terms of physical brick-and-mortar store sites and its growing presence in e-commerce, perhaps the *Wal-Martization* of society. His general answer is basically that the increasing computerization of commerce, hasn't really changed anything in principle. Rather it has just allowed the processes of McDonaldization to continually accelerate.[8] But it might not pay to worry all that much about which labels might be the most appropriate. The introduction of the McDonaldization term was catchy, and things like Amazon.comization can be interesting to discuss, but nothing about the underlying story has changed since the days of Taylor and Ford. *Taylorism, Fordism, bureaucratization, automation, McDonaldization.* They all basically mean the same thing and we've been on the same ride for a little over the last century. It is nothing other than *formal rationality*—the setting out of courses of human action in preset, standardized rules, and procedures whether in written or technological form. And it's all still centered on and driven by the same thing—organizations use various means of controlling action in order to try to maximize the efficiency of the organization, with efficiency defined in terms of organizational needs. Machines are very handy for this because they are far easier to control than humans. And, while they certainly might

---

[8]Ritzer, 2019, pp. 60–66.

malfunction from time to time, they don't get tired or hungry or fall asleep at the switch or whine and complain and go on strike. They are fast, efficient, predictable, and calculable.

But the machines do more than just take over human work tasks in the form of automation. They also control human workers—a process that Ritzer referred to as the replacement of humans with *nonhuman technology*. A *human technology* is a form of technology that a human controls, such as a screwdriver or a pencil. A *nonhuman technology* is a technology or technological system that controls the humans, such as a mass production system, standards of learning (SOL) educational programs, or the fence and crosswalk system described in Chapter 1, which enforces the rule of only crossing at a crosswalk. The building of nonhuman technological systems that control the workers within it was the specialty of the likes of Henry Ford. Our increasing technological capabilities have not changed the general principles. They have simply made it easier for organizations to institute Taylorist and Fordist systems of formal rationality.

Thus at the center of many discussions of the "future of work" for the twenty-first century are the impacts that the continued development of computerization along with in the increasing employment of AI/ML will have on work, workers, and the economy in general. In Chapter 3 we encountered at least one prominent line of thinking which is that the rise of digitization has contributed to increasing labor market dualization. As Taylor biographer Robert Kanigel somewhat poetically put it:

> The coming of the computer has extended Taylorist sensibilities even further; computer programs embody the very split between thinking and doing that is the hallmark of Taylorism. More and more, work bifurcates into two streams—skilled programming, planning and analytical work at the top, and low-skilled program execution...at the bottom. Engineers, economists, planners and systems analysts extract the last fraction of a cent from a fast-food hamburger at one end, while legions of minimum-wage drones peck at cash register touch screens at the other.[9]

But newer questions have also come increasingly to the forefront for organization theory and organizational studies, in general. To be sure, the effects of computerization have been important throughout the post-1970s period. However, more recent developments may also be qualitatively different because of AI/ML. Up until fairly recently, there was really no such thing as having humans controlled by technologies. This is because the technological systems that control humans within them were simply controlled by other humans. Nonhuman technologies, just as with bureaucratic rules, were simply the media through which humans exercised control over other humans. But AI/ML is different in the sense that they operate through algorithms that can alter themselves based on outcomes of their processes. An algorithm is just a list of rules to be followed to calculate or reach some desired outcome. They can appear in written form as they did in scientific management—a specific list

---

[9]Kanigel, 1997b, p. 22. Despite being written in 1997, little has happened to change the basic thrust of this except that even many areas of even the primary labor market seem to be falling to computer control and automation.

of steps would be defined to, say, install and tighten a set of bolts. In scientific management, a worker would follow the instructions and the bolts would be installed. But a manager or consultant would be monitoring the outcome in terms of its efficiency, and if greater efficiency could be found then management would modify the algorithmic instructions.

At this point in time, even if there is still a human worker (as opposed to a robotic one) installing bolts, there often isn't a human on the stopwatch modifying instructions. Rather, the algorithm is programmed into a computer; the computer continually tracks results and recalculates instructions, processes, or procedures. While it is obvious that humans have to initially design and program such systems, it is no longer humans that are controlling and modifying the algorithms after that. Rather, part of the programming is that the algorithms modify themselves—based on their own "learning"—thus the term *machine learning*. The large advantage to this, from the point of view of system designers, is that computers can handle far more data and calculations and do them far faster and with more accuracy than can humans. Hence, ironically the processes of mechanization and automation are themselves well on their way to be mechanized and automated.

The reason that this has become an important issue at the forefront for organizational theory is that the implications of all of this are far from clear in terms of what it means for organizations and organizing, and for humans and work. Certainly one thing that is clear is that increasing computerization continues to feed the Post- and Neo-Fordist trends that were discussed in Chapter 6 with regards to the easier ability to leverage networks relationships (Post-Fordist) or externalize various kinds of costs (Neo-Fordist). As explained in Chapter 6, many of those properties are quite continuous with the past although they also contribute to the reasons that those such as organizational sociologist Gerald Davis has proclaimed "the end of the society of organizations."[10] The ability to easily collaborate with anyone anywhere with nothing but an ICT device could be making the old twentieth century forms of organization increasingly irrelevant. And certainly, the pace of change has increased as well lending something of a permanent and increasing turbulence to economic and social environments, just as they have been since the shake-up of the old, nonadaptive hierarchies of the pre-1970s period.

But as decision-making is increasingly turned over to self-learning algorithms the implications become very unclear. One central issue is that when *machine learning algorithms* (*MLAs*) perform actions and produce outputs, it is often not clearly understood why or how particular decision were reached or actions dictated or carried out. We have truly created systems that we, the system creators, can neither control nor understand, a matter to which we will return in Chapters 10 and 11.

Relatedly, more and more of our lives are tracked by and shaped by what is now generically called *big data*. We have entered a world where everything possible is tracked and stored, largely via our use of various ICT devices, and those data are then analyzed by algorithms and fed into the machine learning. This includes your activity with regards to internet activities, social media use, consumption patterns and habits, and so on for the marketing purposes. In the words of Business Professor Shoshana Zuboff, we have entered an *Age of Surveillance Capitalism* where large technology companies have become

---

[10]Davis, 2009.

panoptic which means all seeing.[11] Every click, every website, every Twitter and Instagram message, every hover over an image, every purchase, and so on is stored and analyzed by *MLA*s to create profiles of people, largely for the purposes of marketing.

But it also increasingly includes what people are doing at work. The tracking of inputs, outputs, and timing of various work processes is easily computerized. Audio, video, radio frequency identification (RFID) and global positioning systems (GPS) can track worker movements including even what they are doing and saying. The use of GPS tracking devices on company vehicles, for example, is now routine. Companies like UPS and FedEx can account for every second of their drivers' routes knowing how long it takes to drive between destinations and how much time is spent at each destination. Amazon made news in 2018 for patenting an RFID wristband for warehouse employees to wear. It provides total tracking of worker movement, including, of course, what they are doing with their hands.[12] There are any number of computer applications available that easily monitor employee computer activity—internet usage, email time, time away from the desk, and so on. Like the Judeo-Christian God, Santa Claus, or the guards in Jeremy Bentham's panoptic prison, the algorithms see it all. It is scientific management increasingly automated and increasingly panoptic.

There are at this point many questions to be asked and answered in organizational studies with regards to what these characteristics mean in terms of the future of organization, organizing, and organizational theory. In other respects, however, all we are watching is the continued march of formal rationality through history—and, arguably its intensification. Our organizational worlds remain significantly shaped by the dreams of the Frederick Taylors and Henry Fords of the turn of the twentieth century. Where this leaves us is simply in the same place we were in Chapter 6 with regards to the question of whether we are in a fundamentally new period with regards to how organizing is done—whether we are in a world of Post-Taylorism/Fordism, or simply in a world of Neo-Taylorism/Fordism with more effective tools for executing formal rationality. In the latter case, even if organizations have become smaller and less bureaucratic, this may simply be because the written rules of the bureaucracy are less and less needed in a world where so much is controlled by automation and algorithm. I suspect Frederick Taylor would be pleased so long as he remained the creator of the algorithms rather than being subject to their control.

The Evolution of Taylorism in Management Science and Consulting

As noted above, the management sciences and their associated institutional business school homes themselves were an outgrowth of the Taylorist impulses of the turn of the twentieth century. And while it is possible to describe the flow of organizational theory as having moved beyond rational systems models of organizing since then, it is also clear that much of organizational studies, and the management sciences in particular, remain steeped in the Tayloristic impulses and this is in very direct ways.

---

[11]Zuboff, 2019.

[12]Yeginsu, 2018. https://www.nytimes.com/2018/02/01/technology/amazon-wristband-tracking-privacy.html

We can begin by briefly revisiting the *Japanese System of Management* (JSM) that took the business and management consulting world by storm during the 1980s and beyond. For many observers, the anti-hierarchical and anti-bureaucratic principles of reliance on skilled shop floor workers operating in self-directed teams represented part of the spirit of Post-Fordism, or we could also say Post-Taylorism. Yet it is just as easy to see much of it as a form of Neo-Fordism. In fact, this becomes much more plausible if we note that the JSM was, at least in part, directly inspired by Henry Ford and his approach to building cars. One of the integral figures in the development of the JSM was Taichi Ohno who spent most of his working life developing the JSM for Toyota, and once claimed in an interview that he learned it all from Henry Ford's book *Today and Tomorrow*.[13] What Ohno and later developers of the JSM had that Ford didn't were just increasingly speedy means of communication and transportation so that greater flexibility was possible in terms of how production was organized and laid out. But we're still talking about the need for very strict means of coordination and control.

Consider the just-in-time (JIT) inventory system which, if it is to be successful, has to be managed much more tightly than just-in-case systems. Coordinating the overall flow of things through the production system to keep them at maximum levels of throughput with minimal amounts of waste isn't a change from Ford's methods. Rather it emulates them. Similarly, recall that another integral part of the JSM is the principle of *kaizen*—or continuous improvement. One part of workers' jobs in the JSM was to always work on figuring out how to do things better and more efficiently (where these value judgments are made in terms of the goals of the organization itself, of course). As such, one part of workers' training in the JSM is usually to learn how to perform time studies—on themselves. In other words, workers were expected to use Taylorism on themselves, and are trained in doing it. The only thing different in the case of Ford was that production line workers were not put in charge of these things. So in some respects, Ohno just kept on taking Fordist principles and making them even leaner.

The JSM took the world by storm, of course, as outlined in Chapter 6, but at least in name it was later supplemented and/or displaced by further development of variations on scientific management—by various means of systematizing the planning, measuring, monitoring, streamlining, and controlling organizational processes. You can easily find names for these all over the management literature and inside of organizations whether business organizations or otherwise: *Management Information Systems (MIS), Planning, Programming, and Budgeting Systems (PPBS), Program Evaluation Review Techniques (PERT), Total Quality Management (TQM)* programs, *Business Process Management (BPM), Six Sigma*, and so on. To some extent the varying and sometimes evolving labels are basically series of fads that run through management and consulting circles, but in one way or another they just remain forms of scientific management that are not different in principle but only in specific form and the power of the available tools. They are all about specifying desired outcomes and setting out the means of reaching them, systematic data-based measurement of performance with regards to efficiency, and constant adjustment to maintain and increase

---

[13]Petersen, 2002, p. 82; Ford, [1926] 2003. As for having learned it all from Ford, that is likely a bit of an overstatement as I will discuss below.

efficiency (*continuous improvement*). For illustration, we can briefly review one of the more popular management approaches referred to as *Lean Six Sigma (LSS)*. In the words of some of its practitioners LSS "has become one of the most popular and proven business process improvement methodologies organizations have ever witnessed in the past."[14]

Lean Six Sigma (LSS)

Lean Six Sigma (LSS) can be seen as something of a marriage between various ideas regarding *Lean Production (LP)*, such as the JSM, joined to another descendant of scientific management called *Statistical Process Control (SPC)*. (This is now also often referred to as *Statistical Quality Control (SQC)*). SPC was developed starting in the 1920s by physicist Walter A. Shewhart at Bell Laboratories. AT&T's Western Electric division, which manufactured most of the phone system's equipment, was having serious quality problems and Shewhart developed SPC as a means of dealing with quality control in manufacturing. The heart of it is the constant measurement and monitoring of quality by the use of statistical methods.

Any work process, whether it is making telephone equipment, making cheese burgers, teaching courses, or processing driver's license applications will contain variations from piece to piece, time to time, process to process, and so on. But variations mean inconsistency, and inconsistencies too far from the needed or desired outcomes represent quality problems and thus waste. Perhaps parts that are produced don't function well enough or at all, student learning outcomes are suboptimal, or more time is taken than is ideal, and so forth. The idea is to try to identify all of the things that contribute to the variations, eliminate those that can be eliminated, and measure the remaining ones that can't eliminated. Shewhart referred to the former as *assignable* or *special* sources of variation, such as worker fatigue or inattention, poor training, suboptimal machinery maintenance, poor layout of work spaces, and things of that nature. The latter kind are just seen to be more natural and inevitable, and were referred to as *common cause* sources of variation. These would be things like minor variations among batches or raw materials, normal variations in wear and tear on machinery, occasional human errors even among experienced and attentive personnel, and so on. In general statistical practice this is quite similar to the distinction between systematic and random sources of variation.

In an SPC approach to quality control you first identify and eliminate all possible *assignable/special*—or systematic—sources of variation. Make sure that all personnel are competent and well-trained, or known sources of problems in raw material supply are fixed, for example. You then engage in production and measure the (largely random) variations that remain. Ideally these are all now from just natural or *common cause* variations and, being from somewhat random sources, if you plot out the variations they should end up with the characteristics of a statistical *normal curve* (a.k.a. *bell curve*, see Figure 7.4). In a perfect normal curve, the mean, median, and mode should all be the same and at or very near your target outcome. The *mode*, of course, is the most common value found in a set of data, and will be equal to the mean in a normal distribution. But because of inevitable variations many outcomes will

---

FIGURE 7.4   **A Typical Normal (a.k.a Bell) Curve**

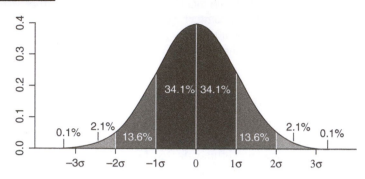

Source: Courtesy of Prof. Wayne W. LaMorte, Boston University School of Public Health, https://sphweb. bumc.bu.edu/otlt/MPH-Modules/PH717-QuantCore/ph717-Module6-RandomError/PH717-Module6-Random Error5.html

be different from the mean. If you measure the differences from the mean and take their average, this is the *standard deviation*. In normally distributed data about 66% of your cases will fall within plus or minus one of the standard deviation. About 95% will fall between plus or minus two standard deviations, and almost 98% will fall between plus or minus three. In statistics the Greek letter *sigma* (σ) is used to represent the standard deviation—and thus the eventual name *Six Sigma*. You constantly measure your output, and make sure that all production and parts and processes and so on fall with ±3 sigma— which adds up to six.

At Shewhart's time this was considered to be new thinking just because it provided a means of constantly monitoring production processes to make sure that they didn't fall outside of allowable limits. Up until then it was more common (and still is for many organizations) to just set out processes and either inspect quality at the completion of the process or only worry about it when problems became obvious. But this can easily result in great deal of waste- —wasted time, materials, energy, and so on. With constant monitoring and measurement, problems are identified and can be corrected immediately. The result is not only overall higher quality, but also less waste and thus lower costs.

Shewhart's work on the development of SPC culminated in what came to be famously referred to as the *Deming Cycle* (see Figure 7.5), after W. Edwards Deming (although it likely should have been labeled the Shewhart Cycle as it originated from a Shewhart book on the subject). Deming was educated as an electrical engineer and came to specialize in statistics working both as a consultant and in University positions. He came under Shewhart's influence when they met at Bell Laboratories in the 1920s. The *Shewhart/Deming Cycle* is quite simple in principle, and goes by the acronym *PDCA—Plan, Do, Check, Act*. It was seen as being analogous to the logic of the scientific method whereby one derives hypotheses from general theoretical principles, designs and makes observations that can check the hypothesis, analyze the results, and then the analysis is used to improve the theory and hypotheses. In other words, science is supposed to operate on a principle of *continuous improvement* in which you constantly plan, do, check, and then act. Thus as much as part of the idea of SPC is to keep variations within ideal limits, it is also to use

FIGURE 7.5   **Principles of the Shewhart/Deming Cycle, Six Sigma, and Lean Production**

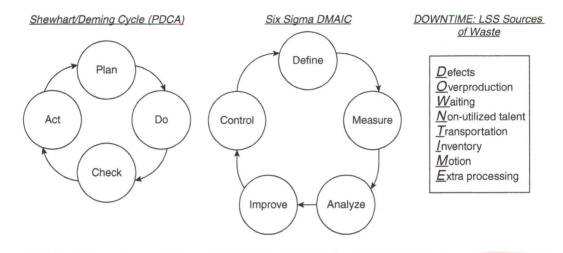

Source: Author's depiction from multiple sources. See notes at the end of the chapter.

data and analysis to continually refine processes and procedures and so forth to continually move toward optimum outcomes.

By most accounts Shewhart and Deming's methods were ostensibly very effective wherever they were implemented, including at Western Electric, and they were also both involved in bringing the methods to the US military during World War II. After the War, Deming apparently found little interest in SPC in the United States and became a very active and influential consultant in Japanese industry. Thus, SPC fed directly into development of the JSM along with Fordism. Thus it is ironic that there is a very real sense in which the Japanese companies that became a competitive problem for US companies beginning in the 1970s were significantly influenced by ideas that originated in the United States. And if we move forward to that post-1970s period, this is where we find the reemergence of SPC in the United States but now under the name *Six Sigma*.

Its development is generally attributed to Bill Smith, a management and engineering professional who was with Motorola in the late 1980s. This was at a time when Motorola was one of those US companies struggling in the face of foreign competition, and particularly with regards to quality control problems. The *Six Sigma* label leaves us no doubt that the core of it remains not too far from the logic developed by Shewhart some 60 years earlier—it is quite simply about keeping business outcomes of whatever kind within ±3 sigma from a desired state. At this point *Six Sigma* is often referred to as more of a "school" that a specific program or method as there is no specific and "official" definition of what it is. (If you want to follow developments, once source is the *Six Sigma Daily*, https://www.sixsigmadaily.com) But the central logic of it is generally summarized as a product and process improvement cycle including five steps: *Define, Measure, Analyze, Improve, Control (DMAIC)* (See Figure 7.5. It was originally just MAIC, but recognition that clear definitions of problems, desired outcomes, and so forth are crucial soon followed). We'll have to imagine that Frederick Taylor would be impressed. Sure, search for the *one best way*. But always assume that you can always make the best better.

While Six Sigma obviously contains emphasis on principles of *lean production (LP)* (as defective products/processes = waste), a more explicit "marriage of Six Sigma and lean"[15] started to come about in the early 2000s. The general idea is that Six Sigma methodologies tend to focus more narrowly than lean production on things like defect rates, whereas lean production takes much broader *enterprise-wide view* of the entirety of organizational operations. The statistical methods at the heart of Six Sigma simply provide very powerful tools to the more general LP attempts to eliminate all forms of waste and thus maximize efficiencies. The addition of LP principles gives an expanded and more comprehensive understanding of the potential sources of waste, which is often captured in the acronym DOWNTIME (see Figure 7.5). Stepping back just a little bit, I think it is easy to say that LSS can just be translated to *Fordist-Taylorism*. The Fordist designation is about designing overall socio-technical systems to eliminate as much waste as possible in the name of productive efficiency. The Taylorism part refers to a focus on intensive measurement and monitoring on the constant search for the *one best way*.

None of this should be too surprising. It is business organizations in a competitive, capitalist economy that basically set the trends for "best practices" for formal organizations. So, for example, LSS techniques can be found not only in private, for profit organizations but also in public and nonprofit organizations. And the fact that business organizations still strive for efficiency in competitive environments, and that this helps to continue and even accelerate the growth of formal rationality should come as no surprise. As Weber observed so long ago, one of the primary movers of rationalization processes is the competitiveness of capitalist market economies. This hasn't changed, so it is unlikely that we should expect to see any declines in the forward march of formal rationality.

But there is more to it than that, and we do need to add some more complications even into the picture of things like TQM or LSS. In Chapter 8 we will learn that ideas about humans and their place and importance in organizations have become more complicated than it ever was for Taylor and Ford. (Although just how much more complicated can be a matter of disagreement). In Chapter 9, among other things, we will also be led back to questions that we have already asked—whether it is truly actual *efficiency* that accounts for organizational success or whether things like SPC or LSS are adopted just as much (or more) for organizational legitimacy rather than for any practical results they may produce. We will then move on to worry a great deal about whether or not this constant pursuit of formal rationality might be the impossible dream (at least for those who dream *that* dream) and may just be leading us to ever more confounding forms of the *irrationality of rationality.*

---

[15]Anthony, et al. 2017, p. 1077.

SOURCES AND FURTHER READING

On *Classical Management Theory (CMT)/* *Ford/Taylor/Fayol* primary sources:

- Fayol, Henri. 1949. *General and Industrial Management.* London: Sir Isaac Pitman & Sons, Ltd.

  - Originally published in French as: Fayol, Henri. 1917. *Administration Industrielle et Générale: Prévoyance, Organisation, Commandement, Coordination, Contrôle.* Paris: H. Dunod et E. Pinat.

- Münsterberg, Hugo. 1913. *Psychology and Industrial Efficiency.* Boston, MA: Houghton Mifflin.

- Scott, Walter Dill. 1911. *Increasing Human Efficiency in Business: A Contribution to the Psychology of Business.* New York, NY: The Macmillan Company.

- Taylor, Frederick Winslow. 1903. *Shop Management.* New York, NY: American Society of Mechanical Engineers.

- ———. 1911/1919. *The Principles of Scientific Management.* New York, NY: Harper & Brothers Publishers.

- Weber, Max. 2013. *Economy and Society: An Outline of Interpretive Sociology.* Edited by Guenther Roth and Claus Wittich. Berkeley, CA: University of California Press.

  - See especially, Chapter III: "The Types of Legitimate Domination" and Chapter XI: "Bureaucracy."

- Wilson, Woodrow. 1887. "The Study of Administration." *Political Science Quarterly* 2: 197–222.

The secondary literature on *Classical Management Theory (CMT)/*Ford/Taylor/Fayol is immense. Most influential here has been:

- Hounshell, David A. 1985. *From the American System to Mass Production, 1800–1932: The Development of Manufacturing Technology in the United States.* Baltimore, MD: Johns Hopkins University Press. See especially Chs. 6–7.

- Hughes, Thomas Parke. 2004. *American Genesis: A Century of Invention and Technological Enthusiasm, 1870–1970.* Chicago, IL: The University of Chicago Press. See especially Chs. 5–6.

- Jacoby, Sanford M. 1985. *Employing Bureaucracy: Managers, Unions and the Transformation of American Industry, 1900–1945.* New York, NY: Columbia University Press.

- Kanigel, Robert. 1997a. *The One Best Way Frederick Winslow Taylor and the Enigma of Efficiency.* Cambridge, MA: MIT Press.

  - A brief highlighting commentary from which the direct quote was drawn can be found in Kanigel, Robert. 1997b. "Taylor-Made: How the World's First Efficiency Expert Refashioned Modern Life in His Own Image." *The Sciences* 37: 18–23.

- Landy, Frank J. 1997. "Early Influences on the Development of Industrial and Organizational Psychology." *Journal of Applied Psychology* 82: 467–77.

- Paxton, John. 2012. "Mr. Taylor, Mr. Ford, and the Advent of High-Volume Mass Production: 1900–1912." *Economics & Business Journal: Inquiries & Perspectives* 4: 74–90.

- Shenhav, Yehouda. 1999. *Manufacturing Rationality: The Engineering Foundations of the Managerial*

Revolution. New York, NY: Oxford University Press.

○ An early paper-length and abridged account can be found in: Shenhav, Yehouda. 1995. "From Chaos to Systems: The Engineering Foundations of Organization Theory, 1879–1932." *Administrative Science Quarterly* 40: 557–85.

• Voxted, Søren. 2017. "100 years of Henri Fayol." *Management Revue* 28: 256–74.

• Daniel A. Wren. 2005. *The History of Management Thought*, 5th ed. Hoboken, NJ: John Wiley & Sons., Inc.

• Wren, Daniel A., Arthur G. Bedeian, John D. Breeze, and David Ross. 2002. "The Foundations of Henri Fayol's Administrative Theory." *Management Decision* 40: 906–18.

On the rise of contemporary **business schools**:

• Conn, Steven. 2019. *Nothing Succeeds Like Failure: The Sad History of American Business Schools.* Ithaca, NY: Cornell University Press.

• Daniel A. Wren. 2005. *The History of Management Thought*, 5th ed. Hoboken, NJ: John Wiley & Sons., Inc.

On **The Continued March of Formal Rationality**, as I headed it:

• Bailey, Diane, Samer Faraj, Pamela Hinds, Georg von Krogh, and Paul Leonardi. 2019. "Special Issue of *Organization Science*: Emerging Technologies and Organizing." *Organization Science* 30: 642–46.

[Note that this was merely a call for papers (CFP) for an issue that had not yet appeared as of this writing. However, the central issues of interest were revolved around issues of increasingly intelligent technologies and the availability of big data.]

• Baum, Joel A. C., and Heather A. Haveman. 2020. "Editors' Comments: The Future of Organizational Theory." *Academy of Management Review* 45: 268–72.

• Curchod, Corentin, Gerardo Patriotta, Laurie Cohen, and Nicolas Neysen. 2020. "Working for an Algorithm: Power Asymmetries and Agency in Online Work Settings." *Administrative Science Quarterly* 65: 644–76.

• Crowley, Martha, Daniel Tope, Lindsey Joyce Chamberlain, and Randy Hodson. 2010. "Neo-Taylorism at Work: Occupational Change in the Post-Fordist Era." *Social Problems* 57: 421–47.

• Gerald, Davis F. 2009. "The Rise and Fall of Finance and the End of the Society of Organizations." *Academy of Management Perspectives* 23: 27–44.

• Faraj, Samer, Stella Pachidi, and Karla Sayegh. 2018. "Working and Organizing In the Age of the Learning Algorithm." *Information and Organization* 28: 62–70.

• Hounshell, David A. 1988. "The Same Old Principles in the New Manufacturing." *Harvard Business Review* 66: 54–61.

• Petersen, Peter B. 2002. "The Misplaced Origin of Just-in-Time Production Methods." *Management Decision* 40: 82–8.

• Ritzer, George. 2019. *The McDonaldization of Society: Into the Digital Age*, 9th Ed. Thousand Oaks, CA: Sage Publications.

• Shestakofsky, Benjamin. 2017. "Working Algorithms: Software Automation and the Future of Work." *Work and Occupations* 44: 376–423.

• Wilson, H. James. 2013. "Wearables in the Workplace." *Harvard Business Review* 91: 23–5.

- Yeginsu, Ceylan. 2018. "If Workers Slack Off, the Wristband Will Know. (And Amazon Has a Patent for It.)" *New York Times.* February 1, p. B3. Accessed December 7, 2020, https://www.nytimes.com/2018/02/01/technology/amazon-wristband-tracking-privacy.html.

- Zuboff, Shoshana. 2019. *The Age of Surveillance Capitalism: The Fight for a Human Future at the New Frontier of Power.* New York, NY: Public Affairs/Hachette Book Group.

  o A review essay can be found here: Kapadia, Anush. 2020. "All That Is Solid Melts into Code." *Economy and Society* 49: 329–44.

In terms of the general flow of "The **Evolution of Taylorism in Management Science** and Consulting" see:

- Feigenbaum, Armand V. 1983. *Total Quality Control*, 3rd Ed. New York, NY: McGraw-Hill.

- Kolesar, Peter J. 1993. "The Relevance of Research on Statistical Process Control to the Total Quality Movement." *Journal of Engineering and Technology Management* 10: 317–38.

- Myers, Lewis A., Jr. 2011. "One Hundred Years Later: What Would Frederick Taylor Say?" *International Journal of Business and Social Science* 2: 8–11.

- Yates, JoAnne. 1989. *Control through Communication: The Rise of System in American Management.* Baltimore, MD: Johns Hopkins University Press.

With regards to the development of **Lean Six Sigma (LSS)**, in particular, see:

- Antony, Jiju, Ronald Snee, and Roger Hoerl. 2017, "Lean Six Sigma: Yesterday, Today and Tomorrow." *International Journal of Quality & Reliability Management* 34: 1073–93.

- Bradford, Phillip G., and Paul J. Miranti. 2019. "Information in an Industrial Culture: Walter A. Shewhart and the Evolution of the Control Chart, 1917–1954." *Information & Culture: A Journal of History* 54: 179–219.

- Deming, W. Edwards. 1951. *Elementary Principles of the Statistical Control of Quality.* Tokyo, Japan: Nippon Kagaku Gijutsu Remmi.

- George, Michael L. 2002. *Lean Six Sigma: Combining Six Sigma Quality with Lean Production Speed.* New York, NY: McGraw-Hill.

- Montgomery, Douglas C., and William H. Woodall. 2008. "An Overview of Six Sigma." *International Statistical Review* 76: 329–46.

- Pepper, M.P.J. and T.A. Spedding. 2010. "The Evolution of Lean Six Sigma." *International Journal of Quality & Reliability Management* 27: 138–55.

- Shewhart, Walter A. 1931. *Economic Control of Quality of Manufactured Products.* New York, NY: Van Nostrand.

- ———. 1939. *Statistical Methods from the Viewpoint of Quality Control.* Washington, DC: The Graduate School of the Department of Agriculture, Reprinted by Dover Publications.

- Snee, Ronald D. (2010), "Lean Six Sigma—Getting Better All The Time." *International Journal of Lean Six Sigma* 1: 9–29.

The Human Organization

While *rational systems* ideas regarding formal organizations were born in and continue to be developed primarily in business organizations, they certainly have always spread throughout organizations of all kinds. I work at a fairly typical state university. We don't operate on a for-profit basis as a fee for service type of a business. We're an educational institution. Yet we are awash in the general principles and logic of formally rationalized *continuous improvement* philosophies. Every organizational unit, for example, is required to have stated goals and objectives and, at the end of each academic year, is required to produce and file an assessment report. The report needs to come complete with data that are presumably designed to measure the extent to which we are meeting our goals and objectives. Deficits are to be noted and ideas regarding improvements presented. We are required to *Plan-Do-Check-Act* as the *Shewhart/Deming Cycle* specified (see Chapter 7). (The assessment report, as should be obvious, is the part where you check.) In addition to the annual assessment, there is one much more extensive *Academic Program Review (APR)* that occurs on a seven year cycle in which we do the same, including much more extensive documentation of how we have improved in meeting our goals and objectives since the prior APR was performed.

But it's not just the academic departments that are regularly evaluated. As the cogs in this larger organizational machinery, every faculty member is required to produce an annual report on their activities. These reports are reviewed each year by the department head, and an assignment of merit is made. (In normal universities, department heads are called "Chairs".) In the annual report we provide an account of the work that we did, and the job description includes three types of work: teaching, research/scholarship (publications), and service. My work on a book like this one, for example, lies at the intersections of teaching and scholarship. (So yes, most of us are "teachers" as people say, but that is far from all that we are expected to do.)

Finishing my first year as a tenure-track faculty member, I pulled up our department's annual evaluation form and was a bit surprised and panicked to see the following as my first order of business for the report: *Briefly describe how your courses contribute to meeting program objectives.* Hmmm…I thought. We have "Program Objectives?" With some degree of trepidation, I opened up the official undergraduate course catalog where one finds program and course descriptions. Sure enough, there they were. Way up front at the beginning of the description of the Sociology major, one learns that we have a "Mission Statement" and a set of stated goals. "Well," I thought, "I'm off to a pretty bad start in my new job since I've been teaching Sociology courses here for a year but didn't know that I was supposed to be meeting stated goals and objectives." There is also a Faculty Handbook. This is the official job description for faculty including all of our duties and obligations and the kinds of authority that we have and don't have. I'm sure that I was provided a copy when I was hired, but I never actually looked at it—until six years later when it was time for me to apply for tenure and promotion. You see, the official rules for tenure and promotion are defined there and when I was trying to find out how to apply I kept seeing references to sections of the Faculty Handbook. So once again with some degree of trepidation I had a look at it, all along hoping that I wasn't going to learn that I had missed something by not knowing the formal rules.

Of course, I wasn't all that disturbed in either instance, nor at any other time when I learned that activities that I had been involved in had some formal rules, procedures, and descriptions that were unbeknownst to me. I wasn't disturbed because I know a thing or two about formal organizations and all of those formal rules and prescriptions and procedures. I know that most any organization really has two faces. One of those is the formal face, and it is found in organizational charts, mission statements, job descriptions, requisition forms, rules and official procedures, and such. This is the ideal-typical picture of an organization as a rational structure that Weber had in mind when he said that one might think of an organization as its filing cabinet. It is also what industrial engineers like Frederick Taylor sought to produce.

But the second face of the organization is its informal side. In all organizations there are formal descriptions of what the organization is and how it operates and who does what and how and so forth. But then there is also what people are actually doing. If one studies organizations with a view to what can actually be observed in practice we often get a very different picture of organizational life from what the formal rules say. There are now quite a few streams of organizational theory and research that take this into account. The earliest, oddly enough, grew out of research being done by Tayloristic industrial engineers who noted that people, both as individuals and in social groups, are quite a bit more complicated to figure out than Taylor and his ilk would give them credit for. This research resulted in a couple of prominent streams of thought in the management sciences that generally go by the names of *Human Relations* and *Humanistic Management* approaches to running organizations. Other streams of research emerged when sociologists turned their attention to the study of formal organizations, beginning roughly in the 1940s and 1950s. Here the emphasis has been less on how to run an organization and more on simply understanding them as forms of human social activity. More recently, many of the themes appear in attention to what is called *organizational culture* which has become a common buzzphrase throughout organizational studies.

It is quite common to take these things as indicating that organizations are best thought of as *human* or *natural* or *organic* systems rather than rational ones. While these labels are not all that precise the *human* reference comes in thinking of organizations not as formalized machines, but as collections of interacting living, breathing, thinking, feeling human beings. Organizations are nothing more than what people construct through their actions. The formal rules and such might matter, but only to the extent that people are attentive to them, and even then they still need to be given meaning and interpretation. The *natural* and *organic* imagery comes from thinking of organization less as systems of preplanned activities and more as patterns of action and interaction that *emerge* out of the activities of all of those humans and take on a life of their own that is often quite different from its formally stated description. A full story covering this kind of thought and research regarding organizations could fill a book on its own. I will pull out some major slices and themes here, beginning with what is often seen as the birth of the human systems perspective, at least for the management sciences.

Industrial Engineering and the Birth of the *Human Relations* School of Management

The Hawthorn Experiments

If you've ever taken a research methods course for social or behavioral science you've probably come across something called the *Hawthorne Effect*. In general form, it refers to a potential problem anytime you put people into experiments to find out how they behave in certain situations. You set up the experiment to manipulate the situations that your research subjects experience, and you expect that they respond to those things that you are purposely designing as experimental conditions. However, being in an experiment is itself a situation, and people can and do alter their behaviors simply because they are in an experiment. They know that they are being observed, for example, and may respond to things in ways that they think they are expected to respond. In research methods terms, this presents a problem of *external validity* which is the question of whether or not what you learn from an experiment applies to anything outside of the experimental context itself. If you notice something about human behaviors in your experiments, have you now learned something about how people, in general, behave? Or have you only learned how they behave if you put them in a particular kind of experimental situation?

The Hawthorne Effect is named after a place called the *Hawthorne Works* which was a production facility for various kinds of telephone equipment for AT&T's Western Electric division. In the 1920s and early 1930s it was the setting for a series of experiments on how to maximize worker productivity. These were very much designed and done in the tradition of Taylor's scientific management. It was, after all, where Walter Shewhart started developing *Statistical Process Control (SPC)*, as we encountered in Chapter 7. In this case, the focus wasn't so much on how to plan out specific work tasks, as it was for Taylor, or to use statistics to monitor output, as it was for Shewhart. Rather it was on the general working conditions such as levels of lighting, understanding how to minimize worker fatigue, the effects of different kinds of pay schemes, and so on. The initial and most commonly described set of experiments was done to investigate the effects of levels of lighting on productivity. Certain workers were separated out from the rest as an *experimental group* and located in a separate room so that researchers could systematical vary lighting conditions while measuring variations in worker productivity. The other shop floor workers who were not in the experimental group would be called a *control group*. For the control group, lighting conditions would remain as they always were. The researchers expected to be able to find optimum lighting levels by simply varying the lighting conditions for the experimental group while leaving them the same for the control group and comparing levels of productivity. While what they actually found is a matter of dispute, there is a common legend that has been handed down since then that worker productivity tended to increase (or at least not decline after observed increases) no matter what they did with levels of lighting.

I say that it is a common legend just because it isn't clear that this is what was found, and more recent analyses of the data collected indicated that the experiments were seriously flawed as was the analysis of data. However, nothing here hinges on what the data truly showed because many things were set in motion regardless. Especially in terms of the contents of this Chapter, we will go by the famous sociological dictum of what is called the *Thomas Theorem*, after early twentieth-century sociologist W.I. Thomas. To paraphrase to gender neutral language, the Thomas Theorem is that *if people define things as real, then they are real in their consequences.*[1] That is, people don't act toward things as they "really are." Rather, they act toward things based on how they understand them to be. Don't look to any ultimate form of objective Reality (with a capital-R) to understand human action. Instead, get a handle on what people *think* reality (with a small-r) to be. It is the latter that feeds into what we think, say, and do. Thus, in the case of the Hawthorne experiments what the data "really" showed is not the issue.

The Hawthorne researchers were expecting to see very straightforward changes in levels of productivity given changes in levels of lighting, and they did not. One thing that was surmised was that other variables were at work. One of those was an, as yet to be named Hawthorne Effect—that output levels reflected a psychological effect of being in an experiment. Output might have just gone up because workers were getting extra attention and felt special, or maybe because there was more attention to their output levels than normal, and they knew that. Initially, the researchers didn't care all that much. They just went on to find ways to get around the potential Hawthorne Effect. So after the illumination studies, the researchers went on to do a series of other experiments to understand the effects of worker fatigue on productivity, but greatly changed up the experimental situation.

In the fatigue experiments, which ran during the late 1920s, a small group of workers were selected and moved to a separate room which was labeled the *Relay Assembly Text Room*. (The history of the Hawthorne Works research includes a long list of various test rooms.) One hope was that eventually being in a separate group would come to feel "normal" and whatever psychological effects might have been created by the experimental situation would fade to elimination. To account for as many variables as possible, records were kept of many things, including even the weather. Perhaps most important, records were kept on the physical status of the workers and their mental states. Periodic medical exams were administered, and the workers were interviewed and asked about what they'd eaten and how long they'd slept, what kinds of things were going on in their lives, their feelings, and so on. When the studies began, and anytime that changes were made to the situation, this was fully explained to the workers who were then given the opportunity to comment. The typical supervisor role was taken over simply by an experimental observer to keep records and maintain cooperation among the workers. This situation also resulted in a relaxing of the typical rules that governed work at Western Electric. There was no typical "boss" around, and the workers were,

---

[1]Thomas and Thomas, 1928: 572.

for example, able to talk freely with one another, whereas conversation on the shop floor had always been discouraged.

The actual experiments were broken up into planned time periods. The first was just the measurement of output under normal shop floor working conditions prior to the start of the experiment, and the second was just maintaining typical working conditions after having been moved to the test room. Presumably, this is when it was hoped that the Hawthorne effect would disappear. The third period was a change in the pay scheme, and all of the others that followed were changes to things like rest breaks and the length of the workday or work week. For example, rest breaks were introduced in the fourth period, lengthened in the next period, and then shortened but increased in their frequency. Many times, earlier conditions were restored after having been changed. It is here that worker output tended to simply increase across time periods regardless of the changes that were made. All of this was very perplexing, and the researchers were once again left unable to interpret how variations in the physical conditions of work would affect worker productivity.

Eventually the dominant interpretation of these patterns—or lack thereof—came to be that applied by Harvard researchers Elton Mayo and Fritz Roethlisberger, of the Harvard Business School, along with William Dickson of the Hawthorne Works. They surmised that the observed changes in worker productivity were not due to the manipulation of the physical work conditions, or physical comfort of workers, or even of worker pay schemes. Rather workers were responding to both the *psychological* and *social* conditions of the work situation. In terms of psychological effects, members of experimental groups were specifically selected and set aside as special from the normal floor workers. As a matter of measuring as many variables as possible, they were given a great deal of attention by the company and researchers in the ways noted above. They were also given the opportunity to comment on working conditions and the changes that were being made, and they were listened to. They felt as if they were involved in doing something important and thus felt important themselves.

The social situation among the group of workers was surmised to have mattered as well. The typical work floor areas at Western Electric were rather large and somewhat nameless and faceless places. As was common in early industry, social interaction among workers was strongly discouraged if not forbidden. Workers were to sit at their work stations and focus wholly on the work. In the test rooms, it was not nameless and faceless, and the ability of workers to interact with each other in many cases made for friendship groups that extended to social relations outside of working hours. The workers got to feeling like a team of sorts, and this motivated them to work toward high output.

Thus what was going on throughout the Hawthorne experiments is that whatever the levels of worker productivity were, they reflected the social–psychological conditions of work more so than mere physical conditions. A Tayloristic logic reduces employees to incredibly simple, rational, and economically motivated little cogs. It assumes that all you need to do to motivate people to reach high levels of productivity is to show them exactly what to do and provide the pay incentives for them to do it. This assumes that a worker's only goal in attending work is their wage and that they will go to work and watch out only for themselves. What the Hawthorne experiments raised was the idea that workers are far more complicated than just being wage calculators, and that organizations are best off when they pay attention to workers as human beings rather than as mere cogs in a larger machine-like system.

In summary form, Elton Mayo argued that management has to abandon assumptions associated with what has come to be called the *rabble hypothesis*. As "rabble," people are seen as atomized and disconnected individuals, acting only in their own individual self-interest and merely according to logical and rational thought. Mayo argued that you must instead recognize that people are primarily oriented to informal social groups and connections, both inside and outside of the work setting; that they largely act according to accepted cultural or subcultural social norms of those informal groups; and that they are heavily motivated by *arational* things such as emotions and sentiments. By *arational* I just mean modes of human action that are not driven by cost–benefit analysis. They are neither *rational* nor *irrational*. Proverbially speaking, you don't help a little old lady across the street by calculating your own personal benefits. Rather you do it because it is the morally right thing to do.

With regards to the management sciences, what this came around to is the idea that any organization has to worry about two distinct things. One is the *technical organization* of work as represented in the arrangement of production processes and/or technologies whatever those happen to be, along with what that means for the physical conditions of work. This was the largest concern of the likes of Taylor and Ford. But the other important aspect is the *social organization* of the work place having to do with the relationships among the people. People are oriented to living in communities of people, and that doesn't change when they go to work. Many of the rules that get followed in any social setting are informal rules of the community and/or those that develop in workplace groups, not the formal rules as written down in bureaucratic form by management. Authority is not a matter of formality in hierarchy and order giving and taking. Rather, it is a matter of getting people *motivated* to *want* to do the work well. Organizational authority then is really a matter of group-building and thus *leadership*. Good leaders build strong working groups and inspire people to willingly follow along with the program.

This all presents a complication for any simplistic conception of organizations as rational systems, among other things because it introduces *multiplicity and complexity of goals*. That is, the workers in an organization actually have fairly complex goals for themselves that exist independently of whatever the goals of the organization happen to be. Certainly workers need to be paid and would want to be paid more rather than less. But they also want to feel like they belong to something larger than themselves, like they are doing something useful, and like they are appreciated. So the challenge for any organization gets much more difficult than Taylorist followers ever had in mind. Not only do you need to engineer the technical side of the organization for the greatest efficiency, but you also have to engineer the social side of the organization to maximize worker *morale*. If the working situation satisfies workers' psychological and social needs, this will maximize worker effort and compliance, and thus raise productivity on behalf of the organization. So the idea is that, up until the Hawthorne experiments, there was a large piece missing in terms of thinking about how to maximize productivity.

Chester Barnard: Some Further Theoretical Grounding

In Chapter 1 we first met up with Max Weber whose writing on bureaucracy and formal rationality could be seen as the origins of the Sociology of Organizations. In Chapter 7 we met up with a great number of people implementing *Rational Systems* ideas about organizations, including Taylor, Ford, and Fayol, who can be seen to have laid the origins of the management sciences. In the present context, we run across another figure, Chester Barnard, who is sometimes given credit for being the first true human management theorist—someone who developed ideas about how to manage humans rather than how to engineer technical systems. Like Fayol, Barnard was in industry rather than in academics, starting out in the statistical department of AT&T in 1909 and later becoming president of the New Jersey Bell Telephone Company. He did study economics at Harvard, though didn't finish his degree. But he had close ties to Elton Mayo and others involved in the Hawthorne studies and read quite widely across the social sciences and humanities.

Barnard's theoretical work regarding organizations doesn't read very much like a rational systems approach theory because it is much more about managing people rather than systems of tasks. (See Figure 8.1 for a summary.) For Barnard organizations are fundamentally systems of human cooperation rather than systems of rules and procedures. In Chapter 1, I summarized Max Weber's ideal type bureaucracy in terms of three main elements: division of labor; hierarchy of authority; and formalization. There's no need for me to summarize Barnard's definition because he actually did define organizations as having three universal elements: (1) willingness to cooperate; (2) common purpose; (3) communication. It's quite a different picture, and willing cooperation of participants is the key.

For Barnard, an organization is established to fulfill some particular goal or purpose, but it can only do that by attracting members into cooperative participation. In other words, it is all about the *collective power*. In Barnard's

FIGURE 8.1   **Chester Barnard on Elements of Organization and Functions of Executives**

Definition of an Organization: "a system of consciously coordinated activities or forces of two or more persons" (Barnard 1968: 81)

Three Elements of an Organization:
  1) The willingness to cooperate
  2) Common purpose among all participants
  3) Effective communication

Three Functions of Executives:
  1) Provide an effective system of communication, both formal and informal
  2) Establish, monitor, and maintain an *economy of incentives* that provides necessary *inducements* to ensure everyone's best efforts (*contributions*) are obtained
  3) Develop, define, and clarify the purpose of the organization, while aligning participant goals with organizational goals (*goal alignment*)

Authority: is fundamentally granted from below, not imposed from above
  • Authority of Position: granted by formal rules and positions (Weberian)
  • Authority of Leadership: earned by the ability to gain trust, inspire, and motivate

words, to achieve the collective power potential of organizing you need all of the individual persons to make *contributions* to the work of the organization. But all of the individual persons are quite likely to have their own goals or purposes that are not the same as those of the organization. So people will have to give of themselves—basically sacrifice and provide their time, energy, and effort toward goals that are not their own. So the organization has to be able to provide various kinds of *inducements* to get people to participate. This is not so different from something like Frederick Taylor who promised that strict order-following (contributions) would be followed by good wages (inducement). But merely thinking in terms of wages was as far as Taylor ever took it—simple and objective rewards in monetary form.

For Barnard, as it came to be for Mayo, people's goals, desires, and motivations are far more complex than that. Obviously people want to be financially secure and thus have their material needs met. But people also have psychological and social needs. We want to feel some manner of self-respect and personal value. And we want to participate as members of cohesive social groups and develop the feeling that we belong to something larger than ourselves. In many respects you might say that Barnard emphasized what later organizational theory would call the building of particular kinds of *organizational culture* where, subjectively speaking, people *feel* good—valued and respected and like they share a camaraderie. Henri Fayol (Chapter 7) called this *esprit de corps*, so while he's generally called a rational system's theorist the idea of an organization as a human system was not foreign to him. When you take into account the web of material, psychological, and social needs of people, the job of securing their complete cooperation comes down to designing and nurturing what Barnard called an *economy of incentives* that involves sets of both material and nonmaterial inducements to draw out the contributions.

For Barnard, setting all of this up and nurturing it to produce a cooperative system is fundamentally what organizational management is all about. In his famous 1938 book called *The Functions of the Executive*, he defined three main executive functions that are needed to establish a healthy cooperative system. The first is to *provide a system of communication*. This would certainly include formal communications that would have a rational systems flavor to them—to clearly define lines of authority, tasks and procedures, and expectations and the like. But informal communications for Barnard are just as important as they are integral to the social nature of the organization and can allow all manner of expression of ideas and concerns that might not easily fit within narrowly defined formal communications. The second function is to *make sure the organization continues to get people's best personal efforts* from them—to maintain that system of inducements that keeps people actively and willingly involved. One of the largest things to watch and maintain was the level of *morale* among participants. You want people feeling positive and energetic with regards to providing their contributions. This function is not all positive, however, as it also involves a punitive side regarding how to address those who do not go along with the program.

Finally, the third function is to *formulate and define the purpose of the organization*. This involves being the organizational decision-maker, setting the overall goals and making the major decisions about how to reach those goals. This cannot be considered as separate from the first two, of course. If an organization meets its goals, then it must have been by securing the willing cooperation of its participants. But clarity of purpose is crucial, so the organizational goals have to be clearly defined and communicated to people. But more importantly the economy of incentives has to be designed in such a way that every individual pursuing their own personal goals meets them by contributing to the organization meeting its goals. There needs to be *goal alignment* as it came to be called later. People need to be able to identify with the goals of the organization and be able to see clearly how offering up their own personal contributions to it also meets their personal goals.

Interestingly for Barnard, none of this executive activity emphasizes the simple giving and taking of orders—or the question of authority. While authority is often seen as a top-down activity, Barnard thought that seeing it that way was backwards. Authority rests with the order-takers, not the order-givers. This is because if orders are not followed by subordinates it means that the superordinate has no authority. Since authority actually has to be given to the higher ups it always rests with those lower down in the organization. And, as with everything else in Barnard, there is both a formal and informal side to this ability to extract order-following from people. Some of the basis for authority is rooted in formal organizational positions—the *authority of position*, as he called it. But the informal side is more about trust and respect—the *authority of leadership*. These correspond roughly to Weber's distinction between *legal-rational* and *charismatic* bases for authority, and, according to Barnard, authority was always granted most willingly where the authority of both position and leadership were combined.

The *Human Relations* School

With the ideas of Barnard in the air, the Hawthorne experiments came to be something of a watershed moment for both organizational studies and for theory in the management sciences. It spawned various streams of research in organizations particularly with regards to things such as worker attitudes toward their jobs, research into small group dynamics, and the kinds of things make for effective leadership and group-building. It also spawned a whole tradition of organizational consulting aimed at helping organizations to manage their *human "resources."* Above all, managing an organization means managing its people. You have to see them and treat them as individual human beings who have various goals and aspiration, have different kinds of personalities, and face various kinds of challenges. You also have to see the workplace as a social setting that will have dynamics independent of whatever the formal and technical systems of the organization are. The social settings need to be nurtured and shaped to make people feel as if they belong with each other, but then also harnessed to function in the interests of the organization's goals. The more satisfied you can make everyone feel at work, and the more they can feel that the organization provides for a meaningful social experience, the more likely they will be to put forward their best efforts toward meeting organizational goals. The key for the armies of *Human Relations* consultants that emerge from this line of work is good leadership from management. It is up to management to provide the leadership necessary to build strong work groups and fulfill worker needs for belongingness and feelings of importance. This point, at least, is shared with Taylor—that the engineering is to be done from the top down.

Over the years, this line of thinking has been consistently developed and expanded and is now most clearly institutionalized in the form what is called *Human Resources Management (HRM)* in schools of business. A closely related field is called *Human Resources Development (HRD)*, a label which can also be found in business schools, but just as commonly in schools of education. It is actually something that you can major in at college, or, at the very least take as a concentration under a business degree. Majors in HRM are quite likely to end up seeking employment in the *Human Resources (HR)* departments of various organizations whether private, public, or otherwise. Mostly any organization of any decent size has one. It is also more and more institutionalized in the growing popularity of various kinds of educational programs in *Leadership*, whether as concentrations attached to other majors or even as entire "schools" of leadership in formalized university divisions. As it was at the beginning Industrial Psychology (now *Industrial and Organizational Psychology (I/O)* remains, in many respects, a more research-oriented arm of HRM in that the focus is on using psychological principles to understand human behavior in the work place. At this point, a lot of this has also melded with various ideas and expansions that would be seen as deriving from a related school of thought called *Humanistic Management*.

Humanistic Management: Did *Human Relations* Sell Workers Short?

The Human Relations perspective has been subject to criticism on many grounds. One of these lines of criticism argues that, while HR thinking gets past the overly simplified rabble hypothesis, it still operates with an overly simplified picture of the human workers in the organization and still just sees them as so many cogs to be manipulated by management. So all that the HR school really did was expand the tools for manipulation and control.

But beginning largely with work by psychologist and management scientist Douglas McGregor in the late 1950s, an extended line of human systems thinking emerged that came to be known as *humanistic management*. McGregor borrowed his starting point from psychologist Abraham Maslow and his famous *hierarchy of needs* (see Figure 8.2). Maslow's theory was basically one of human motivations—what gets people to doing what they are doing when they're doing it. He posited that the most fundamental things that motivate humans are basic *physiological needs*—the need for things like adequate food, clothing, and shelter. To the extent that these needs are not easily met, they will be the primary drivers of human behavior. However, if these needs are generally met, then they will cease to be a strong motivator for behavior. According to Maslow, with physiological needs reasonably well met, people will move on to the satisfaction of *safety and security needs*. If basic safety and security needs are met then they move on to *social needs* of feeling attached to others in social groups and communities.

As far as McGregor was concerned this level of the hierarchy was as far as Human Relations theories went. This was a little better than *Classical Management Theory (CMT)* under the likes of Taylor which only made it to the level of physiological and safety needs—assuming that all you needed to do to motivate people was offer the material incentives of things like pay, benefits, and job security. Human Relations theory added the psychological and social needs of humans—of feelings of belonging and appreciation in social groups. But if you accept Maslow's theory, then there are yet two more levels to human motivation.

FIGURE 8.2   **Abraham Maslow's *Hierarchy of Needs***

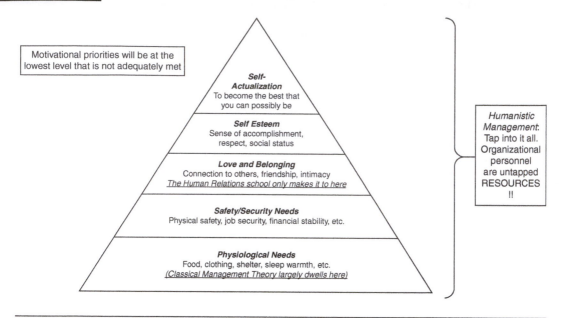

Source: Author's rendering based on Maslow, 1954.

The next level of need in Maslow's hierarchy consists of *ego needs*. These have to do with earning positive self-esteem in the eyes of others. People want to be able to accomplish things in ways that garner praise and make them feel worthy. While present to some extent in HR thinking, the presence is minimal. Finally, even above ego needs are *self-fulfillment* or *self-actualization* needs. This is the need to feel as if one has the opportunity to fully develop her own full human potential. It is what the US Army bills itself as providing through the "be all you can be" slogan.

According to McGregor, even human relations theory remains too Taylor-istic in its logic. Workers are still just so many parts of the organizational system to be manipulated and managed by those above them. And the only reason anyone might care about the needs of people is merely to make sure that the needs of the organization are met. The real "brains" of the operation, and the control, are the province of management which now just manipulates the social along with the technical elements of the organization. According to McGregor's logic, all of that continues to sell people short by cutting off the opportunities for fulfilling ego and self-actualization needs. But the loser is not only the employee. The organization itself also loses out. What employees represent are untapped *resources* for creativity and innovation. He argues that managers are often guided by an implicit view of their employees as being not very bright or motivated, averse to work and responsibility, and rather easy to fool so that they can be controlled. (He dubbed these ideas as aspects of *Theory X*. See Figure 8.3.) Yet, he goes on to say that even if such charac-teristics can actually be observed in many employees, it is *because of* their treatment as mere cogs in the organization. It is something of a self-fulfilling prophesy—assume that people are somewhat dumb and lazy and you will draw exactly that out of them. When the only thing that employers do is appeal to

FIGURE 8.3   Douglas McGregor, *Theory X versus Theory Y*

Theory X:	Theory Y:
• Management is responsible for organizing toward the ends of the organization.	• Management is responsible for organizing toward the ends of the organization (the only one that is the same).
• Participants require direction – they need to be controlled and motivated toward organizational ends.	• People are *NOT* resistant to organizations' needs. If they appear so, it is because management is going by the assumptions of Theory X.
• Without direction, motivation, and control through rewards and punishments people will be passive and/or resistant to the organization's needs.	• The motivation to work (including toward organizational ends), potential to develop, and desire for responsibility are present in all people. It is up to management to allow this to come out.
• Supporting assumptions about human nature and motivation. The average person: – Is lazy and will work as little as possible (*natural soldiering*). – Has no ambition and wants/needs to be led. – Is completely self-centered. – Is resistant to change. – Is not very smart, and is thus easy to fool and control.	• Management's responsibility is to set conditions so that people can best achieve their own goals by directing their efforts toward organizational ends (a.k.a. *goal alignment*).

Source: Author's summary from McGregor (1957).

basic physiological and safety needs through what he calls a *carrot and stick* approach to human motivation, then you're not going to get very much out of your people.

As rooted in Maslow, McGregor proposed *Theory Y* which asserts that (Figure 8.3), given the right conditions, people like to work, seek, and accept responsibility and have much to offer in terms of intelligence and creativity. It is up to management to create the organizational conditions necessary for people to pursue their own higher level ego and self-fulfillment needs in a way that aligns it all with the larger goals of the organization. In this way, all of the persons inside of the organization are able to pursue their own goals while simultaneously pursuing those of the organization. The key thing for managers to realize is that workers are actually untapped resources that can help the organization improve upon what it does. It was a direct attempt to try to overturn Taylor's logic (rooted in Theory X) that all of the thinking should be done by management.

In concrete and practical terms what McGregor (and soon many others as Humanistic Management also became a consulting fad) recommended is basically to flatten out organizations in terms of hierarchy and generally reduce the amount of bureaucracy in all respects. Rather than leaving control and responsibilities in the hands of management who plan and then tell everyone what to do through formalized rules and procedures, you give everyone a stake and a share of the organization's activities. You *decentralize* authority and *delegate* more responsibilities throughout the organization and invite employees to participate in management tasks—a practice called *participative management*. Similarly, you remove narrowly defined work roles and the highly prescriptive rules that often go along with them. Instead you do what McGregor called *job enlargement* where positions, roles, and tasks become more varied, fluid, and flexible. You get rid of all of the vestiges of the old classical management structures and build organizations where the work and processes are planned and carried out by *self-directed teams* of people. Surely there would still be some formal hierarchy, but work is planned and carried out in a highly egalitarian manner rather than by a command and control structure. In Humanistic Management terms, once you charge people up with responsibility and self-determination they will be highly motivated because they will be able to pursue their own ego and fulfillment needs through their work. What you get out of that is an organization of people fully committed to the organization by their own will and desire—a situation of which Barnard would obviously have approved. You no longer have to spend management time and resources on carrots and sticks to cajole people into doing their jobs. They are self-motivated to do their jobs, and the organization gets the extra benefit of a far broader well from which to draw fresh ideas and creativity. One of the common buzz phrases is that organizations are best off moving *from control to commitment*. Building commitment should produce a win-win situation for both worker and the organization.

Thus, humanistic management provides a set of ideas that greatly reduces the extent to which an organization looks like a Weberian ideal type bureaucracy. And it goes farther than a Barnardian cooperative system because Barnard—even with his upside down notion of authority—still had an awful lot of hierarchy in the picture. It was still the case that control was to be designed in from the top down, rather than arising spontaneously from people's existing inner desires. In spreading responsibilities and providing employees in organizations more freedom and responsibility, an organization would become flatter in terms of hierarchy and much less bound up by prescriptive rules. Organizational activities would work a lot less on formal authority and much more on mutual consultation. Rules would become fewer and more flexible, and daily work life would be guided more by human reason and judgment (by *practical* and *theoretical rationality*). Organizations would become less impersonal and rigid, and more capable of adaptation and change.

In other words, the logic fits very well with the ideas involved in the shift from hierarchies to networks discussed in Chapter 6. In terms of the timeline, McGregor may have been a little bit ahead of the curve, but certainly when the 1970s shakeups of big business took place, the ideas of humanistic management that are observed in the somewhat innovative *Japanese Style of Management (JSM)* served as a ready guide for those looking to change business practices. Indeed, the entire line of scientific management techniques from the JSM on through programs like *Total Quality Management (TQM)*, and *Lean Six Sigma* (LSS) do include at least a small dose of HR/HM principles in that gaining the commitment and involvement of all in the organization is emphasized. Of course, in these programs the overall objectives remain those of the organization, and control is not generated from below but, as with Taylor, Shewhart and Deming, remains in the data.

Sociology Gets on the Scene: Organizations as Natural Human Systems

While it's true that I started the introduction to this book with Max Weber, and he makes an appearance in the account of rational systems, most of our actors thus far have either been in business management and/or faculty in business schools, or at least closely related to them. Their questions were rather directly about how to more effectively run business organizations, so the focus is a highly applied one. In many respects, everything from Taylor on through Human Relations (HR)/Humanistic Management (HM) and Barnard could be considered closely related to the rational systems logic where HR/HM simply add on that you have to manage humans as well as technical processes in order to maximize efficiency and thus your competitive position in markets. Oftentimes sociologists have participated in such questions (and too often IMHO), but generally our focus tends to be different and much more broad. As you know, formal organizations "absorbed" much of society around the turn of the twentieth century, and even if that is now less or no longer the case we still live in the shifting aftermath. Sociologists study society, so it is crucial to understand formal organizations in order to understand society. So sociologists often come into organizational studies asking not "how do we make organizations (and people) do what we want them to?" but rather things like "what is going on in these social situations?" "How is it best understood?" And "what does this mean for society?" This was certainly what Weber was doing in seeing the rise and spread of the bureaucratic form as central to the characteristics of the modern industrialized societies. So it's quite possible to see Weber as the starting point for the Sociology of Organizations, but his direct influence was not immediately apparent.

Another candidate for the starting point is sociologist Philip Selznick who, beginning in the 1940s, was instrumental in developing what became a dominant approach to studying organizations called *Institutionalism* which has remained highly influential in the study of organizations up to the present day, whether among sociologists or otherwise.

Selznick's fundamental orientation to asking about formal organizations was largely one of trying to come to grips with the organizational revolution and its aftermath. He was born in 1919, and thus was 10 years old at the onset of the Great Depression, served in the US military during World War II, and completed his PhD in Sociology in 1947 just after the war ended. Among at least some segments of social science at the time, a central puzzle was how to accomplish something like meaningful democratic processes in an age of intensive centralization of power across virtually all segments of society (IEMP power). As described in Chapter 2, the economic and political *zeitgeist* (mood or spirit) of classically liberal societies has always been one that emphasizes widely decentralized and dispersed power because people are given economic and political choice. Philosophically speaking, social power is supposed to be located very closely to the individual level. However, as we have seen, the turn of the twentieth-century period was one in which social power on all dimensions (IEMP) became highly concentrated. Especially in the face of things like the two world wars and the Great Depression that separated them, it didn't look or feel very much like a world of widely dispersed power in the hands of individuals with high degrees of self-determination and choice.

At the most general level, Selznick was heavily influenced by the German tradition that descended down from Weber through Robert Michels and Karl Mannheim (see Chapter 2), especially as it relates to the strong centralizing tendencies of bureaucracies along with the propensity to cover this over with justifying ideologies. As Michels observed so long ago, ideals such as "democracy" and "equality" are often defeated partly because true democracy is largely impossible, and also because organizations tend to take on lives of their own. The needs of the organization—its *structural interests*—end up overriding whatever the ideals happen to be and shape the needs of their participants regardless of the ideals. This is especially the case with those in control. All of this was alive and well in Selznick's mind as he embarked on his research career.

At the same time, the dominant mode of sociological analysis in US sociology was becoming *Structural Functionalism*, and Selznick studied under Robert K. Merton who was one of the most prominent functionalist thinkers of the time. On the face of it, in simplistic understandings, this might seem odd since the likes of Weber, Michels, and Mannheim are associated with the *Conflict Theory* tradition in sociology which is often seen to be the opposite of functionalism in many respects. But simplistic understandings are always just that.

In functionalism, social groups are not seen merely as collections of individual persons, but as organic, structured wholes. In fact, early on there was a tendency to use what's called the *organism analogy* where a society is likened to a complex organism. It is one whole made up of different parts (*structures*), all of which exist to perform some *function* for the whole (thus the term *structural functionalism*). One of the more important implications of this is that societies will be primarily structured, not according to the wishes of the individuals that exist within then, but toward their own health and survival. They are adaptive things, where activities will be geared toward the maintenance and continuance of the system. Thus, one can understand social structures (such as organizations) and change as being shaped and driven by a social formation's survival needs. Far from individuals shaping what a society is, it is exactly the other way around. Individuals end up being socialized into acting in ways that support the functions necessary to group survival. In this respect, the general view fits quite nicely with Michels' picture of the actions and orientations of organizational leadership being shaped toward the needs of the organization itself.

It is also the case that the fundamental basis for social groups is *arational*. Enlightenment philosophers had the idea that the basis of social order among people is rationality. The prominent English philosopher Thomas Hobbes imagined a *state of nature* in which every individual person is free to make their own personal decisions according to what is in their own best interests—in other words according to rational decision-making. He surmised that if this is how things remained, then there would be no society and people would live in a constant state of a *war of all against all*. The solution to that in Enlightenment philosophy was taken to be the idea of the *social contract*. People agree to live together under a common authority with basic rules of the game (such as a Constitution) because the benefits of that outweigh the costs of having to live in the war of all against all. In other words, the ultimate basis of social order is a governmental arrangement that institutes and enforces basic sets of rules.

Rational systems thinking about organizations—obviously seen in what Mayo called the rabble hypothesis—is very much inspired by these kinds of assumptions. Functionalism's starting point is quite different in that what ultimately holds social groups together is a basic shared set of symbolic values among people. The classical theorist Emile Durkheim called it the *collective conscience*[2]—a shared set of values and beliefs among people in the group,

---

[2]Durkheim, [1893] 1984.

along with feelings of *social solidarity* where people feel like they belong to something larger than themselves.

We are already familiar with the idea that a lot of what people do in formal organizations does not reflect their personal decisions. Rather, what they do is spelled out in advance by the bureaucratic rules. In this regard, functionalism is similar, except that people are always like that whether in formally planned settings or not. Their courses of action are instead guided by informal rules—norms, mores, and the like. Very importantly, various modes of acting are also symbolically meaningful to people. They are valued for their own sake rather than for their practical consequences as related to rational evaluation. Social groups that "survive" and do well, in functionalist thought, do so as moral wholes—with what Fayol would have called *esprit de corps* (see Chapter 7).

When it came to formal organizations, in particular, Selnzick was also heavily influenced by Chester Barnard. There is clear recognition that, in their quest to survive, organizations have to be able to attract and motivate participants (inducements to make contributions). This means that organizations will end up doing many things that, on the face of it, appear tangential to their formally stated objectives; that it is crucial for the leaders of organizations to manage all of that, including setting out some manner of moral vision regarding purpose and identity; and that the acceptance of and shaping of a whole host of informal social relations and patterns will naturally evolve inside of the organization.

In the end, Selznick landed at a view of organizations, not as rationally planned tools, but as what he called *recalcitrant tools*. That is, organizations are developed and designed toward particular purposes—as rational systems—but they are very difficult to control in that regard. They inevitably take on a life of their own independently of any formally stated goals or even of the wishes of founders or leaders. Given their survival needs, they will be shaped in unpredictable ways over time by many things such as the differing needs and interests of both formal and informal groups inside of the organization, unforeseen contingencies, the characteristics of leaders and leadership changes, demands from the organizational environment, and so on. This last thing—the organizational environment—will occupy all of our attention in Chapter 9 where I will remind you of Selznick and *Institutionalism*, and you'll learn that there is now a *"New" Institutionalism* (although it isn't clear that it is truly all that new). All of these complexities tend to result in processes now referred to as *goal displacement*—where the original and stated goals of organizations come to be replaced by others—and *organizational drift*—whereby what organizations do or try to do over time becomes shifting and even somewhat unpredictable depending on the particular constellation of forces and conditions that arise. The grandfather of this view of organizations as having ambiguous and shifting goals is none other than Robert Michels.

Philip Selznick, the TVA, and the Exposé Tradition

The Institutional approach to organizations began to take its full shape in Selznick's 1949 book called *TVA and the Grassroots: A Study in the Sociology of Formal Organizations*. This is by now a very old book and an old case study. However, the book laid down so many important foundations and anticipated so much of future organizational sociology; I will go on about it at some length.

The *TVA* is the *Tennessee Valley Authority*. It was started up in the context of the Great Depression as part of the New Deal under President Franklin Delano Roosevelt (FDR). It was a massive set of interrelated projects that were intended to manage and develop the relatively poor and rural Tennessee Valley (TV). The central set of activities was to use dams in the TV watershed to both generate electricity and manage the surface waters of the area. The TV is prone to swings between drought and flooding stages, all of which made farming quite precarious and helped to leave much of the population in economic precarity. The dams provided a way to power hydroelectric plants that could electrify the valley at the same time that they could be used to smooth out the flood/drought cycles. The dams created reservoirs that could hold excess rain when needed, but then supply that surplus of water during periods of drought. Integral to all of this would be improving the navigability of the river for the transport of goods. Around this core set of activities involving river management and hydroelectric power generation arose a vision of a government agency that would do widespread management of the entire region's natural and human capital. So river and dam management was to be integrated with management of all of the natural resources of the region, such as soil and forests, for maximum effect in terms of long-term sustainability and economic development. The dams were even connected to plans for public re-creation opportunities, such as the establishment of national parks. Furthermore, all of the TVA activities would directly generate employment opportunities at a time when this rather poor region of the country was doing more poorly than usual given the Great Depression.

One key issue, if the TVA was to be successful, was seen to have been the ability to avoid resistance from the people who lived in the TV. The TV is rural and agricultural, and was dominated by the same kinds of rural conservatism that we see today. Having large, centralized agencies of the Federal Government out of Washington DC mucking around in people's daily lives was heavily frowned upon. Tensions with regards to such things were already in place as the TVA was just one of the so-called *alphabet soup* programs created under FDR as part of the New Deal. It was a time of the increasing degree of size and centralization of control over more and more political activities, and—as we have already learned—economic activities. The sense that people were losing the ability to maintain local control and autonomy was real and growing. The effects of economic centralization are more subtle, but having nonlocal people from large centralized government bureaucracies active in local affairs is painfully obvious. Furthermore, the skepticism and resistance wouldn't merely come from some disorganized mass of rabble. The region was already populated by existing organizations, many of which were geared toward issues that would likewise be foci for the TVA.

This formed the basic skeleton of *institutional context* in which the TVA needed to operate. It consists of existing organizations that already have ways of doing things, and for various constituencies, those existing organizations and their modes of action are valued. The place, the ways of life of the people there, and their local organizations all had meaning to people in their everyday lives and activities. And this context is joined to and melded with sets of basic cultural values held by the people of the area. Thus, figuring out how to operate in the area was among the first major issues to be handled. Partly because of this, the *TVA* Act (1933) which established the TVA painted the organization's functions in very broad terms setting out only a bare minimum of its organizational structure. It was up to the initial leadership of the TVA to go about filling in all of the blanks.

A Grassroots Doctrine as a "Sustaining Myth"

The approach that the TVA took to setting up and carrying out its programs was to formulate a conception of itself, both structurally and culturally, as a *grassroots* organization. It was not going to operate as a centralized agency taking its orders from Washington DC and imposing them upon people in the TV. Rather, it was going to work with and through local citizens and already existing organizations so that the actual needs and interests of the local people could be the driving force. Thus, while it was a large agency of the centralized federal government, it was going to operate democratically from the grassroots up. The idea was to create and nurture an identity of itself as an assistant to the needs of the people acting on the people's own terms. The TVA would provide financial resources, participate in planning, and generally coordinate its systems of action, but local communities and organizations would be integral to generating the direction and even carrying out a good deal of the work. Thus in both conception and execution, to the largest extent possible, the actors would not be TVA personnel out of Washington D.C., but local people and organizations of the TV.

One of the main messages of the entire book is that, while this is how the TVA came to depict itself, one should not take *the grassroots doctrine* (as Selznick dubbed it) to be an accurate description of how things really worked. For starters, it provides for quite a paradox for the simple reason that the whole existence of the TVA did not grow from the grassroots of the TV. It was, put plainly and simply, an initiative of the federal government of the United States, and it was going to execute its programs in the TV whether people wanted it to or not. Furthermore, there were many aspects of the TVA's practical goals where having intensive grassroots involvement was simply not all that realistic. For example, things like the dams and electrical generation programs, and planning out things like river terminals are highly technocratic activities. Local institutions capable of handling such projects, whether in terms of planning or construction or maintenance, just didn't exist. Given the complexity of managing an entire river complete with dams, electricity generation stations, and river terminals also meant that "the people" could not always get what they want. So, for example, the Douglas Dam that was built in 1942 in eastern Tennessee faced widespread local opposition, but was built in any case.

For Selznick, this wasn't cause for labeling government agencies or their agents as hypocritical. Following from the influence of Barnard and of functionalism, Selznick explains that organizations, just like people, strive to form and present a coherent identity. For organizations, such a self-concept is crucial as what he calls a *sustaining myth* and helps to sustain an organization in two main ways. One is that it provides some sense of internal coherence for actors in the organization. It becomes a shared sense of what the organization is about that helps to maintain commitment and coordinate communications and activities among people in the organization. A second way has to do with how an organization presents itself to constituencies outside of itself. A consistent image that is resonant with cultural values is required in order for an organization to gain legitimacy and trust. For the TVA, the grassroots doctrine was the key sustaining myth for the organization. Virtually all organizations create these kinds of images of themselves, now contained in such things as "visions" and "mission statements." (Click on "About Us" on the website of any organization and you will find an inspiring "story" about the organization's identity which, regardless of how well it depicts reality, is designed as a way of creating a positive image of the organization).

One of the reasons that sustaining myths can continue to function even when they seem to contradict what is happening is that they frequently contain plenty of ambiguity which provides ample room for interpretation. For example, in his discussion Selznick notes that the grassroots concept was tied to the notion that the TVA would remain "close to the people." Well, one might ask, which people? The region is large and contains a lot of people with a lot of different needs and interests and identities and so on. And herein lies another significant aspect of the story, which is that there were ways that the TVA operated whereby some of "the people" were strongly represented in the TVA's activities and others were not. The story involves how the TVA's strategy of involving the grassroots ended up having *unintended consequences* whereby at least some of the TVA's stated goals were not only not met, but sometimes subverted. This generally occurred because of a process called *cooptation* which has a bit of a double meaning. If you want to be able to "win over" or avoid threats from other actors outside of your organization, then you can invite them in and give them a role and a stake in what is going on. You *co-opt* them—it's a little like bribery. But having given over some of the power to actors outside of the organization, they are then able to use the organization's resources for their own purposes—they *co-opt* the resources. The most fateful act of cooptation involved what were called "the agriculturalists."

"The Agriculturalists" of the TVA

One of the more important existing networks of local institutions in the Tennessee Valley was the Cooperative Extension Service (CES) of the United States Department of Agriculture (USDA). Established in 1914, it largely provides research and educational services with regards to issues of agricultural importance. It is run through the US network of land-grant colleges and universities which were established by the 1862 Morrill Act. The most direct purpose was for the development of knowledge and education in practical matters of agriculture and technological development. The program provided grants of land from the federal government to the states in order to fund the establishment of the universities.[3] In simple form, faculty at these universities produce research with regards to agricultural issues (among many other things, of course), and the growing scientific knowledge is distributed out into the field to farmers through networks of Cooperative Extension agents that operate in each county.

When the TVA was first being established, President Roosevelt directed that its three-person board should include a "Southern agriculturalist," and the person who was selected was Dr. Harcourt Morgan, a former President of the University of Tennessee—one of those land-grant universities. As someone

---

[3]If anyone ever reads this book, some may find that they are attending one of the seven land-grant universities in the Tennessee Valley: Auburn University (then Alabama Polytechnic Institute); University of Georgia, Athens; University of Kentucky; Mississippi State University; North Carolina State University; University of Tennessee, Knoxville; Virginia Polytechnic Institute.

with long-standing relations to the land-grant system and thus the USDA CES, the selection of Morgan meant that the TVA agricultural efforts would ultimately end up in line with the interests and needs of that existing set of programs. The resources of the TVA were basically being handed over to existing organizational interests, and those interests were quite powerful. The land-grant institutions were represented by the Association of Land-Grant Colleges and Universities and had a powerful ally in the form of the American Farm Bureau Federation (AFBF) which, since its inception in 1919, had worked closely with the CES. In addition to participating in outreach and educational efforts on behalf of farmers, it remains a powerful lobbying organization representing agricultural political and economic interests.

As it turns out, this constellation of forces ended up being the most powerful segment of the TVA influencing virtually all of its programs and projects, even those not connected to agriculture. Furthermore, this often occurred in ways that were completely unintended by and even contrary to the stated goals of the TVA. The lopsided power of the agriculturalists was not intended, nor even written into its formal structure. It became an *informal power structure* because the CES was so influential over farmers in the Valley that its representatives would be able to make or break the TVA's reputation at the local level. The TVA *needed* the support of the agriculturalists to help create and maintain a positive image and thus gain cooperation.

But the agriculturalists, as represented by the nexus of the land-grant schools/CES/Farm Bureau, did not represent *all* agricultural interests in the area. In fact, they were all much more aligned with the relatively well-to-do farmers of the region. This is because the CES activities, such as experimental research and demonstration trials, generally required larger plots of land and a high degree of stability and predictability over time. This is something of a technical requirement for carrying out effective research, but obviously ends up favoring wealthier farmers. But the region also contained a rather large population of very poor farmers, including sharecroppers, tenant farmers, and migrant workers. Other than perhaps being used for labor, there was not much of a way for them to be involved in agricultural research or trial programs. On the face of it, those poorest of farmers would be among the very people that the TVA's programs should be able to help the most, but that's not how it worked out. The TVA ended up being least likely to help the poorest of farmers largely because the TVA's agricultural programs were so closely aligned with the CES which already excluded poor farmers. And to confound issues even more, those poorest of the TV farmers represented an asset to the more well-to-do farmers in terms of providing for an ample, cheap supply of labor. In at least some respects, helping them would actually be contrary to the interests of more stable farmers. The real workings of power in organizations are nothing if not highly complex.

The extent to which the TVA's orientation came to be rather indifferent to the needs of the poorer farmers of the area was clear in its avoidance of the cooperation with the Farm Security Administration (FSA). The FSA was founded in 1937 as another of the New Deal era alphabet soup of programs and was explicitly geared toward the most desperate elements of the agricultural population. It would seem a natural partner for the TVA in terms of helping with economic development. But the problem it presented with regards to the relation to the TVA was that the FSA set up and carried out its own operations on the ground. In other words, its activities did not have anything to do with the

CES, and thus it actually represented competition to the Farm Bureau. It was by its connection to the CES that the Farm Bureau maintained its membership of farmers. To the extent that farmers became beholden to some other organization in the region, it could potentially weaken the Farm Bureau by drawing people away from membership. Of course, the loyalties of the agriculturalists in the TVA were directly in line with the Farm Bureau, and thus resistance might not be all that surprising—at least once one thinks in terms of the structural interests of organizations rather than in terms of lofty ideals.

The TVA's resistance didn't come so much in the form of direct rejection, but rather more a pattern of avoiding cooperation with the FSA. Direct opposition would not likely occur because on the face of it the TVA and FSA do share some similar goals and both come out of the New Deal programs. In principle, cooperation would have made the most sense. Furthermore, there were divisions of the TVA that were willing to cooperate with the FSA. In 1941, for example, an official from TVA central management forwarded a proposal that the TVA set up a formal understanding to cooperate with the FSA regarding several issues with regards to the agricultural population of the area. The TVA's Department of Agricultural Relations rejected it on the basis that the means by which the TVA and FSA did things were quite different and thus cooperation would be impossible. Furthermore, the Department insisted that any of the people who might be working with the FSA were quite free to participate in CES programs regardless. So the implication was apparently that there was no value to be added in any cooperative understanding. And this was the general pattern—the agriculturalists would resist and generally reject any manner of activity that didn't go through the land-grant and extension system.

In most respects, these matters are very much of the structural interests of the organizations—the notion that organizations will end up having their activities geared toward their own survival. For the TVA to operate successfully at all, the support of the agriculturalists was instrumental for overcoming suspicion or rejection of federal organizations, gaining legitimacy, and securing the cooperation of the people of the region. But the agriculturalists were driven by the organizational interests of the existing alliance between the land-grant universities, CES, and Farm Bureau. This ultimately led to the TVA doing things in ways that were contrary to at least some of its stated objectives.

Other matters were related less to structural interests and more to aspects of the *general culture* of the region. As noted, the CES was much more a representative of the more well-to-do farmers. This also means that they carried their basic political and value orientations which were fundamentally politically conservative. Part of this is represented by the discussion above regarding the value on local autonomy and minimizing the role or place of governmental involvement in people's affairs. Well, the TVA was a giant public works program coming out of Washington DC, so to some extent what was taken on board with the agriculturalists was a whole constituency that would likely resist at least certain aspects of TVA action and it did. One ongoing point of contention was the outright federal ownership of land.

For example, whenever a dam was built, the people living on the land that would be flooded by the resulting reservoir were necessarily displaced. So the TVA had a program for buying private property from people and helping them to relocate suitably. But just how much land needed to be purchased by the TVA for any given project was ambiguous. Initially the TVA plans included relatively large overbuys that, at minimum, included a protective strip of land around what would become the reservoir. This would ensure that whatever benefits that come from the projects, such as recreational access, would be open to the public and also that the TVA could manage the areas for natural conservation purposes. For the earliest dam projects the land purchases were specified in the plans for a dam project and were fairly large. For example, the first TVA dam project was the Norris Dam in Tennessee built between 1933 and 1936. The project included a fairly substantial 120,000 acre overbuy which ultimately became Norris Dam State Park.

However, over the first decade of the TVA's dam building projects, the direct specification of such barriers faded away, and by 1942 the TVA board had entirely reversed the initial policy of acquiring protective strips, directing the purchase of only the bare minimum of land needed for the various projects. The key reason was ultimately that the overbuys of land were opposed by the agriculturalists. The issue was under constant debate inside of the TVA through the 1930s. In 1941, supporters and detractors to the policy were asked to draw up their positions for review by the TVA board which set the stage for the board ruling regarding the bare minimum of land purchases. Selznick notes that the position of those who supported continuing with protective strips of land was quite consistent with the overall goals of the TVA in terms of natural resources management in the region, while the position of those who opposed it was not. The thing that makes sense out of it is though, is that the position opposed to the buys was basically just a politically conservative one regarding the belief that natural resources should be left in private hands to the greatest extent possible. As such, TVA's official policies with regards to some of its central objectives ultimately came to be shaped by the conservative politics of the agriculturalists in ways that contradicted some of the stated goals of the TVA—in this case natural conservation efforts.

In the end, the TVA turned out to be pretty bad at helping poor famers and at many of its conservation efforts largely because of *cooptation*. The alternative, however, would likely have meant the same or worse. That is, without gaining and maintaining the support of the agriculturalists they would have suffered in terms of legitimacy and likely faced much more widespread resistance.

We might say that the key issue for Selznick has to do with the one that was central to Barnard. In order for an organization to be able to pursue its goals, it has to win the cooperation of its participants through *inducements*. In Selznick, this translated to *commitments*—that is, that an organization makes commitments to various constituencies in order to secure cooperation and the buy-in to the needs of the organization. But those commitments mean that an organization will almost always have to do things that are not directly related to its stated objectives and can quite easily run contrary to them. As Selznick put it concisely in a preface to a 1966 reprint of the book: "*Means terrorize when the commitments they build up direct us from our true objectives.*"[4]

The Exposé Tradition in Organizational Research

In general, Selznick's analysis helped kick off what sociologist Charles Perrow dubbed "the *Exposé Tradition*" in organizational research.[5] This generally refers to a large number of following case studies of organizations indicating

---

[4]Selznick, 1966: x.
[5]Perrow, 1986: 159.

that, for many organizations, not all is as it seems. Selznick was part of a cluster of sociologists at Columbia University, sometimes referred to the *Columbia School.* Another was Peter Blau who, in a study of a state unemployment office, showed how a system for the evaluation of interviewers in the organization led to unanticipated and often detrimental consequences. For example, interviewers in the agency who helped people find jobs were evaluated simply on the number of job placements they managed to arrange. This actually put them into competition with one another and that inhibited information sharing that could have helped the actual clients. It also led to a premium being placed on simply getting people placed in jobs in order to enhance one's own numbers, and this meant that the appropriateness of the placement generally didn't matter—a matter of quantity over quality. In a study of agencies that serve the blind Robert Scott found that, in order to best raise funds for their activities, the agencies tended to focus only on a small proportion of the blind population—the relatively young, healthy, and most employable among the blind. Meanwhile, a majority of the blind population is quite elderly and often handicapped in other ways as well. The problem is that it is easier to raise funds from people if they think that those funds will go on to help people gain some independence and become "productive members of society," as the saying goes. Thus, those that needed the most help were the least prone to receive it as a matter of course in terms of what the organizations needed to do in order to survive.

The exposé nature of things is not limited to things like government agencies or nonprofits either. Sociologist Alvin Gouldner produced a very well-known study of a company that mined gypsum and made sheetrock. (A.k.a. "wallboard." It's what covers interior walls in most houses these days.) The production site was in a small town and rural area. It was the kind of place where "everyone knows everyone else," and people who worked at the facilities were generally all connected in one way or another outside of work. As a result, actual bureaucratic rule following for the maximum productivity of the company was not the way things operated. The arrangement of work was highly informal and infused with the local norms and values of the surrounding population. This is what made the place work in generating and maintaining people's cooperation. When supervisors did have to actually use and enforce formal company rules, those rules became used as a bit of a crutch because one could deflect blame to the rules rather than making it personal.

However, a problem arose during a period of increasing competition in the industry. The parent company appointed a new manager whose instructions from the company were to buckle down on things and make the place more efficient. This meant turning the screws on the amount of bureaucracy and order following in the place, and what the new manager did was produce a strike. Prior to this time, the place operated heavily on *informal rules*, many of which were contrary to formal policy, but that is exactly part of what made the place function. Bureaucracy, it seems, is not an all-powerful, technical force automatically controlling actions and producing efficiency. There will always remain a human underbelly that needs to be taken into account in order to understand the formal organization.

The Informal Structure in the Formal Shell

It is now commonplace to see all organizations as having something of dual nature. On the one hand, there is the *formal organization*—this approximates the Weberian characteristics and is what gets put down on paper in terms of what the official goals are, who has power and authority over what, the division of labor and task definitions, and so on. But then there is what is actually going on—the *informal organization*—informally developed modes of thinking and doing, including actual patterns of authority, rules, jobs, and so forth. The idea isn't that formal and informal structures will bear no resemblance to each other, or that the formal structures don't matter at all. It is all relevant to understanding an organization, but it is certainly crucial to not uncritically accept formal descriptions of organizations on their face. For a full understanding of what goes on you have to pull back the proverbial curtain and see what is going on behind.

On the subject of the curtain reference, these days it is not uncommon to use imagery borrowed from social theorist Erving Goffman's strategy of *dramaturgical analysis*. Goffman argued (as did William Shakespeare) that social life is an awful lot like theater and can be analyzed that way. We use things like costumes, props, scripts, and sets to try to portray particular versions of reality to various audiences. If you have a job interview for a corporate position, for example, you will wear some manner of formal business attire (costume), perhaps carry a briefcase (prop), and use very formal language (script). If you go to a friend's afterward to drink beer and watch sports, your *Presentation of Self*, as one of Goffman's book titles phrased it,[6] will be very different. One of the most important things involved in people being able to create convincing *performances* is the ability to use some kind of *back stage* area to prepare. If you are able to watch the actor get into costume and make-up, it becomes more difficult for that actor to convince you that he is Hamlet. You don't want the person interviewing you for the corporate position to come across those pictures of you on Instagram slugging back the beer as it becomes harder to carry off the performance as a professional. The performance takes place on the *front stage*. It is the same with organizations as it is with people. The formal structure of an organization has come to be seen as an *organizational frontstage*, while what goes on behind the scenes is the *organizational backstage*.

The existence of backstages that frequently do not look like the frontstages is inevitable because organizations are, after all, the activities of human beings who tend to not make very good cogs. We don't make great cogs because we are symbolic creatures who act in the world not according to some way that things "really are," but only the meanings that things have for us. Things like rules, orders, and authority can be laid out (and themselves as matters of symbolic meaning), but they cannot actually *interpret* themselves, nor can they really "do" anything. In fact, nothing about anything in the world, whether aspects of organizational life or not, can interpret and give meaning to itself. It is we humans who do that. As such, there is a certain very real respect in which organizations and their processes are not imposed from the top-down as people like Taylor tried to do, and as I have strongly implied at various moments in this book. Rather, organizational reality is generated from the ground up by conscious humans making sense of their situations and engaging in actions according to what things mean to them.

This is the heart of much of *microsociology* where we try to understand how it is that social life is *socially constructed*—that is made by us. This

---

[6]Goffman, 1959.

requires understanding a distinction in our human activities that, as a matter of convention, we can roughly label as *behaviors* versus *actions*. Our human bodies do many things that are simply biological, such as sweating when we get hot or blinking which keeps our eyes clean and lubricated. Take these basic biological things to be *behaviors*. Our bodies engage in many of them, and they occur independently of our will and conscious direction. However, most of what we are doing is not of that nature as it is a matter of our conscious will and conscious direction. We'll call *actions* those things that we do with conscious intention to them. Your body will sweat when you get hot, but that alone does not determine what it means to you nor does it determine your response to it. Being hot and sweaty might be interpreted as a pleasant feeling, as it may be while sunning at the beach or taking some time in a sauna. It would be entirely different, however, if you were hoofing it down a city street on a hot sunny day while late for an important job interview. The *meanings* of being hot and sweaty are very different in those two situations, as are what you would be thinking about your potential responses to it. The important thing is that those meanings are not somehow rooted in "nature," and cannot simply be imposed. Rather the meanings are created by us, although not from scratch and not by us as individuals on our own. They exist as webs of ideas that emerge out of social interaction.

When we do consider meanings, such as what it means to have an important job interview, people are almost always acting on the basis of existing meanings that we take to be commonly shared among other people. For example, you know that you are supposed to show up for a job interview very well-groomed and composed. Dripping sweat and breathless is not the way to make a first impression. These kinds of things are widely assumed among people and just go without saying—no one is going to write out a list of social norms and assumptions to prepare you for a job interview. We refer to these generalized and widely assumed standards and modes of action as being *institutionalized*. However, just because there are commonly understood expectations, patterns, and norms, this does not mean that interpretive work stops. Rather, meanings and related actions in all social situations remain matters of negotiation. How you act toward your hot and sweatiness or how your interviewer does is still not set in stone but is still something that each of you will give meaning to and act toward in the specific situation. Perhaps you were late and hoofing it to the interview because there was a strike among public transit workers, and your interviewer responds with sympathetic understanding as they had the same experience themselves. Or perhaps they do see it as a failure on your part by thinking that your failure to leave extra time was a matter of inattention and carelessness. All of social life, including that within formal organizations, is fluid and shifting. It is rooted in generally shared institutionalized expectations, but it remains a flowing and indeterminate process in which we actually work to accomplish whatever order does emerge.

This may perhaps be nowhere more obvious than in the case of how formal organizations have helped to reproduce and often accentuate things like gender and race/ethnic inequalities as discussed in Chapter 3. While organizations can sometimes gain practical advantages from this practice, as when it helps to keep labor forces divided with a corresponding downward pressure on wages, much of it is also understandable merely as a matter of the enactment of various kinds of social constructions. Neither race nor gender exists in the "nature" of things as the concrete categorizations in which we tend to put people. Those are matters of particular kinds of meanings that have been associated with various biological characteristics. Furthermore, contemporary gender and racial divisions don't exist by virtue of formal organizations, but as larger institutionalized cultural patterns.

Consider, for example, how the *ideology of separate spheres* interacts with the idea of the *ideal worker* in the case of women (from Chapter 3). Both of those concepts are simply sets of social meanings, and they affect the functioning of organizations and the lives of people only to the extent that they are acted upon as meaningful. The terminology these days can vary, but things like gender and race have to be *done*, *enacted*, or *performed*. They don't exist as independent realities that impose themselves on organizational situations and processes.

Given that these things have their origins in human meanings rather than in the nature of things in the world, they vary both over time and across settings. Gender, race, and their intersections still matter significantly, but not nearly as much as they did at the turn of the twentieth century, for example. And the extent to which they matter in any given organizational setting is similarly not a constant. For a host of reasons, different organizations, even if they are in the same industry or sector, can end up manifesting these inequalities in different ways. One significant reason will be that, as an aspect of both their formal and informal structures, formal organizations and/or parts of them can have quite variable *organizational cultures*.

Organizational Cultures

The stuff of culture is generally quite abstract, intangible, and often difficult to define. For simplicity we can follow organizational psychologist Edgar Schein, whose book *Organizational Culture and Leadership*[7] is an oft-cited starting point: "cultures are learned *patterns of beliefs, values, assumptions, and behavioral norms that manifest themselves at different levels of observability.*"[8] There are three levels of observability. The first involves the material aspects of the world (*artifacts*)—things that can be directly observed, such as the physical design and adornment of work spaces, formal organizational documents, styles of dress, modes of speech, forms of technology, the actual activities and interactions of physical human bodies, and so on. But culture is primarily symbolic and about meanings which make it fundamentally invisible in many respects. So the mere existence of physical things doesn't make them culture. Rather it is about what those things mean to people, and that's where things get less visible because the real stuff of culture is about ideas and understandings. In that regard, the second level of culture is about ideals that are consciously represented and articulated. This can occur formally on organizational front stages, such as publicly stated sets of goals, principles, and philosophies. These are often found in things like mission and vision statements of the organization and may be celebrated during various kinds of formal rituals and ceremonies. In universities, for example, formal gatherings such as university-wide faculty meetings to open a new academic year and graduation ceremonies that close them out are exactly those kinds of

---

[7]Schein, 2017. See especially Chapters 1 and 2.
[8]Schein, 2017: 2, emphasis original.

occasions. Speeches are given. Organizational values and virtues are enunciated.

Many other aspects of culture are more informal, but still consciously articulated. Relations among faculty within my own university department, for example, are quite collegial, egalitarian, and collaborative. None of those qualities are specified by any of the formal aspects of the larger organization or of our department. It is simply understood that "that's how we do things around here," and we all constantly work to establish and reaffirm these things in our ongoing interactions with one another, including when we socialize new members of the department.

The third level is the hardest to observe because it is about ideas that lie beneath the surface as unarticulated, taken-for-granted assumptions. I don't recall any time during which it has been consciously articulated, but in my department we do not assume that our colleagues are inherently lazy and seek to avoid work. Quite to the contrary. Thus when it seems that people are having a hard time meeting any kinds of work obligations, in keeping with our collegial atmosphere, the assumption is that some manner of assistance may be required rather than, say threats or punitive measures.

At this point, understanding organizational cultures is seen to be very important for practical reasons in the management sciences according to principles that have descended down through the human systems traditions of thinking. A great deal of what an organization is and what it manages to accomplish in terms of meeting its goals is, of course, a matter of formal organizational design (the technical and formal aspects), so that needs to be optimized. But then a great deal of it comes down to the social organization which by now we can simply take to be organizational culture, and it is important to try to optimize that. What one needs to do is try to build an organizational culture that both generates orientations toward work according to what the organization needs at the same time that it motivates its partici-pants. This often means building commitment and cooperation among par-ticipants as directed toward organizational goals. And it should not only be one where people feel like they "belong," (HR) but where they feel that they can make valuable and important contributions (HM).

Thus we can find various classifications of types of organizational cultures that are empirically developed and largely used for consulting purposes— something like the *scientific management* of organizational culture. One of the better known classifications comes from management scientist Kim Cameron who has identified four *ideal-typical* cultural types.[9] (See Figure 8.4). One is called a *clan* culture which is inwardly focused on the organization's own people and emphasizes things like togetherness, shared values, and teamwork as one might observe in the *Japanese System of Mangement (JSM)*. A second type is labeled *hierarchy* which is a form of organizational culture that values things like stability, predictability, and control, as one might find in fast food restau-rants, government agencies, or public schools. A third type is called *market* cultures that tend to be found in quickly changing and competitive economic markets such as those in the electronics industry. The premium here is on constantly moving forward as quickly as possible and staying ahead of the competition. Finally, the fourth type is called *adhocracy*. Adhocracies are often cast in opposition to bureaucracies. In adhocracies, roles, tasks, processes,

---

[9]Cameron, 2011. See especially Chapter 3.

FIGURE 8.4   Kim Cameron's Typology of Organizational Cultures

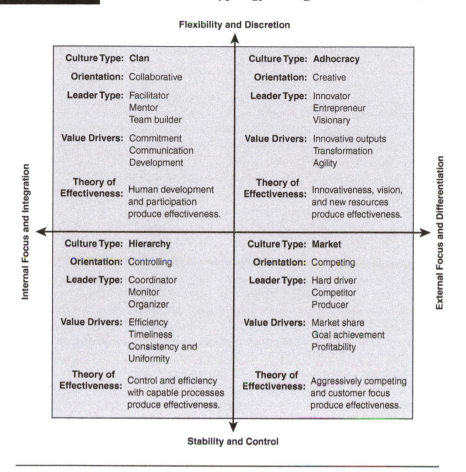

Source: Cameron and Quinn, 2011: 53.

procedures, and so forth can change so fast and to such a degree that no manner of formalization would last for very long. This would be characteristic of organizations such as Google where, in a sense, the future is constantly being reinvented, and there is a value on being at the center of the next new thing. The overriding idea in work like this is to be able to develop tools to analyze existing organizational cultures in order to help organizations align themselves effectively toward meeting their goals. As we'll learn in Chapter 11, work such as this descends from an area of organizational studies called *contingency theory* where the guiding principle is to understand optimal organizational structures as depending on (or being *contingent*) on the kinds of tasks and challenges that organizations face.

But understanding organizational cultures is also very important for more general social science purposes in addressing many social issues. For example, the problem of police brutality, especially toward people of color, is a very old one and obviously remains quite salient. Outside of those who study these issues, assumptions regarding causes tend to be that, where racialized violence by police has occurred, it is simply a matter of some "bad apples." That is that *some* police, as individuals, are racist and the answer is to simply screen applicants better and get rid of existing bad apples. There is ample evidence, however, that both the propensity to engage in violence and to racialize people are deeply ingrained in the general culture of policing. Organizationally speaking, policing organizations in the United States are highly varied and fragmented, so there will be a tremendous amount of variation from department to department, but the degree of general racism in US culture is well-represented and often intensified among members of policing organizations.[10] In addition, many police departments have been increasingly militarized. Officers are drilled in the notion that their jobs are exceptionally dangerous (even though that is less true than is often thought) and that they form the "thin blue line" between order and chaos. Increasingly they are described as being on the front lines of things like a *war* on drugs or a *war* on crime and have tended to be increasingly equipped to operate in similar ways to military organizations. Thus, when you mix pervasive racism together with a militarized understanding of their roles, issues of racialized violence by police become far more complicated than a few bad apples. Rather, it follows quite easily from the kinds of meanings that police officers operate upon.

Similarly, as I noted in Chapter 3, organizational cultures can either highlight and exacerbate or minimize things like inequalities of race and gender. So while the characteristics of formal organizations have frequently intersected with issues of race and gender, there is no automatic or direct translation of culturally defined differences into meaningful differences in terms of organizational dynamics. Variations can stem from many things. There are macro-level factors such as differences in national cultures, the type of industry, or organizational environments that can shape the overall contours. But in the end they will still arise from interaction with the micro-level dynamics of how things like race and gender are defined, thought of, and enacted in ongoing day-to-day interactions. Gaining better understandings of these things is helpful in many cases because it can contribute to making purposeful changes in organizational cultures that help to address many kinds of social issues, particularly with regards to inequalities.

Conclusion

There is much about building organizations as rational systems that is already quite complicated. Yet here we have seen that the complications extend far beyond questions of engineering toward efficiency. And thinking only through the engineering of systems without accounting for the human and social elements means that one will come up short—whether in shaping and running organizations or in just trying to understand them as social entities. Organizations are more complicated things than the rational system builders would like—*recalcitrant tools* as Selznick called them. It may be best to see them, not as rationally planned machines that are carrying out planned and stated

---

[10]Do note that this is more of a discussion of an *occupational culture* rather than any specific organizational culture. Characteristics of occupational cultures inevitably become manifested in particular organizations, but it does happen in highly variable ways. I cannot do the complexity of such things justice in brief form, but see Cockcroft, 2012, especially Chs. 1–2 and 4.

objectives according to specified procedures and methods, but as complex organisms that are adapting toward their own survival. Part of that survival will mean the production of formal descriptions of goals and objectives and procedures and so forth. This is necessary for internal coherence and legitimacy within the environment of the organization. But in many respects those formal descriptions will not offer an accurate view of what is happening as, in order to adapt, organizations will need to do many things that are not directly in line with their rational purposes or procedures. They have to handle their own people who come to the organization, not as easily programmable cogs but as living, breathing pieces of their cultures. And they have to be able to handle various kinds of institutional forces in their environments, in the form of general public acceptance and legitimacy, consistency of image and operation with regards to cultural norms, and other existing organizations. We will dwell more on the latter shortly when we move on to Chapter 9.

SOURCES AND FURTHER READING

The foundational accounts of the **Hawthorne Studies** appeared in:

- Roethlisberger, F. J., and William J. Dickson. 1939. *Management and the Worker.* Cambridge, MA: Harvard University Press.

Elton Mayo's central work on management, including critique of the **"rabble hypothesis:"**

- Mayo, Elton. 1933. *The Human Problems of an Industrial Civilization.* New York, NY: Macmillan Company.

  o Later revised as: Mayo, Elton. 1945. *The Social Problems of an Industrial Civilization.* London: Routledge & Kegan Paul.

Chester Barnard's central initial work on management:

- Barnard, Chester. I. [1938] 1968. *The Functions of the Executive.* Cambridge, MA: Harvard University Press.

The **secondary literature on the Hawthorne Studies** (including how they've been misrepresented) and the **Human Relations** movement is voluminous. Some key sources include:

- Bloombaum, Milton. 1983. "The Hawthorne Experiments: A Critique and Reanalysis of the First Statistical Interpretation by Franke and Kaul." *Sociological Perspectives* 26: 71–88.

- Bruce, Kyle, and Chris Nyland. 2011. "Elton Mayo and the Deification of Human Relations." *Organization Studies* 32: 383–405.

- Franke, Richard Herbert, and James D. Kaul. 1978. "The Hawthorne Experiments: First Statistical Interpretation." *American Sociological Review* 43: 623–43.

- Gale, E. A. M. 2004. "The Hawthorne Studies—A Fable for Our Times?" *Quarterly Journal of Medicine* 97: 439–49.

- Gillespie, Richard. 1991. *Manufacturing Knowledge: A History of the Hawthorne Experiments.* New York, NY: Cambridge University Press.

- Hassard, John S. 2012. "Rethinking the Hawthorne Studies: The Western Electric

Research in Its Social, Political and Historical Context." *Human Relations* 65: 1431–61.

- Jones, Stephen R. G. 1992. "Was There a Hawthorne Effect?" *American Journal of Sociology* 98: 451–68.

- Levitt, Steven D., and John A. List. 2011. "Was There Really a Hawthorne Effect at the Hawthorne Plant? An Analysis of the Original Illumination Experiments." *American Economic Journal: Applied Economics* 3: 224–38.

- O'Connor, Ellen S. 1999. "The Politics of Management Thought: A Case Study of the Harvard Business School and the Human Relations School." *Academy of Management Review* 24: 117–31.

- Smith, John H. 1998. "The Enduring Legacy of Elton Mayo." *Human Relations* 51: 221–49.

- The **Thomas Theorem** is so famous, it almost doesn't need a citation:

  o Thomas, W. I., & Thomas, D. S. (1928). *The Child in America*. Oxford, UK: Knopf.

On the development of ***Human Resources Management (HRM) and Development (HRD)*** (including some critical sources):

- Itani, Sami. 2017. *The Ideological Evolution of Human Resource Management: A Critical Look into HRM Research and Practices.* Bingley: Emerald Publishing Limited.

- Parks-Leduc, Laura, Matthew A. Rutherford, Karen L. Becker, and Ali M. Shahzad. 2018. "The Professionalization of Human Resource Management: Examining Undergraduate Curricula and the Influence of Professional Organizations." *Journal of Management Education* 42: 211–38.

- Obedgiu, Vincent. 2017. "Human Resource Management, Historical Perspectives, Evolution and Professional Development." *The Journal of Management Development* 36: 986–90.

- Ruona, Wendy E. A. 2016. "Evolving Human Resource Development." *Advances in Developing Human Resources* 18: 551–65.

- Schaupp, Marika. 2021. "Understanding the Evolution of the Forms of Carrying Out Human Resource Development." *Human Resource Development International* 24: 262–78.

- Vani, G. 2011. "Evolution of Human Resource Management." *Review of Management* 1: 127–33.

- Vázquez, José Luis and García María Purificación. 2017. "From Taylorism to Neo-Taylorism: A 100 Year Journey in Human Resource Management." In *Menedzsment Innovációk az Üzleti és a Nonbusiness Szférákban* (Roughly: *Management Innovations in Business and Nonbusiness Spheres*), edited by Vilmányi Márton–Kazár Klára. Szeged, Hungary: Szegedi Tudományegyetem Gazdaságtudományi Kar, 496–513. (Faculty of Economics, University of Szeged.)

The origins of **Humanistic Management**:

- McGregor, Douglas. 1960. *The Human Side of the Enterprise*. New York, NY: McGraw-Hill.

  o A very brief synopsis can be found here: McGregor, Douglas. 1957. "The Human Side of Enterprise." *Management Review* 46: 22–28/88–92.

  o The main foundations were in the **hierarchy of needs**: Maslow, Abraham

H. 1954. *Motivation and Personality*. New York, NY: Harper & Row.

On **Institutionalism**, the following **Exposé** tradition, and the **front/back stage imagery**:

- Blau, Peter M. 1955. *The Dynamics of Bureaucracy: A Study of Interpersonal Relations in Two Government Agencies*. Chicago, IL: University of Chicago Press.

- Durkheim, Emile. [1893] 1984. *The Division of Labor in Society*, translated by W. D. Halls. New York, NY: Free Press.

- Goffman, Erving. 1959. *The Presentation of Self in Everyday Life*. Garden City, NY: Doubleday.

- Gouldner, Alvin W. 1954. *Patterns of Industrial Bureaucracy*. New York, NY: Free Press.

- Merton, Robert K. 1936. "The Unanticipated Consequences of Purposive Social Action." *American Sociological Review* 1: 894–904.

- Perrow, Charles. 1986. *Complex Organizations: A Critical Essay*, 3rd Ed. New York, NY: Random House.

- Scott, Robert A. 1967. "The Selection of Clients by Social Welfare Agencies: The Case of the Blind." *Social Problems* 14: 248–57.

- Selznick, Philip. 1966. *TVA and the Grass Roots: A Study in the Sociology of Formal Organization, Harper Torchbooks Edition*. New York, NY: Harper and Row Publishers Incorporated.

On ideas and issues discussed with regards to *organizational culture*:

- Cameron, Kim S. and Robert E. Quinn. 2011. *Diagnosing and Changing Organizational Culture: Based on the Competing Values Framework*, 3rd Ed. San Francisco, CA: Jossey Bass/Wiley.

- Cockcroft, Tom. 2012. *Police Culture: Themes and Concepts*. New York, NY: Routledge.

- Collins, David. 2021. *Rethinking Organizational Culture: Redeeming Culture through Stories*. New York, NY: Routledge. (Chapter 5 is specifically on sexism and racism.)

- Delehanty, Casey, Jack Mewhirter, Ryan Welch, and Jason Wilks. 2017. "Militarization and Police Violence: The Case of the 1033 Program." *Research and Politics* 4: 1–7.

- Gond, Jean-Pascal, Laure Cabantous, Nancy Harding, and Mark Learmonth. 2016. "What Do We Mean by Performativity in Organizational and Management Theory? The Uses and Abuses of Performativity." *International Journal of Management Reviews* 18: 440–63.

- Haas, Linda and C. Philip Hwang. 2007. "Gender and Organizational Culture: Correlates of Companies' Responsiveness to Fathers in Sweden." *Gender & Society* 21: 52–79.

- Kraska, Peter B. and Louis J. Cubellis. 1997. "Militarizing Mayberry and Beyond: Making Sense of American Paramilitary Policing." *Justice Quarterly* 14: 607–29.

- Lyness, Karen S. and Marcia Brumit Kropf. 2005. "The Relationships of National Gender Equality and Organizational Support with

Work–Family Balance: A Study of European Managers." *Human Relations* 58: 33–60.

- Ní Laoire, Caitríona, Carol Linehan, Uduak Archibong, Ilenia Picardi and Maria Udén. 2021. "Context matters: Problematizing the Policy-Practice Interface in the Enactment of Gender Equality Action Plans in Universities." *Gender, Work, and Organization* 28: 575–93.

- Phillips, Scott W. 2018. *Police Militarization: Understanding the Perspectives of Police Chiefs, Administrators, and Tactical Officers.* New York, NY: Routledge.

- Powell, Abigail, Barbara Bagilhole, and Andrew Dainty. 2009. "How Women Engineers Do and Undo Gender: Consequences for Gender Equality." *Gender, Work and Organization* 16: 411–28.

- Rao, Aruna, Joanne Sandler, David Kelleher, and Carol Miller. 2016. *Gender At Work: Theory and Practice for 21st Century Organizations.* New York, NY: Routledge. See especially Chapter 5.

- Shein, Edgar H., with Peter Schein. 2017. *Organizational Culture and Leadership,* 5th Ed. Hoboken, NJ: John Wiley & Sons, Inc.

The Open Organization
ORGANIZATIONS AND THEIR ENVIRONMENTS

Many (or perhaps even all) of my readers will be reading this book because it is required or suggested reading for a college course of some kind. The requirement or suggestion for accessing this book will be included on a syllabus which spells out the basic goals and objectives of the course, what will be required of you, and how you will be evaluated, along with all manner of course policies and procedures. The syllabus is the ultimate piece of formal rationalization for a course, and its logic is one of a rational systems model. The goals and means of reaching them are (ostensibly) spelled out in written form. One of the policies that I include on all of my course syllabi is an attendance policy. Some might find this to be rather odd once I tell you that I don't take attendance in my courses. I'm just one of those people—I think that college level students are adults, or at least need to start acting like they are. I'm not around to be anyone's babysitter and if you'd rather not attend classes and do quite poorly as a result then that is up to you. So if I don't take attendance, then why would I have an attendance policy? It's quite simple really. A lot of the things that are included on my syllabi are not there because they are part of what I have rationally planned out as a means to help people learn. Rather they are required. I did not always have an attendance policy, but my University recently went through an accreditation process by an outside agency and a list of syllabi requirements were generated as a result.

Any college or university that you've heard of goes through accreditation. It's basically a process whereby people check up on you to see if you're legit. There are six regional accreditation agencies in the United States, and those are coordinated and overseen by a national level accreditation body called the Council for Higher Education Accreditation. This umbrella organization and its regional affiliates are, in turn recognized by the US Department of Education as the main accrediting bodies for college and universities throughout the country. As a result of this, you could go to a school in the Pacific Northwest and fill up your course schedule with art and theater and literature courses, but find that your syllabi for these courses—at least in many respects—bear a striking resemblance to those of your friend who has a schedule full of math and science courses at a university in the Southeast. The reason for these similarities will not be found in the rational decision-making of those designing the courses, but will come as requirements from the outside of the organization—or in other words from the organizational *environment*.

My little story about an attendance policy or syllabi generally is a little thing to be sure, and not about whole organizations. But the more you look, the more you'll see things in organizations that are put in place, not directly as part of rational planning of tasks to meet specified goals, but as a reflection of pressures from or the need for access to various things outside of the organization. We have already gotten a glimpse of this in the discussion of *Institutionalism* back in Chapter 8. The key thing to recall is that regardless of what the stated goal of an organization is, there is always one primary goal that comes before all others and that is the organization's own *survival*. And in this chapter we get to ways of looking at organizations whereby you recognize that survival means organizing things toward acquiring and managing *resources from your environment*. Think of an organization as an *input-output* system, where various resources are brought in, worked on and with in various ways, and then some manner of product or service is put out. This is the basic idea of thinking of organizations as *open systems*—their boundaries have to be porous so that resources can get in and out. Resources obviously include *material* things such as labor, capital, raw materials, equipment, and office or janitorial supplies. But organizations also require *symbolic resources* in the form of things like knowledge and information, and—very importantly—legitimacy and trust.

While this was always present in the background for rational and humans systems thinking, understanding organizations as creatures of their environments didn't move to the forefront of organizational studies until around the 1960s and into the 1970s. As of now, it is fair to say that various kinds of *open systems* perspectives dominate the field of organizational studies although with rational and human systems ideas already fully integrated. If you want to understand organizations, whether for social science purposes, or practical matters of organizational design, you have to be able to analyze organizational environments.

Conceptualizing the Environment

The notion of an organizational environment or reference to "things outside of the organization" can seem pretty vague at first, and that's partly because it is. There is no one specific and discrete set of things that we can say constitutes "the environment" of an organization. But the following broad, though not exhaustive, set of ideas should help to put some concrete shape to some major environmental elements. (You can refer to Figure 9.1 for a schematic representation.) We can start with something that is likely obvious. For business organizations, one of the most important elements of the environment are *competitors*. This is one reason that the efficiency concerns of Rational Systems models will generally remain quite relevant to understanding what organizations are doing. Competition, of course, is always taken to be a central mechanism for why market-based economic systems are superior to others. So long as organizations have to compete with others in the same markets, one of their primary objectives will be to become more efficient. But competition isn't limited to for-profit businesses either as most organizations face some manner of competition in their environments. Public universities, for example, compete to attract students and it is fair to say that this kind of competition results in

FIGURE 9.1   **Typical Elements of Organizational Environments**

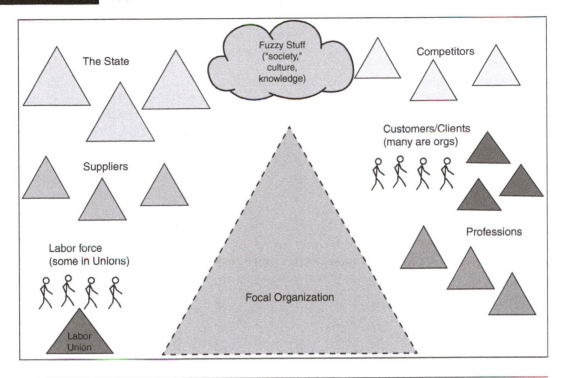

focus on things other than raw efficiencies. In fact, it can often lead to a focus on things that could be called decidedly inefficient if measured by a primary goal of a cost-effective education, such as very large landscaping budgets. Such things do help attract students, but they also represent a great deal of money spent on things that arguably don't directly contribute to the educational mission. Large landscaping budgets do, however, help with survival needs to the extent that nice landscaping helps to attract new students. This can be well-understood through the lenses of Institutionalism as introduced in Chapter 8.

The competition, of course, points to some manner of *customers* or *consumers*. Customers certainly include individual people such as when car companies compete to attract the most consumers as buyers. But many customers are also other organizations. Auto companies don't merely seek customers in the form of individuals, but also compete to supply whole fleets of vehicles to things like rental car companies, military and police forces, universities, and the like. Customers can be seen as located on the *output* side of the organization. On the *input side*, you will find *supplier organizations*. While *vertical integration* may occur on a broad scale under some organizational or economic conditions (see Part II), all organizations will need to procure supplies from outside of their boundaries. Obviously the more vertically integrated and organization is, the more it supplies for itself, but there will always be things that need to be procured from outside of the organization. Manufacturing organizations require various kinds of parts and/or raw materials and whatever equipment is required for doing the work, for example.

This further implies the need for whatever energy source is required to power operations. They also need all kinds of other things from office to janitorial supplies and information technology services.

With just a few minutes of thought, all of this will probably start to seem rather obvious. Competitors, customers, and suppliers are, after all, obvious things with regards to what organizations are about. But there are also less obvious kinds of things that may need more pointing out. One of these is various kinds of *professional organizations*. Organizations require all manner of professional services from legal and accounting expertise to engineering and information technology services. You can actually think about a University as a large collage of different kinds of professions rather than as an insular organization in and of itself. I was trained as a professional sociologist, and we have our own organizational resources, standards, modes of operation, and so on. This includes our own coordinating institutions such as the American Sociological Association (https://www.asanet.org/). In many respects, while I am officially "employed" by my University, I don't really see myself as working for the university so much as I see myself working for the profession. And while a lot of the policies on my syllabi, for example, are dictated by the University the contents of my courses are not. That comes from being in the world of professional sociologists.

On the other hand, my little opening story about attendance policies and syllabi and such represents the influence of various kinds of *regulatory and oversight organizations*. The most common and most powerful of these tend to be governmental organizations. Governmental organizations lay out the basic rules of the game for organizations, including even what forms of organization are legal. Recall from Chapter 5 that the corporate form of the business corporation as we now know it was not always legally possible. But it was eventually made possible through changes in the legal system. But when that helped to bring about widespread concentration of economic power in the form of monopolies and trusts and the like, regulatory measures were taken to try to mitigate those effects. Regulations take the form of both prohibitions (what must not be done) and mandates (what must be done). In addition to the basic rules of the game and regulatory matters, governmental organizations can affect the flow of resources through manipulating tax structures, providing subsidies, granting agencies, and so on. A great deal of what is done in any kind of organization is being done within some legal framework set by governmental agencies.

Oddly, Chapter 8, especially with regards to the Human Relations tradition but also emphasized by Institutionalism, already introduced us to yet another aspect of an organization's environment—the *labor force*. Depending on their tasks and complexity, organizations need a variety of people to actually participate and get the work done; so this means constant interaction with the labor market. Hiring people to work in an organization basically represents importing people from the environment, and this means everything that comes along with those people. It certainly does mean purely personal things, but it can also mean organizational things such as occurs with professional labor forces. Much of the time interacting with the labor market is done on an individual-by-individual basis. But labor markets can also include labor unions in which case the organization has to deal with other organizations. As we glimpsed in Chapter 3, the extent to which labor markets are populated by persons or organizations can be crucial to the characteristics of jobs and the relative power of labor.

Finally, at the most general level, an organizational environment includes the general social context. For the most part we can call that *culture* which doesn't capture everything about the general social context, but is a major portion of it. One major portion of culture that is important involves the current state of knowledge and technological capability relative to what an organization does. Just as importantly, there are generalized sets of norms, values, and expectations by which organizations and their activities will be evaluated. The example of this that we have already visited was in Selznick's study of the Tennessee Valley Authority in Chapter 8. The basic political and value orientations of people in the region was one of local autonomy and skepticism of centralized authority, especially as represented by the federal government. As we saw, this had a very large impact on how the TVA structured itself and ran its operations, but this applies to all organizations. To the extent that organizations do not align their structures and activities with generalized expectations they have a harder time securing buy-in and cooperation on the part of actors both inside and outside of the organization. A good deal of this is about the ability to secure *symbolic resources* such as public trust and legitimacy.

The Ambiguity of Organizational Boundaries

At various points in the above description of environmental elements there may have been some puzzling moments. (If not, then I'll puzzle you with it now.) Consideration of organizational environments assumes that there is an "inside" and an "outside" of an organization. Thus one might have had a moment of questioning when I brought up the issue of the labor force. Aren't the workers on the "inside" of the organization and thus part of the organization rather than part of the environment? The answer is pretty much both yes and no, and what it raises is the tricky issue of just how fuzzy organizational boundaries can get. Recall from Chapter 1 that in ideal typical form, one's personal life is strictly separate from their organizational rights, duties, and obligations. So when we formally participate in an organization, it is only part of us that is on the "inside." Much of us (our personal side) is supposed to remain on the outside. However, the Human Systems traditions show us one reason that it is best to keep in mind that ideal types are only variably manifested in practical action. People obviously do not create and maintain strong separation between those parts of themselves and remain as wholes when they participate in organizational activities. In fact, traditions such as *Humanistic Management* say to count on that by making use of the whole person and setting conditions so that the organizational merges with the personal.

I am currently working on this chapter in July. But in July I am technically not "employed" by my University. Yet work on teaching and scholarship (this book is a hybrid of those) is a major portion of my job description. So in some respects I am doing my "job" right now even though I am technically not employed. So am I on the inside or the outside my university? Furthermore, for whom am I working right now? This book is on my *Curriculum Vitae* (a fancy phrase for "résumé" in some professions), and this will figure into formal performance evaluations at the university. But writing it was my decision. I wasn't told to do it, and whether I complete this project or some other project doesn't actually matter to anything or anyone else at the university. My real hope is that this book is of use to other sociologists and their students—in other words, of use to the profession. Other than perhaps questions regarding what kind of work is being done in the summer, the same issue applies to students. When school is out of session are students on the inside or the outside of the organization?

The ambiguities don't only apply to people but to *interorganizational relations* (IORs) as well. We have come across the use of cooptation with regards to the TVA's strategy for managing its environment, for example. It is fair to say that the Department of Agricultural Relations of the TVA, which was dominated by the agriculturalists, was operating on behalf of the goals and needs of the Cooperative Extension Service system which is presumably part of the TVA's environment. Yet it was obviously both inside and outside of the organization. If you think back to Part II of the book and the grand narrative regarding changes in organizational forms over time, it was very much a story about shifting organizational boundaries. Both horizontal and vertical integration are matters of organizational boundary expansion while something like *Nikefication* is a matter of boundary contraction. But even there ambiguities remain. Holding companies own other companies, but those companies generally operate as independent entities. A step away from that is *multidivisional form* (*M-form*) of organizational structure where divisions operate relatively independently of a head office. Joint ventures produce something of a hybrid organization that is both inside and outside of the organizations involved. Network forms of business produce all manner of IORs that blur the boundaries between firms, and make it clear that boundaries frequently shift. Perhaps the fuzziest picture of all might come from thinking about virtual firms and the increasing degree of *Uberization* (see Chapter 6). Uber drivers are not defined as employees of Uber, but as independent subcontractors (although that is being challenged in various ways).

These ambiguities are just in the nature of organizations and organizing and can become quite relevant to organizational analysis. The issue needs to be raised, but there is no closure to be offered. As with so many other things, don't look for black and white except in discussions of ideal types. Realize that everything is much more likely to be shades of gray because of variability. With regards to organizational boundaries that separate the inside from the outside, always take them to be variable and subject to change. Sometimes boundaries will be clearer than others. Even when clear they can be weakened, or vice versa. They can be moved and changed as when various aspects of organizational activity are either internalized or outsourced. Just assume that organizational boundaries can always be loose, fuzzy, and shifting to varying degrees. But above all else, there are no organizations that can be adequately analyzed as *closed systems*. Resources have to move across the boundaries to make their way in, and outputs similarly have to move across boundaries to make their way out. Organizations are permeable input-output systems.

Basic Forms of IORs

If it wasn't already obvious from the above discussion, while there are exceptions (such as general cultural values), the bulk of what accounts for an organization's environment is other organizations. Thus acquiring and managing resources from the environment involves managing IORs. From Part II we already have a relatively useful general characterization of the forms that IORs take. It is contained in the language of markets, hierarchies, networks, and communities. All of these things refer to various modes of exchange relations among organizations and their participants. Let's review the logics in ideal typical form:

- *Markets:* The typical exchange takes the form of a spot contract. An organization needs a supply of paper, seeks out sources that can supply the paper needs, compares the costs among different sources, and selects the least cost supply of paper. The same process occurs again the next time that the organization needs paper. The boundaries here are relatively clear and paper and money move across them.

- *Hierarchy:* Perhaps the organization uses a lot of paper, and rather than relying on the market (environment) it decides to produce its own paper, whether by starting up a new division or purchasing an existing paper producer. Now the production and distribution of the paper is done by command rather than market exchange. Note that, in this case, at least one part of the environment was internalized, and is thus no longer part of the environment.

- *Community:* An organization is in need of paper and borrows a supply of it from another organization. There is an expectation of reciprocity in such relations whereby the lending organization assumes that it will be able to borrow when it needs to. In this case, there may be boundaries on a formal basis, but not so much on an informal basis.

- *Network:* An organization has a steady need for paper, but rather than relying on any of the above sets up a relationship with another organization that is all of the above. That is, recall that networks are a hybrid form. The purchaser might enter into a long-term flexible purchasing relationship with a supplier. There might be times when it could pay less by going to the market, but the long-term gains are in more intangible things like commitment and trust. In this case, the boundaries between the two organizations have become blurrier because they exist in an ongoing cooperative relationship. You can think of it like having a bridge or even a wormhole connecting two organizations as an ongoing open interface. And obviously boundaries in networking organizations can become blurrier yet. The bookstore at my University is operated by the Follet Corporation, while much of the campus food service is operated by Aramark Corporation—parts of the outside working on the inside.

All of these forms of IOR tend to come with issues for organizations. The most central of interest have tended to be the costs that are associated with various forms, the degree of stability and predictability in acquiring needs, and the question of power relations and thus relative autonomy. As such, there are theoretical and research traditions that deal with trying to understand these issues, especially in terms of where and how organizations locate their boundaries.

Transaction Cost Economics

Economists are an interesting bunch, and I think it is because so many of them start from the mistaken (though usually implicit as well) Enlightenment assumption that there is some kind of "state of nature" whereby individuals lived as individuals rather than being born into and living out their lives in social groups. Thus at least some Enlightenment philosophers found it relevant to ask why there are societies. And in like form, there is a tradition in economics that asks the question of why there are organizations. Why would there not just be pure markets with all individuals acquiring their needs though self-interested, rational exchanges with other individuals? This is the economic state of nature, I guess. One dominant answer largely involves things called *transaction costs*, and thus the tradition in economics that focuses on this, and what it means for organizational structures, is called *Transaction Cost Economics (TCE)*.

Markets work by transactions, which is just another word for exchanges, and it is obvious that all transactions involve costs because you have to give something to get something. What you give is your cost. What you get is benefit. You do the math regarding the costs and benefits of various actions and that's how you decide the what, when, and where of your transactions. What TCE brings to the fore is that the direct cost of the transaction is only part of the total cost. Think of it like this—you want pizza. Perhaps you go through the mail looking for promotional coupons or go to the web to search for current deals offered by local pizza places. You find a deal on a pizza that you'll probably like and order it for $15. So you might think of the cost of buying the pizza (a.k.a. the transaction cost) as being equal to $15. But you would be a little off in your calculations there. For one thing, you used up a bunch of time in looking around for a pizza supply and then in placing your order. You might also have needed to take the time to check your bank balance to find out if you could afford a pizza. These represent costs and would typically be classified as the *search* and *information costs*, and if we include the search for coupons and best prices we can think of that as a corollary of *bargaining costs* (see Figure 9.2). You then also have to actually get your hands on the pizza. This means one of two things. One is that you walk or drive to the pizza place to pick it up. So there is more cost, and that is especially so if you drove to pick it up. Or perhaps you will have the pizza delivered, which also involves a cost, even if that is sometimes only the voluntary cost of providing the driver with a tip. (I delivered pizza while in college and you should tip the driver.)

In addition to the search, information and bargaining costs risks are also being taken with regards to unknowns, such as whether or not the place will get your order right and/or maybe short you on cheese or sauce, or maybe ship you a pizza that's been sitting around under a heat lamp for the last few hours. The latter represent problems of *opportunism* assumed to be potentially present in all market transactions. Actors will only look out for their own best interests and the assumption is that, given the opportunity, at least some of them will cheat. So the monitoring of transactions—often called *policing costs*—also needs to be added on the cost side, and this gets worse if you have to return the thing for any of the above reasons. In order to calculate your total cost for the pizza, you have to add in all of this extra stuff—the *transaction costs*. Once you do that perhaps you might have decided that you would

| FIGURE 9.2 | Basics of *Transaction Cost Economics (TCE)* |

Basic Types of Transaction Costs	*Search & Information Costs*
	   − Locating necessary goods & services on suitable terms
	Bargaining Costs
	   − Establishing terms of exchange, including drawing up of contracts
	Policing Costs
	   − Monitoring exchange partners to avoid problems of *opportunism* (such as cheating)

Variables in Make-Or-Buy Decision
(To *vertically integrate or not*)
	Frequency of the transactions
	   − Occasional transactions are rarely a problem. Persistent need for them can be.
	Uncertainty involved
	   − Anything that gets in the way of predictability and reliability of supply or pricing can be a problem
	Asset Specificity
	   − The degree to which the exchange relation involves assets highly specific to this exchange relation (*sunk costs*)

➤ Where *frequency, uncertainty,* and *asset specificity* are all high, making rather than buying (*vertical integration*) will often be more cost efficient

Source: Author's summary from multiple sources. See notes at the end of the chapter.

have been better off just making your own pizza—if you had decided to *make* rather than *buy.*

You getting a pizza is obviously an oversimplification of the entirety of the issue when it comes to running organizations. Organizations face all of these costs and then some, including the legal costs of arranging, monitoring, and possibly needing to resort to contract enforcement. Furthermore, not receiving adequate or correct products from the market might have devastating consequences for doing business. If you don't get your pizza as specified, this is not that big of a deal. If a manufacturing firm doesn't receive crucial components it can bring a halt to operations. And even if there are no complete disasters the costs are still persistent. But it may be possible to reduce them. You can, for example, reduce or eliminate the transaction costs by *internalizing* whatever the function is. In other words, eliminate at least one way that you need to interact with the environment by bringing the function within your own organizational boundaries. The downside is that this represents costs as well because you'll need to develop or buy an organizational division to perform the function. Thus you have to decide which is cheaper and on that basis arrive at what is called a *make-or-buy decision.* So, among other things, TCE seeks to understand the conditions under which various things will be made or bought. If they are to be made, then this amounts to *vertical integration,* and fewer things are left out in the organizational environment. If they are bought, then they are left in the market.

The key ingredients that influence a make-or-buy decision will have to do largely with three things. First is the degree of *frequency* with which the transactions take place. If you're looking only at things that are needed infrequently, then it is unlikely that the math would ever work out to make it worth internalizing the business function. If, for example, you really only need a true professional accountant once a year at tax time, you're unlikely to put one on staff full time and year around. The second is the degree of *uncertainty*, or predictability with regards to be able to acquire what is needed. Even if your company does go through a lot of paper, if the market is healthy and getting reliable and predictable paper supplies with suitable quality is easy enough to do, then the transaction costs will tend to remain low. The final one is often seen to be the most important and is called *asset specificity*. Asset specificity is basically the degree to which a thing being exchanged is specific to the exchange relationship or business activity. For example, if an auto supplier is making a highly specialized part for only one company and that company can only get that part from that one supplier, then whatever *assets* are maintained on the part of both companies are *specific* to that relationship—thus the term *asset specificity*. This certainly applies in the case of physical assets like buildings or equipment, but it can apply to people too if there are highly specialized skills or forms of knowledge involved in the relationship. This situation leaves the exchange parties vulnerable due to their co-dependence and makes it more likely—because it is less costly—to bring things under the same organizational hierarchy. Thus in the logic of economics, the question of organizational boundaries comes down to rational decision-making with regards to how to manage relations with the environment.

It is worth noting that the logic of TCE fits like a glove into Alfred Chandler's explanation of the rise of big business (Chapter 4), and this would partly be because Chandler was likely influenced by economist Ronald Coase who is generally credited with originating TCE in his 1937-book *The Nature of the Firm*. The basic idea is that managerial hierarchies overseeing vertically integrated enterprises eliminate, or at least greatly reduce, many of the transaction costs for any function that could be internalized. The need for all of the searching, information gathering, bargaining and (especially) policing virtually disappear or become much easier. TCE has thus played a role in saving Chandler's basic approach to understanding the structure of business organizations. Back in Chapter 5 I mentioned that one of the best reasons to question Chandler's interpretation was that by the 1970s–1980s it was looking pretty clear that large, vertically integrated, and hierarchical was *not* actually efficient as Chandler had argued. However, perhaps it was the most efficient *at that time*, and times do change. So just because the large, bureaucratic form fell in the latter part of the twentieth century, that doesn't necessarily kill off efficiency explanations for their rise.

Economic historians Naomi Lamoreaux Daniel Raff and Peter Temin, among others, have argued that Chandler was basically right, but that his accounts were largely descriptive rather than being driven by an underlying theory that could account for change. Into that perceived theoretical void, goes TCE. The root problem for all transaction costs is seen to be deficits of information for parties to the exchange. We always have imperfect knowledge about things like the future and what exchange partners will really do, and whether or not they will try to cheat. (This is called *bounded rationality* which we will look at in some depth in Chapter 10.) Information problems are what allow opportunistic actions. If you go back to the turn of the twentieth century, the economic institutions that grease the wheels of market economies, such as regulatory and oversight agencies and a stable monetary and banking systems, weren't all that well developed yet. Furthermore, technologies of communication and transportation were quite rudimentary as compared to what they would eventually become. These kinds of things are generically referred to as *coordinating mechanisms*. At the turn of the twentieth century, with many fewer coordinating mechanisms, transaction costs were a major issue and putting things under managerial coordination in the classic hierarchy solved those information problems and thus the problem of high transaction costs. Big and vertically integrated really *was* the most efficient at the time, as the argument goes. However, by the 1970s period the development of coordinating mechanisms was such that those transaction costs that had made hierarchy so much more efficient initially were so greatly reduced that now hierarchy was *comparatively* less efficient than things like the network form.

As a corollary to some aspects of the ideas presented in Chapters 4 and 5, efficiency explanations of organizations and organizing have frequently been challenged by explanations that emphasize inequalities of social power. And so it is generally with TCE which helped give rise to a theoretical challenger called *Resource Dependence Theory (RDT)*.

Power in IORs—Resource Dependency Theory (RDT)

Based on the material presented in Part II, especially in Chapter 5 you should already have an inkling that many social scientists, outside of the economists, are quite skeptical of understanding organizations through the logic of economics. In simple terms this is because the logic of economics operates in a fictional world where all manner of social relations among actors are erased save those based on rational, self-interested exchange. This includes relations of inequality among social actors. Economic analyses, including TCE, tend to share some of the problems seen in the *rabble hypothesis* that we learned about in Chapter 8. One of the things that this means is that economists tend to not be very good at dealing with questions of social power. Assumptions are made regarding how all parties to all exchanges are free and equal to participate or not and on their own terms. On the other hand, sociologists (among others) have no such illusions, and more often than not are likely to see societies, and perhaps especially, economic relations, as being shaped by unequal power relations. Partly as a reaction to TCE in the 1970s there emerged a perspective on organizations and their relations with their environments that was explicitly focused on questions of variable power called *Resource Dependency Theory (RDT)*, or just *Resource Dependence*.

The landmark work that first defined the approach appeared in 1978 in a book called *The External Control of Organizations: A Resource Dependence Perspective* by Jeffrey Pfeffer and Gerald Selancik. The basic starting point of the perspective is that the most significant factors that shape organizational structures and actions are not be found internally in such things as the nature of the organization's tasks or the ideas and values of its leadership as it would be with Rational and Human Systems orientations. Rather they are to be found in the relationship of the organization to other organizations in their environment in terms of what kinds of resources the organization depends on to survive. Depending on resources means depending on other organizations and that creates variable kinds of power relations among organizations. For Pfeffer and Salancik, much of what an organization is up to is geared toward trying to avoid constraints and increase their own autonomy.

In order to analyze specific power relationships, they borrowed from a very famous and very simple logic for understanding social power among various actors first outlined by sociologist Richard Emerson in 1962. Emerson begins by making clear that power is a type of social relationship rather than a "thing" of sorts that some actor possesses. (Though obviously all kinds of "things" can provide the basis for power in a relationship.) Power is generated by *relationships* of mutual dependencies among actors. You can think of the logic that he laid out as something of a Q&A tree (see Figure 9.3). Imagine two companies—ACME Widgets, Inc. and Apex Supply Co. In order to establish whether a power relation exists you ask a basic set of questions:

- Does Apex have something that actor ACME needs (or wants)? Y/N.

- If yes, how badly does ACME want or need it? Very badly/No big deal. (Pfeffer and Slancik label this *resource importance*, though it is also frequently called *criticality*.)

- Does ACME have something that Apex needs (or wants)? Y/N. (This is the question of *asymmetric dependence*. If the answer is yes, then this becomes a source of *countervailing power* for ACME and the dependence may be *symmetric*.)

- Can ACME get this need filled from actors other than Apex? Y/N. (This is called *resource concentration*. If Apex is the only supplier, that is high resource concentration. If there are many suppliers, then it is low resource concentration.)

FIGURE 9.3   Determinants of Unequal Power/Resource Dependence

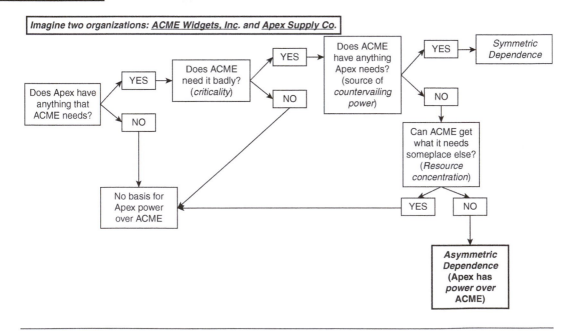

If you just mull that over, it's not hard to see how the logic works. If Apex has something that ACME needs badly (*criticality*); and if ACME doesn't have anything important that Apex needs in return (ACME has no source of *countervailing power*); and if ACME can't get what it needs anyplace else (environmental *resource concentration*), then ACME is dependent on Apex. Thus Apex has *power over* ACME, and the organizational analyst will do best to understand that a good deal of ACME's decisions and activities and even internal dynamics will be driven by its dependence on Apex.

Of course, if neither Apex nor ACME has anything that the other wants or needs, then there is no basis for a power relationship, or a relationship of any kind for that matter. Apex and/or ACME might be very powerful actors in some other kinds of relations with other actors, but neither has any power over the other. Similarly, if ACME has multiple sources to fulfill its needs, then it is not dependent on Apex and Apex thus has little to no power over ACME. If there is *symmetrical dependency*, where both Apex and ACME have something crucial that the other needs, and the other can't easily get it elsewhere, one can call that equality—but it is not an absence of power. It means that each has power over the other. In this case, it would also do the organizational analyst well to attend to this relationship in understanding what these organizations are doing.

Do note that a situation symmetric dependence largely equates to what TCE calls strong asset specificity (above) among trading partners, and for TCE produces conditions that make it more likely that an organization will self-supply—often by absorbing or otherwise merging with the trading partner. In other words, it will produce a tendency toward at least some degree of *vertical integration*. However, what RDT would emphasize is that the way this relationship unfolds will not be driven by rationality or efficiency, but rather by power considerations. Organizations will act to manage their dependencies and, whenever possible, avoid or alleviate them, although it will never be possible to get rid of interdependencies entirely. If an organization exists, then it is dependent on resources from its environment and it must organize toward that above all else.

There are a large number of different strategies that can be used to manage dependencies. Mergers and acquisitions—a.k.a. horizontal and vertical integration—can reduce competitive pressures and alleviate dependencies on suppliers or buyers. Various forms of business networking arrangements such as joint ventures and strategic alliances can increase interdependencies and thus reduce lopsided power differences. There is also ample evidence that organizations actually structure their boards of directors toward management of environmental relations, including having large boards made up of many outside directors with links to organizational sectors that are environmentally crucial, and by the use of interlocking directorates, discussed in Chapter 2. Organizations can also try to manipulate their operating environment in various ways. Attempting to influence the state and its regulatory structures is often done through lobbying, political campaign contributions, and the circulation of industry personnel through governmental posts. And this can be enhanced if done through collective action organizations such as industry and trade associations where organizations with similar environmental challenges join forces to press their interests in both formal and informal ways.

On the whole RDT has proven to be a very useful perspective in Organizational Studies. It was one of the dominant approaches during the 1980s, and continues to be fruitfully used, often now in combination with other approaches. For some purposes, however, it may be still too narrowly focused on particular organizations and their strategic and contextualized decisions. In fact, it may be possible to understand organizations and their structures by largely ignoring what is going on in particular organizational activities. RDT assumes that organizations can change over time to manage the varying constellation of their interdependencies over time. But we also know that organizations often find it quite difficult to change—and sometimes even because of those dependencies. But obviously there is a good deal of organizational change over time and it is possible to understand this without assuming that organizations themselves change.

Organizational Ecology

One of the more intriguing approaches to understanding organizations in terms of environmental constraints is known as *organizational ecology* (a.k.a. *population ecology of organizations*). It is an approach that completely shifts the level of analysis away from particular organizations or organizational relations to the analysis of *populations* of organizations. The entire logic of this approach is borrowed from population ecology in biology, which itself is rooted in evolutionary biology. All living things must be able to extract necessary resources—things like food, water, and frequently shelter—from their environments to be able to survive. Following from that we can deduce a couple of things. One is that any given environment will impose limits on the number of members of a species that it can support. This is called an environment's *carrying capacity*. If every elephant needs 50 gallons of water per day to survive, and you have an *ecological niche* in which water availability totals 5,000 gallons per day, then over the long term that niche can support only 100 elephants. If there are more than 100 elephants, then some will inevitably die or will need to move elsewhere to a different niche. The second thing is that certain members of a species may be better able to acquire access to and use resources in that environment. This is, of course, linked to the theory of evolution. Populations of elephants will naturally come to take on characteristics that make surviving members well suited to exploit available resources and to survive. Those without the best characteristics for the environment will not survive long enough to reproduce.

And perhaps this is how it is with organizations as well. In a landmark paper from 1977 called "The Population Ecology of Organizations," sociologists Michael Hannan and John Freeman propose that very thing, and this paper went on to spawn a new specialty area within organizational studies. The context of the paper came from a couple of existing things in Organizational Studies. One was basically the *contingency theory* tradition which we will come to in Chapter 11. *Contingency theory* is concerned with explaining the wide range of variability that can be found in organizational structures, and environmental conditions figure into it prominently. The other inspiration was from a tradition of seeing organizations as adaptive structures that change with the times to maintain themselves, whether this was in terms of rational systems images involving strategic decision-making, or natural systems notions of organizational drift.

Hannan and Freeman wanted to be able to explain organizational variability and change, but argued that this was unlikely to be explained by any manner of adaptive processes, whether rational or natural, for the simple reason that established organizations find it hard to change things very much. They are subject to all sorts of pressures that produce *structural inertia* such as *sunk costs* in facilities, equipment and personnel, existing internal power relations, built up commitments among participants to existing conditions, and external constraints regarding things like the need for legitimacy and normative obligations. They argue that organizational change will more likely occur by the foundings of new organizations rather than by change among existing organizations. As such, whatever variability is found among organizations will occur by the appearance of new forms and the *selection* of certain forms by the environment ("survival of the fittest"), rather than from *adaptations* made by existing organizations.

If you want to think about the argument that they are making, you can go back to the elephants. The basic structures, capabilities and processes that are important to survival in the case of any given elephant body are largely set at the time that the elephant is born. There is only so much adaptation that an elephant can do in terms of getting by in its environment. It can't, for example, develop better hearing or shrink or grow its trunk. Rather if such changes occur to elephants it will occur, not at the level of changes to individuals of the species, but at the level of the population where only certain elephants with the most advantageous characteristics are selected out based on their environmental fitness. That is, individual organisms of a species don't change very much, but over time populations of a species can and do based on variations found with the birth of new members of the species.

Thus in organizational ecology, the key thing to look at to understand existing organizational structures and organizational variability and change is organizational *births (foundings)* and *deaths (disbandings/failures)*. In this approach, there is not much attention given to what generates new organizational forms. Rather there is just a general assumption of *entrepreneurship* where there will always be various actors looking to capitalize on some manner of opportunity or setting out to achieve some goals via formal organization. Thus new kinds of organizations will continually be "born" just as new members of any species of animals are.

For organizational forms that do end up being successful at some point, early growth tends to be very slow. This can be because not many are being founded, but is also because of a condition dubbed *the liability of newness*. Basically, newer organizations are more likely to fail than older, more established ones. The liabilities of newness can come from any number of things, such as questionable legitimacy, difficulties in access to capital, a lack of an adequate pool of qualified personnel, unreliable supplies in terms of raw materials, tools or equipment, and uncertainty regarding the most viable operating strategies. For new types of organizations, there just might not yet be conditions in the environment that will support them adequately.

But if foundings continue and some new forms of organization manage to survive, eventually that liability of newness might decline. Surviving organizations establish the legitimacy of the new type, and new entrants to the population find it easier to access resources such as funding, supplies, personnel, clientele, and the like. In addition, basic structures and processes for new foundings can be established by the emulation of successful models. Thus survival becomes much more likely, and while foundings very well may increase, the key is that with a decreasing failure rate there is typically rapid growth in the new form of organization. This cannot go on indefinitely, however, because as the *population density* increases, available resources eventually become more scarce. As the population hits the *carrying capacity* of the environment, founding rates will likely decline and death rates will increase, and thus the population of now not-so-new organizational forms levels off at that carrying capacity of the environment, or sometimes declines.

This process results in a growth shape that can be drawn as an S-shaped curve as shown in Figure 9.4. This basic dynamic has been dubbed *the density model of legitimation and competition* because the survival of organizations is *density dependent*. With the emergence of new forms, if the density is too low organizations have a harder time surviving because of problems of *legitimacy*. But once the new form becomes viable, density can also become too high, and organizations have a hard time surviving because of *competition* for scarce resources.

It might sound like these processes would mostly be applicable in the case of business enterprises, especially in light of the emphasis on competition as a central regulator of population characteristics and size. And indeed organizational ecology has been successfully applied to a wide range of business areas, from semiconducting manufacturing and automobile companies to microbreweries and hotels. But it has also been used to study such things as labor unions, social service agencies, political activist organizations, and intergovernmental organizations (IGOs). There is no such thing as an organization, whether it operates for profit or not, that doesn't need to acquire things from its environment in order to survive, and thus the model is widely applicable to all populations of organizations. It is probably fair to say the approach had its most vigorous period of development from its origins in the late 1970s up until about the early 2000s. But it remains an important and useful logic for various kinds of analyses, and is still put to use, especially in a form that has been broadened by its melding with (and many would say eclipsing by) yet another form of open

FIGURE 9.4   **Population Growth to Ecological Carrying Capacity**

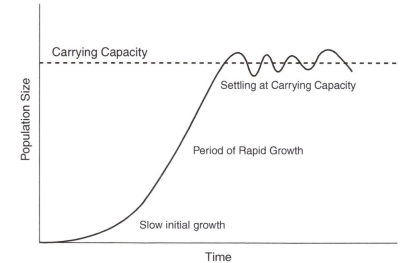

systems analysis that emerged (or perhaps just reemerged) during the late 1970s called *Neoinstitutionalism.*

Neoinstitutionalism

Like organizational ecology, virtually all of the ideas introduced in this chapter remain quite relevant in the world of organizational studies. But at this point it is probably fair to say that, especially among organizational sociologists, one of the dominant approaches has come to be what is called *Neoinstitutionalism* (or *New Institutionalism*). We were introduced to the roots of this back in Chapter 8 with Philip Selzick when we learned about how the TVA had to design itself toward conformity with various kinds of environmental forces. Because this was one important aspect of the original (or "old") institutionalism, I could have saved that story for this chapter but it really does belong in both places. The breakdown of theoretical imageries into Rational/Human/ Open systems is ideal typical. Many things don't come in neat boxes. Transaction Cost Economics, for example, is very much a Rational Systems approach since organizational forms are largely seen to be driven by rational decision-making with regards to maximizing efficiency. However, it is also an Open Systems approach because the primary focus is on environmental relations. And, in fact, it is generally classified as an approach in *New Economic Institutionalism* because it sees the rise and form of economic institutions—like banking systems, laws regarding property rights, regulatory and oversight agencies, and the like—as coming from the need to reduce transaction costs. In contrast, Institutionalism and Neoinstitutionalism most developed from Selnick and onward could be called both Human and Open Systems. The main focus is on the environment, but the primary drivers of activity are social and cultural patterns rather than matters of rational planning toward efficiency. In fact it is an explicit hallmark of institutional theory that organizational structures, processes, and activities are driven more by social and cultural forces than they are by rationality, unlike the approach of TCE.

The word *institution* is a widely used, but notoriously slippery term that has no single standard and agreed upon definition. One might summarize the whole idea of in the same way that you can summarize what it means to think of organizations having cultures—"there are ways that we do things around here." There's basically a *status quo*, and organizations have little choice but to conform to that *status quo*. Furthermore, they have to do so *even if it is inefficient* in some respects with regards to whatever their central goals and tasks are. The elements of the *status quo* are manifested in various ways, from taken-for-granted assumptions to self-consciously understood informal rules, and, of course, formal rules. They are ideas and expectations about how things are supposed to be and what people are supposed to do or not do.

Any of my University student readers will immediately be familiar with certain kinds of things that are highly institutionalized with regards to higher education. For example, while you can find occasional variations in some schools, college grading usually works on a highly standard A, B, C, D, F scale, including a +/- system, with each grade level linked to a 4.0 Grade Point Average (GPA) scale. This standard is *institutionalized* in the sense that it is widely used, has been for a very long time, is well understood, and taken for granted—people just expect it to be used without giving it any conscious thought. In this case, it is both a taken-for-granted scheme for grading scales, and is formalized in the written rules of organizations. I am not allowed to decide that it makes no rational sense that the scheme skips over the letter E and assign that as a failing grade instead. Heck, the computer system into which I enter grades doesn't even provide that as a choice—the ultimate form of deterministic rationalizing. If you go on a job interview and are asked for your transcript or just your GPA, you won't need to explain anything about it to the interviewer. However, if you went to one of the schools that does operate with a different kind of grading system, you would likely need to explain how that system works. And, depending on the system, it might even count as a mark against you as it could stand a chance of making your degree more questionable than those of others because it's not so much "how we do things around here."

This latter point with regards to conformity to existing institutionalized patterns is about the question of *legitimacy* which has been one of the central themes in neoinstitutional analyses since the beginning. What counts as "the beginning" can be rather fuzzy, and there has been some discussion of what actually makes Neoinstitutionalism new. Like Philip Selznick, I would put the beginning with him and the rest of the Columbia School.[1] But since the use of the "neo-" prefix is now itself *institutionalized*, it is typical to point to a 1977 landmark paper by Sociologists John Meyer and Brian Rowan called "Institutionalized Organizations: Formal Structure as Myth and Ceremony."[2] Recall from Chapter 8 that formal organizational structures often do not provide a good representation of what is actually going on inside of an organization. There is always a spontaneously generated informal structure consisting of what people are actually doing. This presents a bit of a puzzle. Why would the formal description of an organization not match up to its actual activities (or *vice versa*)? According to Meyer and Rowan, those formalized rational structures—consisting largely of the principles of Weberian ideal-typical Rational Systems bureaucracies—are not adopted because they provide the optimum means to ends for organizations. Rather they are put in place as a matter of conformity to expectations. Ever since the organizational revolution, the rational, bureaucratic form is, itself, an institutionalized expectation in contemporary societies. Even if the reality is that organizational life is just one damned thing happening after another, it can't appear that way. Organizations must look like rational systems bureaucracies in order to gain and maintain legitimacy. They must be able to state their goals, clearly, describe a set of means that are intended to efficiently reach those goals, and they have to constantly monitor and review their own performance to see that it meets efficiency expectations, and present this to various audiences. Rationalization is a powerful set of expectations "enforced by public opinion, by the views of important constituents, by knowledge legitimated through the educational system, by social prestige, by the laws, and by the definitions of negligence and prudence used by the courts," as Meyer and Rowan put it.[3] The ghost of Frederick Taylor is alive and well in all sorts of ways.

One central problem that arises, however, is that many aspects of formal structure can be detrimental to the organization in terms of getting things done. Thus organizations are frequently subject to conflicting demands. The

---

[1]See Selznick, 1996.

[2]Sometimes another 1977 paper by sociologist Lynn Zucker titled "The Role of Institutionalization in Cultural Persistence" is included as well.

[3]Meyer and Rowan, p. 343.

general argument is that organizations solve these problems of conflicting demands by *decoupling* their formal structures from their informal structures. If you recall the language from Erving Goffman introduced in Chapter 8, then we can simply say that organizations maintain a highly Weberian and rational looking *frontstage* which can be decoupled from their *backstage*. Frontstage activities remain out in front as what the audience (the general public, the clientele, the state, other regulatory organizations, and so on) sees, but frontstage activities serve as those things that Selznick called *sustaining myths*. Meyer and Rowan refer to *rationalized myths* since, in this argument, rationalization is the key institutional expectation of our times. Because of that, the appearance of being a rational system must be upheld, even if that provides a poor description of actual structures and activities. The real business of the organization can be found in the informal organization which takes place on the backstage. The formal elements are carried out as ceremony and ritual in the interests of maintaining legitimacy, and function to shield the far messier backstage of the organization from too much scrutiny.

A key overarching concept with regards to understanding how organizations get their form and function, whether with regards to many formal or informal characteristics, is *environmental* (or *institutional*) *isomorphism*. Taking the word apart, *iso*—is from the Greek *isos* which means equal to or the same as. *Morph* is also from Greek and means form or shape. So *isomorphism* just means to take on the same form, shape, or structure. Organizations take on a form or structure that basically molds them to the environment they are in. A systematic development of the forces that produce isomorphism is found in a 1983 paper by Paul DiMaggio and Walter Powell called "The Iron Cage Revisited: Institutional Isomorphism and Collective Rationality in Organizational Fields." This paper along with the one from Meyer and Rowan discussed above are frequently taken to be the foundational statements for Neoinstitutionalism, and are still widely used and cited. They themselves have become institutionalized entry ways for the discussion of Neoinstitutionalism.

As their main title suggests, DiMaggio and Powell's jumping off point was to revisit Weber's initial reasoning for the rise and continual spread of bureaucracies (see Chapter 1). They don't dispute Weber in terms of the initial importance of efficiency, nor in the observation that the spread of formal rationality continues apace. But they do argue that the reasons for the continued spread of formal rationality (or at least the appearance thereof) have changed. The world continues to become more and more rationalized not because of the efficiency of the bureaucratic form, but because of institutionalized forces, most centrally driven by governmental "rules of the game" and the rise and spread of professionalization. In essence, rationalization itself became institutionalized and now organizations will inevitably be molded by this.

These were things present in Meyer and Rowan's argument, but DiMaggio and Powell develop a specific typology of forces leading toward isomorphism along with the now common idea of an *organizational field*. The organizational field is basically a way of conceptualizing, with regards to any particular kind of organization, what counts as its environment and conceiving of the dynamics within it. My opening story of the chapter was about things that are required on my syllabus, and many of those requirements come from an outside source—in this case an accreditation agency. These are part of the organizational field for universities as are the professional associations for all of the various disciplines (majors), educational agencies of state and federal governments, academic publishing companies, and so on. All of these kinds of organizations exist in particular kinds of relationships (including some of *resource dependency*) that take on and maintain a relatively stable form over time, and that is even regardless of which specific organizations are the focus of analysis. If you wanted to be able to understand what was going on in any particular kind of organization, then the only way to do it is to understand its whole field. And because the same types of organizations inhabit the same fields, the argument is that they will all end up with similar structures—isomorphism.

DiMaggio and Powell define three mechanisms that provide isomorphic forces in fields that make this all rather inevitable. The first they call *coercive*, which has to do with things that organizations are required to do if they are to survive. They come in both formal and informal forms. The central set of coercive organizations are governments that set various kinds of rules and policies that prohibit or proscribe certain kinds of organizational activities. Yet these formal proscriptions can come from nongovernmental organizations (NGOs) as well—such as accreditation agencies for schools. Informal coercion comes from basic social norms and expectations. There has been a great deal of discussion and activity over recent years regarding *corporate social responsibility (CSR)*, for example. CSR is about the extent to which businesses have obligations beyond merely providing returns to shareholders, such as to workers, the environment, or the communities in which they operate. Thus concerns about CSR usually have to do with things such as environmental responsibility, fair labor practices, and the like. There is little in the way of legal requirements to focus on CSR, but giving it attention helps with issues of legitimacy among various constituencies outside of the organization.

The second isomorphic mechanism is *mimetic*. Just note the root of the word—to *mime* or *mimic*. A lot of the time organizations adopt various aspects of structure, processes, or procedures by copying what other organizations do. This will tend to occur under conditions of high uncertainty—where something needs to be done and it isn't clear how to go about it. This uncertainty can come from many kinds of sources including changes in technology, in the competitive environment, in new rules of regulations, and so forth. Faced with new or changing tasks when the course of action is not clear, organizations will start casting about looking for existing models. The widespread adoption of various aspects of the Japanese Style of Management in US industries, discussed in Chapter 6, is often regarded to have come about through mimetic isomorphism. Processes like this are also assumed to occur as part of the growth of populations of new organizational forms as highlighted by population ecology models. Part of the liability of newness (discussed above) is that, for new kinds of organizations, the routes to success can be unclear. But once there seems to be a model that works, it will often get copied by others. As we saw in Chapter 5, bureaucratic organization itself spread in this way when many organizations copied the organizational strategies of the Pennsylvania Railroad. Similarly, Fordism spread by the easy ability to copy Henry Ford's methods.

Finally, other isomorphic forces are called *normative*, and the primary driver for that is the proliferation of professionalization. The professions are specialized areas of knowledge and practice that are basically self-maintaining and self-policing. The principles of professional work are developed systematically, very often in Universities, by professionals who then educate and certify new professionals. The key thing is that organizations of all types require specialized knowledge, such as legal and accounting services at the very least. Accounting is a profession—an area of specialized knowledge and practice developed by and overseen by accountants. As such, in terms of how accounting gets done across various organizations, the primary principles by which an accountant operates are not generated by the organization in question. Rather, they come from standards and principles that are set on the outside of the organization by the profession of accounting. In many respects, hiring one accountant is going to be very much like hiring any other accountant, and so accounting practices will be very similar across different organizations. The same goes for most any area of specialized knowledge including all of the disciplines. This is perhaps easiest to see with Universities. While people tend to make a lot of what makes each school special or unique, they are arguably more remarkable in their similarities containing reasonably standardized kinds of divisions and offices, similar policies, procedures, and practices, very similar line-ups of majors that all have similar structures in terms of requirements, and so on. To be sure, some of the similarities are from coercive and mimetic forces. But much of the time is because these things represent different professional areas. A Sociology program, for example, is designed, administered, and overseen by people with advanced degrees in Sociology (usually PhDs) and those degrees were granted by other Sociology departments under the oversight of professional sociologists. The American Sociological Association, the primary professional association for Sociologists in the United States, issues general guidelines for the design of undergraduate programs.[4] Thus what is happening inside of a Sociology program in any given university has little to do with the specific university organization that it is in. Instead, most programs look very similar across schools because the principles come from the same professional source in the environment.

These three mechanisms fit well with what sociologist W. Richard Scott later classified as three basic elements that make up institutions: *regulative systems*, *normative systems*, and *cultural-cognitive systems*.[5] They also nicely fall along a continuum from the most to the least formalized elements. Regulative systems are the most formal elements in that they are explicitly made up of formal regulatory rules, including systems of sanction for the enforcement of the rules. Quite obviously, the state will be one of the most important *institutional agents*, as such things are often called, but there are plenty of other organizations with regulatory abilities, such as accreditation agencies or professional associations. The American Bar Association, for example, is a voluntary organization of professionals, but plays a fairly strong regulatory role in terms of the oversight of legal education and practice. Given formal rules and sanctions, this is, of course, where the coercive isomorphic mechanism operates.

Normative systems are quite similar in that they are about rules, expectations, and sanctioning. However, these are composed of the more informal rules of society. It's more about social *norms* and thus the normative label. While a great deal of normative importance is actually written into formal regulative systems, the vast majority of it is not. And in a regulative system

---

[4]Pike et al, 2017.
[5]See Scott, 2014: especially Chapter 3; Scott and Davis, 2007: especially pp. 258–61.

the question is whether or not something was done in accordance with or within the boundaries set out by the written rules, not whether it was considered to be correct in moral terms. If you are speeding while rushing a sick friend to the hospital, you are acting in accordance with basic moral norms, but at the same time you are breaking formal, written rules. As noted above, for DiMaggio and Powell, the key thing about the normative isomorphic mechanism is now the professions. This is at least partly because the notion that organizations should operate according to professionalized expertise, as guided by ethical guidelines, is now a normative expectation—an aspect of rationalization as an institutionalized part of our world. But normative systems as a whole are broader than that as they also include general conformity with social norms. This is the case with the question of CSR, noted above. It is not, for example, illegal by the formal rules to outsource various kinds of labor needs to the lowest bidder who is likely not paying living wages to workers. But the question of whether or not people find that to be ethical or moral is a whole different story.

Finally, *cultural-cognitive systems*, the least formalized element of institutional systems, can still be thought of as providing some manner of rules—ideas about things that ought or ought not be. But these are the most hidden kinds of rules because they are generally just taken for granted. Because of their taken-for-grantedness, many things get done in particular ways simply because there is no thought of doing them in any other way. If you went to visit a college and learned that it has no specific curricular requirements and there weren't things to major in, then the response wouldn't be something like "that's against the rules" or "that's morally wrong." But it very well might create some confusion because, well, "that's not how we do things around here." It would be sort of like trying to have Christmas without trees and symbols of Santa Claus or having Hanukkah without a menorah and dreidel and the like. A good deal of things in social life are just assumed without thinking. There are already taken-for-granted models which represent, in the language of institutional theory, *constitutive schema*. Don't let the lofty and weird term confuse you. Constitutive schema is just another way of saying that certain kinds of social arrangements are institutionalized—they are basic "schemes" that are assumed, expected, taken for granted, and at some level also enforced whether formally or informally.

To come back to organizational ecology for a moment, this can be an important aspect of the liability of newness for new organizational forms, and is a reason that they might initially lack legitimacy. If people have never seen a particular model before, then they will be skeptical and less likely to accept it until it might be shown to "work." So above I mentioned that the ecological perspective was broadened by neoinstitutional ideas, and it was by incorporating some of these ideas, such as the importance of legitimacy. The initial impetus was in thinking about organizational populations as being conditioned by scarce resources, such as funding or clientele or expertise and the like. But it is apparent that many of these things can be conditioned by institutional forces, such as the link between legitimacy and the ability to secure funding or the available pool of professionals who know how to do things. In simple terms, we can just say that organizational ecology came to think about the conditioning of populations according to the availability of both *material* and *symbolic* resources.

While Scott notes that these three basic elements tend to get varying amounts of attention across different disciplines, he is also clear that any well-established institutional area of society simultaneously contains all three in interaction. When this is a case, institutional theorists tend to see what is happening with regards to organizations—how they are structured, the types of processes and procedures they use, and so forth—as occurring according to an *institutional logic*. If a neoinstitutional view of organizations was to be summed up one could probably just say that, contrary to a Rational Systems view, organizations are not primarily oriented toward designing the most efficient means to meet whatever are their stated goals. Rather, they are oriented toward taking on a form that makes them fit best with expectations found in the general social environment. Many of those expectations must appear to be rational and based on assumptions about what makes for what are called the *best practices* in some area of activity (such as which business practices that will produce the highest return on investment or Sociology program curricula that will best pass on the canon). Or they might be more generalized ideas rooted in general cultural values, whether those are manifested in formal, informal, or taken-for-granted form. In essence, we live more in a world of general cultural expectations, some manifested in formal rules, rather than in a world of rationally planned activity. Yet even so, the appearances of rationally planned activity still must be maintained even if only on organizational frontstages.

Moving Forward

So here is where we are: We started the twentieth century with the rise and spread of organizations explicitly built in rational systems form exemplified but such things as scientific management and Fordism. These ideas and practices spread rapidly throughout all sectors of society and brought us into the iron cage. A rational system organization is meant to be an efficient means to an end—goals are clearly spelled out, and organizational structures and processes are designed to most efficiently meet those goals. Goals and means must be specified, outcomes measured, and adjustments made. But we soon learned that this vision, while in some instances and for at least some period of time might be able to produce narrow efficiencies (bigger, faster, cheaper, more), is too oversimplified for a generalized understanding of how organizations do, can, or even should operate. The human elements of a system are difficult to rationalize as they just simply won't act as good little cogs (although this varies). And we now know that "the environment," however it happens to be conceptualized, is also a constant wild card. We find that organizational goals are often multiple and conflicting. We find that any organization's primary goal is its own survival in whatever environment it finds itself in, and that meeting this goal may very well result in the need to do things that are contrary to efficiency concerns and the organization's own formal, stated goals. We find that survival ultimately means an orientation toward managing the environment in a multitude of ways. This can mean calculating where boundaries need to be placed in the name of efficiency as with TCE; or it may mean trying to control the environment as highlighted in RDT; or conforming to the overall *status quo* in the environment as institutional/neoinstitutional theory would have it.

Yet, even as we learn that rational systems approaches might not be the best way to understand organizations, Neoinstitutionalism highlights the point that the model is assumed. The rational, bureaucratic form is a requirement for legitimacy—it has become a *constitutive schema*. Thus rational systems thinking and action are ongoing and, where possible, use insights gained from both human and open systems orientations in the continued hopes of the Tayloristic dreams of rationality and control. We now move on to perhaps the biggest question of all: even under ideal conditions, is rationality even possible at all?

SOURCES AND FURTHER READING

In many respects, the focus on organizational environments began in the late 1960s with two seminal works typically classified as forms of *contingency theory* which will be a main focus in Chapter 11:

- Lawrence, Paul R., and Jay W. Lorsch. 1967. *Organization and Environment; Managing Differentiation and Integration.* Boston, MA Graduate School of Business Administration, Harvard University.

- Thompson, James D. 1967. *Organizations in Action.* New York, NY: McGraw-Hill.

  o (The use of **the term open system** could have had its origins in many different ways, but Thomson explicitly contrasts thinking of organizations as closed systems as rational and human systems thinking tended to do, and was among the first to say that we need to see organizations as open systems. See especially pp. 3–24.).

On **Transaction Cost Economics (TCE):**

- Coase, Ronald H. 1937. "The Nature of the Firm." *Economica* 4: 386–405.

  o (This is widely regarded as the founding paper, though it was neglected for many years until picked up again, largely by Oliver Williamson).

- ———. 1960. "The Problem of Social Cost." *Journal of Law and Economics* 3: 1–44.

- Kay, Neil M. 2015. "Coase and the Contribution of 'The Nature of the Firm.'" *Managerial and Decision Economics* 36: 44–54.

- Rindfleisch, Aric. 2020. "Transaction Cost Theory: Past, Present and Future." *AMS Review* 10: 85–97.

- Williamson, Oliver E. 1981. "The Economics of Organization: The Transaction Cost Approach." *American Journal of Sociology* 87: 548–77.

- ———. 1975. *Markets and Hierarchies, Analysis, and Antitrust Implications: A Study in the Economics of Internal Organization.* New York, NY: The Free Press.

- ———. 1985. *The Economic Institutions of Capitalism.* New York, NY: Free Press.

- ———. 2010. "Transaction Cost Economics: The Natural Progression." *American Economic Review* 100: 673–90.

- Tadelis, Steven, and Oliver E. Williamson. 2013. "Transaction Cost Economics." In *The Handbook of Organizational Economics*, 159–89, edited by Robert Gibbons and

John Roberts. Princeton, NJ: Princeton University Press.

- o (Short shrift has been given here to economic approaches to organizations, but this edited volume is a good starting point for the curious).

On how **TCE** may inform and enrich **Chandler's** perspective on organizational change:

- Lamoreaux, Naomi R., Daniel M. G. Raff, and Peter Temin. 2003. "Beyond Markets and Hierarchies: Toward a New Synthesis of American Business History." *The American Historical Review.* 108: 404–433.

- See also:
  - o Richard N. Langlois. 2003. "The Vanishing Hand: The Changing Dynamics of Industrial Capitalism." *Industrial and Corporate Change.* 12: 351–85.

  - o _____. 2004. "Chandler in a Larger Frame: Markets, Transaction Costs, and Organizational Form in History." *Enterprise & Society.* 5: 355–375.

On **Resource Dependence Theory (RDT)** past and more present):

- Casciaro, Tiziana, and Mikolaj Jan Piskorski. 2005. "Power Imbalance, Mutual Dependence, and Constraint Absorption: A Closer Look at Resource Dependence Theory." *Administrative Science Quarterly* 50: 167–99.

- Dalziel, Thomas, Richard J. Gentry, and Michael Bowerman. 2011. "An Integrated Agency–Resource Dependence View of the Influence of Directors' Human and Relational Capital on Firms' R&D

Spending." *Journal of Management Studies* 48: 1217–42.

- De Prijcker, Sofie, Sophie Manigart, Veroniek Collewaert, and Tom Vanacker. 2019. "Relocation to Get Venture Capital: A Resource Dependence Perspective." *Entrepreneurship Theory and Practice* 43: 697–724.

- Drees, Johannes M., and Pursey P. M. A. R. Heugens. 2013. "Synthesizing and Extending Resource Dependence Theory: A Meta-Analysis." *Journal of Management* 39: 666–1698.

- Emerson, Richard M. 1962. "Power-Dependence Relations." *American Sociological Review* 27: 31–41.

  - o (As noted, this view of relational power provided the root logic for power relations among organizations).

- Hillman, Amy J., Michael C. Withers, and Brian J. Collins. 2009. "Resource Dependence Theory: A Review." *Journal of Management* 35: 1404–27.

- Lin, Liang-Hung. 2018. "Vertical Ally-Or-Acquire Choice and Technological Performance: A Resource Dependence Perspective." *R&D Management* 48: 552–65.

- Pfeffer, Jeffrey, and Salancik, Gerald R. 1978. *The External Control of Organizations: A Resource Dependence Perspective.* New York, NY: Harper & Row.

  - o (This is seen as the founding piece of work. It was reprinted in 2003 by Stanford University Press with a new Preface).

- Schnittfeld, Nicole Luisa, and Timo Busch. 2016. "Sustainability Management within Supply Chains–A Resource Dependence View." *Business Strategy and the Environment* 25: 337–54.

- Tashman, Peter. 2021. "A Natural Resource Dependence Perspective of the Firm: How and Why Firms Manage Natural Resource Scarcity." *Business & Society* 60: 1279–311.

  o (While natural resource issues have not been a major focus all along, this paper is one that shifts the focus to that issue.)

- Verbruggen, Sandra, Johan Christiaens, and Koen Milis. 2011. "Can Resource Dependence and Coercive Isomorphism Explain Nonprofit Organizations' Compliance With Reporting Standards?" *Nonprofit and Voluntary Sector Quarterly* 40: 5–32.

- Zheng, Yanfeng, and Jun Xia. 2018. "Resource Dependence and Network Relations: A Test of Venture Capital Investment Termination in China." *Journal of Management Studies* 55: 295–319.

- Zona, Fabio, Luis R. Gomez-Mejia, and Michael C. Withers. 2018. "Board Interlocks and Firm Performance: Toward a Combined Agency–Resource Dependence Perspective." *Journal of Management* 44: 589–618.

For some of the classic defining work on **Organizational Ecology:**

- Aldrich, Howard E. 1979. *Organizations and Environments.* Upper Saddle River, NJ: Prentice-Hall.

- Carroll, Glenn R. 1984. "Organizational Ecology." *Annual Review of Sociology* 10: 71–93.

- Carroll, Glenn R., and Michael T. Hannan. 2000. *The Demography of Corporations and Industries.* Princeton, NJ: Princeton University Press.

- ———. 2015. "Organizational ecology." In *International Encyclopedia of the Social and Behavioral Sciences*, 2nd ed., 358–363, edited by James D. Wright. New York, NY: Elsevier.

- Carroll, G. R. 1987. *Publish and Perish: The Organizational Ecology of Newspaper Industries.* Greenwich, CT: JAI Press.

- Hannan, Michael T., and John Freeman. 1977. "The Population Ecology of Organizations." *American Journal of Sociology* 82: 929–64.

- ———. 1984. "Structural Inertia and Organizational Change." *American Sociological Review* 49: 149–64.

- ———. 1987. "The Ecology of Organizational Founding: American Labor Unions, 1836–1985." *American Journal of Sociology* 92: 910–43.

- ———. 1989. *Organizational Ecology.* Cambridge, MA: Harvard University Press.

Some **more recent commentary/applications regarding Organizational Ecology:**

- Abbott, Kenneth W., Jessica F. Green, and Robert O. Keohane. 2016. "Organizational Ecology and Institutional Change in Global Governance." *International Organization* 70: 247–77.

- Bertoni, Fabio, Massimo G. Colombo, and Anita Quas. 2019. "The Role of Governmental Venture Capital in the Venture Capital Ecosystem: An Organizational Ecology Perspective." *Entrepreneurship Theory and Practice* 43: 611–28.

- Cui, Yu, Jie Jiao, and Hao Jiao. 2016. "Technological Innovation in Brazil, Russia, India, China, and South Africa

(BRICS): An Organizational Ecology Perspective." *Technological Forecasting & Social Change* 107: 28–36.

- Eilstrup-Sangiovanni, Mette. 2020. "Death of International Organizations: The Organizational Ecology of Intergovernmental Organizations, 1815–2015." *The Review of International Organizations* 15: 339–70.

- Getz, Donald, and Tommy Andersson. 2016. "Analyzing Whole Populations of Festivals and Events: An Application Of Organizational Ecology." *Journal of Policy Research in Tourism, Leisure and Events* 8: 249–73.

- Lake, David. 2021. "The Organizational Ecology of Global Governance." *European Journal of International Relations* 27: 345–68.

- MacMillan, Karen, and Jennifer Komar. 2018. "Population Ecology (Organizational Ecology): An Experiential Exercise Demonstrating How Organizations in an Industry Are Born, Change, and Die." *Journal of Management Education* 42: 375–97.

  o (This paper describes a useful exercise for teaching organizational ecology.)

- Morin, Jean-Frédéric. 2020. "Concentration Despite Competition: The Organizational Ecology of Technical Assistance Providers." *The Review of International Organizations* 15: 75–107.

- Olvera, Jacqueline, and Stacey A. Sutton. 2021. "An Organizational Ecology Approach to New Food Marts in New York City Neighbourhoods." *International Journal of Urban Sciences* 25: 252–71.

- Tran, Hien Thu, and Enrico Santarelli. 2020. "Successful Transition to a Market Economy: An Interpretation from

Organizational Ecology Theory and Institutional Theory." *Industrial and Corporate Change* 29: 1–26.

Some classics in **Neoinstitutionalism**:

- DiMaggio, Paul J., and Walter W. Powell. 1983. "The Iron Cage Revisited: Collective Rationality and Institutional Isomorphism in Organizational Fields." *American Sociological Review* 48: 147–60.

- ———. 1991. "Introduction." In *The New Institutionalism in Organizational Analysis*, edited by Paul. J. DiMaggio and Walter. W. Powell, 1–39. Chicago, IL: University of Chicago Press.

- March, James G., and Johan P. Olsen. 1984. "The New Institutionalism: Organizational Factors in Political Life." *The American Political Science Review* 78: 734–49.

- Meyer, John W., and Brian Rowan. 1977. "Institutionalized Organizations: Formal Structure as Myth and Ceremony." *American Journal of Sociology* 83: 340–63.

- Zucker, Lynn. G. 1977. "The Role of Institutionalization in Cultural Persistence." *American Sociological Review* 42: 726–43.

Some selected more recent commentary/ applications regarding **Neoinstitutionalism**. Alvesson and Spicer (2019) is particularly useful for a brief review and assessment:

- Alvesson, Mats, and André Spicer. 2019. "Neo-Institutional Theory and Organization Studies: A Mid-Life Crisis?" *Organization Studies* 40: 199–218.

- Abrutyn, Seth, and Jonathan H. Turner. 2011. "The Old Institutionalism Meets the

New Institutionalism." *Sociological Perspectives* 54: 283–306.

- Baum, Joel. A. C., and Christine Oliver. 1991. "Institutional Linkages and Organizational Mortality." *Administrative Science Quarterly* 36: 187–218.

- Beckert, Jens. 2010. "How Do Fields Change? The Interrelations of Institutions, Networks, and Cognition in the Dynamics of Markets." *Organization Studies* 31: 605–27.

- Currie, G., and Spyridonidis, D. 2016. "Interpretation of Multiple Institutional Logics on the Ground: Actors' Positions, Their Agency and Situational Constraints in Professionalized Contexts." *Organization Studies* 37: 77–97.

- Davis, Gerald F., and Aseem Sinha. 2021. "Varieties of Uberization: How Technology and Institutions Change the Organization(s) of Late Capitalism." *Organization Theory* 2: 1–17.

- Dobransky, Kerry Michael. 2014. *Managing Madness in the Community: The Challenge of Contemporary Mental Health Care.* New Brunswick, NJ: Rutgers University Press.

- Du, Shuili, and Edward T. Vieira Jr. 2012. "Striving for Legitimacy Through Corporate Social Responsibility: Insights from Oil Companies." *Journal of Business Ethics* 110: 413–27.

- Greenwood, Royston, C. R. Hinings, and Dave Whetten. "Rethinking Institutions and Organizations." *Journal of Management Studies* 51: 1206–20.

- Gümüsay, Ali Aslan, Laura Claus, and John Amis. 2020. "Engaging with Grand Challenges: An Institutional Logics

Perspective." *Organization Theory* 1: 1–20.

- Lawrence, Thomas B., Bernard Leca, and Tammar B. Zilber. "Institutional Work: Current Research, New Directions and Overlooked Issues." *Organization Studies* 34: 1023–33.

  ○ (This is an introduction to a special issue of Organization Studies on the question of creating institutional change.)

- Meyer, John W., and Patricia Bromley. 2013. "The Worldwide Expansion of 'Organization.'" *Sociological Theory* 31: 366–89.

- Risi, David, and Christopher Wickert. 2017. "Reconsidering the 'Symmetry' Between Institutionalization and Professionalization: The Case of Corporate Social Responsibility Managers." *Journal of Management Studies* 54: 613–46.

- Scott, W. Richard. 2008. "Lords of the Dance: Professionals as Institutional Agents." *Organization Studies* 29: 219–38.

- ———. 2014. *Institutions and Organizations,* 4th ed. Washington, DC: Sage.

  ○ (This book is an evolving classic).

- Scott, W. Richard, and Gerald Davis. 2007. *Organizations and Organizing: Rational, Natural, and Open System Perspectives.* Upper Saddle River, NJ: Pearson/ Prentice Hall.

- Selznick, Philip. 1996. "Institutionalism 'Old' and 'New.'" *Administrative Science Quarterly* 41: 270–7.

- Shabana, Kareem M., Ann K. Buchholtz, and Archie B. Carroll. 2017. "The Institutionalization of Corporate Social

Responsibility Reporting." *Business & Society* 56: 1107–35.

- Townley, Barbara. 1997. "The Institutional Logic of Performance Appraisal." *Organization Studies* 18: 261–85.

The following is a useful and interesting **bibliometric analysis** tracking what seemed to be **dominant theoretical schools in Organizational Studies** from 1980 to 2009:

- Vogel, Rick. 2012. "The Visible Colleges of Management and Organization Studies: A Bibliometric Analysis of Academic Journals." *Organization Studies* 33: 1015–43.

The issue of defining a **Profession** is not a central preoccupation here, but much ink has been spilled on it. For a reasonably recent and useful discussion, see the following along with the citations within:

- Saks, Mike. 2012. "Defining a Profession: The Role of Knowledge and Expertise." *Professions and Professionalism* 2: 1–10.

I mentioned the **American Sociological Association's curricular guidelines** found here:

- Pike, Diane L., Teresa Ciabattari, Melinda Messineo, Renee A. Monson, Rifat A. Salam, Theodore C. Wagenaar, Jeffrey Chin, Susan J. Ferguson, Margaret Weigers Vitullo, Patrick Archer, Maxine P. Atkinson, Jeanne H. Ballantine, Thomas C. Calhoun, Paula England, Rebecca J. Erickson, Andrea N. Hunt, Kathleen S. Lowney, Suzanne B. Maurer, Mary S. Senter, and Stephen Sweet. 2017. *The Sociology Major in the Changing Landscape of Higher Education: Curriculum, Careers, and Online Learning.* Washington, DC: American Sociological Association.

The Prospects for Rationality

We have already seen much that presents challenges to thinking of organizations uncritically as rational systems. Humans, it turns out, are more difficult to turn into cogs than people like Frederick Taylor would like, and no organization operates within a vacuum in which it is free from constraints of its environment. But the issues with attempting to build rational systems go deeper still because, as we will soon see, rationality itself is not even possible regardless of all else. In fact, there are many conditions under which trying to be rational might actually turn out to be irrational. This can be problematic since, as Neoinstitutionalism tells us, attempting to build rational systems—even when it might not be warranted—is a very powerful cultural expectation needed for legitimacy. It is time to crack open the central nut and see what is inside.

Do note that in bringing up these issues now, I have shaken up what has thus far been a rough timeline in Part III of the book. Roughly speaking, everything got started with the rational systems thinking of the turn of the twentieth century which was soon supplanted by human systems ideas. Attention started to shift strongly toward the environment starting in the 1960s. The stuff of this chapter emerged starting in the 1950s out of what is sometimes called the *Carnegie School* in organizational theory because it originated with an influential group of social scientists at Carnegie-Mellon University—Herbert Simon, James March, and Richard Cyert. It is also often referred to as the *Behavioral Theory of the Firm (BTF)* after a famous book by Cyert and March by that title.[1] In some respects it grows out of *wanting* organizations to be rational systems, but takes its central starting point to be that rationality is actually impossible. So how are we to handle the problem that organizations and organizational actors want and need to be rational, but can't be?

The Woes of Homo Economicus

We start with one of the most famous analyses of the issue of rationality which comes from the late social scientist Herbert Simon. Much of the entire discipline of economics is based on the assumption that human behavior largely represents the purposeful, rational decisions of individuals. As we've already

---

[1]Cyert and March, 1963.

noted, to be rational involves decision-making where one weighs the costs and benefits of various alternatives and then chooses the alternative that represents the best cost/benefit ratio. In the typical jargon of economists, rational actors *maximize their utility* (get the most use or benefit). These are the assumptions of what is now usually called *neoclassical economics*.

Simon basically thinks through the hypothetical, perfectly rational actor referred to as *homo economicus* ("economic human"—*homo sapien* is "thinking human"). In order for a person to make a perfectly rational decision they need several basic, yet very complicated, things. (See Figure 10.1.)

First, *homo economicus* needs a full list of clearly ranked *goals* or *ends*. In economics these are usually called *utility functions*. Actors always have a lot of these. They include normal, mundane, everyday goals like finding a cup of coffee or buying socks. They also include larger, more general goals such as building a solid retirement account or paying off one's mortgage early. Mixed in with those goals may be yet more general and abstract goals such as only consuming coffee or socks that have been produced in an environmentally responsible way. In addition to being clear on what all of those goals are, one also needs to know the importance of each relative to others. Achieving some goals frequently comes at the expense of others. You might not have time to both get breakfast and pick up the mail before work or class, so you have to be clear about which of these is more important. Or your desire for a new car might go against your desire to build a stronger retirement portfolio. Furthermore, multiple goals are always in play at once, so one also has to know about various combinations of additive benefits. It might be that being able to get both breakfast and the mail provides a more desired outcome than being on time to work or class. To make it worse, for many decisions you would also need to know how your preferences might change in the future.

The second thing that *homo economicus* needs is full knowledge of all of the possible *means* of reaching all of the goals. Even for something as simple as an itchy nose, there are multiple ways of scratching it and thus multiple means for reaching the goal. Evaluating those means is especially tricky, of course, if your nose is itchy on the inside. Many of my readers are probably college students and are quite familiar with how difficult it can be to have full knowledge of all of the possible means to reach a goal. For the college student, the goal is generally a college degree. (Although note that many other goals are wrapped up in that, such as having a decent social life, living in a reasonably secure environment, and having a reasonably good time.) The potential means of obtaining the

FIGURE 10.1   **The Needs of *Homo Economicus* ("Rational Man")**

Clearly ranked *goals* (a.k.a. *ends* or *utility functions*)

Complete knowledge of potential *means*

Complete knowledge of *costs / benefits* associated with choices of *means*

The ability to calculate the results that *maximize utility* degree are the choices among all of the colleges and universities that are available. As most anyone who has been faced with such choices well knows, the *search procedure* for appropriate means can get very complicated. There is an awful lot to learn and to know—too much in fact to discover all of it.

Third, for each possible means, one needs full information regarding all of the *consequences* that come along with the choice of various means. The consequences bring the *costs* and the *benefits*. Note that this has to include not only the direct benefits and costs from things that you choose, but also the *opportunity costs. Opportunity costs* are benefits that you lose by the courses of action that you did not choose. If you decide to go to college, for example, the costs are not only represented by the time and money directly spent on college. You are also losing whatever income and experience you would gain by going straight to work instead. (Note that these days it is sometimes looking more and more rational to perhaps find a career without college, so long as you avoid the secondary labor market. If you're interested may be try something like welding, HVAC certification, plumbing, or the like.)

Finally, with all of the options in front of you and the costs and benefits of each laid out, the last thing that you need is to be able to do is perform the calculations that reveal which options provide the best cost/benefit ratio—the ones that *maximize your utility.* This can sometimes be rather simple, especially to the extent that various kinds of costs and benefits can be quantified—expressed in numerical terms. If you need to fill your car with gasoline, given a few gas stations clustered together, it is pretty easy to tell which one is selling at the lowest price. This is one of the reasons that organizations are prone to try to turn so many things into numbers, such as when standardized testing tries to turn learning into numbers. But generally it is not so simple. Even if a lot of things can be turned into numbers, many other things cannot and the ability to actually perform any manner of reliable calculation can become quite impossible.

Even on the face of it, this should all start to look pretty complicated. To simplify the difficulties for now we are going to take the first three elements and just say that rational calculators have problems of *information,* and that those problems are of two opposing kinds. On the one hand we are frequently working with *too little* information, and many relevant things do not end up in our calculations. This includes that fact that many costs and benefits cannot be easily quantified, and many of those can't even be predicted. However, we simultaneously face the opposite problem—having *too much* information. Too much information overwhelms the ability of the calculator to figure in all of the relevant things, and that can easily be the case even if everything can be quantified. It is important to note that, in terms of real world decisions, both of these problems tend to be simultaneously ever-present. That is, we will almost always have too little information to make perfect calculations. But even while operating with too little information, we will frequently still have too much information to be able to make clear calculations. Once again, this will resonate with anyone who has tried to choose a college or university.

Once this is all fully out on the table, perfect rationality should start to look quite impossible. You can choose even the simplest of things such as the need to buy ketchup. You can even grossly oversimplify the context of the situation and forget about how you decided to get to the store, which store you decided to go to, what it would really detract from your life to not have ketchup, whether or not you will get home and find a 50% off coupon for ketchup in the mail, what it would take to just stay home and make your own ketchup, and so on. Forget all of that and just put yourself in the store on your shopping trip examining the ketchup shelf. Many stores provide handy little labels on the shelves that provide costs per unit for various items. You don't even need to do any calculations yourself! For the ketchup you can use the cost per ounce on the label to find out whether the bigger bottle really costs less per unit than the little bottle.

(Hmmmm...But we know all about economies of scale and thus the biggest bottles are often cheapest by the ounce. But for the moment let's also leave aside the question of how large a bottle you can fit in your refrigerator and whether or not you will use it all before it goes bad).

You can also use the cost per ounce to compare across different brands.

(Hmmmm...But for the moment, let's also leave aside the sticky problem of whether Brand A has better flavor than Brand B, and, if so, how many cents per ounce the better flavor is worth; how many cents per ounce the risk is worth on buying a Brand C that you've never tried; whether one has more preservatives than the other and whether or not that matters anyway; whether the organic Brand D is really better or more healthy in some way, and so on).

So if you can leave aside and ignore some of the complexities even in this simplified situation, and just use the helpful little cost per ounce on the store labels, you can happily pick up the bottle of ketchup that you know gives you the most product (benefit) for the least cost.

Satisfied with your rational decision, you go home, perfectly grill your burger just the way you like, crack open the ketchup and find that it is rancid. Whether though a breakdown in quality control or some form of post-packaging contamination you now have a perfectly grilled burger that you can't fully enjoy. Beyond that you now have to either throw the ketchup away—a thoroughly irrational outcome because it produces all cost and no benefit—or take it back to the store and get a new bottle. If you take it back to the store, you now need to add the time, money, and aggravation of a return trip along with the loss that came from a ruined meal into the initial cost of the ketchup.[2] Your cost per ounce has now gone through the roof. Of course, the situation would be even worse if the ketchup *appeared* to be fine and you ate it, only to find out later that it was contaminated with *e coli* bacteria.

Intended and Bounded Rationality

The point here is not that you should become *panophobic*, or be afraid to buy things from the store. It's just to provide a simple illustration of how complicated rationality can be (see Figure 10.2.) In getting the ketchup you *intended* to make a rational decision. However, there were limits, or *boundaries*, on the information that you had in making the decision. Your knowledge

---

[2]To take a brief aside back to *Transaction Cost Economics (TCE)* that we encountered in Chapter 9, these are unanticipated *transaction costs*. Oliver Williamson received his graduate education at the Carnegie School and TCE's central starting point was the problem of *bounded rationality* which I am in the process of explaining.

| FIGURE 10.2 | The Woes of *Homo Economicus* |

Goals	Numerous, often conflicting, often ambiguous, difficult or impossible to rank, especially in combination
Means	Numerous, with ambiguous and often completely unknown consequences.
Complete knowledge of *costs / benefits* associated with choices of *means*	Even if one could possibly assemble all of the information the costs of the *search procedures* would often become irrational.
The ability to calculate the results that *maximize utility*	Too little information makes calculations imperfect, so there are always unknown consequences. To much information overwhelms the decision maker.

of the goals, means, costs, and benefits were all limited. When people engage in rational decision-making, they can only be *intendedly rational*. We do have goals and often even some semblance of a ranking among multiple goals. We do evaluate alternative means and try to calculate costs and benefits. But our knowledge and abilities with all of these things is always limited. We have *multiple* goals and many of them are *ambiguous*. We frequently don't know just how the goals rank relative to each other, especially if we worry about different additive combinations. Many of the *goals conflict* with each other.

We face similar difficulties with the means. There are usually a lot of them. Many of them are not particularly well understood. There are many different kinds of consequences that potentially follow from the various means. We are aware of some of those outcomes, though often imperfectly. But there are plenty of outcomes that we don't know about and can't predict. And then, of course, if you were able to amass all of that information about goals and means and consequences so that everything was on the table, then the amount of information would frequently overload the ability to calculate the courses of action that would maximize your utilities.

According to Simon, when decisions are actually made, we make them based on highly simplified pictures of reality, or according to a simplified *definition of the situation*. The *definition of the situation* is a social science buzz phrase for the notion that people do not act toward an objective world as it "really is." Rather we always act toward the world as we understand it to be. Our understandings of things will always be selective oversimplifications. We don't pay attention to everything at once. We can't. And even if we could, we would quickly find that it was too much to handle. Thus, we are not capable of perfect rationality, but only of *bounded rationality*—a degree of rationality that is limited by (bounded by) the information that we have, can pay attention to, and are able to deal with it.

Satisficing and the Irrationality of Rational Decision-Making

Once you follow the thinking far enough you end up with an intriguing paradox. A rational actor will rarely pursue maximizing utilities by making rational decisions because it is actually *irrational* to try to do so. Let's call trying to get everything you need to know about goals, means, costs, benefits, and calculations a *search procedure* (because that's what it's called in this context). You may have experienced such a thing most vividly when you were going through high school (or now college or any other life stage). What are your goals in life? If those goals might involve the need for education of some kind beyond high school, what kind of education? If you decide on the kind of education you need, then which specific schools or training programs will you seek? What will those places cost, and how will you get the money together? What will you lose by not choosing alternative options (*opportunity costs*)? Given what you are trying to accomplish, how likely are these things to produce success? As you probably know, trying to sort all of these things out is very difficult. It takes a lot of time. It often costs money. It often creates stress. These are all *costs of the search procedure.* You may even experience the same thing as you stand in front of the ketchup rack at the store. Should you buy the organic brand? What does it mean to put "organic" on a food label? What are the risks of not using organic brands? If you really want to worry about these things you might have to spend the better part of a day—or more—online tracking down the necessary information. How much does all of that time and effort cost and what has been gained in the end?

So we always have a set of hidden costs that have to be calculated into any decision-making procedure—the costs of the decision-making activities themselves. The fact that this is often not noticed does not make the costs go away. Rational decision-making is a costly thing to do, and sooner or later the costs of the search alone outweigh the benefits of continuing to do the search. (Of course, you will almost never be able to calculate exactly when you pass the point of diminishing returns either.) As Simon argues, rational actors do not tend to continue a search procedure until they have certainty that their course of action has maximized their utilities. Rather they search until they have reached a *satisfactory* decision. In the lingo of the field, decision-makers do not *maximize*, they *satisfice*. To paraphrase one way that Simon put it, one does not go through the haystack looking for the sharpest needle. One goes through the haystack until a needle is found that is sharp enough for sewing. If you do decide to go on for higher education, and manage to choose a college, earn a degree, and land a reasonable job you will never know that your decisions about what to do maximized your benefits. But you will have obtained a satisfactory outcome. If you managed to get a cup of coffee this morning you will never know whether or not it would have been fresher or better or cheaper had you gotten it someplace else. But you will have reached a satisfactory outcome.

But even more to the point, rather than reflecting decision-making geared only toward *satisficing*, a lot of human activity actually comes down to avoiding decision-making altogether. A great deal of human activity takes place by following pre-set routines and habits. Or, if you prefer to leave it couched in terms of rational decision-making, people often *decide to operate according to pre-made decisions*. Many of these are just habits that one falls into such as always stopping at the same place every morning for coffee. You probably don't comparison shop every day with regards to changing prices, coffee varieties, specials, and so on. You don't know whether you might have missed running into your soul mate or potential future employer by going someplace else. What you do know is that you get satisfactory results there. There may have been an initial decision-making point for choosing the place, but the place is not explicitly chosen each time one visits it. It becomes a pre-made decision—a rule to follow, even if this is just your own informal rule, routine or habit.

But at other times people deliberately set up routines as when one makes an explicit daily schedule to follow. This is, in fact, the heart of formal rationality. All of the classical, ideal-typical features of bureaucracy are exactly that—preset rules and procedures to follow so that actors just follow preset programs *rather than making decisions*. For the BTF, organizations purposely produce a simplified set of definitions of situations for actors. Perhaps no one was more explicit about this than Frederick Taylor (see Chapter 7) who plainly stated that workers should make no decisions, and should just follow the preset rules. The difference, of course, is that Taylor did have faith in something like perfect rationality, at least with regards to the superior intelligence of management. For Taylor, the economic or rational man (*homo economicus*) was still possible. For Simon, we need to come to grips with *administrative man*. Administrative man often faces ambiguities with regards their actual goals and interests. He also does *not* search for the *one best way* and doesn't even explore all of the possible options. In reality people work from within simplified and bounded definitions of situations, thus choosing from a limited set of options and selecting courses of action based on finding satisfactory solutions. This often included opting for solutions that are already in existence—pre-made decisions whether in the form of habits or more formally established procedures.

Organizations and the Multiplication of Complexity

At this point we have been thinking about a person as an actor and decision-maker. In order to get to organizations as rational actors, we have to add extra layers of complication. Even if you take something simple—like buying ketchup—and add in all of the complexity involved such as whether Brand A's quality is really worth more money and whether it might go bad before you can use it all, and so on, the difficulties still pale in comparison to the ones you hit when you think about organizations as actors trying to maximize utilities.

I work for a fairly large university. Like most Universities, it has a stated primary goal. It is called a "mission statement." Ours probably looks like most others and it goes like this: "*We are a community committed to preparing students to be educated and enlightened citizens who lead productive and meaningful lives.*"[3] Wow. Where to begin? Getting ketchup is pretty concrete and clear. Once you're home with the grocery bags you can be quite clear about whether you've met your goal or not, even if you're not sure that you maximized your utility. You either have ketchup in the bag or you don't. How would one know whether or not "educated and enlightened citizens" have been produced? What does that even mean? Here we have a degree of *ambiguity* about the goal itself which wasn't really present in the ketchup problem, and is very common in formal organizations.

This is one of the reasons that the formally stated goals of organizations operate more as *sustaining myths* as Selznick put it (Chapter 8), or *rationalized myths* as the terminology goes with Neoinstitutionalism (Chapter 9).

---

[3]https://www.jmu.edu/jmuplans/about.shtml, retrieved 11/11/2020.

Organizations like universities will proclaim such inspirational and lofty goals as "enlightenment and meaning," but such ambiguous goals largely serve as part of creating a legitimizing *frontstage*. In reality an organization will actually direct its operations toward much more concrete and measurable goals, such as increasing the four year graduation rate. (My own university is also fond of touting its own equivalent of a "customer satisfaction" rating.) Because they are much more influential in how organizations actually operate, in the language of the BTF, these more concrete and measurable things are called *operational goals*. This is one of the primary drivers of the process of *goal displacement* in organizations as introduced in Chapter 8. You start off wanting to produce educated and enlightened citizens, but then to meet the demands of conforming to the general cultural expectations of rational systems assumptions you need to provide "metrics" that show your results in some concrete form. But, of course, the percentage of students passing a standards of learning exam only provides one means of legitimation. In terms of broader cultural values regarding the value of liberal education, it's thoroughly uninspiring. Thus the lofty mission statements about enlightenment and meaning are still necessary and valuable for frontstage legitimacy.

Leaving that aside for now, even if we focus on concrete operational goals we still have to deal with all of the complexity and ambiguity of the tasks required. If we want to focus on an operational goals like the four year graduation rate, we need to find a means of recruiting applicants, evaluating applications, offering admission, and inducting new students into the organization. We need to maintain basic facilities such as libraries, classrooms, student housing, and food services, and offices for university personnel. We need to make students feel good psychologically and socially. We need various departments to satisfy the different intendedly rational decisions the students might want to make with regards to majors and minors. We need record keepers to keep track of students and their statuses and grades. We need people to collect the data on entering students and produce the analyses that will track graduation rates. We need to figure out how all of this will be financed. The list of general tasks goes on, and we haven't even begun to consider the more specific tasks in each of these general areas, such as how to do student orientation or what kinds of readings or assignments are appropriate to our courses. In most universities, of course, there are specific organizational divisions for the different tasks. In an organization of any size, these divisions tend to be yet other large organizations in their own right. As the divisions are constructed we add more and more complexity. The goals multiply. The means multiply. There is even uncertainty about the organizational structure itself since it is supposed to be the means to an end.

So now when it comes down to selecting means and evaluating costs and benefits the difficulties just multiply. What aspects of the entire organization contribute what to the goal? If we increase operating budgets to academic departments by 10% next year, will we get a 10% improvement in education and enlightenment? Would we even get a 10% improvement in four-year graduation rates? Or would that be an irrational decision? Perhaps we should take the dollars represented by that 10% and start a new program or department instead. Or perhaps we should take the 10% and reduce tuition costs by that much because it makes the students' decision to attend that much more rational, and allows some to spend more time on school and less time on working for money to cover costs. Or perhaps we should give the 10% to faculty salaries because it will provide them more time and energy to devote to the students "satisfaction."

To be sure most universities and many other organizations have "planning" offices where people specialize in dealing with such issues (yet another task). But they are working with much more complicated things than bottles of ketchup, and neither the people, nor the offices, nor their associated professions have any kind of magic for dispelling the uncertainties. All they have is more limits on their ability to make fully rational decisions given complexity and ambiguity regarding almost all aspects of the activity. Organizations have many goals. Divisions within organizations have many goals. The persons that occupy the organization have many goals. Various parts of the organization's environment also have things to say both about the goals, how to interpret them, and what kinds of means and outcome measures might be most appropriate. As a faculty member, I know that at least one means to increase the four-year graduation rate is for everyone in the academic divisions to make classes easier. But if we do that, will this now detract from the ultimate goal of maximizing education and enlightenment? At a personal level for faculty, making classes easier and giving better grades (a.k.a. *grade inflation*) saves time. In terms of personal goals this might sound pretty good except that challenging students with difficult material is often a professional value and seen as critical to producing education and enlightenment. The situation is nothing if not complex.

Formal Organization: Avoiding Decision-Making

Simon's work on rationality was later expanded to a theory of organizations through work with James G. March, and then with both March and Richard Cyert. They argue that organizations aim to simplify situations for those working in them by developing pre-set routines and habits. As noted, this is the heart of *formal rationality*—structures that provide routines and habits and definitions of situations for occupants of various offices. Organizations provide the bounds for actions by defining simplified sets of means, goals, and decision-making procedures, where those are relevant—simplified definitions of situation. It is a picture of organization that resonates with Taylor's idea that organizational leaders set up an organization as a preset piece of machinery. Organizational divisions and offices are provided with sets of goals, all of which are intended to be sub-goals that contribute to the overall goals of the organization. This includes *goal alignment*—the alignment of the personal goals of the participants with organizational goals, commonly via monetary incentives, though obviously it can include needs for social belonging, recognition, and sense of accomplishment, as the Human Relations/Humanistic Management tradition emphasized. At each point within the organization goals are aligned with tasks in an attempt to make it all fit together. The formalization of tasks amounts to what are called *standard operating procedures (SOPs)*. If this is all done well, then an organization can function very smoothly. By reducing uncertainty and complexity, it can go into autopilot and produce the machine-like efficiency, predictability, and calculability of the McDonaldized form. However, due to bounded rationality, everything can't be specified in advance according to the formal rules. The rule makers can't account for all possible situations and contingencies. Thus informal structures, including organizational cultures evolve for many reasons, but one is often to fill in those gaps. All of it provides the boundaries. Wherever possible, decision-making is to be avoided because it is costly. But where decisions do have to be made organizational characteristics, both formal and informal, provide the simplifying premises on which decisions are made.

It is here that we can get a clear view of why it is not always best to see things in our social world as the result of reasoned actors making decisions. It is often quite inaccurate, unless you simply want to say that following the *SOP* for a given situation was a rational decision made by an actor. That is certainly possible to argue, but it still leaves us in a world where many of the things that we see around us are the outputs of standardized organizational plans, or more loosely, institutionalized patterns of assumptions rather than the reasoned decisions of actors. One might say reasoned actors should only follow an *SOP* if it is judged to be the correct option, and should do something better when it is not. But that is to ignore the fact that following *SOP*s is generally a *requirement* of positions in organizations. People are not free to just do as they please in most organizational contexts, and it causes trouble for them when they do. And if we move beyond the formal SOPs to more informal cultural patterns and expectations, then we run into issues of the boundedness of rationality and the difficulty of search procedures.

One also might instead say that organizational leaders will always be in a position to alter procedures, and good ones will only be letting *SOP*s operate as usual if they are the most appropriate means of approach. Thus, to the extent that *SOP*s are left to flow, this will always represent a decision. But this is also frequently a misguided assumption. No one escapes the problems associated with decision-making. In most any large organization there is too much going on—much more than any leaders will be able to track and observe and understand on a day to day basis. Specialization inside of organizations also frequently represents areas of special expertise and organizational leaders are typically not experts in everything. There are many aspects of organizational operations that are not understood well enough by leadership and frequently formal barriers to the ability of leaders to dictate tasks and changes to tasks. There is also the sticky problem that *SOP*s across an organization generally do not exist in isolation from one another. Making changes in one area easily creates complications and clashes with other areas of the organization. This is among the reasons that formal organizations are so difficult to change. It can often be the case that everything affects everything else (which we will eventually learn to call *tight coupling*), and no one escapes the boundaries of rationality. This is also not to say that once SOPs, whether formal or informal, are established that nothing changes. The idea is, as with the Institutional school, that organizations are constantly trying to adapt to changing circumstances. However, they are always doing so from inside of the bounds of rationality.

The bottom line is that trying to see organizational activity and actions as the intended outcomes of purposeful, rational decisions made by people rather than mostly following procedures is just going to take one back to the problems of rationality itself, the irrationality of decision-making, the tendency to satisfice and thus to create routines and procedures. In an odd way, following procedures is often the most rational thing to do. So the fact is that taking things that occur in the world as the outcome of human decision-making is often quite simply incorrect. Many things that occur in the world are simply the result of organizational actors following procedures—or organizational *SOP*s.

Organizing from the Garbage Can

One prominent and useful extension of the line of thought begun by Simon's analysis of bounded rationality can be found in what is called the *Garbage Can Model* of organizations. Initially proposed by James March in collaboration with Michael Cohen and Johan Olsen,[4] this model takes things like goals and means, decisions and decision-makers, and consequences and *decouples* them. A rational model assumes that all of these things are *tightly coupled* and linearly related. An actor first has a goal, then identifies and evaluates means, performs the utility *maximizing* (or at least *satisficing*) calculus, and finally carries out the decision. The consequences of that decision are then generally assumed to be both attributable to that decision, and the intended outcomes. What the garbage can metaphor suggests—as the name clearly implies—is that you can think of what an organization does like a shifting collage of the contents of the organization's garbage can. Floating around inside of the garbage can are many of the things that have been relevant to the organization's past and present activities, including various kinds of goals and means, organizational actors with varying amounts of time, energy, attention, feelings, and issues, and various *choice opportunities*, *decision-situations*, and so forth (discussed below). All of these things just float around in the can as bits of paper and come together and coalesce into various kinds of organizational actions and activities. Much of what is done is actually quite haphazard and unplanned.

Imagine someone showing up to work in the morning. For the first activity of the day they reach into the garbage can and pull out a slip of paper. The slip of paper might contain a goal—anything that might need to be done. Because decision-making itself is costly, the first response to having this task emerge is not to make a decision. Rather you just dive back into the garbage can to fish around for pre-existing solutions. The solutions are ones that already exist within the organization in the form of *standard operating procedures* and other past actions, along with various participants that, with varying skills and resources and varying amounts of time and energy, might make for good decision-makers if it comes to that. Given the costs associated with the search for the solution that will *maximize* utility, the organization's garbage can will serve as the source for finding an existing solution that is *at least satisfactory*—satisficing. The only "decision" here is best seen as an attempt to avoid making any new decisions, which includes avoidance of having to set up any new procedures or processes. The garbage can already holds past decisions that can be borrowed and re-implemented.

In practical (rather than metaphorical) terms it may be represented by an email from a supply clerk who indicates that the latest shipment of widgets has been causing quality control problems on a production line. In such a case the first course of action might be to just go back to a prior widget supplier, or even to actually fully enforce an existing, un-monitored policy regarding the inspection of incoming supply shipments. (Recall that just because things are written down doesn't mean that anyone is following along. Informal procedures are often the real rule.) Or the goal to fall out of the can may appear in the form of a new memo from the Senior Management stipulating that your division is required to produce a set of procedures for the monthly evaluation of the performance of personnel. The "search" in this case may begin by

---

[4]Cohen, March, and Olsen, 1972.

shopping around to other divisions in the organization that already have such procedures. This strategy, incidentally, is a common basis for *mimetic isomorphism* (see Chapter 9). A first response to uncertainty is generally not to institute a search procedure for decision-making. Rather it is to just go to the garbage can to find existing decisions or procedures. Oddly, that is often far more efficient and thus more rational than engaging in more costly search procedures that invent new wheels.

It is also possible, however, that what comes out of the garbage can is not a goal or a problem to be solved, but it may be that it is actually a solution. In this case, you end up with solutions that are looking for problems to solve rather than the reverse. One of the more popular names for such things is the *law of the instrument* or *law of the hammer*.[5] If all you have is a hammer, then everything starts to look like a nail. Information Technology (IT) divisions on University campuses often tend to operate in this way. The latest piece of instructional technology or software that the university has purchased results in the establishment of various programs, seminars, and instructional events that demonstrate how these things "solve" problems that in many cases people didn't even know that they had. This is because these kinds of things can *create* goals, such as integrating more video or animation into one's lecture periods—a "need" that I never had until a "solution" presented itself. It is often like that with technologies. In the *rational* model action starts with a goal, followed by a search for means. In the *garbage can* goals and means and actors and such are *decoupled*. In terms of the flow of time and the instigation of organizational activity, they can appear in any sequence.

Other things that may spur organizational activity are called *decision-situations*. These are events or processes that create an expectation that "something needs to be done." This can come in the form of crises such as falling stock prices, unexpected budget deficits, or events in the organizational environment. Very prominent and disturbing events such as terrorist attacks or natural disasters frequently create decision situations for governmental actors and agencies, for example. Sometimes decision situations are actively sought out by actors looking for *choice opportunities*. Certain actors within an organization may find that are overflowing with time, energy and attention. Or perhaps some might feel as if they need to find a way to distinguish themselves in some way or even clearly justify their existence. They might actually seek to *create* problems or goals or solutions and even more *SOPs*. It may be that for the sake of public legitimacy an organization greatly increases its budget for IT resources and staff. Even if those staff find no real problems to address, they will have to invent problems and goals solutions simply to justify their own existence. At other times there are not actors who are flush with time and energy and large budgets in which case many issues or potential issues (goals) just lay around in the bottom of the garbage can. There is often an ebb and flow in these terms. Problems might arise that gain attention for a while but then fade away as actors and their energies are taken up elsewhere.

As Cohen, March, and Olsen summarized it, *"an organization is a collection of choices looking for problems, issues and feelings looking for decision*

---

[5]Usually attributed to our old friend Abraham Maslow of the *hierarchy of needs* from Chapter 8. As he wrote: *"I suppose it is tempting, if the only tool you have is a hammer, to treat everything as if it were a nail."* (Maslow, 1966, p. 15).

situations in which they might be aired, solutions looking for issues to which they might be the answer, and decision-makers looking for work."[6]

Note, however, that this particular mode of operation is not considered to characterize *all* forms of organizational activity. Rather, it is likely to be associated with particular kinds of organizations that have been called *organized anarchies*. That is, some manner of formal organization will exist on paper, but the actual day-to-day activities will bear little resemblance to the formal description and will appear to be somewhat disorderly and haphazard. The conditions that produce this type of situation are all things that contribute to ambiguity and complexity with regards to the requirements for rationality. As Cohen and colleagues specify, the three main conditions include first, *problematic preferences*, or simply ambiguous and/or complex goals. The second is *unclear technology*, or more generally, lack of clarity regarding means by which things should be done. The organization's own processes and procedures are not well understood, either in terms of how to do things or in terms of consequences produced. The third condition is *fluid participation* where it is not always clear which actors in the organization are relevant to decision situations, how they are relevant, and how much time or attention any of them have at any given time. The more these conditions exist, the more likely an organization's activities will be to conform to the *garbage can model*—or, in other words, be organized anarchies.

The message of the garbage can metaphor is not that organization life is simply chaotic. It is generally presented as a more accurate way to capture the messy empirical reality of many complex organizational situations and activities. But even then, the extent which it applies is variable depending on the conditions noted above, although virtually all organizations will exhibit garbage tendencies in some respects. But, of course, organizations generally do not appear to operate in this fairly fluid and haphazard fashion. To the extent that that this mode of operating captures organizational action, it will generally be kept on the backstage. Consistent with the expectations of Neoinstitutional theory (Chapter 9), even if the backstage is somewhat anarachic, on the front stage organizational actors always will produce accounts of what happens that reorder events and activities in order to conform to rational model expectations. It is rare that one would find an organization that could risk appearing to have its activities appear to be one damn thing happening after another. Regardless of how messy actual activities are, there is a cultural premium placed on the appearance of rationally coordinated action. As such *ex post facto* rationalized accounts convince organizational actors themselves as well as those in the environment that organizational outputs are the result of purposeful and rational action, regardless of how things really unfolded. We constantly work to convince ourselves and others of the fact that we engage in rational action, build rational structures, and strive to reach rational ends. But in the end, that's not how it works, although the extent to which it is true is only a variable. The BHT provides useful ways of thinking about that variability.

---

[6]Cohen et al., 1972, p. 2.

Normal Accidents: Rational Organizations and Irrational Outcomes

So far in this chapter, the idea has been that formal organizational structures can be interpreted as being responses to problems of imperfect human rationality. The Weberian characteristics of bureaucracy are designed to provide boundaries that decrease complexity and thus increase the possibilities for rationality, even if maximal rationality is not entirely plausible. Things like formally defined hierarchies of authority, specialization of tasks and procedures, and written job descriptions are in place to tame the complexities associated with the organization's tasks, personnel and organizational environments. The garbage can metaphor tends to be most applicable when complexities are particularly difficult or even impossible to tame. At the extremes of complexity and uncertainty, we may end up with organizational systems that outstrip our ability to control or predict their outcomes. A great deal of the time the deficits of control and predictability are not obvious because whatever actions and consequences emerge are re-ordered by accounts that produce rationalized myths.

However, in many other instances unintended and negative consequences emerge that cannot easily be swept under the rug or reinterpreted as rationally intended. This occurs when systems produce various forms of disruption and disaster. There are certain kinds of systems in which we should expect breakdowns and accidents—*normal accidents* as organizational sociologist Charles Perrow called them.[7] *Normal accidents* include certain kinds of catastrophic systems failures such as nuclear power plant meltdowns and space shuttle explosions, though the concepts can be and have been generalized beyond highly complex technological systems. Perrow calls some of these kinds of accidents *normal*, not because they are frequent or common, but because they should just be counted as among the expected properties of certain systems. Some systems are so complex that we cannot anticipate or prepare for every contingency. Expect the unexpected.

Perrow argues that there are two key features of organized systems relevant to the analysis of normal accidents. One is the nature of the interactions among system parts. This can be seen as varying between two poles from *linear* to *complex*. Linear systems are relatively easy to understand and would be represented by a typical assembly line where something is built up over a series of planned and discrete steps in a set sequence from beginning to end. Any one element in the system is only related elements directly before and after it. If something goes wrong it is relatively easy to isolate the problem and understand how it relates to other parts of the system. *Complex* systems include multiple kinds of connections among system elements, including branching, feed forward and feedback effects, and often even some degree of random contingency—unanticipated interactions between different elements. Different elements in the systems are related to other elements in numerous ways, and all possible kinds of interactions between system parts can't always be predicted. If something goes wrong at any point in the system, it isn't

---

[7]This was coined in a book by that title (Perrow, [1984] 1999), although Perrow later expressed a preference for the term *system accident* (Perrow, 2004, p. 10). I will stay with the phrase normal accidents as this has been more the standard reference.

always possible to tell what the consequences will be at other points in the system. The effects can reverberate in unpredictable ways.

The second feature has to do with the *degree of coupling* between system elements. Coupling is about how tightly tied together the elements of the system are. Some systems, such as Universities are quite *loosely coupled*. How we structure and run our major requirements in our department have little to no impact on any other part of the organization. Other systems, such as nuclear power plants, have many elements that are *tightly coupled*. Loose coupling provides some degree of buffering, or slack between events in different parts of a system. If something goes wrong in one place, the consequences are not immediately felt elsewhere and there is time to react, isolate problems and address them. In tightly coupled systems, things that happen in one part of the system can have very rapid consequences for other parts of the system. These things can reverberate very quickly and unpredictably throughout the whole, and there is little or no time to react to, isolate and address problems.

For illustration sake, take as a metaphor any stretch of interstate highway that you know. On a stretch of highway with relatively light traffic where everyone is (mostly) obeying the rules, the highway would resemble a linear system with loose coupling. Everyone is moving along in the same direction with no sudden turn offs or cross cutting traffic. There is only one basic path to take. The direction of flow and points of entry and exit are well marked and easy to understand. If anything does happen to go wrong there is ample time for other parts of the system (other drivers) to adjust. If a vehicle ahead is entering the roadway, there is ample time and room to adjust speed and/or make way for entering traffic. If a vehicle ahead of you has a tire blow out, there is time and room to slow down and/or move away from harm. A blown tire on a highway would be called an *incident*, and these will occur in all socio-technical systems from time to time. The central question is basically, what is the likelihood that incidents will end up leading to *accidents*?

For that you can imagine a stretch of highway with heavy traffic at an interchange where multiple highways converge and then disperse. The heavier traffic means much tighter coupling. There is now little time to adjust speed or position in the event that unexpected things happen. The presence of other roadways also increases complexity. It becomes much more difficult to predict what other vehicles will be doing, especially as each vehicle is adjusting both to where it needs to be and to other vehicles attempting to be where they need to be. Here the system approaches something that looks more like a complex and tightly coupled system (though please note that this discussion is illustrative and metaphorical rather than literal). Now a tire blowing out—a normal *incident*—has a much higher chance of leading to an *accident*. The proximate cause of the accident could be called the tire blowing out, but that alone would be insufficient to explain it because it had to come together with other aspects of the system in just the *wrong* way to result in an accident. Thus the issue is in the system, not in whatever incidents might occur.

According to Perrow, *normal accidents* are integral properties of systems with both high complexity and tight coupling. The issue is that anything that sets a system out of balance can have effects that reverberate very quickly in ways that are very difficult to understand or predict. According to Perrow, there is no way around this for some system designs. Obviously engineers are smart and understand a lot of things about potential failure modes of overall systems and all of their parts. So systems are always designed with elements, such as warning devices, monitoring systems and redundancies (back up devices or systems) that are added to try to avoid accidents by increasing safety, manageability, and predictability. However, once we have confronted the problem of bounded rationality, it should be clear that it is not truly possible to predict all possible outcomes and to plan for every possible contingency. In fact, all of the safety elements and redundancies that get added can very well lead in the opposite direction because they only serve to increase the complexity of the system.

Smarter humans or human systems for overseeing these kinds of systems might help in some respect, but won't eliminate the issues either, and for similar reasons.[8] Technological systems are, of course, built and run by human organizational systems—formal organizations. And complex technological systems tend to require complex human organizations to oversee them, and this actually adds to the issues. In this regard, Perrow identifies an inevitable conflict regarding what is required for organizations that oversee complex systems. On the one hand the organizational systems require *centralization* of oversight and decision-making because the system has to be observed as a whole in order to maintain an understanding of what is going on with it and deal with the tight coupling. However, the complexity also means that knowledge, both of the systems' normal operations as a whole and during crisis or disturbance periods, is distributed rather than being held in one place. Thus complex systems also require *decentralization* of oversight and decision-making because actions must be quick and guided by the most up-to-date information and expertise regarding system states at the site of problems. The root of those conflicting demands are our two kinds of information problems. Those close to the problem(s) *lack the information* needed to have a system-wide view. Yet anyone with a more complete view of the system can be quickly overwhelmed by having *too much information* at the same time that they lack necessary information.

A Note on Public Understandings versus Normal Accidents Interpretations

In many cases, thinking of some disasters as normal accidents will run quite contrary both to standard cultural understandings and even standard cultural values because, in the face of humanly produced disasters, we want to know what went wrong. This normally means identifying and isolating the specific cause of the problem. More often than not, the assumption is that someone did something wrong—that there was some kind of a human failure in decision-making and performance or just flat-out deviant behavior. This follows from our propensity to see things in rational systems terms. Our systems are designed, built and run my decision-making persons. If those systems fail, then the roots must be found in decisions and decision-makers. One approach to this has been called an *amoral calculator model* for deviant events.[9] The *amoral calculator* is the decision-maker who merely calculates

---

[8]Do note, however, that partly in reaction to the normal accidents conception of systems, a competing perspective has emerged that typically goes by the name *High Reliability Theory (HRT)* so there has been an ongoing debate between NAT (normal accidents theory) and HRT. The central claim in HRT is that complex systems can be tamed and kept safe and reliable, and research is geared toward achieving that end. See Sources and Further Reading at the end of the chapter.

[9]Vaughan, 1998.

costs and benefits and bases decisions purely on utility maximization. The utility maximizing path is chosen regardless of whether or not it is legal or illegal, moral or immoral, and so on. Questions of whether a course of action is culturally or humanly "right" or "wrong" are simply irrelevant to the decision-maker. Or if they are relevant, the anticipated costs of the illegal or immoral actions are not calculated to outweigh the benefits.

To this, I will also add that there is also an *incompetent calculator model*. The *incompetent calculator* is the human decision-maker that made errors in their decisions or execution, whether by lack of proper training, laziness, incompetence, inattention, haste, or all of the above. People do make mistakes, after all, and poor decisions must be the things that lead to system failures. There is not necessarily any attribution of morality or immorality in terms of the incompetent actors' intentions. However, there is generally an implication that the inattention or incompetence or lack of training or preparation—or whatever the case may be—is itself a moral failing on someone's part. As such, *operator errors* are often blamed for system failures.

Sometimes focus will arrive at specific part failures inside of systems—a faulty gauge or valve or containment system and so on. Yet this often turns the question of the part designer, part maker, or maintenance and inspection personnel. In the question of equipment failures, we just find other amoral or incompetent calculators maximizing their own utilities and making errors. The explanations are sometimes appropriate and are culturally palatable. But they are often not very good explanations. Operator errors occur all of the time in all kinds of systems, and sometimes do produce incidents, but not system accidents. Who thinks that humans won't make mistakes? Similarly, part failures occur all of the time in all sorts of systems and remain incidents without generating accidents. Things will occasionally break, and no one doubts this. *Ex post facto* analyses of systems failures will always identify things like operator errors and part failures because they will be there.

Yet more careful and holistic analyses that don't proceed on the assumption that some*one* or some*thing* is to blame often discover that the problem is not to be found in any specific failure within the system, but with the ways that different kinds of failures interacted in unpredictable ways. It is an outcome of the system's complexity. At any given moment, assume that all of the different aspects of these systems are akin to items floating around in the garbage can that, if they happen to come together in just the wrong way, produce sequences and courses of action that are well beyond any of the intended outputs of the system or participants. Perrow points to giving attention to six aspects of systems that can be abbreviated as DEPOSE: Design, Equipment, Procedures, Operators, Supplies and materials, and the Environment (whether "natural" or social). (See Figure 10.3.) The key is that a holistic analysis of a system accident will generally not find that any *one* of these things alone was the cause, but rather that it was an unexpected confluence of multiple elements that come together in unexpected and often incomprehensible ways. This does not, however, stop the tendency of people single out specific sources of the problem, and especially the operators.

Analyses of many systems failures that assign blame to the decisions of persons are generally *ex post facto* attributions made by greatly over-simplifying the elements that contributed to the failure. This is not surprising as these systems are approached as rational systems, and intendedly rational investigators are looking for breakdowns in rationality. Thus, after the fact

FIGURE 10.3   **Elements of Systems that Can Contribute to *Normal Accidents***

<u>D</u>esign
<u>E</u>quipment
<u>P</u>rocedures
<u>O</u>perators
<u>S</u>upplies & Materials
<u>E</u>nvironment
Failures occur in each regularly, are expected, not surprising, and merely produce *incidents*. In a *Normal Accident* the failure comes from their interconnections in a system ~ like elements in the *garbage can* coming together in an *unexpected way*.

decisions about how to explain an event occur by the same boundary setting that occurs in everyday action. Definitions of situations are constructed to reduce complexity and allow decisions about blame to be made. Just as *rationalized myths* function as front stages for messy garbage-can-like back stages, many explanations of systems failures are rationalized myths that gloss over and ignore actual complexities.

The Space Shuttle Challenger *Disaster*[10]

For the purposes of clarity and illustration regarding many of these points, I will lean heavily on some of the work that Diane Vaughn has done in studying the space shuttle *Challenger* explosion. This occurred in 1986, and represented a dramatic set-back for the US Space Program. At the time, the Space Shuttle program was the center of the US space program, and this particular launch was a very high-profile event as the crew of seven included Christa McAuliffe, a school teacher from New Hampshire. The launch was hyped quite a bit by the National Aeronautic and Space Administration (NASA), and made all the more visible because it had gone through a series of delays. When it finally did launch on the morning of January 28, 1986, all eyes were on it as it lifted off from Kennedy Space Center, and was enveloped by a dramatic explosion over the Atlantic Ocean a little more than a minute after liftoff. All seven crew members aboard, including the school teacher Christa McAuliffe, were lost.

---

[10]Note that there can be plenty of disagreement with regards to what truly classifies as a normal accident. I will describe the *Challenger* even though it is an old case because it is very good for highlighting the confluence of both technical and organizational complexity. Yet, Charles Perrow did not think it a normal accident (Perrow, 1999, pp. 379–380) while organizational sociologist Diane Vaughan, who studied the case most intensively, did classify it as one (Vaughan, 1996, p. 414). Addressing the ambiguities is useful, but beyond the scope of an introductory level account.

The official and best known story coming from the investigation of this event is that the explosion was caused by the breach of o-rings that sealed sections of the shuttle's solid rocket boosters (SRBs). The shuttle looks a bit like a giant airplane. In order to get it into space it basically gets strapped to a couple of rockets—the SRBs—along with a large external fuel tank to supply the shuttle motors with fuel during liftoff (see Figure 10.4). On the top of the SRBs (up with the cone) are control technologies for flight and ignition, while the bottom segment is the actual motor. All of the middle segments, which take up most of the length, are basically just big tubes filled with rocket fuel. The rockets and all of that fuel are required to produce enough thrust and lift to get the shuttle out of the atmosphere. The boosters are built in segments and assembled near the launch site, and when assembled the different segments have to be sealed, and this was done by pairs of giant o-rings. In the 1986 *Challenger* launch a breach occurred in an o-ring seal leading to a leakage of exhaust gasses which, following a chain of somewhat odd events (see below), led to the dramatic explosion and the loss of all life onboard the shuttle.

The explosion obviously resulted in a long investigation in which o-rings were specified as the technical cause of the explosion. And it turns out that there were already known issues with the o-rings. The morning of the launch

FIGURE 10.4   **Space Shuttle Launch System**

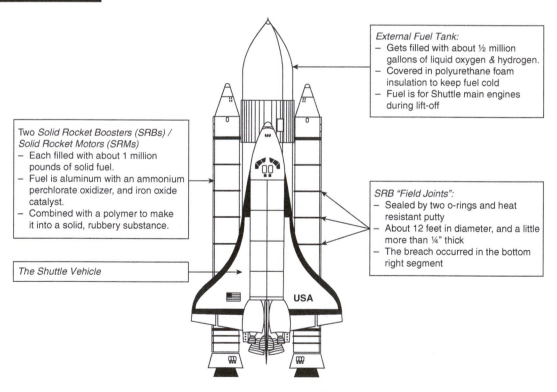

Source: NASA/MSFC, Public domain, via Wikimedia Commons.

was unseasonably cold at the launch site in Cape Canaveral, Florida, and on the night before the launch the cold temperatures and potential o-ring problems were discussed by engineers and managers involved with the project. The main cause for concern was that the o-ring material was basically a form of rubber and these materials lose resiliency and flexibility as they get colder. On this basis, there was concern among the SRB engineers regarding whether or not the o-rings would hold up under the forecast launch conditions. If they couldn't remain flexible enough, they might not be able to seal up the joints. Initially, a recommendation against launch was made which was later reversed, although at least some of the engineers involved in the review of the issue remained adamantly opposed to the launch.

There were multiple problems with regards to delaying the launch, but one was that having the "school teacher in space" had made this particular flight into a very high profile event. In addition, the launch had already been delayed several times for various other reasons, and NASA was constantly under time pressure because the shuttle program was supposed to maintain efficiency and strive for self-sufficiency. In order to do so, it was supposed to keep a regular launch schedule because most missions included fees being paid to carry forms of payloads into orbit. With the high publicity, the continual launch delays, and the pressure to stay on schedule, there was strong pressure to go ahead with the launch rather than delay it again.

Thus all of the pieces fell into place for either an amoral and/or incompetent calculator explanation for the disaster. In the interests of protecting themselves and the organization from the negative effects of yet another delayed launch NASA management decided to plow ahead despite the dangers. As a result, seven astronauts, including New Hampshire school teacher Christa McAuliffe lost their lives and hundreds of millions of dollars were lost. In this interpretation, this was a preventable event had more knowledgeable, responsible and moral heads prevailed. An accident occurred—and *someone* must be at fault.

However, to leave it at that can easily be seen as a quite over simplified—and arguably just plain inaccurate—interpretation. We can begin with the o-ring issue, which was the most *proximate* cause of the accident. It's true that NASA had information about o-ring issues, including potential problems related to cold temperatures. Rubber gets harder and less flexible when it is cold and it doesn't seal as well. This was famously demonstrated at congressional hearings by physicist Richard Feynman who dunked a sample o-ring material into a glass of ice water. Presumably he was trying to imply that everyone involved in the launch *should have known* of this issue, but didn't so they were either incompetent, immoral, irresponsible or all of the above. So why did NASA launch knowing about the o-ring issue and temperatures?

Well, this was the 25th launch of a space shuttle. It was to be the 10th for the *Challenger* vehicle. The rocket booster o-rings had frequently been damaged during launch, but there didn't appear to be any particularly clear pattern in the types of damage and the conditions under which it occurred. If knowledge of o-ring issues should have stopped the *Challenger* launch, then there never should have been any space shuttle launches at all once the first forms of damage were found on prior launches. The problem with that, of course, is that some o-ring damage was, in fact, expected some of the time. Otherwise there wouldn't have been a built in redundancy (the second o-ring at each joint). A perfect o-ring in a perfect world would not need a backup in place.

It is also worth noting that another high profile shuttle disaster was when the *Columbia* broke up upon reentry to the earth's atmosphere in 2003. The proximate cause of that disaster was damage to the shuttle's wing during launch. The external fuel tank is insulated with special foam insulation to keep the fuel cold and to avoid having ice form on the tank. During the launch pieces of foam broke off of the tank, struck the *Columbia's* wing, and caused damage to some of the insulating tiles that protect the shuttle from the heat generated by reentry into the earth's atmosphere. This was *also* a known problem that was not infrequent in its occurrence. The *incident* was assessed by shuttle engineers during *Columbia*'s flight but nothing clear emerged regarding the danger it posed to the shuttle vehicle, at least partly because it was yet another recurring kind of *incident* that had not resulted in disaster. Yet it's not as if o-rings and foam were the only two problems. It was a *normal* part of shuttle missions to encounter various kinds of anomalies and failures with many different aspects of the system. There wasn't *always* o-ring or foam damage. But there were *always* incidents in some form.

In any case, returning to the o-ring issue, there was some evidence that the amount of damage was related to air temperature, and based on the unseasonably cold temperatures engineers had raised very strong concerns on the night before the launch. Furthermore, it really wasn't a mystery to the engineers that temperature and o-ring resiliency are related as Feynman seemed to want to imply. It was one aspect of the o-ring materials and design that was given direct attention from the inception of the SRB design. But the evidence that was on hand with regards to temperatures and o-ring damage was quite ambiguous—as much evidence tends to be. The worst o-ring damage on a shuttle launch was from a launch that took place at 53° Fahrenheit. It was largely this, coupled with the general knowledge that the o-ring material loses resiliency as it gets colder, which had raised the concerns of the engineers. Yet just behind that 53° launch in terms of severity of o-ring damage was a launch that took place at 75° Fahrenheit. In between those two temperatures was a large number of launches with either no damage or, occasionally, some minor damage. Furthermore, during development of the SRBs engineers had tested SRBs down to 47° with no sign of o-ring damage, and technical analysis of the system indicated that the o-rings should seal down as low as 30°. While overnight temperatures were supposed to be below that, launch time temperatures were not. Finally, there was also a *redundancy* built in because there was a secondary o-ring in place should the primary ring fail.

Soon after the disaster, well-known statistician Edward Tufte produce a re-analysis of the data that were on hand and produced a graph (not including the test rockets) that many claim provided the *proof* that was needed regarding the o-ring and temperatures.[11] Thus the implication is that we were dealing with incompetent calculators—SRB engineers who couldn't properly handle their own data. But in the course of the actual decision-making process nothing was that simple or obvious, and hindsight always make things so much easier.

And even the way that accident actually unfolded was not as would have been predicted or expected given an o-ring failure. The notion that the disaster

---

[11]Tufte, 1997, pp. 38–53.

was a simple as an o-ring failure is oversimplified. Engineer Allen McDonald, who was in charge of the SRB program on the project, had been among those who didn't think the shuttle should fly and wouldn't sign off on launch approval. However, once the shuttle launched and flew successfully for 73 seconds before exploding he assumed that the accident was not, in fact, due to the o-rings because the expectation was that it would have exploded right on the launch pad. When someone told him that they had film evidence of an SRB leak on the launch pad he initially declared that to be absurd. As he later recounted saying: "solid rocket motors don't continue flying around with holes burned through the side of them. They explode!"[12] Well it didn't explode because the breach was immediately sealed up by aluminum oxide from the combustion of the fuel. As such, the launch actually did go off with initial success. Even the instruments that monitored conditions with the SRBs showed nothing out of the ordinary. Furthermore, it wasn't even the SRB that exploded in the end as both SRBs kept flying. The breach was eventually blown back open by high wind shears that began at about 37 seconds into flight. Even then, this is *still* not when the explosion occurred. The newly escaping exhaust gasses blew out onto one of the brackets that holds the SRB to the external fuel tank. When that bracket finally failed from the heat, the SRB became unstable and ended up rupturing the external fuel tank. That is when the explosion occurred. Obviously, the o-ring failure was the root proximate cause, and the thing should not have been launched. But even so, there is no simple "an o-ring failed and the shuttle system blew up" account to be had. It's complicated.

So let's back up a minute. The space shuttle had something on the order of 60 million parts to it. Many of those parts were crucial to the safety of the vehicle and underwent severe stresses every time a shuttle was launched and flown. The fact that there were issues with parts was not a surprise to anyone. Incidents regarding things like o-rings and foam insulation—and many other parts—were well known by engineers. People such as Richard Feynman have the benefit of hindsight. There was no way to *guarantee* the safety of any space shuttle mission and still fly them. Rather all shuttle launch decisions were made based on performing *risk analysis* which itself is based on the assumption that *certainties* are not possible—there were always plenty of *uncertainties* and so only levels of risk to be calculated. NASA went through an extensive Flight Readiness Review (FRR) process each time the shuttle was launched. That is, there was a set of *standard operating procedures* for evaluating the shuttle and risks prior to every shuttle launch, and those procedures were followed prior to the shuttle decision just as they were for all launches.

That doesn't mean that accident investigators didn't find fault with the execution of the FRR procedures prior to the *Challenger* launch. They did. As noted above, SRB engineers did raise concerns about the o-rings and air temperatures, and at least one was adamantly opposed to launch. The problem was that NASA managers in charge of the final launch decision never had full information regarding those concerns. Once again, we must be looking at either incompetence or perhaps even immorality—do you smell a cover up? But not so fast. To the technical complexity of the shuttle system including its 60 million plus parts, and launching it into space, and getting it back we can add organizational complexity. For any technical system as complex as this

---

[12]McDonald (2009, p. 130). See generally Chs. 10–11.

one, organizational complexity is bound to be very high as well. But in the case of the shuttle program there was extra complexity added largely due to political and economic issues. So let's back up even a little bit more to see the larger context.

Messing around with space is very expensive. To this day questions and criticism rain down on programs that have to do with space exploration, largely on a rational cost/benefit basis. Many people say that the amount of money that goes into space exploration is very much out of line with what we might be able to get out of it. There is little practical payoff. The space shuttle program was born during the early years of Ronald Reagan's first term as president at a time when scrutiny of government spending (some of it anyway) was the word of the day. So the shuttle program was explicitly designed to be one that could potentially be self-supporting. It was supposed to operate more like a business than a government agency. This included the widespread use of subcontracting and competitive bidding for the goods and services that the program needed. As businesses were moving to network form (see Chapter 6), so too were many agencies of government, including NASA. The shuttle was supposed to operate partly as a networked form of transportation company that outsources for many of its needs and delivers payloads to orbit for various customers.

So for the space shuttle program, NASA was acting as a *lead firm* having many of the parts and subsystems of the shuttle built by a network of sub-contractors. The subcontractor that developed and supplied the SRBs Morton Thiokol, Inc. whose manufacturing facilities were in Utah. Space shuttle launches occur in Florida. This meant that the SRBs had to be shipped, but they are huge. So they had to be built in pieces, shipped in pieces, and later assembled at the launch site. This is not all that uncommon in rocket design, and the design of the boosters would have required some assembly anyway. But it is at least partly because of this political/organizational fact that the SRBs had the segmented design for the solid fuel portion of the boosters. With a different organizational structure, the SRBs may have had a different technical structure that reduced or eliminated the need for o-rings in the first place.

But even if we put that aside and take o-rings as a given, we have to seriously consider how capable this entire socio-technical system would be of being able to handle all of the information that needs to flow through it for perfect evaluation of risks (for we already know we must abandon the quest for certainty, even if that's just in buying ketchup). We can start by asking who the "knower" is. A formal organization such as NASA is an abstraction, not a person. It can't know or think or perceive or evaluate. Certainly there are those who are decision-makers in the organization. Serious decision-making tends to concentrate at the top. For the launch decision this meant NASA managers. The NASA managers are dependent upon information from other levels and divisions inside of NASA, and from managers in the multiple sub-contracting organizations that built different parts of the system. Inside of those subcontracting organizations, those managers are dependent upon information from other divisions and levels. If you want to know what turns up on the desk of those in charge of the final launch decision, just think of it like a very large game of telephone that is made even nuttier by the fact that there isn't only one message, and that one message doesn't flow in a linear fashion. Rather there are many messages and they flow up and down and backwards and forwards and sometimes in feedback circles.

Multiple organizations, multiple divisions within each organization, multiple layers of hierarchy within each. All of these generate information issues and concerns. The garbage can becomes something like a fountain of confetti. In the end there is *no one decision-maker* nor even one decision-making situation where all of the information and knowledge come together on the entire operation. No one knows or grasps the whole. Rather specialization across and within organizations leaves information and knowledge fragmented. This is partly by design under bureaucratic logic. Complex systems involve many different kinds of technical expertise and even if there was a central point for all of this to go, the amount of information would quickly overwhelm any decision-maker that is presented with it. This is why launch decisions were handled through SOPs in the form of the FRR.

Given issues of bounded rationality, all of the parts of an organization—people, offices, divisions, etc.—have to do what March and Simon labeled *uncertainty absorption.* There is really no way around that and it is, in fact, built into the structure of organizations. Departments and offices generally send information about activities through organizations in the form of standardized reports on activities. Those reports oversimplify the actual information that is present and so many things in organizations are simply unknown by decision-makers. In her writings about the *Challenger* launch Vaughn has called this *structural secrecy* but that can suggest a level of intent to hide information. There may or may not be an intent to hide information at various times and places, but the disappearance or unavailability of information is inevitable. Information has to be selected, summarized and presented. As such, one key thing that occurred on the night before the *Challenger* launch was that engineers at Morton Thiokol initially recommended against the launch based on temperature concerns despite the fact that everything had already cleared the FRR process. The overnight temperatures were forecast to be in the 20s (Fahrenheit), and they issued a new recommendation not to launch below 53° Fahrenheit. One problem with that is they couldn't definitively explain why or defend that specific number. It just happened to be the lowest launch temperature to date that had also seen the most severe o-ring damage. Not only were their own data incomplete and often conflicting with regards to the question at hand, but when analyses were hastily produced to discuss with management, errors were made and identified. Another problem was simply that it was outside of normal procedures to suddenly introduce new rules or standard on the fly during or after a FRR.

But the ultimate issue became that the engineers are not directly involved in the launch decision. NASA management consulted with Morton Thiokol management, and Morton Thiokol management was provided information and recommendations by their engineers. And everyone has to do uncertainty absorption. In the midst of a hastily drawn phone conference among NASA managers at two different locations and two levels of hierarchy at Morton Thiokol (management and engineering) at yet another location, problems, and issues were identified in the engineers' analyses. The Morton Thiokol management dropped off of the call to have a separate meeting with engineers who, in the end, couldn't present definitive and conclusive evidence that launch would be a problem. As such, Morton Thiokol management returned with the recommendation to accept risk and fly. NASA managers never received the full information on the concerns of the Morton Thiokol engineers, not even knowing that engineers still objected, filtered as all of this was through multiple organizational locations and divisions.

At this point, one might say (as some have) that it was Morton Thiokol management that did the wrong thing in giving into pressure from NASA and suppressing information from its own engineers. But there are a couple of problems with that interpretation as well. One is that the engineers could provide no definitive proof or probability that launch would be a problem. Contrary to various *ex post facto* claims, they simply did not have the data needed to demonstrate the actual effects that the temperatures would have on the launch. Faced with political and public pressures to launch, and absent any ability of engineers to provide definitive information regarding safety management, Morton Thiokol management had no clear foundation to stand on if they wanted to recommend against a launch. The second problem is that knowing that there were uncertainties and risks was not exceptional, but routine. It is built into this kind of activity. Since the risk is ever-present, it is dealt with by particular routines and procedures embedded in the FRR process. Every launch of the space shuttle was approved by following the FRR processes and the same occurred in the case of the *Challenger*. In other words it is possible to say that everyone, from NASA management down to Morton Thiokol engineers, did what they had done every time the shuttle was launched. They produced analyses of risk and followed the FRR procedures.

As Perrow has observed with regards to normal accidents, the presence of *warning signals*, such as the concerns of the Morton Thiokol engineers, is part and parcel of normal accidents. It's just that they often don't help, because they only become clear warning signals in retrospect. It's not that there are no persons or decision-makers who see them as warning signals at the time. Morton Thiokol managers heard the warnings of the engineers. It is rather that warning signals are very common—they are *normal* in dealing with risky complex systems. In many instances the presence of a warning signal does not make clear what the appropriate course of action is. It is also the case that if the mere presence of warning signals should trigger action this can quickly become irrational. These kinds of systems operate all of the time and do not fail, even in the presence of warning signals. The systems contains procedures for dealing with them and they are most frequently followed without any irrational consequences. Given that warning signals are routine, after any kind of serious breakdown *ex post facto* observers, such as Feyman or Tufte, will find the warnings and see them as clear indicators of impending doom. This is, however, only possible in retrospect. The central message of the normal accidents argument remains the same—short of not building or operating certain kinds of systems at all, you cannot completely rule out the accidents. They are simply characteristics of the systems themselves—thus a *normal* part of complex systems. If we build them, they will always hold the possibility of disaster.

Conclusion

The message from all of this should not be that we are incapable of designing rational systems and will just produce chaos and disaster when we try it. Rather, with the problems of rationality in clear view, we can simply begin to shift our basic perspectives on formal organizations. They are best seen as *intendedly rational* systems where the prospects for control are easily disturbed depending on the presence of uncertainty and complexity. We should keep in mind that the more we introduce complexity, the farther away we might be taking ourselves from the ability to produce expected and rational outcomes. Or, to go back to the basic characteristics of formally rationalized systems introduced in Chapter 1, we intend to create systems that deliver *efficiency, calculability,* and *predictability.* However, if we aren't careful we may just produce the opposite—aspects of the *irrationality of rationality.* But this is not the Ritzer argument that "[r]ational systems *inevitably* spawn irrationalities that limit, eventually compromise, and perhaps even undermine their rationality."[13] Rather, as with all else, the potential for irrationalities is best thought of as variable. Luckily, organizational theory already has a fairly well-developed way of thinking about such things and I turn to that in Chapter 11.

Post-Script Note on *Behavioral Economics*

It is possible to see the work of the likes of the Carnegie School and the BTF as having been supplanted, or perhaps merely supplemented by a relatively new sub-field of economics called *Behavioral Economics (BE)*. The core idea of BE is simply that economics has always operated on the basis of assumptions where rationality is taken to be a real, operative possibility, but that we now know that real decision-making is far more complicated than that. As such, sometimes the initial work on bounded rationality by Simon and others is now actually just referred to as behavioral economics, perhaps it is the *old behavioral economics (OBE)* by contrast to a *new behavioral economics (NBE)*.[14] I have outlined the OBE as the root thread of this chapter. The NBE is less about trying to account for organizational structures, processes, and practices than it is about bringing psychological processes into the study of human decision-making. And it is not so much concerned with issues of information and information processing as it is with figuring out why people are so bad at making rational decisions, even when information problems aren't a large issue. The overriding concern is actually one of being disturbed that people aren't better at being *homo economicus*, and research is geared toward finding ways to manipulate situations and *nudge*[15] people into making better decisions.

The NBE tends to operate on a highly individualistic basis, both theoretically and methodologically. Thus it largely focuses on discrete decisions by persons and much of the work is done by experimentation to learn about what truly goes into the decisions that people make. It does share much with the OBE, such as the fact that complexity and uncertainty make things worse, and that people are forced to operate by simplified mental models of decision situations. The knowledge gained is largely seen to be of use for policy-making, both general social/political policies, and for organizational policies. With regards to organizations, it hasn't changed a whole lot about organizational theorizing. Rather it tends to offer up ways to do things like

---

[13]Ritzer, 2019, p. 167, emphasis added.

[14]On the former see, for example, Augier (2013) and on the latter see Heukelom and Sent (2017).

[15]To use the title word from one of the more well-known books on the subject which is now in common use among the NBEs. See Thaler and Sunstein, 2009.

help managers avoid the pitfalls of *irrational* decision-making. But is also looks to offer up analyses of "flawed" decision-making among humans to better manipulate both consumers and workers in organizations. As one account put it:

> The baseline assumption in this literature is that consumers make systematic mistakes and firms are rational actors. This is reasonable because experience, specialization, larger resources, sorting, and market competition all work in the direction of enabling organizations to train and choose managers who are expert at exploiting mistakes by consumers-and by their own workers.[16]

In this way, it is much more a descendant of the old traditions of scientific management as supplemented by things like Industrial/Organizational Psychology (see Chapter 7) and the Human Relations movement (see Chapter 8). But it doesn't modify the picture of organizations presented here.

SOURCES AND FURTHER READING

On Herbert Simon, **bounded rationality** and the development of the **Behavioral Theory of the Firm (BTF)** see:

- Argote, Linda, and Henrich R. Greve. 2007. "A Behavioral Theory of the Firm—40 Years and Counting: Introduction and Impact." *Organization Science* 18: 337–49.

  o (This is an introduction to a special journal issue).

- Augier, Mie. 2013. "The Early Evolution of the Foundations for Behavioral Organization Theory and Strategy." *European Management Journal* 31: 72–81.

- Augier, Mie, and James. G. March. 2004. *Models of a Man: Essays in Memory of Herbert A. Simon.* Cambridge, MA: MIT Press.

- Bromiley, Philip, Rouslan Koumakhov, Denise M. Rousseau, and William H. Starbuck. 2019. "The Challenges of March and Simon's Organizations:

Introduction to the Special Issue." *Journal of Management Studies* 56: 1517–26.

  o (This is an introduction to a special journal issue).

- Cohen Michael D. 2007. "Administrative Behavior: Laying the Foundations for Cyert and March." *Organization Science* 18: 503–50.

- Cyert, Richard M., and James. G March . 1963. *A Behavioral Theory of the Firm.* Englewood Cliffs, NJ: Prentice Hall.

- Gavetti, Giovanni, Henrich R. Greve, Daniel A. Levinthal, and William Ocasio. 2012. "The Behavioral Theory of the Firm: Assessment and Prospects." *The Academy of Management Annals* 6: 1–40.

- March, James G., and Herbert A. Simon. [1958] 1993. *Organizations*, 2nd Ed. Cambridge, MA: Blackwell Publishers.

- March, James G., and Johan P. Olsen. 1979. *Ambiguity and Choice in*

---

[16]Camerer and Malmender, 2007, p. 271.

Organizations. Berger: Universitetsforlaget.

- Maslach, David, Chengwei Liu, Peter Madsen, and Vinit Desai. 2015. "The Robust Beauty of "Little Ideas": The Past and Future of A Behavioral Theory of the Firm." *Journal of Management Inquiry* 24: 318–20.

  o (This is also an introduction to a special journal issue).

- Simon, Herbert A. 1957. *Models of Man: Social and Rational.* New York, NY: Wiley.

- Simon, Herbert A. [1947] 1997. *Administrative Behavior: A Study of Decision-Making Processes in Administrative Organizations*, 4th Ed. New York, NY: Free Press.

On origins and later assessment of the *garbage can model* of organizations:

- Bendor, Jonathan, Terry M. Moe, and Kenneth W. Shotts. 2001. "Recycling the Garbage Can: An Assessment of the Research Program." *American Political Science Review* 95: 169–90.

- Cohen, Michael D., James G. March, and Johan P. Olsen. 1972. "A Garbage Can Model of Organizational Choice." *Administrative Science Quarterly* 17: 1–25.

  o (The originating paper for the garbage can model).

- Glynn, Peter W., Henrich R. Greve, and Hayagreeva Rao. 2020. "Relining the Garbage Can of Organizational Decision-Making: Modeling the Arrival of Problems and Solutions as Queues." *Industrial and Corporate Change* 29: 125–42.

- Lomi, Alessandro, and J. Richard Harrison, eds. 2012. *The Garbage Can Model of Organizational Choice: Looking*

Forward at Forty. (*Research in the Sociology of Organizations, vol. 36*). Bingley: Emerald Books.

- *Cited merely in connection with the "law of the hammer":* Maslow, Abraham H. 1966. *The Psychology of Science: A reconnaissance.* New York, NY: Harper & Row.

On *Normal Accidents Theory (NAT)*, some of its applications, and controversies, see:

- Le Coze, Jean-Christophe. 2015. "1984–2014. Normal Accidents. Was Charles Perrow Right for the Wrong Reasons?" *Journal of Contingencies and Crisis Management* 23: 275–86.

- Marley, Kathryn A., Peter T. Ward, and James A. Hill. 2014. "Mitigating Supply Chain Disruptions: A Normal Accident Perspective." *Supply Chain Management: An International Journal* 19: 142–52.

- Naor, Michael, Nicole Adler, Gavriel David Pinto, and Alon Dumanis. 2020. "Psychological Safety in Aviation New Product Development Teams: Case Study of 737 MAX Airplane." *Sustainability* 12: 8994.

- Nunan, Daniel, and Marialaura Di Domenico. 2017. "Big Data: A Normal Accident Waiting to Happen?" *Journal of Business Ethics* 145: 481–91.

- Palmer, Donald, and Michael W. Maher. 2010a. "A Normal Accident Analysis of the Mortgage Meltdown." In *Markets on Trial: The Economic Sociology of the U.S. Financial Crisis (Research in the Sociology of Organizations, vol. 30, Part A)*, edited by Michael Lounsbury and Paul M. Hirsch, 219–56. Bingley: Emerald Books.

  o See also: Palmer, Donald, and Michael W. Maher. 2010b. "The Mortgage

Meltdown as Normal Accidental Wrongdoing." *Strategic Organization* 8: 83–91.

- Perrow, Charles. (1984/1999). *Normal Accidents: Living with High-Risk Technologies.* Princeton, NJ: Princeton University Press.

- ———. 2004. "A Personal Note on Normal Accidents." *Organization & Environment* 17: 9–14.

- ———. 2008. "Disasters Evermore? Reducing Our Vulnerabilities to Natural, Industrial, and Terrorist Disasters." *Social Research* 75: 733–52.

- ———. 2010. "The Meltdown Was Not An Accident." In *Markets on Trial: The Economic Sociology of the U.S. Financial Crisis (Research in the Sociology of Organizations, vol. 30, Part A)*, edited by Michael Lounsbury and Paul M. Hirsch, 309–30. Bingley: Emerald Books.

  ○ (This is a response to Palmer and Maher (2010a)).

- Tufte, Edward R. 1997. *Visual Explanations: Images and Quantities, Evidence and Narrative.* Cheshire, CT: Graphics Press.

- Turner, Stephen P. 2010. "Normal Accidents of Expertise." *Minerva* 48: 239–58.

- Vaughan, Diane. 1989. "Regulating Risk: Implications of the Challenger Accident." *Law & Policy* 11: 330–49.

- ———. 1996. *The Challenger Launch Decision: Risky Technology, Culture, and Deviance at NASA.* Chicago, IL: University of Chicago Press.

- ———. 1998. "Rational Choice, Situated Action, and the Social Control of Organizations." *Law & Society Review* 32: 23–61.

With regards to **High Reliability Theory (HRT)** including contrast to **NAT** see:

- La Porte, Todd R., and Paula M. Consolini. 1991. "Working in Practice But Not in Theory: Theoretical Challenges of 'High Reliability Organizations'." *Journal of Public Administration Research and Theory* 1: 19–47.

- Le Coze, Jean-Christophe, ed. 2020. *Safety Science Research: Evolution, Challenges and New Directions.* Boca Raton, FL: CRC Press/Taylor & Francis Group.

- Leveson, Nancy, Nicolas Dulac, Karen Marais, and John Carroll. 2009. "Moving Beyond Normal Accidents and High Reliability Organizations: A Systems Approach to Safety in Complex Systems." *Organization Studies* 30: 227–49.

- Roberts, Karlene H. 1989. "New Challenges in Organization Research: High Reliability Organizations." *Industrial Crisis Quarterly* 3: 111–25.

On **Behavioral Economics** (the Postscript), see:

- Augier, Mie. 2013. "The Early Evolution of the Foundations for Behavioral Organization Theory and Strategy." *European Management Journal* 31: 72–81.

- Camerer, Colin F., and Ulrike Malmendier. 2007. "Behavioral Economics of Organizations." Chapter 7 in *Behavioral Economics and Its Applications*, edited by Peter Diamond and Hannu Vartiainen. Princeton, NJ: Princeton University Press.

- Frantz, Roger, Shu-Heng Chen, Kurt Dopfer, Floris Heukelom, and Shabnam

Mousavi, eds. 2017. *Routledge Handbook of Behavioral Economics*. New York, NY: Routledge.

- Heukelom, Floris. 2014. *Behavioral Economics: A History*. New York, NY: Cambridge University Press.

- Heukelom, Floris, and Esther-Mirjam Sent. 2017. "Behavioral Economics: From Advising Organizations To Nudging Individuals." *Journal of Behavioral Economics for Policy* Vol. I: 5–10.

- Pope, Devin G., and Justin R. Sydnor. 2015. "Behavioral Economics: Economics as a Psychological Discipline." Chapter 28 in *The Wiley Blackwell Handbook of*

Judgment and Decision Making, edited by Gideon Keren and George Wu. Hoboken, NJ: John Wiley & Sons, Ltd.

- Thaler, Richard H., and Sunstein, Cass R. 2009. *Nudge: Improving Decisions About Health, Wealth, and Happiness*. New York, NY: Penguin Books.

The **Ritzer quote on the inevitable irrational consequences** of rational systems is from:

- Ritzer, George. 2019. *The McDonaldization of Society: Into the Digital Age*, 9th Ed. Thousand Oaks, CA: Sage Publications.

Rationality as Constant and Variable

The ideas and issues introduced in Chapter 10 should not lead one to simply abandon the whole idea of rationality or rationalized organizations. While truly rational decisions and structures are technically impossible, they are not all equally so. What we may want to take away from this analysis of rationality is to learn to see actors, whether individuals or organizations, as only *variably* engaged in attempts at rational decision-making, and then only *variably* capable of achieving predictable and desired outcomes. That is, people and organizations are not rational, a-rational or irrational in any essential sense. A good deal of human action is not guided by cost–benefit decision-making, but by things like norms, emotions, sentiments, habits, and routines. When intendedly rational decision-making is actually done, sometimes the require-ments for rationality are relatively easy to achieve. The goals and potential means, along with the ability to understand and calculate the consequences can be relatively clear and concrete. This is the case if you're trying to buy ketchup. My nightmare scenario in Chapter 10 notwithstanding, in these cases rationality can be approximated fairly well.

But at other times the goals and/or means and/or consequences can be very difficult to clearly state, understand and calculate. Things can get to be very ambiguous, complex, and difficult to predict or control. Rationality becomes more difficult to achieve and attempts at rational decision-making or rationally designed systems become more costly and perhaps even irrational, as occurs in the case of overly prolonged *search procedures* for non-routine problems or in the instance of *normal accidents*.

Of course, not all complex actions, systems or processes end up producing obvious disaster even when the consequences are unintended or undesirable according to some set of criteria. In cases of high complexity where goals and their evaluation are particularly ambiguous, one may not even be able to tell how rational various processes are. To make such an attribution would require clarity about goals along with the ability to precisely measure outcomes, both of which are often part of the complexity to begin with. This is the case when one tries to produce educated and enlightened citizens that lead productive and meaningful lives. There are all sorts of activities that go into providing a University education. Grades are assigned, GPAs calculated, degrees awarded, jobs accepted by graduates, buildings constructed or renovated, the grass is cut, and so forth. Certain kinds of outcomes are also measured. Assessment exams are given, four year graduation rates calculated, and the careers of alumni tracked. But the typical mission statement is not about the proportion that graduate in four years or get a job in their field of study. *"We are a University committed to achieving a high four year graduation rate"* is just not very inspiring. Favorable numbers on such items *might* represent things like the production of enlightenment and meaning. And then again they might not. Any difficulty in measuring outcomes, of course, spills over into the search for the most rational means. With highly ambiguous goals that are hard to specify and measure, one generally ends up with organizational garbage cans (Chapter 10) that are covered over by rationalized myths (Chapter 9)—as Universities tend to be.

Yet, not all organizations deal with goals that are this complex. Some organizations make toothpicks. At an industrial level I don't want to overstate the simplicity of mass producing anything. But, as compared to making educated and enlightened citizens, making toothpicks can be much more rationalized. The goal is pretty clear and easy to measure. The means can similarly be made clear. And calculations of costs and benefits can be made in fairly concrete ways. Most costs and benefits are easily quantified and one can tell whether or not toothpicks have been produced, how many there are at the end of the day, and then end up with a reasonably accurate idea of whether or not any benefits have been accrued from producing them. In the rationalized world, if your thing is to make toothpicks, then the job of organizing efficiently toward that is far easier than if you have to produce education and enlightenment.

The problem is that you don't get a break just because your goals and means and outcomes are difficult to define and to measure. As Neo-institutionalism (Chapter 9) alerts us, you still have to try to achieve the rationalized form in at least some respects, even if it is only ceremoniously on the frontage. This form is a matter of deeply held cultural expectations. Of course, competition in markets, which is not limited merely to business organizations, also brings the same kinds of pressures on the basis of efficiency concerns. If we follow power based understandings we can also add in that the rationalized form is frequently in the interests of organizational elites as a means of the few controlling the many. The forces that push rationalization are many and strong. But we now also know that the forces that push back against it can also be many and strong. The humans that inevitably populate the systems are difficult, and environmental issues can seriously hamper and alter any or all aspects of the institution structures, processes and procedures that might be most rational for the organization. And above all of that, no one escapes the problems of bounded rationality even if you can simplify your tasks, your people and the environment. Thus, this chapter jumps off from a particular image of organizations[1]—that the pressures to achieve a formally rationalized form are a *constant*, and this has been the case since at least the turn of the twentieth century. Yet the ability to accomplish the rational form along with its intended and utility maximizing outcomes is *highly variable*. Fortunately, organizational theory already contains the seeds of the thinking and research tools that can help sort things out.

---

[1]Many "images of organization" (Morgan, 2006) can be sketched. The rational/human-natural/open systems images are among them. There is not *one best way* to describe perspectives in organizational theory.

Contingency Theories of Organization

The intensive focus on the variability of organizational forms is a core aspect of what are called *Contingency Theories (CT)* of organization (also often in the singular). In a very general sense its origins lie in the lineage of impulses that go all the way back to *Classical Management Theory (CMT)* as originated by Frederick Taylor and others that we met up with in Chapter 7. Recall that Taylor's goal was always to find *the one best way* to accomplish any task. In later CMT this turned into searching for *one best way* to organize. People like Chester Barnard, Henri Fayol, and others, sought to lay out an optimum set of principles by which to structure human organizations. Weber's ideal type with which we started the book also entered the picture, and is sometimes seen in the same way. Initially Weber's discussion of bureaucracy was not widely known because it wasn't translated into English until the late 1940s. But once it was available to the English-speaking world, where most of CMT was developed, it also became a bit of a benchmark for thinking about the optimal characteristics for formal organizations. The classical theorists, including Weber, didn't actually collect systematic data on existing organizations to find out what observed characteristics of organizations provided the optimal forms. People like Barnard and Fayol worked from their own personal bases of experience. And Weber merely observed that the emerging bureaucratic forms were more efficient than past forms, and described what he saw as their typical and defining characteristics. Furthermore, his intentions were not normative in that he was trying to claim that there is a one *best* way in which things *should* be done. His interests were more those of a social scientist attempting to understand emerging complex social realities rather than a management scientist interested in organizational design.

But beginning in about the late 1950s, this CMT project was turned into the intensive comparative and empirical study of organizational structures in a quest to find the most effective form(s). The starting point for conceptualizing and measuring aspects of structure was typically drawn from concepts like those found in the Weberian ideal type such as the characteristics of hierarchy, the degree of division of labor, the degree of formalization and so on. The basic thrust of such research was to directly measure aspects of organizational structure in samples of multiple organizations alongside of indicators of organizational performance (e.g., stock price performance, dividend production, profitability, etc.) to discover what kind of structural design is the most effective. For instance, one might think that there is an optimum number of levels for an organizational hierarchy. Perhaps too many levels can become inefficient by hampering effective communication and supervision, and by wasting money on salaries at the middle management levels. Perhaps too few levels of hierarchy are also inefficient because you end up with too many generals and not enough soldiers, so goal clarity and the coordination and monitoring of activities become difficult. So what is the optimum, most efficient height of a hierarchy?

As a related feature, one might also ask about the shape of the hierarchy—should it be tall and narrow or shorter and wider? This involves things like the optimum number of supervisors to supervisees at each level, which is called the *span of control*. That's not too hard to think about. If your spans of control are too large (too many supervisees under a supervisor), then supervisors are not able to supervise very well because there is too much for them to pay attention to. If your spans of control are too small then you might end up with a lot of micromanagement by supervisors, duplicated efforts, and certainly end up with inefficiencies related to putting out more supervisory level pay and benefits than is necessary. Measures for these kinds of things are fairly straightforward. For example, you just count the number of people under each office in the organization and calculate ratios and averages and such.

Similarly, the degree of formalization is fairly straightforward to measure by just looking at how many things get defined in writing. Are there employee handbooks? How large are they? Are there regularly planned meetings and, if so, are minutes of the meetings kept? Does each office have written job descriptions and if so, how long are those? How highly specified are the duties and obligations associated with various positions? How many forms are required to be filled out for how many tasks? The list can go on both for measures of formalization and for the characteristics of organizational structures that can be measured.

For many the start of the contingency tradition is marked by the work of organizational sociologist Joan Woodward in the 1950s.[2] Woodward started out with the intent of finding out whether or not the management theory being taught in business schools at the time held up under empirical investigation. She collected data on a sample of nearly 100 British manufacturing businesses and measured various aspects of their structures along with how successful they were. She didn't necessarily expect to find the textbook teachings of the time to be spot-on, but she did expect to find that success was tied to particular kinds of structural characteristics that were held in common. But that is not what the data showed. The most successful firms in the sample had quite different structural characteristics which came as quite a surprise both to her and to most everyone else at the time.

One thing that you might think is that this means that it doesn't really matter all that much how an organization is structured. Maybe organizations are just about what all of the people do in them rather than their formal structures. But that didn't quite turn out to be the story either. In terms of accounting for variations in success, the noise in Woodward's data turned to signal once companies were sorted out based on the kind of production work that they did. While she grouped production systems into 10 different categories, three styles of production seemed to correspond to particular kinds of organizational characteristics. Comparatively speaking companies that did either custom *unit or small batch production* (e.g., fabrication of large equipment one piece at a time) tended to have relatively short hierarchies, a low ratio of management staff to non-managerial workers (*managerial intensity*), relatively small spans of control, and generally operated with a lot of skilled labor rather than a great deal of formalization and bureaucracy. By comparison, production systems geared toward *large batch* or *mass production* (e.g., automobile assembly lines) had more levels of management, higher managerial intensity, and quite broad spans of control. Wider spans of control are at least partly afforded by the fact that more of the control was built into production machines and processes as the work was lower skilled and more bureaucratic. In contrast, firms that engaged in *continuous process production* where materials are transformed from state to state along the way

---

[2]See Woodward, 1958; 1965.

(e.g., petroleum refining or chemicals manufacture), while they tended to have the highest number of levels of management, had low managerial intensity, the smallest spans of control and relied more on the exercise of discretion among skilled workers than on bureaucratic processes. All of this produced conclusions that remain a central idea for the contingency tradition to this day—there is *no one best way* to organize. The "best way" depends—or is *contingent* upon the kind of production processes, tasks or technologies that an organization deals with. This might seem obvious once it is pointed out, but at the time it actually came as quite a surprise.

At about the same time that Woodward was making waves with a focus on an organization's technological contingencies, attention to the organizational environment entered the picture as well. Another of the originating pieces of research in the contingency tradition appeared in a 1961 book by Tom Burns and G. M. Stalker called *The Management of Innovation*. Burns and Stalker also did an empirical study of the characteristics of a number of British companies in different industries—textiles, heavy industry, and electronics. Their data showed that some organizations looked a lot like the Weberian ideal type of bureaucracy with lots of job specialization and standardization and commands up and down a clearly defined hierarchy, and so forth. These kinds of firms would make Frederick Taylor proud, and Burns and Stalker labeled these *mechanistic* forms of organization because they do resemble a Weberian ideal type—organizations that operate like predictable, bureaucratic pieces of machinery. However, they also noted that many firms had quite different characteristics. Control in some organizations was based much more on collegial consultation than it was on the giving and taking of orders. Tasks were often rather fuzzy and shifting. As such tasks and job descriptions were not highly standardized. Workers in the organization were not geared to obedience of hierarchal authority and faithfully carrying out pre-defined tasks. Rather they were more likely to be guided by the overall goals of the organization itself, and much of the way that work was done was left to the discretion and judgment of workers themselves. Firms such as this simply didn't look much like Weber's ideal type. Weber, of course, would not be surprised to find this. He built ideal types because he knew that the actual empirical world contained much variation. So Burns and Stalker, in essence, produced a complementary ideal type to the mechanistic bureaucracy, and called it *organic*. The general idea is that some organizations work more like organisms—as adaptive, decentralized and variably coupled parts of a system in reciprocal exchanges. I have summarized the key features of the distinction between mechanistic and organic organizational forms in Figure 11.1. (I would be good to pause and dwell on it for a while.)

As with Woodward's study the data didn't support an idea opposite from the *one best way*—that perhaps it just doesn't matter how you organize. Rather, the variability among mechanistic versus organic organizations was systematic. The textile firms in Burns and Stalker's sample operated in very stable and predictable markets with very well known, standardized technologies, raw materials and products. These were the ones that had more mechanistic structures. Where there is little need to change rapidly or adapt to changing or complex technologies or environments, much can be standardized and the efficiency benefits of the bureaucratic form can be realized. In the electronics industry, however, there was a great deal of innovation going on in terms of products and production technologies, which went along with a much

FIGURE 11.1   Burns and Stalker: Mechanistic versus Organic Organizational Forms

		Mechanistic	Organic
WORK TASKS	Division of Labor	Specialized Tasks	Specialized Knowledge/Experience
	Worker Focus	Vary Narrow/Own Task	Overall Enterprise Goal
	Standardization	Highly Specified/Stable	Unclear/Shifting
	Accountability	Clear and Hierarchical	Fuzzy/Uncertain/Shared
CONTROL	Authority/Communication Style	Hierarchy	Network
	Information Control	Hierarchical	Dispersed/Diffused
	Predominant Interactions	Vertical	Horizontal
	Governance	Directives	Advice/Consultation
WORKERS	Performance Expectations	Obedience/Loyalty	Commitment to Overall Objectives
	Prestige Basis	Internal Position	External Criteria and Judgement

Source: Author summary from Burns and Stalker ([1961] 1994): 119–122.

more dynamic and fast-moving market. It was electronics firms that tended to exhibit the organic characteristics. As we first encountered with regards to the *competitiveness crisis* among US companies in the 1970s, bureaucracies are great for doing the same thing over and over again and can do well when things are stable and predictable. But they're not very good at adaptability and change, and thus have trouble if they face high levels of *environmental turbulence*.

Combining Woodward with Burns and Stalker, we already have what eventually became (and largely remains) the primary focus of research in the contingency tradition—understanding the variability of organizational structures according to characteristics of their technology and environment. If both work systems and organizational environments are relatively stable and well understood, then organizations tend toward the Weberian bureaucratic form.

Increasing degrees of complexity, uncertainty, and instability tend to lead organizations to take on alternative forms. The picture was likely solidified by some further foundational work in the contingency tradition from 1967. Along with Woodward and Burns and Stalker, just as frequently cited as key to the dawn of the contingency tradition is a 1967 book by Paul Lawrence and Jay Lorsch (who first labeled this approach as Contingency Theory) called *Organization and Environment*. The title leaves little to the imagination in that the focus was on the effects of the environment on organizational structures. It is an entire book, and we don't need to review everything about it here. The core of the findings and argument are that organizations will take on characteristics that are induced by the degree of environmental complexity. In highly complex environments, there will be many different and potentially difficult demands that an organization will need to navigate. Therefore, if it is to do it well, it needs to become more and more *differentiated* in order to deal with the complexity. That is, it will end up with many different divisions and a great deal of division of labor as the environmental demands require a great deal of specialized expertise and attention. In order to deal with all of that resulting internal differentiation, the organization will also need to develop more and more intensive mechanisms for internal *integration*. The subtitle of the book is, in fact, *Differentiation and Integration*. The imagery is not at all unlike the notion of *isomorphism* that we learned of in Chapter 9. Successful organizations will develop a complexity in their structures that mirrors the complexity of their environment.

But Lawrence and Lorsch's findings went farther and they point out that it is not always wise to treat organizations as singular entities where the same environmental forces apply to the organization as a whole. In large, complex organizations with multiple divisions one will also find variations in structure across different divisions in the same organization. Different divisions themselves need to deal with very different kinds of *tasks* and different *environments*. Some divisions, for example, are explicitly *boundary spanning* divisions such as sales and marketing and are regularly interacting with and managing environmental elements. Others mostly operate within the boundaries of the organization with more buffering from environmental disturbance, such as a manufacturing division. Yet others might be focused on research and development (R&D) where task complexity and uncertainty can be quite high. Lawrence and Lorsch found the same kinds of variation across divisions as can be found across different organizations, largely based on complexity of task and environment. Some divisions become very mechanistic and bureaucratic. Others remain more organic in form.

This latter point should really come as no surprise once you recall that there is nothing essential that puts different kinds of tasks in the same organization (recall discussions of vertical and horizontal integration from Part II). Any of the functions that take place inside of an organization could always be outsourced. Just because a company manufactures and sells doesn't mean that it has to design and market. With all of these considerations in mind it should come as no surprise that Lawrence and Lorsch are often recognized as giving an important early push to the emergence of *open systems* thinking in organizational studies. *Population Ecology* (Chapter 9), for example, was at least partly inspired by asking the question of how these variable organizational structures come to be as they are, and the answer was basically variation, selection, and retention by the environment—some manner of natural selection. It is also the case that the entire framing that I am using for this chapter could be attributed to Lawrence and Lorsch because they argued that one can reconcile the differences between *rational* and *human systems* perspectives of organizations by seeing them, not as competing models for best practices or for how to best characterize organizations, but simply as different kinds of systems that might exist under different environmental conditions. Their idea was to take organizations, above all, as *open systems* where it is the nature of the environment that determines whether they will be structured more as rational (mechanistic) or human/natural (organic) systems. Organizations do operate like rational systems if their environments are relatively simple and stable. But the more complex they become, the harder and harder it gets to implement rational systems principles in which case one must leave more to the situational decision-making of humans in the system.

While Lawerence and Lorsch's primary focus was on the organizational environment, also in 1967 Charles Perrow, one of our "friends" all along in the book, provided an important early paper contributing to what was once called *the technological school*[3] in the contingency tradition. This work was very much influenced by the Carnegie School and the ideas that went into the *Behavioral Theory of the Firm*, and later fed directly into his later work on *normal accidents* both of which were discussed in Chapter 10.

Building on the growing recognition of the importance of technological forms to organizational structures that started with people like Woodward, Perrow started from the assertion that the kinds of tasks an organization performs will most centrally condition how it is structured. He posited two characteristics of technology that are crucial, and it should all seem familiar after Chapter 10. One characteristic is the number of *exceptions* that are encountered in the course of doing the work. In the lingo of organizational theory, *exceptions* are basically about when you have square holes, but you keep ending up with round pegs (or triangles or stars or trapezoids...). The wrong shaped peg is the *exception*, and it can't be handled with existing routines or programs—the *standard operating procedures*. Falling outside of existing routines, exceptions are the kinds of things that trigger *search procedures*. Thus Perrow argues that the second dimension is the degree to which search procedures are "analyzable"—basically just whether or not there are clear understandings of the problems and well-known and reliable principles for finding solutions. In general, if there are very few exceptions so that work tasks are highly predictable and stable (few, if any of the wrong-shaped pegs), then you are very likely to find a "well-programmed production process."[4] Organizations with such technological forms are likely to be formalized and centralized—mechanistic if we wanted to use the vocabulary of Burns and Stalker. At the opposite extreme—where you find both many exceptions and "unanalyzable" searches—it is not possible to produce or maintain the programming. Rather, highly experienced personnel have to be able to use professional judgment and expertise to deal with unpredictable and changing work processes. It is not possible to institute a lot of bureaucracy in such cases, and organizations will need to remain flexible and can't successfully institute central authority. They will more approximate what Burns and Stalker called organic.

[3]Perrow, 1967.
[4]Perrow, 1967: 200.

However for Perrow, it can't be as simple as two poles of a single continuum because the two dimensions of exceptions and the analyzability of the searches can vary independently. Perrow summarized the whole picture of types of production in a four box model by cross-classifying the frequency of exceptions with analyzability (see Figure 11.2). The two conditions I noted above—few exceptions that are easily analyzed versus many exceptions that are not—were labeled *routine* and *non-routine*, respectively. The former will tend to have a highly *centralized and formalized* structure, while the latter will tend to be *flexible and polycentralized* (generally, multiple centers—neither entirely centralized nor decentralized). Under conditions where there are few exceptions but with unanalyzable problems you find work that is characteristic of many *craft industries* where organizational structures will tend to remain *decentralized*. While exceptions are not overly common, when they do appear skilled workers need to be able to work out a means of proceeding that will often involve tacit knowledge, intuition and—Frederick Taylor's old enemy—the dreaded rule of thumb. On the other hand, many exceptions but with analyzable search procedures would be encountered in *engineering* types of tasks and tend to produce structures that are *flexible* but *centralized*. Flexibility is required to be able to deal with all of the exceptions. But a good deal of centralized control is afforded by the fact that problem solving is somewhat standardized and contains few mysteries.

In many respects early contingency work turned into the comparative study of organizational structures along with the search for effective typologies of organizations. All organizations were not Weberian bureaucracies, so were there other *ideal types* of formal organizations that needed to be

FIGURE 11.2   **Perrow's Classification of Organization by Technical Complexity**

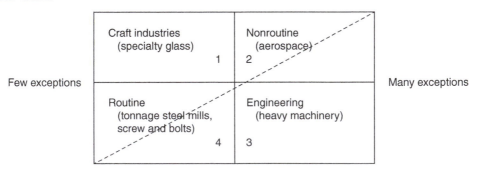

Source: Perrow, C. (1967). A Framework for the Comparative Analysis of Organizations. *American Sociological Review*, 32(2), 194–208.

defined? The Burns and Stalker distinction between mechanistic and organic was perhaps the earliest but others were soon added that captured more than just two poles. One of the more well-known came from management scholar Henry Mintzberg for whom characteristics of technology and environment loomed large. Mintzberg defined five basic organizational types, four of which will be typical under different degrees of technological and environmental complexity (see Figure 11.3). Something approximating the Weberian ideal type of bureaucracy, which Mintzberg dubs the *Machine Bureaucracy*, will tend to found under *stable* environmental conditions with *simple* technical systems. These are exemplified by things like large mass production organizations operating in a manner that approximates the Fordist model. If technical systems are simple, but the environment is *dynamic*, organizations will tend toward a *Simple Structure* which includes centralization and direct supervision, but it will have a more organic form with little bureaucracy. These organizations are often relatively young, small, entrepreneurial, and operating in fast moving new markets. *Complex* technical systems in stable environments will tend to be *Professional Bureaucracies* and contain a good deal of standardization and bureaucracy, but remain decentralized as the expertise to deal with complex work processes are difficult to standardize and remain under the discretion of skilled workers. With complex technical systems in dynamic environments, one often ends up with *Adhocracy*. Little can be systematized, at least for very long, and work has to be continually reinvented by skilled personnel operating more on the basis of creativity and mutual consultation rather than order giving and order taking. The Burns and Stalker mechanistic-organic dichotomy is most like a Machine Bureaucracy-Adhocracy dichotomy.

There is a fifth type in Mintzberg's typology called the *Divisionalized Structure* such as that taken by those large integrated and/or conglomerated organizations that we met in Chapter 4 with Alfred Chandler. In Divisionalized Structures the headquartering organization that controls the divisions is more of a structure that is imposed over the top of other structures. Each division has to carry out its own operations quasi-independently and each will encounter its own particular kinds of circumstances. Thus, to some extent, each will need to have its own structure, and organizational divisions can take on any of the four ideal types shown in Figure 11.3. However, there is a strong

---

FIGURE 11.3   **Henry Mintzberg's Contingency Typology**

	Stable environment	Dynamic environment
	Professional bureaucracy	**Adhocracy**
Complex technology	Decentralized	Decentralized
	Bureaucratic	Organic
	(standardization of skills)	(mutual adjustment)
	Machine bureaucracy	**Simple structure**
Simple technology	Centralized	Centralized
	Bureaucratic	Organic
	(standardization of work processes)	(direct supervision)

Source: Based on Mintzberg, 1983: 144.

tendency for divisions to take on the Machine Bureaucratic form over time for the simple reason that the headquartering organization needs means for control and monitoring. This tends to involve careful training and surveillance of division management, but more importantly the monitoring of outputs through bureaucratic reports which need to be clear, easy to measure, and quantifiable. All of this creates constant pressures toward standardization and bureaucracy. Thus Mintzberg would say that under a Divisionalized Form, divisions would typically, but not always, be organized as Machine Bureaucracies.

In any case, the contingency literature is vast and for our purposes a basic introduction rather than a full review of the development will do. Its beginnings are to be found in a rational systems quest to find the optimal structure for formal organizations—the proper "ideal type" that provides the one best way to organize. But when researchers started to carefully measure the characteristics of real organizations and their structures they found a lot of variety. Yet the variety is not random. It's not that it does matter how you organize. Rather organizations need to end up with structures that are best adapted to the organizational situation—to the complexity of the work that they do and the environments within which they operate. In other words, the *best way* for any particular organization to structure itself and lay out its activities just depends—it is *contingent*. The central contingency factor is the extent to which an organization faces complexity and/or uncertainty with regards to its *tasks* and/or *environment*. Generalizing from Perrow (above), the reason this is important is because of the issue of exceptions, and the resulting need for search procedures for ongoing decision-making. With many exceptions and anything but simple search procedures, attempts to implement formal rationality—the standardization of tasks, simple work-by-orders plans, or *standard operating procedures* will become overwhelmed. Hierarchies will then tend to flatten out, decision-making becomes more and more decentralized as it has to be left to skilled and experienced people at the site of the issues. In other words, in a general sense, organizations are pushed toward more and more organic forms. In their least bureaucratic and thus most organic they can come to be characterized as organized anarchies, adhocracies, or simply garbage cans.

The contingency tradition took up a central place in organizational studies starting by the 1960s and continuing on into the 1980s. At this point, the tradition did not disappear. In terms of organizational theory, the insights and findings were largely just absorbed and came to be taken for granted. As noted above, the tradition was also instrumental in turning theoretical attention to organizational environments and the flowering of *open systems* theorizing that began in the 1970s (Chapter 9) and that now predominate in organizational studies. In organizational studies more generally speaking, contingency approaches do continue to be directly used in various applications such as the best way to organize a *Human Resources Management (HRM)* division, whether all of the same applies to small and medium sizes enterprises (SMEs), or best practices with regards to instituting *continuous improvement* programs.[5] Much of this appears in conjunction with very practical and applied matters in the management sciences, where the contingency tradition never truly left center stage for dealing with matters of *Organizational Design*

---

[5]See, respectively, Verberg et al., 2007; Ali and Varoğlu, 2021; McAdam et al., 2019.

(OD). In many respects it has remained highly empirical and statistical where design consultants use complex statistical models to align organizational structures and processes with demands.[6] It also can be seen as perhaps having an explicit resurgence in recent years—or at least the need for one.[7] In any case, to be sure, if you are ever in a position of making decisions about OD, such as whether or not to set up a new division or specific job classification, add or remove layers and supervisory levels of hierarchy, implement more participatory management practices or produce more bureaucracy, or the like, then contingency research is an excellent place to go for information on specific research findings that would be helpful.

What I plan to do here is just wrap up the ongoing discussion of Part III by providing a simple heuristic for thinking about organizations, their structures, and complexities in flexible and variable form. Following the initial lead of Lawrence and Lorsch, we will take all formal organizations as having a very strong tendency to try to approximate the form of rational systems—well oiled, predictable, and efficient machines. I think that it is fair to say that this has been the essence of formally organizing all along, and there are multiple forces that push organizations in that direction. Yet the problem is that other forces and various kinds of conditions can make it impossible to achieve the rational form and rational outcomes from organizational activity.

Generalized Contingency Thinking as an Orienting Tool

As a distinctive research tradition, contingency theory occupies a somewhat ambiguous place in organizational studies. Sometimes it is associated with a *rational systems* perspective (Chapter 7) because of its relation to the concerns of CMT, and primary preoccupation with optimal organizational designs. Organizations are seen as means and must be designed to meet their challenges in the most effective way possible, whether that means taking a more mechanistic or organic form given whatever contingencies are faced. Sometimes it is associated with an *open systems* perspective (Chapter 9), largely because of the central importance of the environment in shaping organizational structures. Contingency theory, particularly of the *technological school* in the hands of Perrow, was also something of an extension of concern with issues of bounded rationality, and was later highly influential in shaping the development of *normal accidents theory* (Chapter 10).

Regardless of where or how people want to place it, what I am going to do in the remainder of this chapter is make contingency theory out to be the central starting point for any kind of thinking about formal organizations, whether driven by practical issues of effective design and strategy or by social science issues of understanding organizations as actors and/or as arenas for action in the world. Most, if not all, of the complexities of organizing dealt with by organizational theory, including most issues presented here in Part III, can be effectively ordered and understood through the general logic of contingency theory.

Too often organizational theories or images are thought of in essentialist terms as if one is supposed to figure out whether organizations are (or *should*

---

[6]See Donaldson, 2010.
[7]Van de Ven, et al., 2013.

be) more like machines or human groups or adaptive organisms navigating an environment of potential resources and so forth. The different ideas are lined up on a book shelf like so many alternative "perspectives." But the key, as organizational theorist Gareth Morgan put it, is to see that "Organizations are many things at once. They are complex and multifaceted."[8] By having an explicit focus on *variability*, contingency thinking provides the roots for a reasonably simple heuristic for analytically ordering the multifaceted complexity and seeing that formal organizations are all of these things at once. I am not claiming that it provides for some manner of complete and totalizing theory of organizations. That is not likely possible (certainly not in a simple, introductory book), and probably not even desirable. But the world of organizational studies is nothing if not complex. For beginners to the field, the logic of contingency thinking can simply provide a way of maintaining some signal amid what can sometimes seem like noise.

One Constant: The Quest for Rationalization and Encounters with the Variable Limitations

Whether it seems obvious or not, the history of formal organizing and of organizational theory is a sustained grappling with the problem of rationality itself. We started with confronting the Weberian *rationalization thesis* and it is quite obvious that the iron cage continues to grow in many respects even if not in the forms it took through the first part of twentieth century. We also have several ways of thinking about why the march of formal rationalization is so persistent. One is that it can produce great gains in certain kinds of efficiencies as Weber initially argued, as we saw with the likes of Frederick Taylor and Henry Ford (Chapter 7), and as was celebrated by Alfred Chandler (Chapter 4). Another is that it can be a great tool for organizational elites in terms of instituting control, as we saw with regards to power-based explanations for the rise of hierarchy and the corporate form (Chapter 5). Formal rationalization provides "*unobtrusive, inexpensive, pervasive, and impersonal control devices, the best elites have ever discovered*" as Charles Perrow put it.[9] The two goals of efficiency and control are, of course, not mutually exclusive. Finally, the rational and bureaucratic form is now a deeply ingrained cultural expectation (Chapter 9). Organizations cannot appear to just be one damn thing happening after another, but are expected to be rationally designed means to meet ends and must appear so to maintain their legitimacy. So even where a rational systems approach to organizing might not seem applicable or even be valued, some semblance of it will generally need to be instituted.

So begin with the fundamental assumption that whatever else they may be formal organizations and the larger networked systems of which they may be a part are *intendedly rational* means to achieve certain ends. Just whose ends are in play should itself remain completely variable, along with the question of whether or not formally stated ends are truly the focus of practical organizational activities. The extent to which rationalized structures are merely symbolic displays should also remain a variable and seen as the degree to which the front and back stages of organizational activity are coupled. If

---

[8]Morgan (2006: 337).
[9]Perrow, 2002: 163.

rationalization was easy, then there would be no need for decoupling. Informal and formal structures would always match up pretty well, and we might truly stay with the rather dark and dreary *iron cage* notion from Weber. But the formal rationalization of human action, while it is a dream for many and an expectation of most, is frequently not easy, as we have seen.

As the contingency tradition made clear, what stands in the way of rationalizing are basically uncertainty and complexity. We face varying degrees of uncertainty and complexity with regards to setting and defining goals. Even if we can specify the goals reasonably well, we will still face varying degrees of uncertainty and complexity with regards to our means (technologies) in terms of both making them function as expected and the potential consequences that emerge. We face varying degrees of uncertainty and complexity from whatever counts as the environment in any given form of action. From the position of the organization as an actor, all of the issues that tasks (Chapter 7) people (Chapter 8) and organizational environments (Chapter 9) present are things that can hamper the ability of an organization to operate as predictable and smooth machinery. They are all potential sources of uncertainties and unpredictability, although to varying degrees. They are things that feed into the basic difficulties of rationally planned action that we encountered in Chapter 10. They represent elements that exacerbate the extent of the multiplicity and ambiguity of goals, and things that produce unknowns with regards to means and their consequences. And much of the flow of organizational studies over time, especially in the management sciences and applied areas more generally, has been geared toward questions of how to manage and tame the complexity—from taming the tasks to taming the humans to taming the environment, all in the interests of increasing the ability to accomplish formally rationalized control.

The life's dream of the Taylors and Fords of the world was to tame the complexity of tasks. It was to take the uncertainty and rule-of-thumb *heuristics* out of craft work and replace it with known certainties. This quest has not slowed. The current frontiers of the dream of Taylorism is likely the use of *machine learning algorithms (MLAs)* as we saw in Chapter 7. As part of the quest for *artificial intelligence (AI)*, people implement softwares as more effective handlers of information and calculators for decision-making. Where the boundaries of our cognitive abilities stop, in order to more closely approximate our desired ends we hand over Taylorism to machines that can handle more information and calculations than we limited humans are able to. This taming of the tasks at the same time often amounts to taming of the humans. Consider, for instance, the question of whether *deskilling* strategies *within* organizations (or now sometimes *platforms*) are not attempts to exert more control over the *environment* by making workers into something closer to a bunch of round pegs. By systematizing tasks, deskilling removes complexity and unpredictability from the human aspects of the technology. Taking deskilling as standardizing aspects of the environment is not an outlandish way to think about it. Organizations have to design themselves to tame that complexity and better control the humans.

But not all tasks can be tamed and even when they can be, not *everything* about the humans can be. The management strategies of both the Human Relations (HR) School and Humanistic Management (HM) (Chapter 8) enter here as they are geared toward how to harness the goals of persons to direct them toward becoming more effective means for the organization. Humans come in from the environment and bring complexity and unpredictability with them, although that varies as well depending on the characteristics of the labor force and degrees of technological standardization. If we take HM to be an advance over HR, then it would be in the HM recognition that humans are even more complicated than they are for HR. We have more goals that are even more complex. Taylor, of course, figured that you can harness the humans with simple calculations of material rewards. The HR school merely added the goal of social belonging. The HM school accepts both of those things, but also adds all of those more difficult and ambiguous psychological "higher needs" of self-esteem and self-actualization. In either case, the thinking is not far from what we get from the Carnegie School—that organizational structures are there to shape the premises on which the humans act so that they will decide as the organization wishes.

But therein also lies an important source of variation. For HM the employees of an organization are untapped resources. If you provide working conditions whereby they are given the freedom to pursue their own self-esteem and self-actualization needs, then you will get a well-spring of creativity that ultimately benefits the organization. Thus you do things like decentralize and delegate, provide job enlargement, participative management and the like. It is anti-Taylorism. Management does not monopolize what is to be done and how while the workers just receive and carry out orders. Taylorism, in the eyes of Humanistic Management, not only robs workers of their agency, autonomy, and creative potentials but also more importantly robs the organization of what it can gain my leveraging those potentials. It's a compelling story where human agency rather than organizational structure is celebrated and given a central role.

But under what conditions are such ideas even relevant? What would Frederick Taylor think about handing discretion and control back to workers? And how would it play out on the ground among line workers in your local McDonald's? Or similarly with regards to working under the control of algorithms as is the case with Uber drivers? Maybe there is some room to move at the fringes for the human elements. But your local Uber driver or employee at your local McDonald's is not going to be invited into the conversation, nor are they even relevant to start other than being a part of the machine that has not yet been completely automated. On that note, where will Uber drivers be once motor vehicles are purely driven by software rather than by actual humans? They are a step away from being replaced by machines and their degree of agency, at least with regards to work, reflects that as it always has where mechanization is able to be done. Where systems can be intensively rationalized the humans *actually are* appendages to the machines. In such systems, if there is any relevance of the humans asserted it will be in terms of largely *de facto* empty placations that come from the impulses of HR ideas, like employee of the month plaques, company picnics, and the like. Or it might manifest as *symbolic* invitations to participative management where the open questions are issues of little true consequence with regards to the conditions of work. Other than ways to placate alienated workers with ice cream and cake (which was actually involved in some of the Hawthorne experiments), any management ideas based in Human Systems thinking are of highly limited relevance. If they are made to seem relevant, then that will largely be in symbolic, front stage terms.

To the extent that HM ideas genuinely make sense and apply, it would be under more complex work conditions where tasks have not been tamed (whether in terms of technology or environment) and the actual exercise of discretion and judgment remain relevant—largely conditions found in *primary labor markets*. This book began by going rather heavy handed on both the prospects for true human agency and the degree to which social power is concentrated. It was a way of describing the world where most, if not all humans are mere cogs in much larger machineries simply following larger programs. But this, of course is a variable itself and herein lies some room for human agency and the importance of individual persons. Organizations are human systems under certain kinds of conditions and not all aspects of the world of formal organizing are bound up completely by the iron cage.

If rational systems logic is about taming the tasks, and human systems about taming the humans, open systems ideas, of whatever type, are obviously about understanding and managing the complexities and uncertainties of organizational environments. In terms of contingency theories proper—if narrowly construed as the tradition that deals with questions of organizational design—organizations have to design themselves toward grappling with uncertainties produced by tasks and environments if they are to be successful. This includes how they manage the tasks and the humans. The routes to doing this can actually be quite variable. As we saw in Part II, a major part of the story of the *organizational revolution* at the turn of the twentieth century was the use of large amounts of capital to simply absorb as much of the environment as was possible—competitors in the case of *horizontal integration* and suppliers and buyers in many cases of *vertical integration*. In the case of company towns such as those built by the Boston Associates (Chapter 5), even the humans are nearly fully internalized. In many respects, some of these moves were responses to issues of *resource dependence* or *transaction costs* (or both) before these perspectives on organizations had names. Of course, integration (whether vertical or horizontal, but certainly both) produces very large organizations, and becoming large like this tends to produce high levels of bureaucracy as a means of control. And as long as "bigness" can be used to dominate and tame the environment, rationalizing can be maintained as it was for much of the twentieth century—the *hierarchy* phase of organizing. However, as we learned, it was during the 1970s that the situation for large, bureaucratic business forms may have begun to come apart in the face of increasing global competition. Too much bigness and bureaucracy result in difficulty in adapting to changing circumstances.

In contingency theory terms this period just represented increases in *environmental turbulence*. What were once stable and predictable environments became subject to rapid change and thus higher degrees of uncertainty. Big and *mechanistic* would no longer do, so the new business logic for organizing seemed to shift to being smaller, more *organic*, and thus more adaptable. The extent to which many organizations were open systems increases as more and more functions were spun back out into the organizational environment rather than being absorbed. The *best way* became the network form rather than the hierarchy. But of course, it's not that *either* hierarchy *or* network is the best way in any essential sense. It is more that hierarchy is better for stability, and network for instability, at least if "better" is judged in terms of narrow organizational efficiencies. We have plenty of reason to question whether hierarchy in the forms it took by about the turn of the twentieth century was "better" in some broader social sense, at the very least because it brought vastly concentrated economic power along with producing other negative externalities (Chapter 5).

Of course, along the way we also learn that rationalized structures might need to be seen as more of a front than a reality. A formal description of an organization as a set of rationally designed means often bears little resemblance to the actual day to day activities inside of the organization. But there is nothing essential or constant about that either—except for the persistent cultural expectation of the rational form. The extent to which an organization's front stage presentation resembles its backstage activities is itself a variable. When our goals and means and calculations remain simple, the inexorable push toward rationalization produces mechanistic forms of organization that deliver fairly predictable and intended outcomes. Here organizational front stages *will* tend to look a lot like organizational back stages. The more complex things become, especially with regards to tasks and environments, the lower is the ability to produce forms of personal or organizational action that approximate rationality and are subject to programming via standard procedures. This pushes organizational activity to become less bureaucratic and more organic, and can necessitate at least some degree of decoupling of the front stage from the back stage. It is here that you find the kinds of processes that took up much of the attention of the *expose tradition* (Chapter 8) where the idea was generally to look behind the curtain to observe informally structured organizational realities.

At some point we can reach issues of complexity and unpredictability that completely outstrip our abilities to fully control, understand, or predict what we are actually doing or what will come out of it. Where complexity is high, the coupling between different technical and organizational elements remains loose, and/or the stakes for failure are either low or perhaps undetectable largely because of goal ambiguity, we end up with *garbage cans* covered over with a veneer of rationality as a front stage myth such as is often found in universities. But where complexity is high, the coupling is tight, and the stakes become high, we end up with *normal accidents*—noticeably *irrational* disasters of various kinds. In such complex systems formally rationalized processes have to be constructed, used, and maintained as a part of handling the dangers and complexities of the system. In other words, you still need a lot of real as opposed to merely *symbolic* bureaucracy. Working out of the garbage can just won't do. But the complexities of the system can outstrip our ability to control, predict, avoid, contain, or prevent all possible negative interactions and consequences, and when things do go completely sideways failure does not go unnoticed. In terms of thinking about formal organizations and organizing, these issues may very well be the most important general focus. We constantly seek rationality via formalized controls even though many things cannot be brought under formally rationalized control. Thus an ultimate question we need to ask is whether or not the distinctive feature of the continual push toward more and more rationalization isn't better thought of as the inexorable march toward the potential for more and more *irrationality.*

The Rationalized World as Golem

Sociologists of science and technology Harry Collins and Trevor Pinch have a book series on science, technology and medicine that is centered on the metaphor of a golem.[10] A golem is a creature of Jewish mythology. You make it out of clay and then breathe life into it. It is thus a human creation that becomes a new actor in the world. A golem can be particularly useful because they are very powerful creatures that will do your bidding. The problem is that they can also be quite dangerous because they tend to be rather clumsy, not terribly smart and are difficult to control. Their power can be unleashed in very destructive ways even without any intent on anyone's part to do harm. They are, in other words, *recalcitrant tools* to use one descriptor that Philip Selznick applied to organizations (Chapter 8).

In addition to science, technology, and medicine, this is a reasonably good way to think about formal organizations, and not merely in the singular—as golem—but also in the plural—as glamim, tied together into various kinds of larger level systems that make up society. Recall that the organizational revolution not only increased the size and complexity of individual organizations but also created greater interdependencies between them (Chapter 2). This increased complexity and coupling has only continued in important respects, and was accelerated by the post-1970s trends discussed in Chapter 6. Companies became more likely to source their needs from others, creating political economies that are more and more like webs of interdependencies among different organizations. Throughout the entire global economy those interdependencies operate by the strategies of *just-in-time (JIT)* production and inventory management principles, which explicitly reduces all slack possible in systems and thus more tightly couples them. Much of this is enabled and managed by the growing power of computing and information technologies. The spread of written bureaucratic rules as observed by Max Weber is increasingly done by the spread of invisible algorithmic rules pulsing through information and communications technologies and their networks. This not only continues to increase the degree of formal rationalization of human action but also simultaneously allows our webs of social and economic relations to effortlessly cross the entire globe creating more complexity. At the same time it increases coupling as information and the consequences of events produce system-wide effects at near the speed of light. As such, the increasing degree of complexity and coupling applies to organizations in the singular, but also to our larger interconnected global systems. At this point in time, conditions for most people on the planet are entangled with the workings of a highly interconnected global political-economy, and the potential for small issues to lead to *cascading failures*, as they're called, has increased in many important respects.

At the center of that global system of political economy is a system of finance which by most accounts is highly complex and very tightly coupled, and thus constantly ripe for events that fit the profile of the *normal accident*. The 2008 global financial crisis, where disruptions in one sector of the home loan market in the United States rapidly created a global crisis in banking and finance, has been analyzed in just such a way. And the same had already been done about 15 years prior with regards to a savings and loan banking crisis in the 1980s. Although Charles Perrow denied that the 2008 crisis counted as a normal accident, seeing self-interested and reckless risk-taking and malfeasance at its core instead, in a 2010 interview he did say that the financial system is more complex than nuclear plants upon which the Normal Accidents

---

[10]Collins and Pinch, 1998a; 1998b; 2005.

Theory (NAT) was initially based. Years after the 2008 crisis, sociologist Mauro Guillén did a more complete analysis of the global system of political economy characterizing it as an *architecture of collapse*, which gave his book its title.[11]

Guillén's account has a more holistic view than the global financial system alone as that lies at the core of larger sets of tightly interconnected global economic, political, and social systems and subsystems. At the level of countries—the nodes in global networks in Guillén's analysis—we have witnessed both increasing complexity and coupling. The spread of democratic forms of rule, for example, have made political and administrative actions within countries more complicated, while things like ever-increasing degrees of urbanization have made populations and many social issues much more tightly connected to each other. Economically speaking, industrial structures have become more and more diversified increasing economic complexity and that can be an economic strength. But growing levels of government debts resulting from a myriad of issues increases coupling in the sense that states have fewer and fewer options in dealing with disruptions and crises, whether those stem from economic sources or not.

These increases in complexity and coupling at the node level have also occurred at the level of the entire network of the global political economy. Especially since the 1980s a number of things have come together to increase global complexity. The sheer number of countries involved in the global political economy, as measured by things like membership in the United Nations or the International Monetary Fund, has increased greatly as have levels of global trade, cross-border economic investments, global migration (including of refugees) and tourism, and flows of information. One of the key things that has simultaneously increased coupling is the reliance on supply chains that stretch around the entire globe and rely on the JIT systems noted above. Our ability to access many everyday things from computers to cars to clothing to just about anything made of plastic and so forth are daily dependent on the smooth flow of goods around the planet and disturbances in one area can easily reverberate around the planet.

The most recent set of events to vividly expose many of these issues, and to have been flagged as understandable through Normal Accidents Theory, is likely the global coronavirus pandemic and its other derivative crises that emerged in late 2019-early 2020[12]—events that continue to unfold as of this writing. The constant flow of people around the globe is what allowed a new virus that appeared on one part of the planet—really just one market in Wuhan, China—to spread very rapidly and unpredictably around the globe. The resulting and later unfolding effects on workers and on consumer demands then collided very uncomfortably with JIT production and inventory management strategies. With regards to the pandemic effects, for many people in the United States this was perhaps most directly experienced early on as shortages of things like toilet paper and cleaning supplies. As we know, the idea in JIT is to more or less have everything operate as a continuous flow system. You never want to have too much slack in your systems and need to

---

[11]On the question of 2008 see Cebon (2009), Palmer and Maher (2010a; 2010b), Guillén and Suarez (2010) and Perrow (2008). The savings and loan analysis is in Mezias (1994). Perrow's interview comments are from Harford (2011), cited in Clearfield and Tilcsik (2018: 40). On the later, larger analysis see Guillén, 2015).

[12]See, e.g., Tomaskovic-Devey, 2020 and Roberts, 2020.

keep production capacity (*capacity utilization*) matched up as well as possible with predicted levels of demand, so as to avoid the costs of having to hold excess inventory. You provide supplies *just in time* to meet existing demand. Thus when demand for things like toilet paper, cleaning supplies, and personal protective equipment suddenly soared, there was no place from which to pull extra capacity.

Less noticeable, unless maybe you were trying to buy new car, was that automakers around the world had to cut or even halt auto production due to a computer chip shortage from Asian suppliers. Those same chip problems also created problems with regards to a surge in demand for electronics as many people became more reliant on working from home. Part of the reason for the chip shortage is from production slowdowns due to virus related restrictions and illness on the part of workers. But another was a sudden increase in market unpredictability (*environmental turbulence*). When it first became clear that the globe faced a dangerous pandemic auto makers cut orders for chips assuming a dip in demand. The dip occurred but was short lived, and when demand increased again it did so much faster than the ability to bring chip production back online.

But even in areas where production may have been able to keep up with demand, shipping things to where they needed to be became a large problem as well. Many of the world's main shipping ports had their operations disrupted, and this certainly includes those in China which is central to the global supply chains. Virus related lockdowns significantly slowed operations as did illness and/or quarantining among port workers, the need to follow virus related safety precautions, and difficulties in finding workers when needed. The shipping port disruptions went on to snarl shipping all over the globe on both land and sea. At the outset of the pandemic, consumer demand for many things dropped and global shipping companies cut back on their regular routes. But by the summer of 2020 demand surged, partly aided by governmental economic stimulus programs. At the same time, much of the demand surge was in online shopping rather than at stores so more shipping needs to be done even than normal. The demand was also shifted away from services (like eating out and travel) and more toward goods which have a much higher level of dependence on reliable shipping for everything from raw materials to the finished goods. Many of the shipping containers needed to move goods around were not where they needed to be, so that caused shipping delays. Labor shortages at ports persisted even while the volume of goods moving around was increasing. Major ports had backups of ships needing to be unloaded, containers piled up in the way at ports further slowing down operations, and that was only for shipments where shipping containers that could be found.

The labor shortages that hit ports also hit the trucking and warehousing industries in many places which slowed down domestic transportation and distribution even further. Those slowdowns just exacerbated the issue for many domestic shippers and contributed to the congestion at many ports. The demand for shipping containers to load up goods in China was so high, and domestic shipping so significantly slowed that shipping containers, normally sent back out of the United States loaded, were going back to Asian ports empty.

Some unrelated and unexpected events fed into supply issues as well. In February of 2021 an uncharacteristically severe winter storm in Texas caused massive power outages—themselves worthy of a Normal Accidents analysis—leading to an extended shutdown of major petrochemical plants, and feeding into global shortages of supplies for plastics production. In March of 2021 a large container ship became stuck in the Suez Canal—a very busy and crucial shipping passage between Europe and Asia—for almost a week, halting a good deal of shipping traffic. All of this adds up to widespread global shortage of goods and price increases across a huge array of products from cars and electronics to heavy equipment, various food items, building supplies, bottles and cans, anything made of plastic and so on. A June 2021 *New York Times* article title put it quite succinctly: "How the World Ran Out of Everything."[13]

Of course, periods of crisis also bring to light how well things work much of the time, at least with regards to those who benefit from a system in question. Normal accidents weren't named "normal" because they occur frequently, but only because they should be seen as a normal property of the systems rather than as exceptions. At the heart of making so many things work in large, interconnected global systems is *formal rationality* itself whether instituted in traditional bureaucratic or technological form. Over the course of the last century and a half or so we have brought a lot of it into the world, and we continue to do so. And like glamim, the systems that have been built are incredibly powerful. However, also like glamim they can be rather unpredictable at times, clumsy, difficult to control, and disaster prone. The issues associated with bounded rationality obviously loom large. In sufficiently complex systems it becomes impossible to imagine all of the different kinds of things that can go wrong. And when they do go wrong, it can be very difficult to understand just what is happening. If we add in tight coupling, then when problems do occur their effects propagate so quickly that there is little time to figure things out and decide on the best courses of action. We have truly come to depend on systems that escape our ability to fully comprehend and control. In the end, we have created and come to rely on a great deal of formal rationality. But this does not necessarily mean that we created a lot of *rationality*.

SOURCES AND FURTHER READING

Some of the standard "classics" cited as the roots of the **contingency theory tradition**:

- Burns, Tom, and G. M. Stalker. 1961. *The Management of Innovation.* London: Tavistock.

- Lawrence, Paul R., and Jay William Lorsch. 1967a. *Organization and Environment: Managing Differentiation and Integration.* Boston, MA: Division of Research, Graduate School of Business Administration, Harvard University.

o What amounts to a paper-length synopsis: ———. 1967b. "Differentiation and Integration in Complex Organizations." *Administrative Science Quarterly* 12: 1–47.

- Mintzberg, Henry. 1979. *The Structuring of Organizations.* Upper Saddle River, NJ: Prentice Hall.

- ———. 1983. *Structure in Fives: Designing Effective Organizations.* Englewood Cliffs, NJ: Prentice-Hall.

[13]Goodman and Chokshi, 2021.

- Perrow, Charles. 1967. "A Framework for the Comparative Analysis of Organizations." *American Sociological Review* 32: 194–208.

- Woodward, Joan. 1958. *Management and Technology: Problems and Progress in Technology, Vol. 3.* London: HMSO.

- ———. 1965. *Technology and Organization.* New York, NY: Oxford University Press.

For ***more contemporary*** commentary, development, application and so forth in the ***contingency tradition***:

- Ali, Muhammad, and Mehmet Abdülkadir Varoğlu. 2021. "Revisiting the Mintzberg, Lawrence, and Lorsch Theories about Organisational Structure, Strategy, and Environmental Dynamism from the Perspective of Small Firms." *Technology Analysis & Strategic Management.* doi: 10.1080/09537325.2021.1880003.

- Battilana, Julie, and Tiziana Casciaro. 2012. "Change Agents, Networks and Institutions: A Contingency Theory of Organizational Change." *Academy of Management Journal* 55: 381–98.

- Burton, Richard M., Børge Obel, and Dorthe D. Håkonsson. 2015. *Organizational Design: A Step-By-Step Approach.* New York, NY: Cambridge University Press.

- Donaldson, Lex. 2001. *The Contingency Theory of Organizations.* Thousand Oaks, CA: Sage.

- ———. 2006. "The Contingency Theory of Organizational Design: Challenges and Opportunities." In Burton Richard M., Dorthe Døjbak Håkonsson, Bo Eriksen, and Charles C. Snow, eds. *Organization Design. Information and Organization Design Series, vol 6,* 19–40. Boston, MA: Springer.

- ———. 2010. *The Meta-Analytic Organization: Introducing Statistico-Organizational Theory.* Armonk, NY: M. E. Sharpe.

- Klein, Lisl. 2006. "Joan Woodward Memorial Lecture Applied Social Science: Is It Just Common Sense?" *Human Relations* 59: 1155–72.

- McAdam, Rodney, Kristel Miller, and Carmel McSorley. 2019. "Towards a Contingency Theory Perspective of Quality Management in Enabling Strategic Alignment." *International Journal of Production Economics* 207: 195–209.

- Meyer, Alan D., Anne S. Tsui, and C.R. Hinings. 1993. "Configurational Approaches to Organizational Analysis." *Academy of Management Journal* 36: 1175–95.

- Qiu, Jane X. J., Ben Nanfeng Luo, Chris Jackson, and Karin Sanders, eds. 2017. *Advancing Organizational Theory in a Complex World.* New York, NY: Routledge.

- Siggelkow, Nicolaj, and Jan W. Rivkin. 2005. "Speed and Search: Designing Organizations for Turbulence and Complexity." *Organizational Science* 16: 101–22.

- Van de Ven, Andrew H., Martin Ganco, and C. R. Hinings. 2013. "Returning to the Frontier of Contingency Theory of Organizational and Institutional Designs." *The Academy of Management Annals* 7: 393–440.

- Verburg, Robert M., Deanne N. Den Hartog, and Paul L. Koopman. 2007. "Configurations of Human Resource Management Practices: A Model and Test of Internal Fit." *The International Journal of Human Resource Management.* 18: 184–208.

- Volberda, Henk W., Niels van der Weerdt, Ernst Verwaal, Marten Stienstra, and Antonio J. Verdu. 2012. "Contingency Fit, Institutional Fit, and Firm Performance: A Metafit Approach to Organization–Environment Relationships." *Organizational Science* 23: 1040–54.

Works cited generally with regards to the *classification of the contingency tradition*:

- Davis, Gerald F. 2009. "The Rise and Fall of Finance and the End of the Society of Organizations." *Academy of Management Perspectives* 23: 27–44.

- Handel, Michael J., ed. 2003. *The Sociology of Organizations: Classic, Contemporary, and Critical Readings*. Thousand Oaks, CA: Sage Publications.

- Morgan, Gareth. 2006. *Images of Organization*, Updated Edition. Thousand Oaks, CA: Sage Publications.

- Perrow, Charles. 2002. *Organizing America: Wealth, Power, and the Origins of Corporate Capitalism*. Princeton, NJ: Princeton University Press.

- Scott, W. Richard, and Gerald F. Davis. 2007. *Organizations and Organizing: Rational, Natural, and Open Systems*. Upper Saddle River, NJ: Pearson/Prentice Hall.

On the *Golem* metaphor and book series:

- Collins, Harry, and Trevor Pinch. 1998a. *The Golem: What You Should Know About Science, 2nd Ed.* New York, NY: Cambridge University Press.

- _____. 1998b. *The Golem At Large: What You Should Know About Technology*. New York, NY: Cambridge University Press.

- _____. 2005. *Dr. Golem: How to Think About Medicine*. Chicago: The University of Chicago Press.

On *global complexity and coupling* and the *accident prone* nature of the global system:

- Cebon, Peter. 2009. "Innovating Our Way to a Meltdown: To Understand the Financial Crisis, View It as a Systems Accident." *MIT Sloan Management Review.* 50: 13–15.

- Clearfield, Chris, and András Tilcsik. 2018. *Meltdown: Why Our Systems Fail and What We Can Do About It*. New York, NY: Allen Lane/Penguin Random House.

- Guillén, Mauro F., and Sandra L. Suárez. 2010. "The Global Crisis of 2007–2009: Markets, Politics, and Organizations." In *Markets on Trial: The Economic Sociology of the U.S. Financial Crisis (Research in the Sociology of Organizations, vol. 30, Part A)*, 257–279, edited by Michael Lounsbury and Paul M. Hirsch. Bingley, UK: Emerald Books.

- Guillén, Mauro F. 2015. *The Architecture of Collapse: The Global System in the Twenty-first Century.* New York, NY: Oxford University Press.

- Harford, Tim. 2011. *Adapt: Why Success Always Starts with Failure*. New York, NY: Farrar, Straus, and Giroux.

- Mezias, Stephen J. 1994. "Financial Meltdown as Normal Accident: The Case of the American Savings and Loan Industry." *Accounting, Organizations and Society.* 19: 181–92.

- Palmer, Donald, and Michael W. Maher. 2010a. "A Normal Accident Analysis of the Mortgage Meltdown." In *Markets on Trial: The Economic Sociology of the U.S. Financial Crisis (Research in the*

Sociology of Organizations, vol. 30, Part A), edited by Michael Lounsbury and Paul M. Hirsch. Bingley: Emerald Books.

o   See also: Palmer, Donald, and Michael W. Maher. 2010b. "The Mortgage Meltdown as Normal Accidental Wrongdoing." *Strategic Organization.* 8: 83–91.

•   _____. 2010. "The Meltdown Was Not An Accident." In *Markets on Trial: The Economic Sociology of the U.S. Financial Crisis (Research in the Sociology of Organizations, vol. 30, Part A)*, 309–30, edited by Michael Lounsbury and Paul M. Hirsch. Bingley: Emerald Books.

o   *(This is a response to Palmer and Maher (2010a)).*

To the best of my knowledge no complete analysis of the **COVID-19 pandemic** with regards to Normal Accidents Theory has been published. Explicit suggestions that it applies can be found in Tomaskovic-Devey (2020) and Roberts (2020). Those and other sources in my brief (and largely only suggestive) commentary:

•   Goodman, Peter S. and Niraj Chokshi. 2021. "How the World Ran Out of Everything." June 1. https://www.nytimes.com/2021/06/01/business/coronavirus-global-shortages.html, Retrieved 7/20/2021.

•   Matthews, Christopher M., Austen Hofford, and Collin Eaton. 2021. "Texas Freeze Triggers Global Plastics Shortage." *The Wall Street Journal.* March 17. https://www.wsj.com/articles/one-week-texas-freeze-seen-triggering-monthslong-plastics-shortage-11615973401. Retrieved 3/17/2021.

•   Remes, Jaana, and Sajal Kohli. 2021. "Shortages of everyday products have become the new normal. Why they won't end soon." *Barron's.* September 14. https://www.mckinsey.com/mgi/overview/in-the-news/shortages-of-everyday-products-have-become-the-new-normal-why-they-wont-end-soon. Retrieved 9/14/2021.

•   Roberts, Anthea. 2020. "How Globalization Came to the Brink of Collapse." *Barron's.* April 2. https://www.barrons.com/articles/how-globalization-came-to-the-brink-of-collapse-51585865909. Retrieved 9/13/2021.

•   Sajjad, Aymen. 2020. "The COVID-19 Pandemic, Social Sustainability and Global Supply Chain Resilience: A Review." *Corporate Governance.* 21: 1142–54.

•   Sizov, Pavel, and Zinaida Khmelnitskaya. 2021. "Supply Chain Management in a Global Pandemic." *E3S Web of Conferences.* 291: 07006. https://doi.org/10.1051/e3sconf/202129107006. Retrieved 10/6/2021.

•   Tomaskovic-Devey, Donald. 2020. "The COVID-19 Pandemic: Normal Accidents and Cascading System Failures." *ASA Footnotes.* 48: 25–6.

•   Vakil, Bindiya. 2021. "The Latest Supply Chain Disruption: Plastics." *Harvard Business Review.* March 26. https://hbr.org/2021/03/the-latest-supply-chain-disruption-plastics. Retrieved 8/10/2021.

Final Reflections
LIVING WITH ORGANIZATIONS

Human beings have spent most of their time on the planet without living in a global web of formally rationalized systems. In the grand scheme of things, the state of affairs is strikingly new and most would probably say for the better. Yet even if one decided that it not all for the better, there is no turning back the clock. Our daily lives depend on the smooth operation of the *Glamim* (*Golem* in the plural, as you'll recall). Our systems are very powerful, and this is both for our good and our detriment. In using the Glamim metaphor, I am certainly not saying anything new. The idea that formal organizations are simultaneously empowering and useful but also problematic and even dangerous goes all the way back to Max Weber's initial observations, and it is present in virtually all introductions to and discussions of bureaucracy and formal rationalization. On the whole, it is easy to recognize the benefits of the bureaucratic form of organization and the formal rationality that defines and animates it. It can and often does bring all manner of efficiency, predictability, and calculability that provide various benefits to people. Even some of the things that are often counted as drawbacks of formal rationalization, such as its impersonality where people become cogs, numbers and lines on their résumés, carry elements that most find desirable, such as "equality before the law." We like to know, for example, that people get hired for jobs because they are technically the best, not because they are someone's nephew or have the "right" colored skin. Technical merit is only biased toward performance, and we like that because it is fair and functional.

Similarly, the proliferation of rules can certainly have its dark side when life does come to feel like so much *red tape* and hemming in by the iron cage rather than the ability to make our own choices according to our own values, needs, preferences, and will. But on the other hand, people also like knowing how things work and what is expected of them in various situations. They like to know the rules of the game and often like the authority that comes with it—to know not only who is in charge, but that someone *is* actually in charge. It provides order and certainty. This certainly applies to schools and workplaces. My students, for example, constantly ask me for more "bureaucracy" in the sense that they want their tasks laid out very clearly for them so that they know exactly what to do. They actually want more rules. (I resist this because it generally produces *goal displacement* where the question isn't "how do I learn?" but "how do I get the points?") In his description of these processes as the *McDonaldization* of society, George Ritzer notes that many people find the iron cage of rationality to be a *velvet cage*, where all of the predictability and calculability is comforting.[1]

The fact that organizational characteristics contain these simultaneous contradictions is so much a matter of discussion and interest that there is now a research tradition, generally referred to as *Organizational Paradox Theory (OPT)*, that focuses on at least some aspects of this very thing. OPT is less of a particular, specifiable theory than a basic orientation to the various paradoxes that come with formal organization. Organizations need to be innovative and adaptive at the same time that they have to maintain stability and order, for example. They also have to accomplish their own ends while also allowing participants to accomplish theirs, even where those ends might be different or even conflict with each other. They frequently need to produce both collaboration and competition. In the interests of operating on the basis of technical competence, they need to maintain impersonality, yet this can produce dehumanization that detracts from getting the best out of people.

OPT is often presented as a move beyond *contingency theory* (Chapter 11), which is seen to have been about making appropriate choices between poles. For example, *mechanistic organizations* emphasize control and stability, while *organic organizations* emphasize innovation and change and there is basically a correct direction to take based on the contingencies faced by the organization, or organizational division. The OPT approach is to take these tensions as simply being normal and unavoidable issues of organizing rather than either/or choices. You can't do away with the paradoxes, so you learn how to manage and even leverage them for the benefit of the organization. This all makes perfect sense as these paradoxes are likely somewhat inevitable and in the nature of organizing. And since our organizations are crucial to our existence, organizational research oriented toward learning of the ups and downs of organizing and how to best control them is valuable. Indeed this has been the dominant orientation or organizational studies all along.

There are also dangers in this orientation, however. For one thing, as has been pointed out in several places throughout the book (see especially Chapters 5, 7, and 8), in asking how to make organizations better tools for human action, we often end up taking on the perspective of organizational elites. This was especially evident in the development of *Classical Management Theory (CMT)* all the way from its beginnings with the likes of Frederick Taylor on through its morphing into *Human Relations* and *Humanistic Management*, whereby we begin to care about the humans in the system, but mostly to better manipulate them as means to ends ultimately defined by management. This orientation does not apply to the entirety of work that falls under the vast umbrella of organizational studies and is generally not the explicit focus or purpose of research activities. It just follows from a frequent narrow focus on the question of organizational efficacy, where ends are set by some combination of *structural interests* and the preferences of organizational elites. Questions about organizational effectiveness are important. But they are still questions about means and not about ends.

An intertwined issue is highlighted well by OPT and has to do with questioning just what kinds of organizational processes have been and continue to be built into the world. Brushing aside contingency thinking and taking various

---

[1]Ritzer (2019: 199).

organizational characteristics as inevitabilities tends to turn them into constants and thus does lose sight of important things. This is at least partly because, while there may be some inevitabilities, there is still a great deal of variation in the extent to which different characteristics of formal organizations manifest themselves. Take for example the tension between the centralization and decentralization of authority. As we saw in Chapter 11, some organizational contingencies call out for more centralization of authority and rationalized control while other contingencies call for less. Through the lens of contingency thinking, this recognition doesn't lead to the conclusion that the tension between the need for centralization and decentralization disappears once an organization takes the form best suited to its circumstances. Rather it just means that it performs better than if it doesn't have an appropriate balance. The tensions may very well still remain in some respects. But it also allows us to think about how different organizational conditions can impose certain social relations.

As we saw with organizations that build and operate systems that are highly complex and tightly coupled, there is a heightened contradiction and tension between centralization and decentralization. The oversight of tightly coupled systems requires centralized authority and decision-making because coordination is needed from organizational positions that are able to provide a system-wide view. However, in order to deal with the complexity, the organization simultaneously needs to be decentralized so that specialized expertise can be put to use when and where it is needed. Centralized leadership often lacks the requisite expertise to adequately grapple with all aspects of the system, while specialized operatives lack the system-wide view that allows seeing the whole. So while this tension between centralization and decentralization might just be an inevitable tension in most or even all organizations, its salience and intensity depend on what kinds of systems we build. This is an issue that it is best to not lose sight of. It is one for which contingency thinking remains useful and was certainly one that did interest Charles Perrow in his work on Normal Accidents. One of his conclusions was that there may just be some kinds of systems that we should avoid building altogether, if at all possible. But in the largest sense of all, for at least some things and in some respects, it might be too late.

This is because early on during the organizational revolution, a path was laid down that generally favored organizational systems that were very large, complex, and tightly coupled. As we have seen, this tendency has not slowed. During much of the nineteenth century the economic and political lives of people were largely shaped at the local level. By comparison to today, political and economic units remained fairly small, simple, and loosely coupled. Throughout the organizational revolution and beyond, economic and political organization went increasingly regional, then national, and is now very much globalized. This has ushered in highly centralized forms of social power along with the propensity for crisis. However, our dominant ideas about how economic and political life work—or at least *should* work—are still stuck in the prerevolutionary nineteenth century leading to what may be the greatest paradox requiring our attention.

The Greatest Paradox?

Early on in our journey—in Chapter 2—we came across the basic roots of concern over what may be one of our most fateful paradoxes of rationalization and formal organization, and thus of our current times. It involves Robert Michels' concerns over the prospects for mass democracy. As initially discussed in Chapter 2, we live in a culture whose basic values were shaped during an intellectual period called the *Enlightenment*. At its core was a faith in the ability of humans to use human reason to intelligently shape our world into what we want it to be. Thus the Enlightenment is also known as the *Age of Reason*. Processes of formal rationalization that lay at the heart of the organizational revolution share that spirit and faith in some respects. The amazing capabilities that were developed through the First and Second Industrial Revolutions were a reflection of that—the purposeful application of our intelligence to master our world (including other people wherever that was relevant).

At the same time, the Enlightenment was very much a reaction against older ideas of social order based in beliefs about natural inequalities among classes of people. In the old aristocracies of Europe only certain hereditary lines of people were understood to be capable of intelligently exercising power—of reason we might say. But in the new age of Enlightenment, everyone was made equal because everyone possesses the capacity to use reason. This provides the basis for what came to be a philosophy of political philosophy called *Liberalism*, now often referred to as *Classical Liberalism* to distinguish it from present day connotations which are related but very narrow. Recall from Chapter 2 that *liber* is from the Latin for *free*, so Liberalism simply means "freedom-ism." It is a philosophy of political economy that values the maximization of liberty and self-determination at the level of each individual. It is the equivalent of valuing "power to the people"—or just *democracy*. In matters of political life (Political power), it means that we all have the same basic civil rights—to speech, press, religion, and the like (Ideological power). And it means that governance is not only limited, but also done according to our wishes by representatives elected for that purpose. As much as we are governed by a system of laws, they apply *equally* to *all*, and "we the people" are ultimately the governors of the governors (Political power). In matters of economic life (Economic power), it is similar. We decide what to demand and what to supply in the economy according to our own wishes as opposed to receiving commands from some centralized authority. Across the board, we are able to participate in determining the conditions under which we live our own lives.

It is a very attractive value system and one to which I myself adhere—at least in terms of ideal values. Who doesn't want the power of self-determination? I am largely antiauthoritarian and seek as much self-determination as possible. In *value* terms, I am a Liberal in the classical sense (and rather *Libertarian* in the contemporary classification sense). I don't want to be ordered around and subject to the will of others. I want political and economic liberties that allow me to be able to participate in determining the conditions under which I live my own life. This also means that I want some bureaucracy because I want my liberties protected by laws and stable organizations for overseeing them. I want to live under the rule of rules, not of persons, or even of a "majority." In that respect, I must also be a fan of formal rationality which I am to a degree. But there are kinks in the works.

Technocracy Versus Democracy

One direct kink, which is likely inevitable to some extent, is that formal organizations and all of their efficiency, predictability, and calculability are predicated on *technocracy*—rule by technical expertise—which is quite at odds with *democracy*. Put somewhat wryly by Political Scientist of technology Langdon Winner,

> *Whatever claims one may wish to make on behalf of liberty, justice, or equality can be immediately neutralized when confronted with arguments to the effect: "Fine, but that's no way to run a railroad" (or steel mill, or airline, or communications system, and so on).*[2]

In other words, there is no room for "the people" in running complicated systems because in order to function well they require cold, hard expertise. "Opinions" and "values" will not do in the face of the need for efficient time schedules and well-planned coordination of all of the different functions. Winner's focus was not on formal organizations *per se*, but rather on technological systems. However, we have already seen that there is not much of a real distinction to make there. Technological systems and formal organizations are heads and tails of one another and are largely cut from the same cloth of the formal rationalization of human action. It also just so happens that in saying this Winner was partly in the midst of a critique of Alfred Chandler's argument regarding the fact that the new technological systems of the turn of the twentieth century, such as rail systems, necessitated control by a *visible hand* of management (Chapter 4). Recall that the foil for this was the *invisible hand* of the market where everyone is making their own choices. Rather than freedom of choice on the ground, the stuff of "modern" life would instead require the organized direction (domination) of the many by the few. "The system must be first," as Frederick Taylor wrote in his 1911 book *The Principles of Scientific Management*,[3] and managerial and technical expertise must rule the day. In many respects, then, by the turn of the twentieth century, the old European aristocracies were not being replaced by equality, democracy, and individual liberty as our ideals have it. Rather formal organizations would bring into the world a new aristocracy consisting, at least in part, of technocrats—trained experts.

Perhaps fatefully, by the time the *organizational revolution* and its technocratic needs were coming to the fore, the Liberal impulse was already in full swing in the United States, and was expanding. Initially the individual rights of the Liberal society of the United States only applied to property-owning white males—people who were already relatively powerful in economic, political, and often ideological terms. Eventually, the property ownership criterion fell by the wayside, followed the criteria of race/ethnicity and gender. Similar trends, in fits and starts, were simultaneously taking hold throughout Europe. And thus there were two conflicting trends at the same time. One was the growth and spread of large formal organizations that were centralizing power and control. Some of that control was technocratic. But, of course, the technocrats were often merely the employees—the technical instruments—of economic elites who were busy centralizing control over economic power resources via the growth of *Big Business*.

A second trend was the growth and spread of mass democracy which, in many respects, merely threw more fuel on the fire. As Robert Michels'

---

[2]Winner (1980: 133).
[3]P. 7.

observed, mass democracy is impossible without formal organizations as a means of coordination. Additionally in the face of the intense concentration of economic power that came with the growth of big business, how else would "the people" gain any true power except through their own countering organizations, such as labor unions and certain kinds of political parties? This was the very subject of Michels' 1911 book *Political Parties* (see Chapter 2). As we learned from Michels', the very tools that might allow "the people" into mass democracy come to defeat democracy via the *iron law of oligarchy.* Some of the reasons are, of course, technocratic ones. Running large organizations such as labor unions and political parties is very difficult and requires the development of all manner of knowledge and skills that are neither possessed by nor understood by the masses. Democratic ideals are turned into so much symbolic fodder for organizational elites to use in whipping up support among followers. To use Philip Selznick's term (Chapter 8), these ideals become *sustaining myths.* They don't reflect actual reality, but they are put forward on *organizational front stages* to maintain legitimacy and support.

Hitler's Shadow?

The recognition of this paradoxical historical confluence by now has a long history. Sociologist Karl Mannheim, writing *in Hitler's shadow,*[4] placed it at the center of the extreme "Modern" crises of the early part of the twentieth century. The Enlightenment had seemingly set us on a path of the application of human reason to learn how to produce the "good society." Yet a little more than a century into the new age of "Enlightened progress," we ran straight into World War I, followed by the Great Depression, the rise of Hitler, Fascism and the Holocaust, along with World War II. It was a strange and crisis-ridden episode in Western history which does not at all look like the culmination of the application of Enlightenment Reason to make progress.

Mannheim was a German sociologist who was grappling with understanding the crises of the period. His book *Man and Society in the Age of Reconstruction* was first published in German in 1935 (two years after Hitler was appointed German Chancellor), and translated to English in 1940. In it he argues that the ills of the modern age could be traced to the two basic trends of the spread of mass democratization and the growing concentration of power in and interdependence between the large bureaucracies of society. The growth and interdependence of organizations left us much more vulnerable to various kinds of crises. But it also left us politically that much more incapable of dealing with them.

The economic, political, and military machineries of the early twentieth century were not only increasing the complexity of how the world works, but also *de facto* removing any real power from the level of individuals on the ground. The main decision-making ability for serious matters of the political economy fall into the hands of what C. Wright Mills eventually called the *power elite* (also Chapter 2). The conditions that affect our lives are more and more shaped by forces that we do not have a chance to participate in, and can no longer see or comprehend. The ability of the average person on the street to be able to know and understand what is going on so that they may be able to

---

[4]To borrow a rather provocative chapter title from Randall Collins and Michael Makowsky (2010): Ch. 13.

exercise Reason with regard to political and economic decision-making is completely outstripped. People more and more realize that they don't truly understand what is going on, and don't have much of an ability to control it.

There follows a growing appeal to leaders who do profess to know and seem to be able to do something about it. And since the masses lack any real way to gain insight into the dynamics of our political and economic machineries, and leaders do require their support especially in terms of electoral politics, politics comes to be reduced to *demagoguery*—the appeal to people's sentiments and emotions rather than to their Reason in matters of political economy. Simplistic, "common sense" answers and appeal to ideals come to substitute for informed and reasoned insight. It becomes Michels' iron law of oligarchy writ large, and this is the very thing that opens the door for mass dictatorship such as that which we saw with the likes of Hitler. Our means (the expansion of formal organization) and our ends (those of Classical Liberalism) had been running at cross-purposes—and they continue to do so.

One could hope that power elites, since they do possess a good deal of power over organizations, would act responsibly in the public interest and for the best of all; that they remain, for example, democratically responsive. But we can't forget the kinks there either, clearly elucidated by the likes of Michels and later Selznick. In the end, organizational elites will come to be primarily driven by the *structural interests* of the organizations that they oversee. Often by necessity, they tend to act in the interests of the organization itself, even if those actions run contrary to stated goals and ideals. This can easily be, and often is, on the basis of pure self-interest, and the arenas of power come to be ripe for opportunistic leaders who simply seek to advance their own interests. The ideals of Liberalism are reduced to sustaining myths that help to maintain the loyalties of the masses—merely so much ideological fodder for *demagogues*.

Reflecting on Mannheim's ultimate diagnosis of the times, sociologists Randall Collins and Michael Makowsky provide a particularly apt and concise summary:

> *Mannheim's theory comes down to this basic issue. Modern industrial society will necessarily consist of powerful, centralized bureaucracies, run by their elites. The only question is: Will it be an intelligent and humanistic elite or a shortsighted and irrational elite? Mannheim views advanced industrial society through the lenses of Weber's and Michels' theories, which see supposedly rational organizations blindly drifting, following the imperatives of their internal functioning regardless of their consequences for the larger society. Business corporations, government bureaucracies, political parties, the military, the police, all follow their own patterns of self-aggrandizement, regardless of the disasters they may lead us into. Thus, we come into the modern era of enormously concentrated social power, controlled by blind and irresponsible elites who cloak their irrationality with the outdated ideologies of liberalism. The result, says Mannheim, is bound to be crisis – economic depression, senseless war, domestic disillusionment, and panic.*[5]

---

[5] 2010: 209.

Mannheim was not simply complaining or expounding upon what would now often be called *Weberian pessimism*—a dark and dreary vision of the future where people are largely the powerless, nameless, and faceless masses whose lives hold no genuine meaning. Rather than giving in, he was on the search for what it might be best to do next. One of the alternatives to Liberal order and to Fascism that emerged during the crisis period was the Russian revolution, whereby people tried to institute a socialist order.[6] But there was no hope to be found there. Weber had already predicted that any such move would result in a larger bureaucratic nightmare than was to be found in societies remaining with Liberal ideals—and so it was. But things were not going fabulously well in the Russian experiment in any case. What Mannheim saw was that neither the development of Liberal nor Socialist ideas were in any way in line with the realities of the time. They were systems of social thought founded on the basis of eighteenth- and nineteenth-century social realities. Of the two, Liberalism was the most out of touch with the times resting, as it did, in the assumption that power could be located at the level of the will of individuals. This actually did make sense early on in the development of capitalism and industrialization when economic and political units were relatively small and localized. So the idea wasn't that Liberalism was "wrong." There was a time when it was workable and relevant, but the ideas no longer applied to social realities by around the turn of the twentieth century and after.

Mannheim's hope, which will likely sound a little bit scary because it is, is that a new elite might be able to arise—an elite that was trained in social science and understood the complexities along with the promise and the perils of our modern, complex sociotechnical machineries. The scary part would be having something of a dictatorship of technocrats, but to Mannheim in important respects, this was already the state of affairs. By values he was basically a Liberal, but he understood that the social world to which Liberal values were relevant was long gone. So given that technocracy was already the rule, he argued that we just needed a different kind of technocratic elite.

As much as Mannheim's technocratic elitism seems contrary to Liberal values, in another respect, he was also simply expressing other aspects of the Enlightenment spirit. One is simply that of having people gain their place in society based purely on their merits. Competence in terms of getting the job done best is the only thing that matters in terms of where one ends up in life, and who ends up being in charge of what. A second is the idea that we should use science to gain understandings of how the world works, and use that knowledge to make the "good society." This absolutely suggests the submission of the individual will to a higher authority—that of scientific Truth. This was actually Frederick Taylor's idea—that science rules over everyone, including even over the rulers (management). Of course, Taylor was an engineer, not a social scientist, so therein lies that problem. Something much closer to Mannheim's eventual position, in terms of the need to understand human needs and human societies first and foremost, was conceived a century earlier with what can be regarded as the first stirrings of formal Sociology. Working around the turn of the nineteenth century, French intellectual August Comte is sometimes called the "Father of Sociology" because he is credited as being the

---

[6]This was supposedly about instituting the ideas of Karl Marx. But contrary to many popular and even academic interpretations, Marx's dictum was also "power to the people" and not "power to the state" which is what the USSR became instead.

first who declared that the world needed a science of society. Comte's shadow was of the violent and bloody mess that was the French Revolution, and he argued that the world should be overseen by a hierarchy of scientific knowledge with Sociology as the "queen" of the sciences. It does represent a form of technocratic dictatorship, but for the likes of Comte and Mannheim, it was a depoliticized benign dictatorship—a *stateless state* as it would often be called today. Science ruled the day rather than the power interests of various elites.

Technocracy and Populist Resurgence

As Mannheim envisioned it, this state of affairs has never come about, although there has been and remains plenty of technocracy involved in governing. Our (post)industrialized Liberal societies rely on a great deal of specialized expertise and few would question that this continues to increase. The duly elected representatives of a Liberal democracy generally lack the needed expertise to grapple with many of society's issues, from how to handle problems of infrastructure, to public health issues, foreign policy, environmental and economic crises and so forth. Some issues, such as economic or public health crises, also frequently require rapid and decisive action to avert worse problems, just as with Normal Accidents. So expertise is constantly being fed into governance, and solely takes the lead in more and more regulatory and policy setting issues and arenas.

All along, some manner of social science has been involved in technocratic policy setting, but it has been dominated largely by the logic of economics where the thinking continues to be through basic Liberal principles heavily shaded by a value on *laissez-faire* ideas—by now a good century and half out of date. Thus not so much is different now from Mannheim's time and, as we come to see more and more clearly, feeding technocratic knowledge into ostensibly Liberal politics can easily stoke anger on the part of the general population. Through the latter part of the twentieth century and on into the early twenty-first, the Western Hemisphere in particular has seen the rise of highly influential *Populist* movements. The specific definition of populism can be a bit of a fuzzy target in social science discussions, but generally speaking, it is a form of engagement in politics where people see the world as divided into two opposing groups. On the one had there are "the people"—the rightful sovereigns of their own lives and of society—and on the other there is a corrupt elite that rules for its own benefit and power, trying to control "the people," and thwart their will and their wishes. Such movements bring the tension between technocracy and democracy directly into the political arena.

One interesting and not-so-savory characteristic of populism is that the idea of the people versus elites pretty much accounts for the bulk of the orientation. This means that leaders wishing to capitalize on these sentiments can fill out the picture with most any kind of political ideas that they wish. The incomprehensibility of the world means that you can't appeal to the rational side of people, but you can find all manner of symbolic ideas that lie close to the heart and thus move them with sentiments and emotions. This works particularly well if one stokes things like fear and a sense of injustice. As such, strong populist movements have arisen throughout the Liberal democracies of Western Europe and in the United States on both the political left and right. In US electoral politics of the early twentieth century, two leaders have frequently been referenced. One is Bernie Sanders, who declares himself to be a Socialist (which he is not, really) and thus he leverages sentiments on the political left. The other is Donald Trump, who largely leverages sentiments on the political right, and who rode a wave of those sentiments all the way to the presidency of the United States in 2016. While Trump lost the subsequent 2020 election, as of this writing, he continues to lead a popular mass movement of largely right-wing populist sentiment in a quest to potentially return to the presidency.

It is fairly easy to motivate the political left, as Sanders does, with images of a world characterized by radical economic inequality that stems from domination by economic elites acting in their own self-interests and using their economic power to control the political system. This all amounts to a clear violation of our Liberal values regarding equality and justice for all. Likewise, it is equally easy to stir up the sentiments of the political right with shrill warnings about political elites robbing people of their individual rights and liberties, while deflecting whatever economic concerns people have toward nationalist sentiments where "the nation" is the equivalent of "the people" who are under threat, not only by a global political and economic elite (e.g., "the globalists" and the Chinese), but also by some manner of "others," such as political opponents, immigrants and refugees (e.g., Latin American migrants).

Yet another unsavory characteristic of populism is that even while it so often feeds off of Liberal values, it turns against Liberalism itself, although that is not typically the way that those caught up in the movements think of it. Having lost faith in the basic system of political economy, and not really trying to grapple with its true complexities, populists often place their faith in strong and charismatic leaders who promise that they are *not* in cahoots with elites and know how to overcome them. In other words, there comes to be something of a craving for and promise of dictatorship—for a leader to gain control of the machinery and set things right on behalf of "the people."

As should be obvious by now, starting this discussion with Karl Mannheim writing *in Hitler's Shadow* was not a discussion of long ago. We remain in just about the same quandary and for the same fundamental reasons. National Socialism, as it came to be under Hitler, occurred as the organizational revolution was in full swing. While it was totalitarian and autocratic, it was at its roots basically a populist mass movement, complete with the Jews as scapegoats for Germany's problems and the promise to purify and make great the Nation on behalf of "the people" of Germany. This does not mean that I am currently predicting the rise of a new Hitler or of a new round of fascism emerging from Western Liberal democracies, although there is good reason to not leave it outside of the realm of distinct possibility. Many of today's populist movements carry the very same sentiments including direct adherence to Nazi principles. But populism has also been an unavoidable aspect of politics for at least the last century (if not just always and everywhere). It is an indispensable tool in vying for political power these days. It speaks to those who feel downtrodden, excluded, oppressed, powerless, confused, and so forth. In today's world this is not hard to find whether on the right or the left. And during times of disruption and crises, of which people continue to see plenty, it becomes more and more intense as it has recently.

The short story here is that we have not moved far beyond the quandary observed by the likes of Michels and Mannheim. The (post)modern world operates on an awful lot of formal rationality in large, complex, and interconnected systems where true political and economic power are highly concentrated. But people's minds remained gripped by the old Liberal values emerging from the Enlightenment. Yet those values are largely unrealizable given the structure of the political economy and come to serve as sustaining myths for populist movements in which emotions win out over reality. In our minds, we believe we should have some power over our own lives. But in the reality of today's world we mostly feel a sense of "terrified helplessness" as Mannheim put it,[7] and people's irrational and illiberal impulses become easy to stir up. The situation is not heartening.

An *Inevitable* Paradox or a Faustian Bargain?

It should be obvious by now that I am in most respects a Weberian pessimist. I don't think that the world is currently in a good place or on a good path, especially if one is interested in basic Enlightenment values of societies that work on the basis of the widespread empowerment of all and operating on the basis of the exercise of reason. Instead I see that things work on the basis of formal rationality rather than reason, and thus in ways that concentrate rather than decentralize social power. I think that Weber's predictions of a world governed by *formal* rather than *substantive* rationality were spot on. I similarly think that the observations and arguments of the likes of Michels, Mannheim, C. Wright Mills, and others of similar stripe best capture the state of things since the turn of the twentieth century. But unlike for some, my pessimism is not necessarily a hopeless one that would come from taking the current state of affairs to be inevitable. It would seem that Robert Michels did feel that way. He ended up on the faculty at an Italian University and eventually fell in behind Benito Mussolini's Fascist movement there. In other words, his pessimism was so great that he basically gave up in the face of the dominance of the iron cage.

I'll not follow Michels there, at least not all the way. I do think it is fair to say the basic paradox of the conflict between democracy and technocracy is inevitable to a degree, and for reasons well explained by Michels. However, I also think it is fair to argue that the intensity of the conflict can be dialed up or down depending on what kinds of organizational structures are built in the world. Increasing organizational size, complexity, and coupling all tend to centralize power and to call out for increased levels of technocracy. They also increase risks with regard to system accidents and other unintended consequences. These things all increased dramatically at the turn of the twentieth century with the organizational revolution and a pattern was set there that continues apace. This remains so even if we take changes of the post-1970s period into account. Organizations may have shifted form in important ways, but not in ways that have created less centralized forms of social power, or lower levels of systemic complexity. Quite to the contrary.

If we follow the logic of efficiency arguments such as those laid down by Alfred Chandler (Chapter 4) and at least some Post-Fordists (Chapter 6), then there are no further choices to be made. It is efficiency that inevitably delivers us our current state of affairs, and that is all for the best even regardless of whatever warts may have appeared. If that is the orientation, then there is nothing left to do but accept the inevitabilities and figure out how to grapple with them. Herein does lie the orientation of a healthy proportion of work in organizational studies, although that is frequently left implicit. In my read, if I thought that efficiency arguments were sound enough to explain organizational structures and dynamics, then I *would* be as pessimistic as Michels and

---

[7]Mannheim, [1935]1940, p. 59.

could simply finish up by saying that we are doomed. (Half of me does want to end that way...)

However, we might also do well to keep in mind the traditions of research, addressed most directly in Chapter 5, that present arguments and evidence that our organizational trajectory has been driven much more by power interests than by economic efficiencies. First, recall that efficiency questions cannot be value free unless one can first specify the ends. But ends are matters of values. Typical efficiency arguments operate from very narrow views regarding things like speed, output volumes, and reducing unit costs for each unit of a good or service that is produced. This narrow view also tends to deflect attention away from negative externalities, which just might interfere with the math. If stuff gets cheaper and more plentiful, then this is simply deemed as being good. It is apparently the only end worthy of consideration, and when you strip it down to its simplest form, that's pretty much the Chandlerian orientation.

But imagine that the "We" of the mid-nineteenth century were able to engage in a choice among our ultimate *ends*, while understanding that the chosen *means* might defeat some of our ends. To oversimplify the choice: (1) Do we want to maximize on cheap and plentiful goods and services by pursuing things like *economies of scale and scope* while accepting the associated *externalities of scale*, such as environmental degradation and inequalities of political power and wealth? This has to come with the specification that one *opportunity cost* will involve some significant degree of abandonment of our Liberal values. Or, (2) do we want to maximize on the ability to live up to our Liberal values in a way that reduces externalities to our natural environment and to the least powerful segments of our labor markets? In this latter case, it doesn't necessarily mean that we'd now all be poor. But an *opportunity cost* would likely be that all of our stuff probably couldn't be as cheap because with smaller and fewer negative externalities, more *real costs* would actually be included in prices. It is quite possible that history has delivered something of a *Faustian bargain*[8] in this regard, and the former path was taken.

The problem is that it technically wasn't a bargain. Options were potentially there and were subject to dispute, but the terms were not laid out on the table and subject to a vote. In essence, especially if we follow the argument of sociologists such as William Roy and Charles Perrow (Chapter 5), the taking of the former path was engineered by people holding enough economic power to make over the economy (by way of the legal system) into the form that worked best for them. The key tool was the corporate form of business as we now know it, and this introduced a whole new kind of "person" into the world which now carries all of those same constitutional rights as you and me. These were indispensable in the spread of Big Business which became the hub around which the organizational revolution turned. Eventually some of the benefits of Big Business did become widely spread, but only to some, and then only by the expansion of other organizations such as growing agencies of federal government and industrial labor unions which brought their own negative externalities along with them.

The potential alternative path would have been one that limited the ability to concentrate economic power and thus, potentially, limited the concentration of other forms of power across society as a whole. The ideal typical imagery,

---

[8]Faust was a character in Medieval German folklore who, in a pact with the Devil, traded his soul for unlimited knowledge and worldly pleasures. In short, it's about selling your soul to the Devil.

introduced in Chapters 5 and 6, would be that of a world organized more along the logic of nineteenth-century industrial districts with smaller, proprietary businesses, a more independent labor force, less concentration and economic and political power, and so forth. It is a model that delivered the proverbial goods, but with smaller and fewer negative externalities. I'm not trying to be nostalgic or romantic about times past. Nor am I indicating that there was some route to utopia that we missed in the past and should try to recover. Utopian ideas are nice, but all of our modes of organization and all of our activities will always carry their warts.

Technocracy in some regard will remain indispensable, and is—frankly—a good thing in many arenas. This also goes for its partner formal rationality, generally speaking. Similarly, power inequalities are more than likely inevitable and can also be found to have their virtues, especially when they are functional for all rather than the few, which they sometimes are. Our systems will sometimes break down and fail. And even when they don't all sorts of externalities are still unavoidable. But the bigger and more complex are the systems, the more problematic these issues become. The question isn't how to make the perfect world, because that is not possible. Rather, it is more about how to dial up or down toward different kinds of ends. Liberal values are not perfectly realizable under any conditions. But they are *more or less* realizable under different kinds of social conditions, and the most important factor since the organizational revolution is what kinds of organizational structures are built into the world.

If our primary driving desires are merely about bigger, faster, more, and cheaper, then accept *hierarchy* and *Neo-Fordism* along with all of its warts. It means a complex system of global political economy in which true power is not located anywhere near "the people." It means externalities of scale, which have always been easy to brush under the rug because they are experienced far more by the poorest and least powerful among us. It means learning to live with periodic, systemic crises such as global financial crises, global pandemics, and associated "supply chain" disruptions. It means learning to see certain of our issues, not as the result of situated human decision-making, but as outcomes of *standard operating procedures* and often unintended consequences including Normal Accidents. Yet, even where issues are generated by poor, immoral, unethical, and/or self-interested elite decision-making, it means accepting that the effects are that much larger. And, honestly, if we're going to get through it, it also means the abandonment of the Enlightenment dreams and the derivative Liberal values. To accept bigger, faster, more, and cheaper *is to ask for an elite* that has far more power than "the people." If the choice is to continue the Faustian bargain, then learn to see it as a choice and accept it with some manner of understanding and informed insight into the current state of affairs. Lie in the bed that you make.

Yet there is good reason to think that things could have gone a different way and that we aren't driven by any manner of inevitable natural laws that keep us accelerating down the same tracks. But as of now that's what we're doing and no *one* is actually at the controls, so there is no simple answer for making any distinct shift of speed or direction. I just do what I can where I am with what I've got. I can't avoid my participation in, or exercise any true control over the very systems that are integral to the issues. But I do minimize it as I can. Economically, I avoid fast food, Wal-Mart, Amazon, Uber, and so forth. Politically, whether at my own workplace or at any level of politics from local through national, I vote against any manner of action, policy, candidate, and so on that is likely to increase centralized control whether in governance or in the economy. (This does mean that I favor labor unions because even with all of their substantial warts they generally provide some degree of reduction of general power imbalances.) But "be the change" in a society of organizations is a rather empty sentiment in the grand scheme of things.

So I guess the best I have to offer is that I try to bring the world of sociology and of Organizational Studies to a wider audience—to help as many people as I can develop a *sociological imagination* and "to grasp what is going on in the world and to understand what is happening in themselves as minute points of the intersections of biography and history within society."[9] I may have overemphasized the extent to which the Sociology of Organizations alone can do this. But I do know that it cannot be done without it.

SOURCES AND FURTHER READING

The "velvet cage" imagery appears in the closing chapter of Ritzer:

- Ritzer, George. 2019. *The McDonaldization of Society: Into the Digital Age*, 9th ed. Thousand Oaks, CA: SAGE Publications. (The original/first edition was published in 1993).

On **Organizational Paradox Theory** see, for example:

- Andriopoulos, Constantine and Marianne Lewis W. 2009. "Exploitation–Exploration Tensions and Organizational Ambidexterity: Managing Paradoxes of Innovation." *Organization Science* 20: 696–717.

- Berti, Marco and Ace V. Simpson. 2021. "The Dark Side of Organizational Paradoxes: The Dynamics of Disempowerment." *Academy of Management Review* 6: 252–74.

- Lewis, Marianne W. 2000. "Exploring Paradox: Toward a More Comprehensive Guide." *Academy of Management Review* 25: 760–76.

- Lewis, Marianne W. and Wendy K. Smith. 2014. "Paradox as a Metatheoretical Perspective: Sharpening the Focus and Widening the Scope." *Journal of Applied Behavioral Science* 50: 127–49.

- Putnam, Linda L., Gail T. Fairhurst and Scott Banghart. 2016. "Contradictions, Dialectics, and Paradoxes in Organizations: A Constitutive Approach." *Academy of Management Annals* 10: 65–171.

- Schad, Jonathan, Marianne M. Lewis, Sebastian Raisch, and Wendy K. Smith. 2016. "Paradox Research in Management Science: Looking Back To Move Forward." *Academy of Management Annals* 10: 5–64.

- Smith, Wendy K. and Marianne W. Lewis. 2011. "Toward a Theory of Paradox: A Dynamic Equilibrium Model of Organizing." *Academy of Management Review* 36: 381–403.

Langdon Winner is best known as a critical thinker in the somewhat parallel interdiscipline of *Science, Technology and Society (STS)*. The strongest parallels have to do with concerns about the triumph of our means (formal rationality) over concerns about our ends (substantive rationality). The quote I pulled in the context of a critique of valorizing

---

[9]Mills ([1959]2000: 7).

Chandlerian accounts is from a widely read and cited essay:

- Winner, Langdon. 1980. "Do Artifacts Have Politics?" *Daedalus* 109: 121–36.

- Also see an updated version in Chapter 2 of Winner, Langdon. 1986. *The Whale and the Reactor: A Search for Limits in an Age of High Technology*. Chicago, IL: University of Chicago Press.

With regard to **Karl Mannheim's** grappling with his own age, the *Man and Society* book followed *Ideology and Utopia* which is where he most fully developed the idea that ideologies of political economy were not right or wrong, but only more or less realizable given the circumstances. See:

- Mannheim, Karl. [1929] 1985. *Ideology and Utopia: An Introduction to the Sociology of Knowledge*, translated by Louis Wirth and Edward Shils. New York, NY: Harcourt, Inc.

- ———. [1935] 1940. *Man and Society in an Age of Reconstruction: Studies in Modern Social Structure*. London, UK: Routledge and Kegan Paul Ltd.

The **Hitler's Shadow** phrase is from Chapter 13 of the following and was quite influential in what was framed out here:

- Collins, Randall and Michael Makowsky. 2010. *The Discovery of Society*, 8th ed. New York, NY: McGraw Hill.

For **some contemporary commentary on Mannheim's** thought, including consideration of concerns with regard to things like Fascism and Populism:

- Hammersley, Martyn. 2021a. "Planning versus the Market: The Dispute between Hayek and Mannheim and Its Contemporary Relevance." *The British Journal of Sociology* 72: 1464–78. DOI: 10.1111/1468-4446.12893

- ———. 2021b. "Karl Mannheim on Fascism: Sociological Lessons about Populism and Democracy Today?" *Sociological Research Online* 1–16. DOI: 10.1177/13607804211042032

Contemporary commentary regarding the clash between **technocracy** and **democracy**, including the idea of the **New Technocracy**, and the dim prospects for **Liberalism** has been much more a subject of conversation for political scientists and political philosophers. It's time that it was more a subject of conversation in organizational studies (although see Hammersley, above). For now, see:

- Bertsou, Eri and Daniele Caramani, Eds. 2020. *The Technocratic Challenge to Democracy*. New York, NY: Routlege.

- Brennan, Jason. 2016. *Against Democracy*. Princeton, NJ: Princeton University Press.

- Deneen, Patrick J. 2018. *Why Liberalism Failed*. New Haven, CT: Yale University Press.

- Esmark, Anders. 2020. *The New Technocracy*. Bristol, UK: Bristol University Press.

- Mudde, Cas and Cristóbal R. Kaltwasser, Eds. 2012. *Populism in Europe and the Americas*. New York, NY: Cambridge University Press.

The closing reference to the **sociological imagination** is from the well-known introductory piece by C. Wright Mills:

- Mills, C. Wright. [1959] 2000. *The Sociological Imagination*. New York: Oxford University Press.

Index